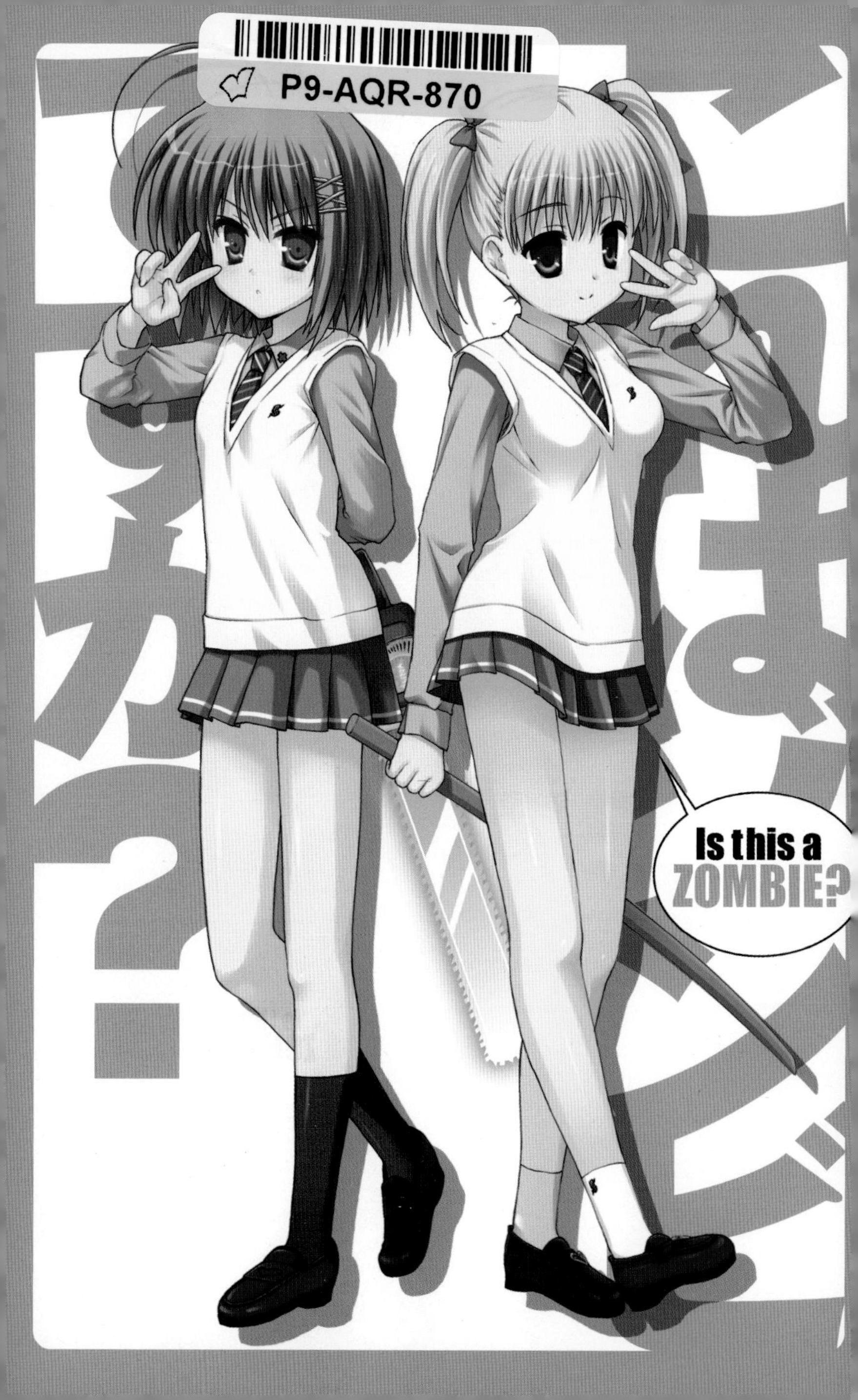
Is this a
ZOMBIE?

CONTENTS

Is this a ZOMBIE?

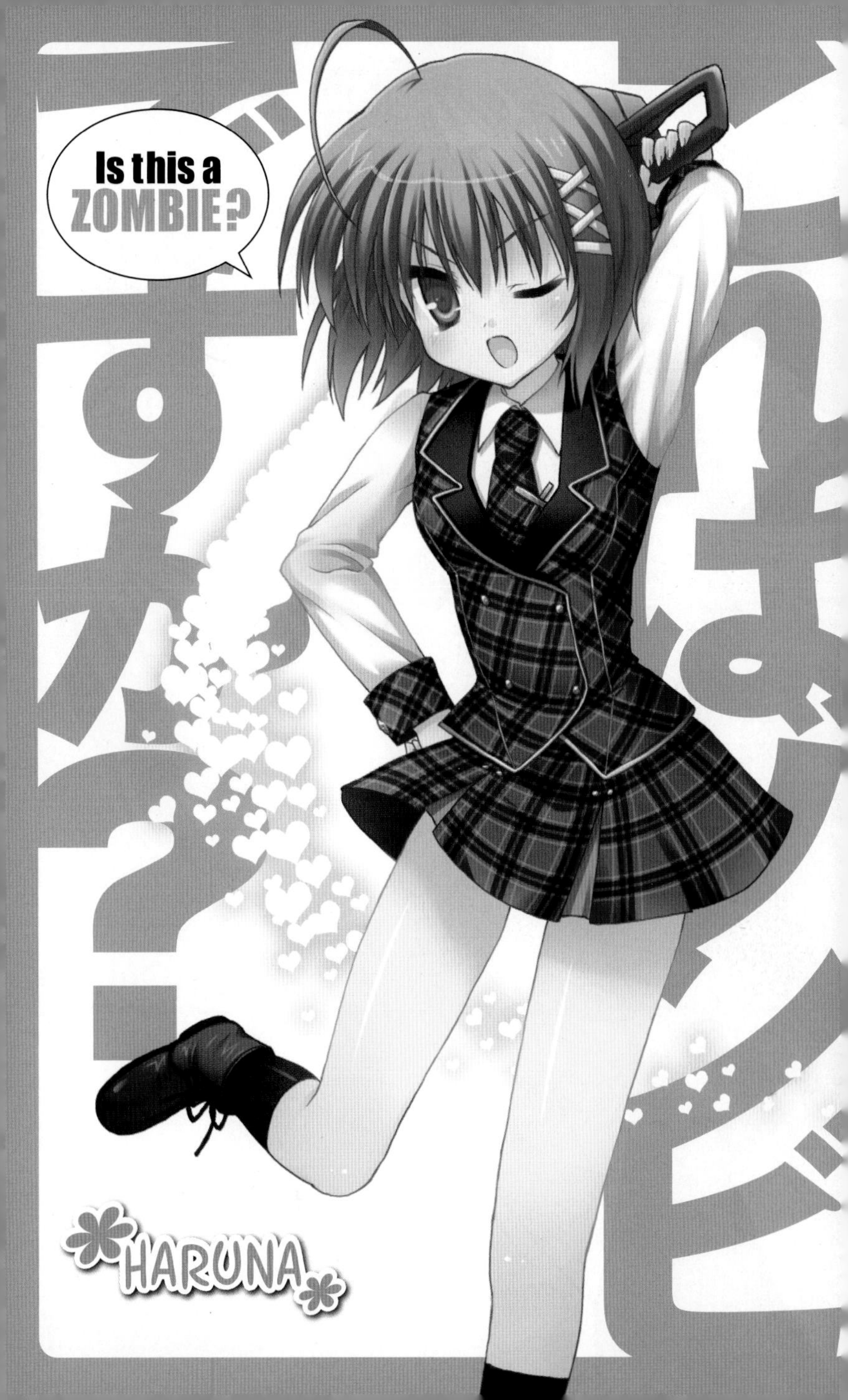
Is this a ZOMBIE?
HARUNA

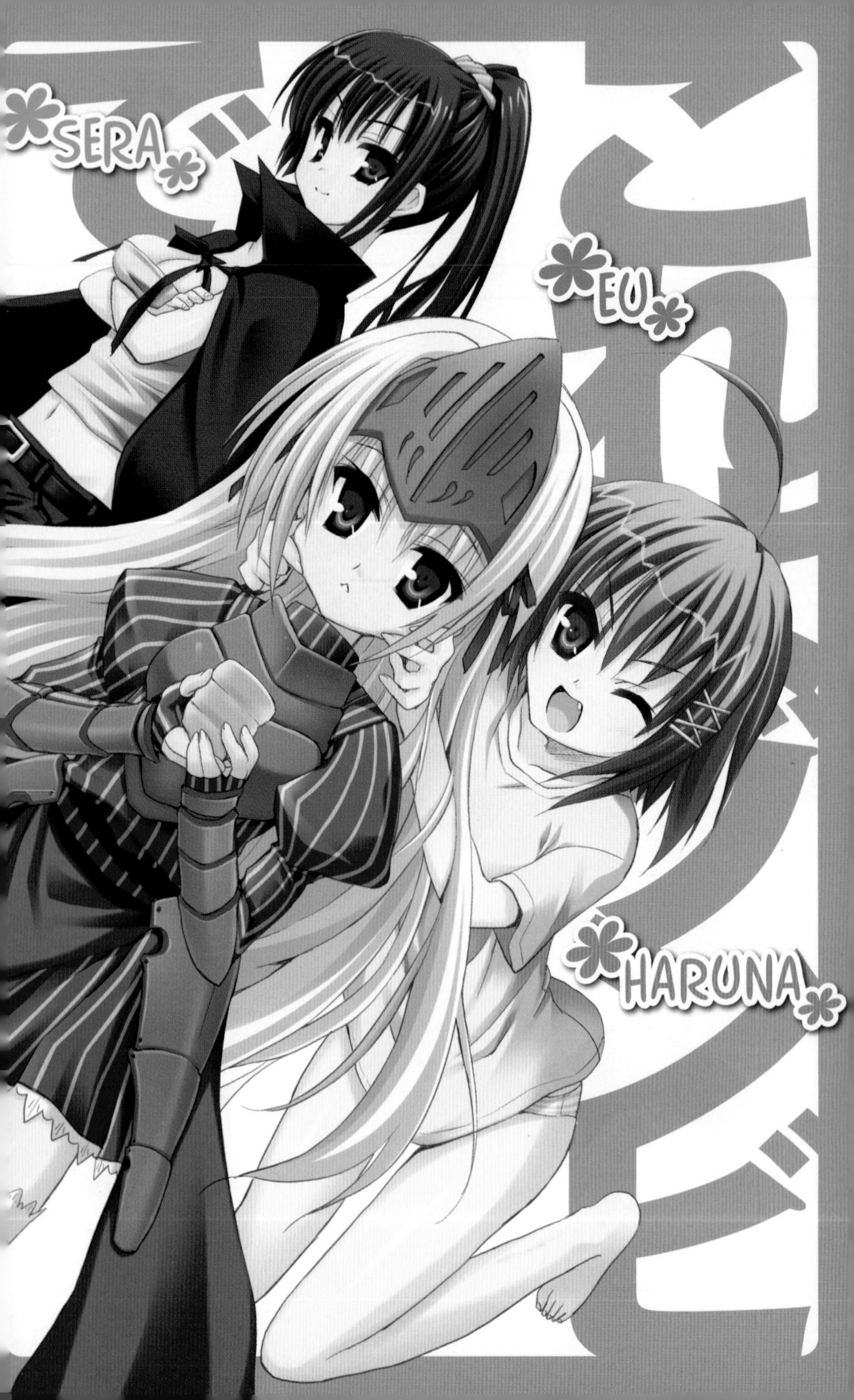
SERA
EU
HARUNA

YES, THIS IS THE STORY SO FAR!

AFTER BEING MURDERED BY A SERIAL KILLER, I WAS BROUGHT BACK TO LIFE AS A ZOMBIE BY THE NECROMANCER EU, THEN ORDERED TO BE A MAGIKEWL GIRL BY THE MAGIKEWL GIRL HARUNA, AND FINALLY HAD A VAMPIRE NINJA NAMED SERA SHOW UP ON MY DOORSTEP. BEFORE I KNEW IT, THEY ALL STARTED LIVING WITH ME. FAREWELL, SWEET DAYS OF PEACE AND QUIET...

WE ALL PROMISE EU THAT WE'LL PROTECT HER FROM A MYSTERIOUS MAN WHO GOES BY THE NAME KING OF NIGHT AND HATES HER FOR HAVING TURNED HIM INTO A ZOMBIE.

THEN ONE DAY, HARUNA SAYS THE MOST OUTRAGEOUS THING AFTER SHE FINDS OUT THAT TOMONORI AND I ACCIDENTALLY LOCKED LIPS!

"KISS ME!"

OF COURSE, WHEN I ACTUALLY BELIEVE HER AND TRY TO FULFILL HER COMMAND, I'M MET WITH A HIGH KICK TO THE FACE. NICE.

AND EVEN THOUGH WE'VE BEEN GETTING ALONG SO WELL, PRACTICALLY LIKE A FAMILY, WHY IS SERA SUDDENLY ISSUED THE ORDER TO

"KILL EU"!?

TO TOP IT ALL OFF, TOMONORI TURNS OUT TO BE A MAGIKEWL WEAPON HERSELF, AND DAI-SENSEI GETS WHISKED AWAY OF HER OWN FREE WILL BY THE KING OF NIGHT.

THEN EU FOLLOWS CLOSE BEHIND......

AAAARGH! TOO MUCH HAPPENED TO FIT ON JUST ONE PAAAGE!!!

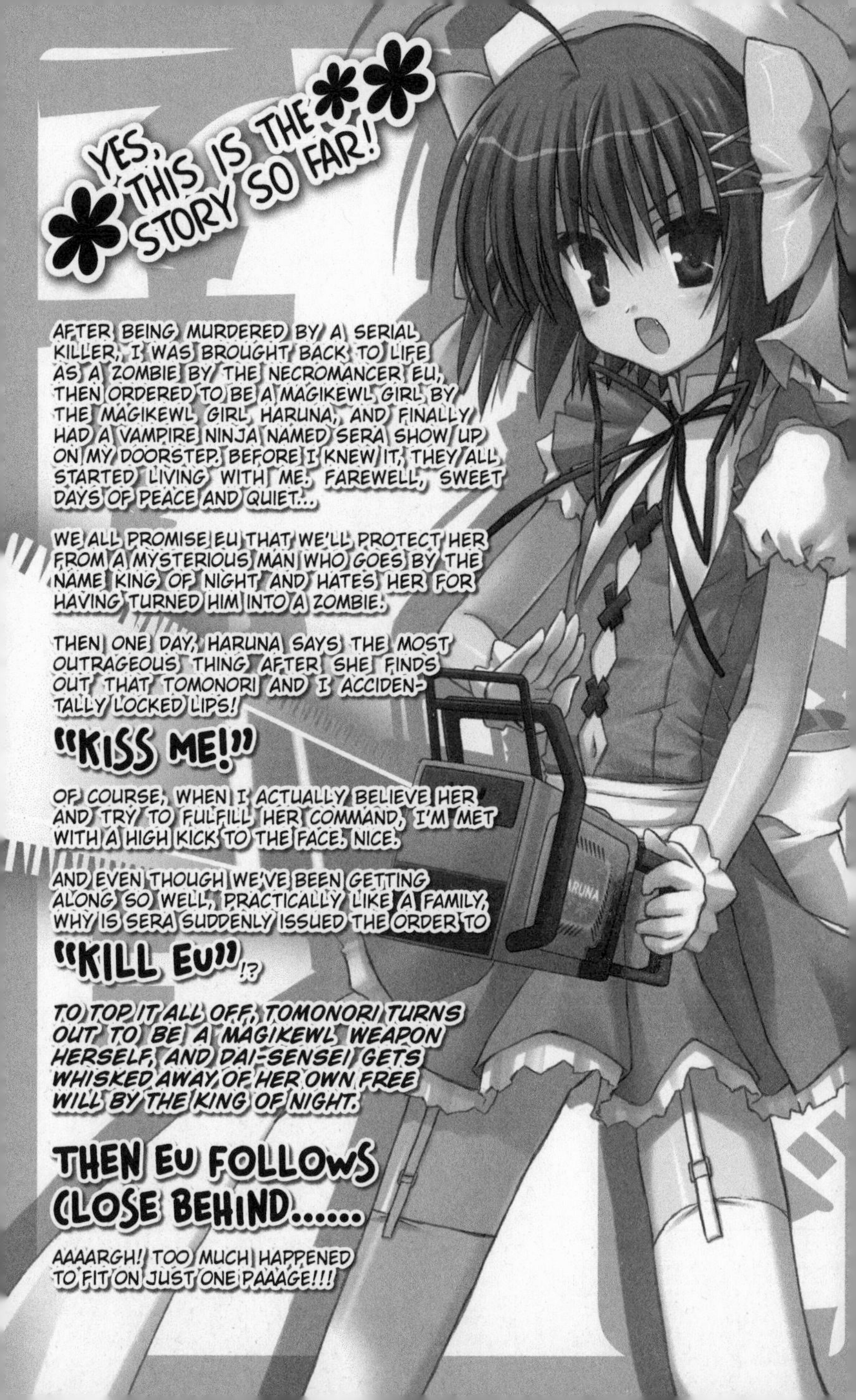
HARUNA

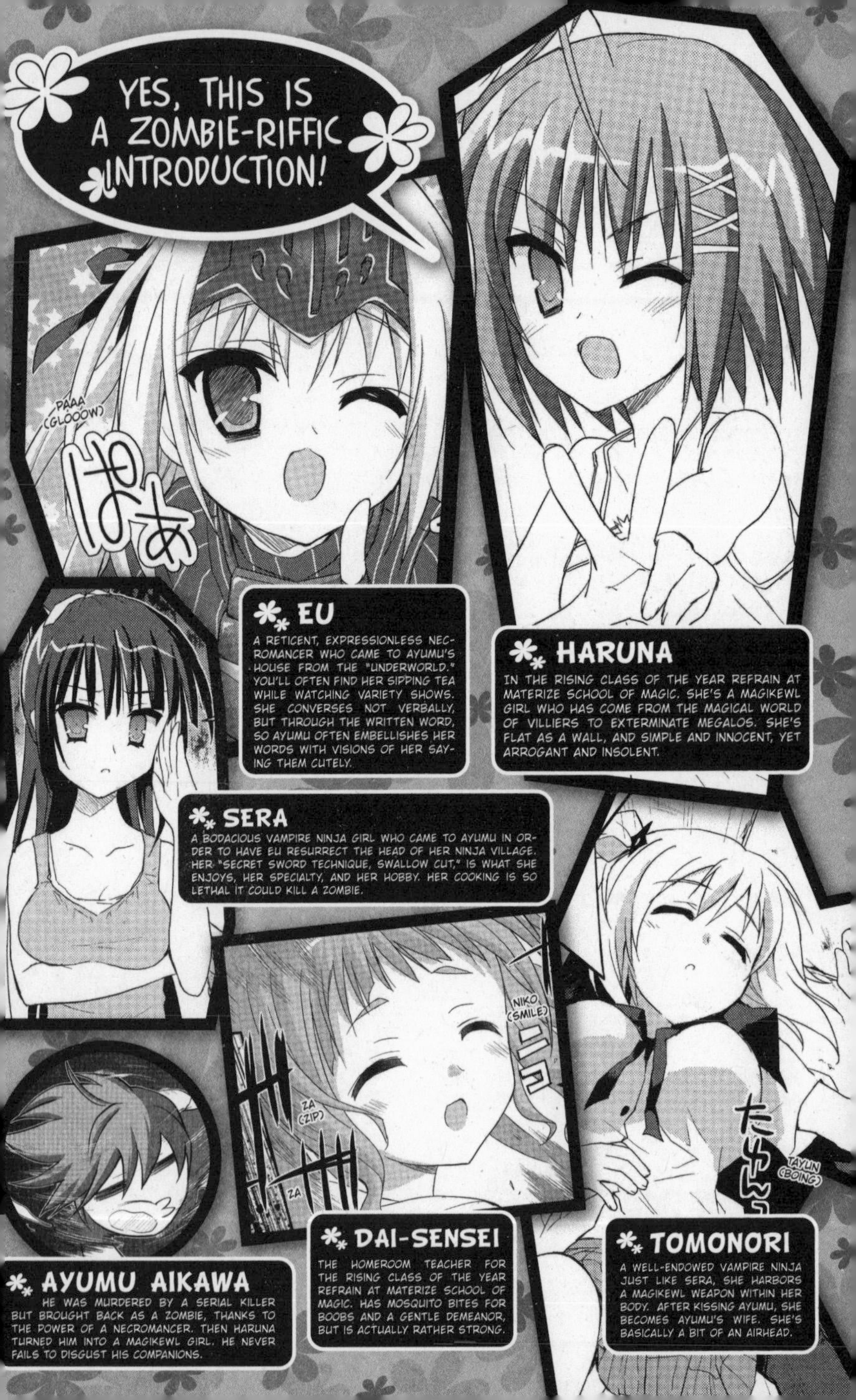
YES, THIS IS A ZOMBIE-RIFFIC INTRODUCTION!
PAAA (GLOOOW)
ぱあ
EU
A RETICENT, EXPRESSIONLESS NECROMANCER WHO CAME TO AYUMU'S HOUSE FROM THE "UNDERWORLD." YOU'LL OFTEN FIND HER SIPPING TEA WHILE WATCHING VARIETY SHOWS. SHE CONVERSES NOT VERBALLY, BUT THROUGH THE WRITTEN WORD, SO AYUMU OFTEN EMBELLISHES HER WORDS WITH VISIONS OF HER SAYING THEM CUTELY.
HARUNA
IN THE RISING CLASS OF THE YEAR REFRAIN AT MATERIZE SCHOOL OF MAGIC. SHE'S A MAGIKEWL GIRL WHO HAS COME FROM THE MAGICAL WORLD OF VILLIERS TO EXTERMINATE MEGALOS. SHE'S FLAT AS A WALL, AND SIMPLE AND INNOCENT, YET ARROGANT AND INSOLENT.
SERA
A BODACIOUS VAMPIRE NINJA GIRL WHO CAME TO AYUMU IN ORDER TO HAVE EU RESURRECT THE HEAD OF HER NINJA VILLAGE. HER "SECRET SWORD TECHNIQUE, SWALLOW CUT," IS WHAT SHE ENJOYS, HER SPECIALTY, AND HER HOBBY. HER COOKING IS SO LETHAL IT COULD KILL A ZOMBIE.
NIKO (SMILE)
ニコ
ZA (ZIP)
ZA
たゆん
TAYUN (BOING)
AYUMU AIKAWA
HE WAS MURDERED BY A SERIAL KILLER BUT BROUGHT BACK AS A ZOMBIE, THANKS TO THE POWER OF A NECROMANCER. THEN HARUNA TURNED HIM INTO A MAGIKEWL GIRL. HE NEVER FAILS TO DISGUST HIS COMPANIONS.
DAI-SENSEI
THE HOMEROOM TEACHER FOR THE RISING CLASS OF THE YEAR REFRAIN AT MATERIZE SCHOOL OF MAGIC. HAS MOSQUITO BITES FOR BOOBS AND A GENTLE DEMEANOR, BUT IS ACTUALLY RATHER STRONG.
TOMONORI
A WELL-ENDOWED VAMPIRE NINJA JUST LIKE SERA, SHE HARBORS A MAGIKEWL WEAPON WITHIN HER BODY. AFTER KISSING AYUMU, SHE BECOMES AYUMU'S WIFE. SHE'S BASICALLY A BIT OF AN AIRHEAD.

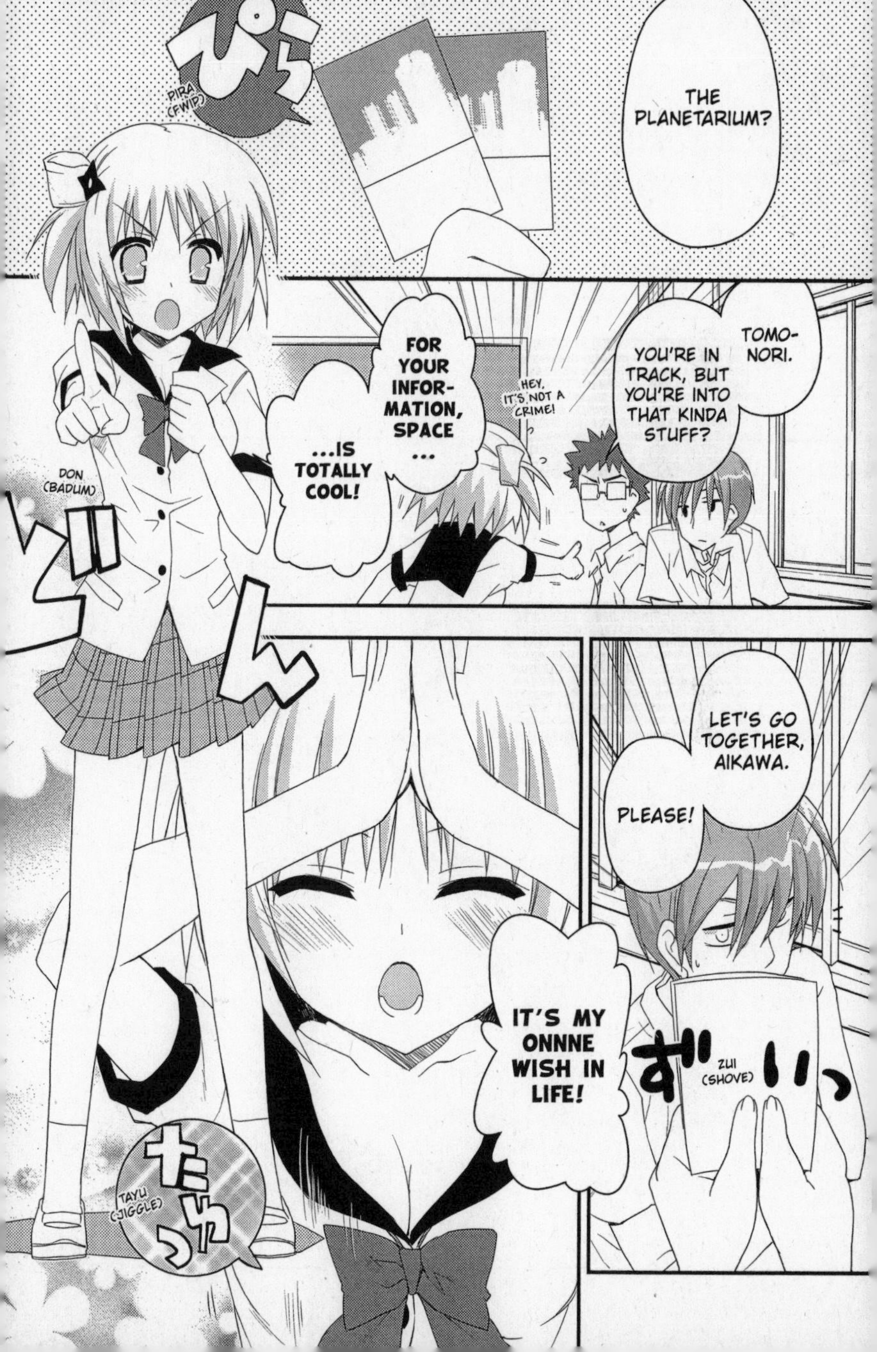
THE PLANETARIUM?
PIRA (FWIP)
TOMO-NORI.
YOU'RE IN TRACK, BUT YOU'RE INTO THAT KINDA STUFF?
HEY, IT'S NOT A CRIME!
FOR YOUR INFORMATION, SPACE...
...IS TOTALLY COOL!
DON (BADUM)
LET'S GO TOGETHER, AIKAWA.
PLEASE!
IT'S MY ONNNE WISH IN LIFE!
ZUI (SHOVE)
TAYU (JIGGLE)

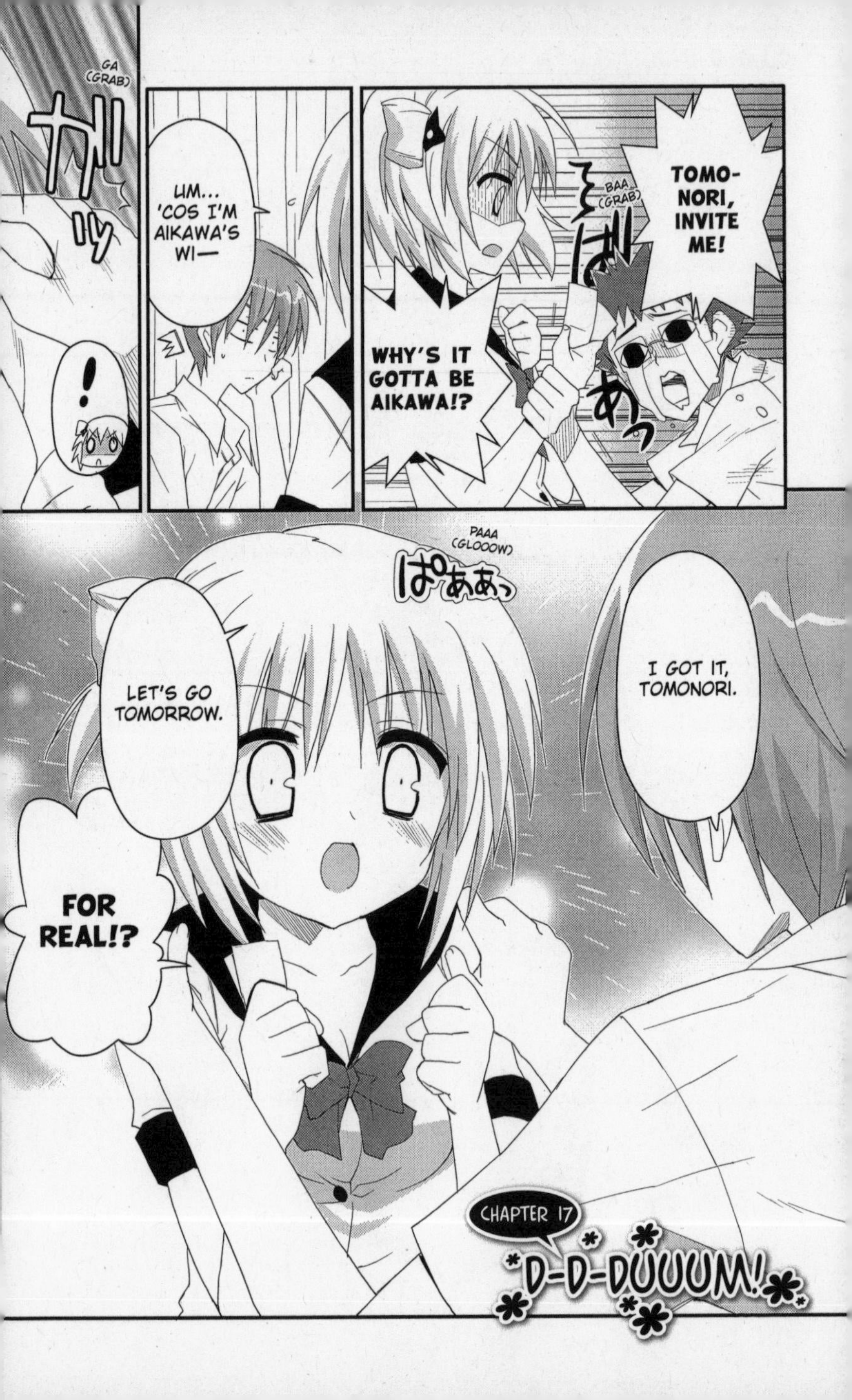
BAA (GRAB)
ばっ
TOMO-NORI, INVITE ME!
WHY'S IT GOTTA BE AIKAWA!?
あっ
UM... 'COS I'M AIKAWA'S WI—
GA (GRAB)
ガッ
!
PAAA (GLOOOW)
ぱあぁっ
I GOT IT, TOMONORI.
LET'S GO TOMORROW.
FOR REAL!?
CHAPTER 17
D-D-DUUUM!

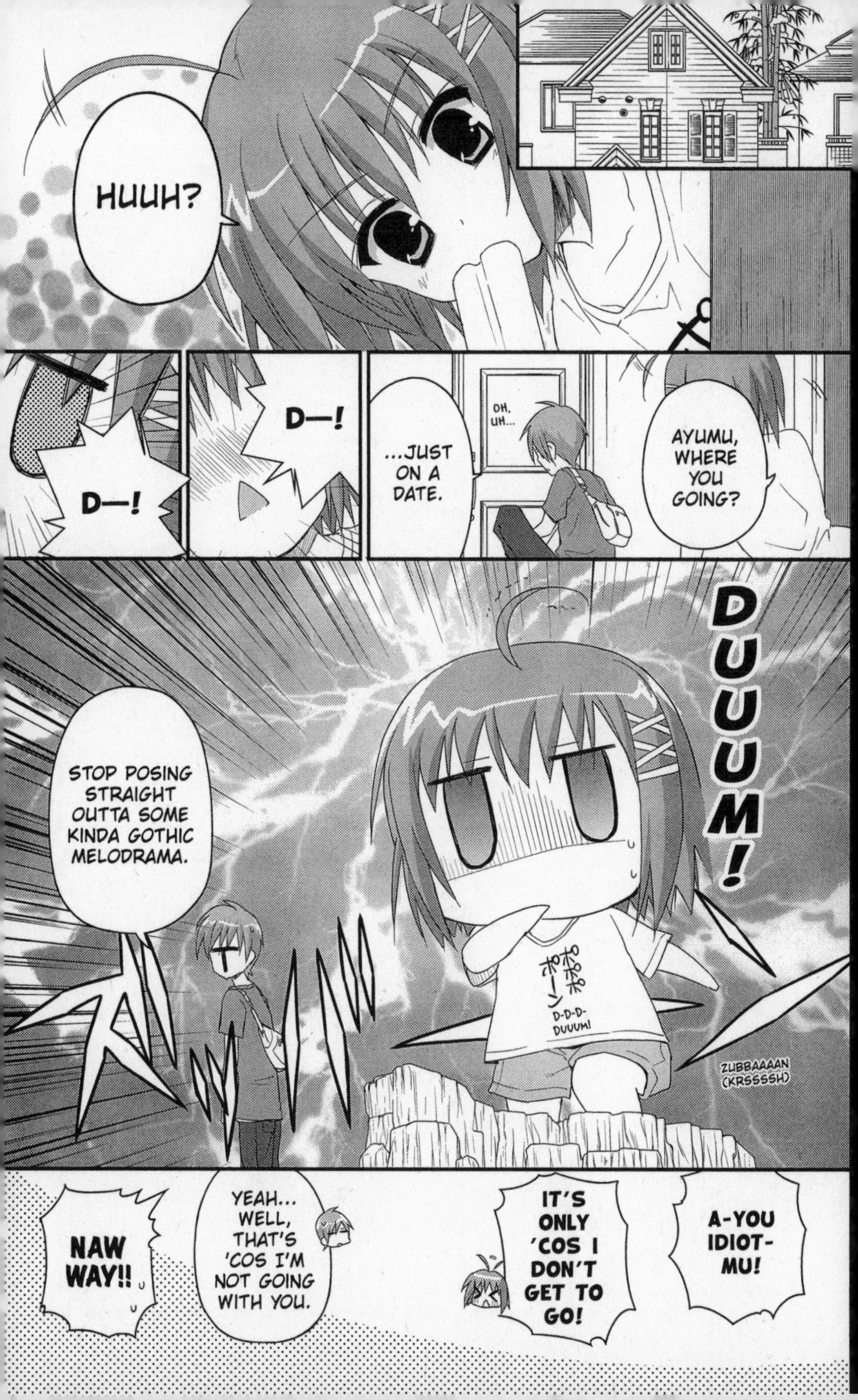
HUUH?
AYUMU, WHERE YOU GOING?
OH, UH...
...JUST ON A DATE.
D—!
D—!
DUUUUM!
STOP POSING STRAIGHT OUTTA SOME KINDA GOTHIC MELODRAMA.
ポポポポーン
D-D-D-DUUUM!
ZUBBAAAAN (KRSSSSH)
A-YOU IDIOT-MU!
IT'S ONLY 'COS I DON'T GET TO GO!
YEAH... WELL, THAT'S 'COS I'M NOT GOING WITH YOU.
NAW WAY!!

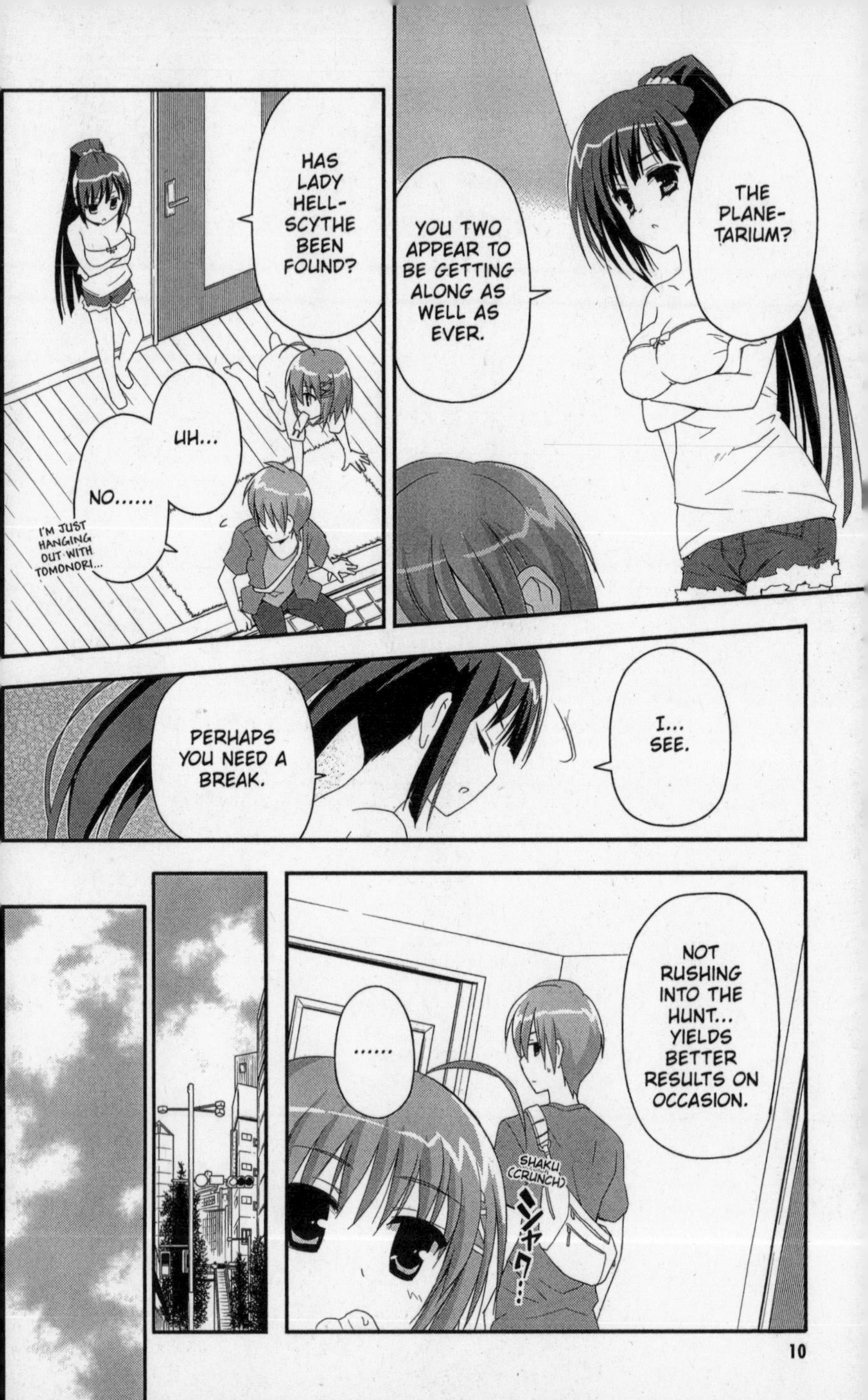
THE PLANE-TARIUM?
YOU TWO APPEAR TO BE GETTING ALONG AS WELL AS EVER.
HAS LADY HELL-SCYTHE BEEN FOUND?
UH...
NO......
I'M JUST HANGING OUT WITH TOMONORI...
I... SEE.
PERHAPS YOU NEED A BREAK.
NOT RUSHING INTO THE HUNT... YIELDS BETTER RESULTS ON OCCASION.
......
SHAKU (CRUNCH)
シャク...

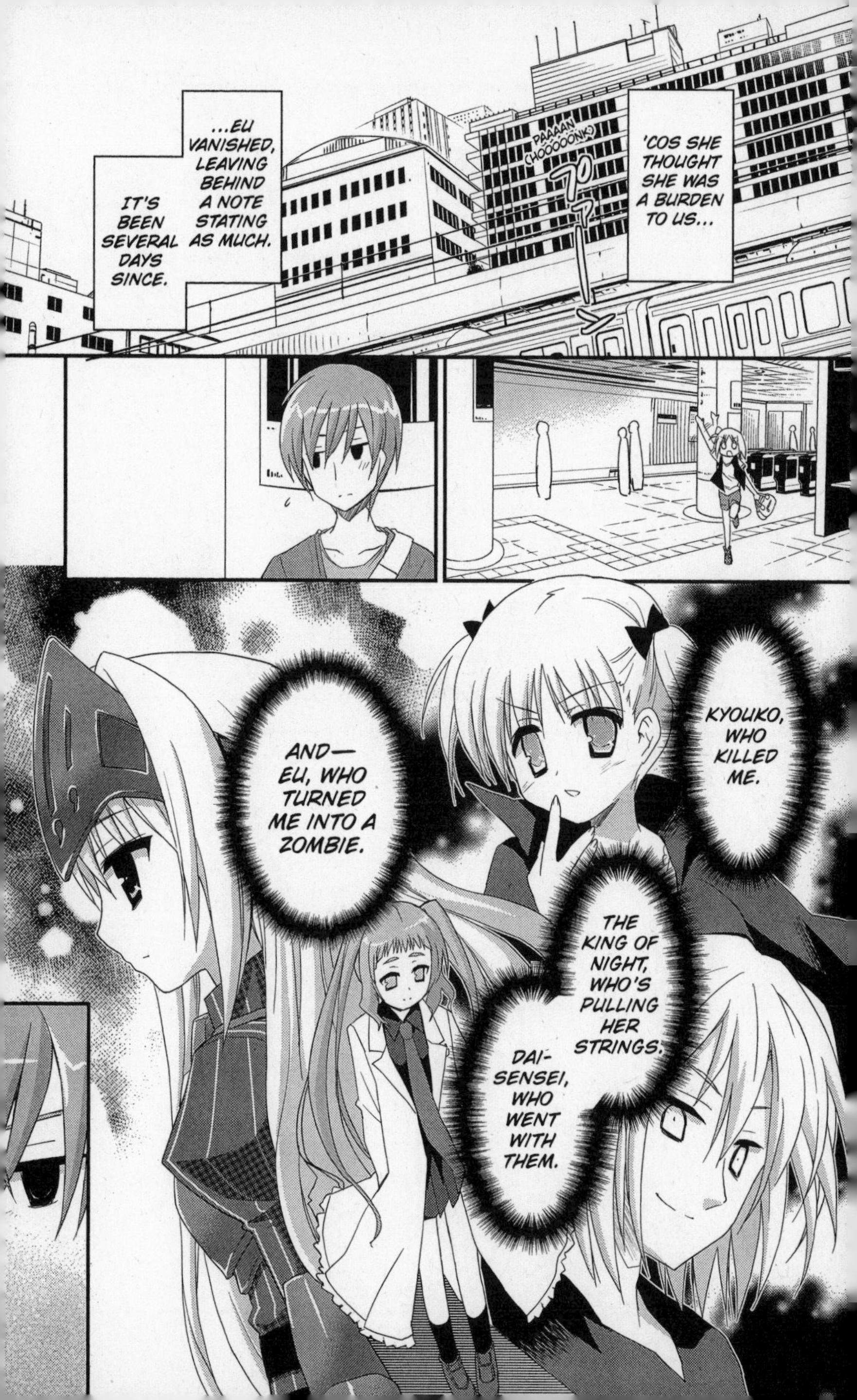
'COS SHE THOUGHT SHE WAS A BURDEN TO US...
PAAAAN (HOOOOONK)
...EU VANISHED, LEAVING BEHIND A NOTE STATING AS MUCH.
IT'S BEEN SEVERAL DAYS SINCE.
KYOUKO, WHO KILLED ME.
AND— EU, WHO TURNED ME INTO A ZOMBIE.
THE KING OF NIGHT, WHO'S PULLING HER STRINGS.
DAI-SENSEI, WHO WENT WITH THEM.

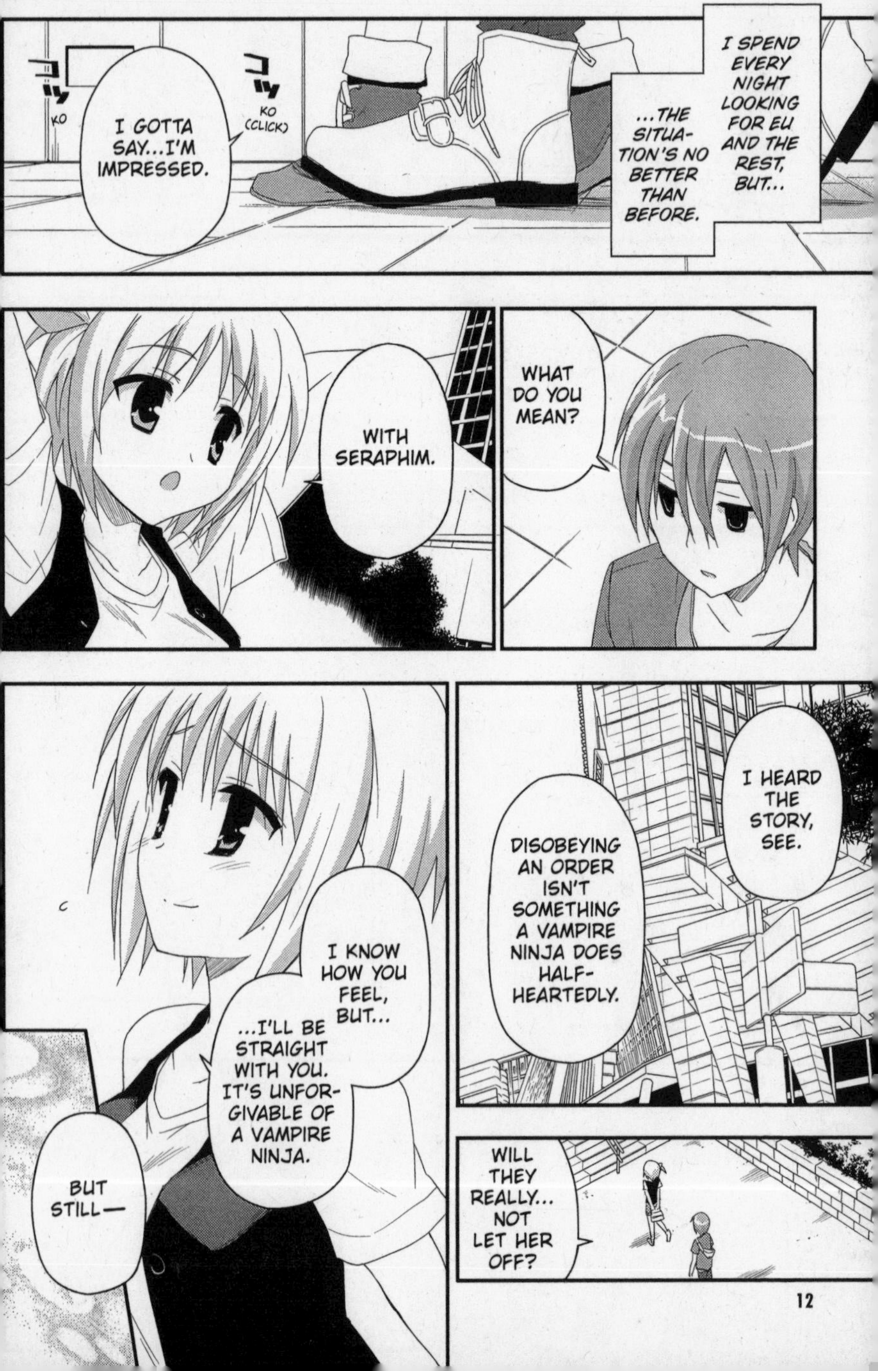
I SPEND EVERY NIGHT LOOKING FOR EU AND THE REST, BUT...
...THE SITUATION'S NO BETTER THAN BEFORE.
KO (CLICK)
I GOTTA SAY...I'M IMPRESSED.
KO
WHAT DO YOU MEAN?
WITH SERAPHIM.
I HEARD THE STORY, SEE.
DISOBEYING AN ORDER ISN'T SOMETHING A VAMPIRE NINJA DOES HALF-HEARTEDLY.
WILL THEY REALLY... NOT LET HER OFF?
I KNOW HOW YOU FEEL, BUT...
...I'LL BE STRAIGHT WITH YOU. IT'S UNFORGIVABLE OF A VAMPIRE NINJA.
BUT STILL—

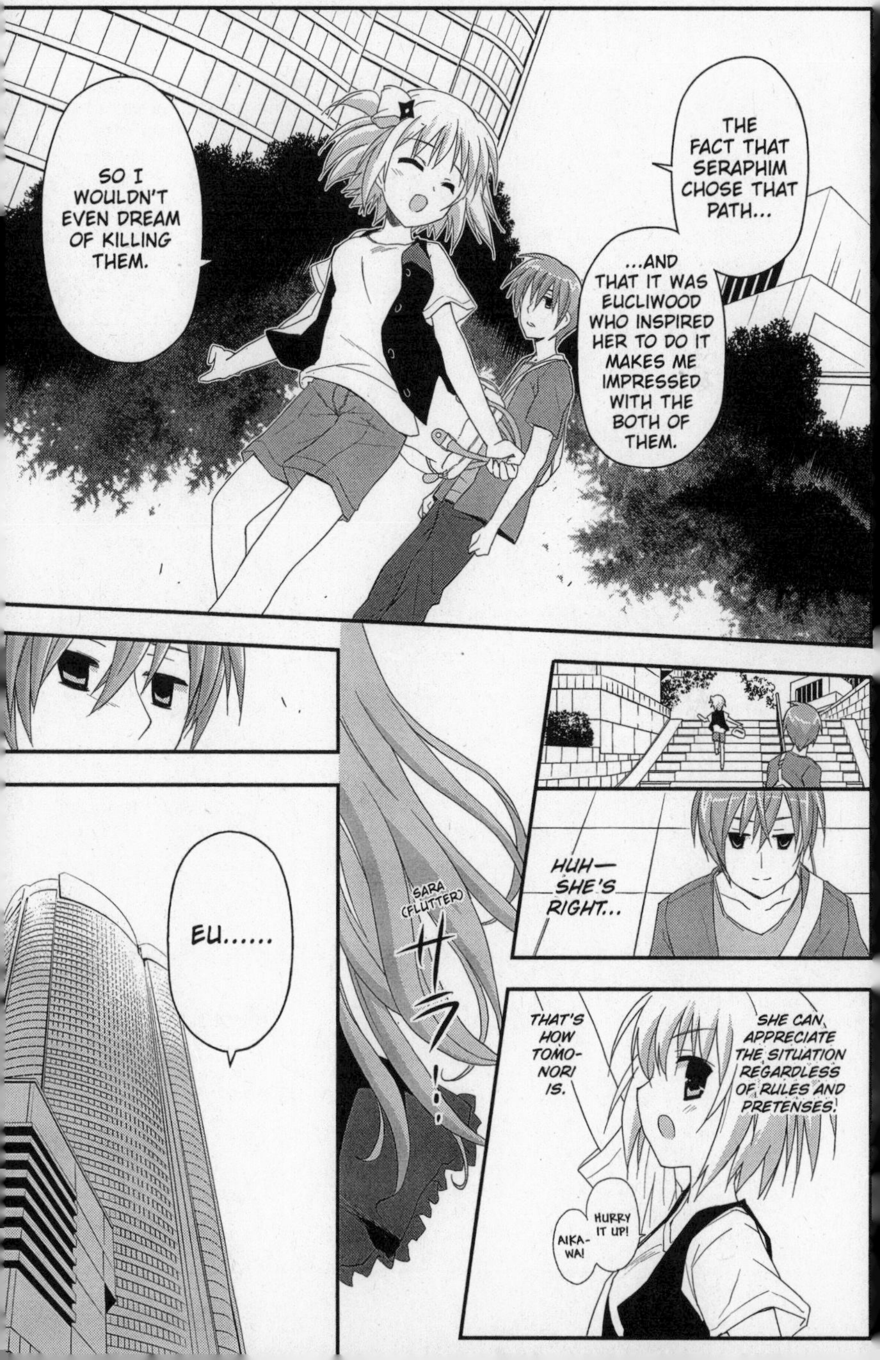
THE FACT THAT SERAPHIM CHOSE THAT PATH...
...AND THAT IT WAS EUCLIWOOD WHO INSPIRED HER TO DO IT MAKES ME IMPRESSED WITH THE BOTH OF THEM.
SO I WOULDN'T EVEN DREAM OF KILLING THEM.
HUH—SHE'S RIGHT...
SARA (FLUTTER)
EU......
SHE CAN APPRECIATE THE SITUATION REGARDLESS OF RULES AND PRETENSES.
THAT'S HOW TOMONORI IS.
HURRY IT UP!
AIKAWA!

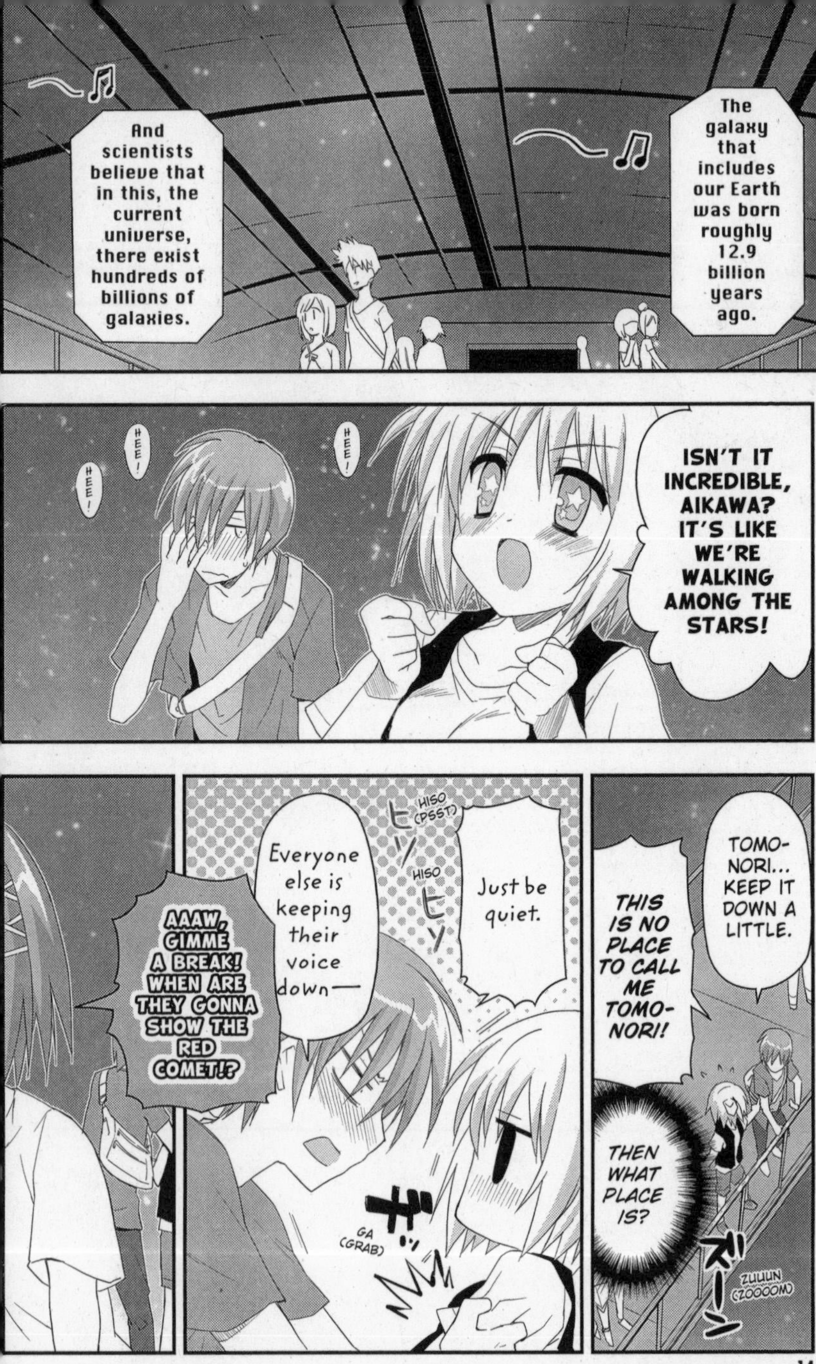

The galaxy that includes our Earth was born roughly 12.9 billion years ago.
And scientists believe that in this, the current universe, there exist hundreds of billions of galaxies.
HEE!
HEE!
HEE!
ISN'T IT INCREDIBLE, AIKAWA? IT'S LIKE WE'RE WALKING AMONG THE STARS!
TOMO-NORI... KEEP IT DOWN A LITTLE.
THIS IS NO PLACE TO CALL ME TOMO-NORI!
THEN WHAT PLACE IS?
ZUUUN (ZOOOOM)
Just be quiet.
HISO (PSST)
HISO
Everyone else is keeping their voice down—
GA (GRAB)
AAAW, GIMME A BREAK! WHEN ARE THEY GONNA SHOW THE RED COMET!?

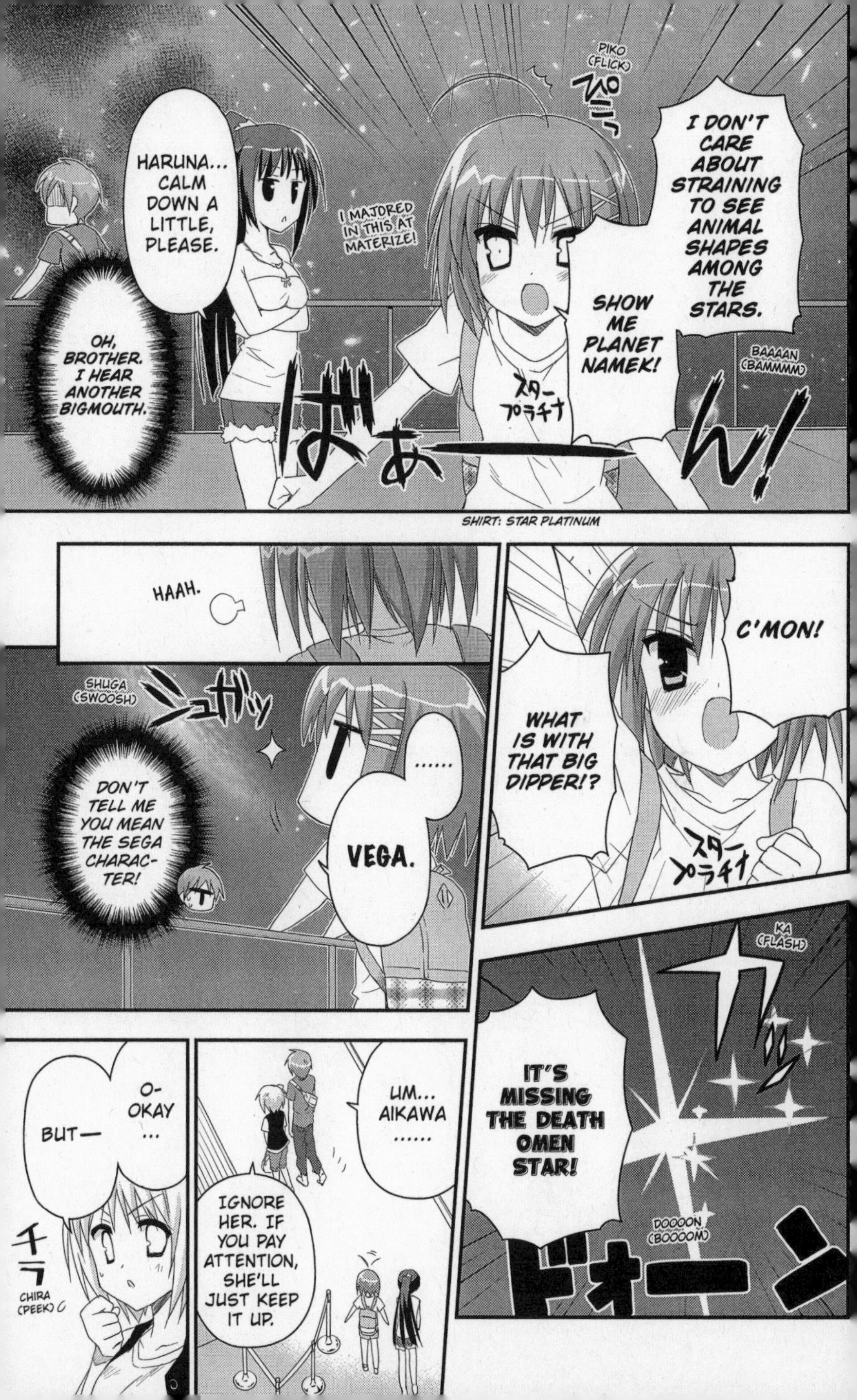
PIKO (FLICK)
I DON'T CARE ABOUT STRAINING TO SEE ANIMAL SHAPES AMONG THE STARS.
SHOW ME PLANET NAMEK!
BAAAAN (BAMMMM)
I MAJORED IN THIS AT MATERIZE!
HARUNA... CALM DOWN A LITTLE, PLEASE.
OH, BROTHER. I HEAR ANOTHER BIGMOUTH.
スタープラチナ
SHIRT: STAR PLATINUM
C'MON!
WHAT IS WITH THAT BIG DIPPER!?
スタープラチナ
HAAH.
SHUGA (SWOOSH)
......
VEGA.
DON'T TELL ME YOU MEAN THE SEGA CHARACTER!
KA (FLASH)
IT'S MISSING THE DEATH OMEN STAR!
DOOOON (BOOOOM)
UM... AIKAWA ......
IGNORE HER. IF YOU PAY ATTENTION, SHE'LL JUST KEEP IT UP.
O-OKAY ...
BUT—
CHIRA (PEEK)

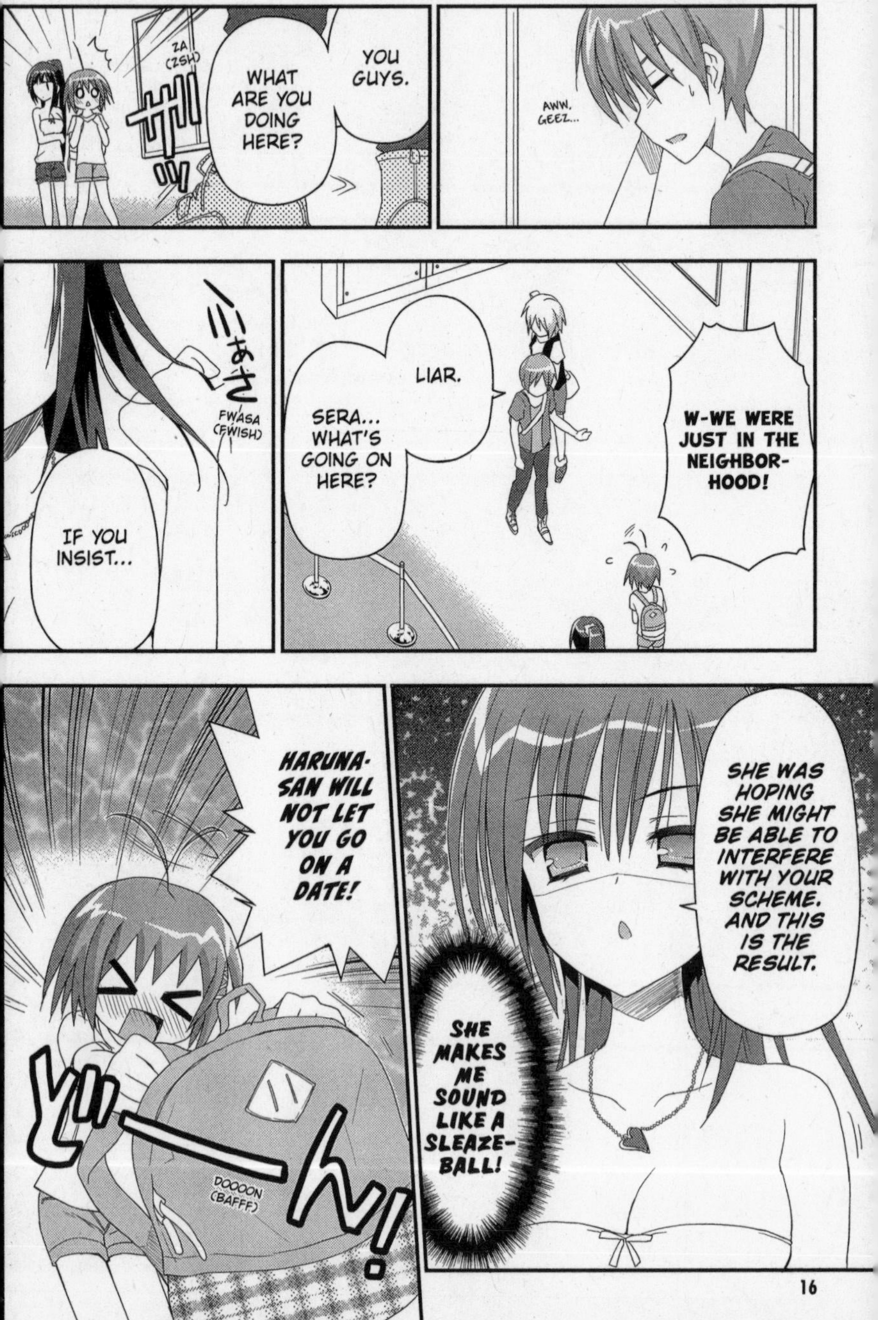
AWW, GEEZ...
YOU GUYS.
WHAT ARE YOU DOING HERE?
ZA (ZSH)
W-WE WERE JUST IN THE NEIGHBOR-HOOD!
LIAR.
SERA... WHAT'S GOING ON HERE?
FWASA (FWISH)
IF YOU INSIST...
SHE WAS HOPING SHE MIGHT BE ABLE TO INTERFERE WITH YOUR SCHEME. AND THIS IS THE RESULT.
SHE MAKES ME SOUND LIKE A SLEAZE-BALL!
HARUNA-SAN WILL NOT LET YOU GO ON A DATE!
DOOOON (BAFFF)

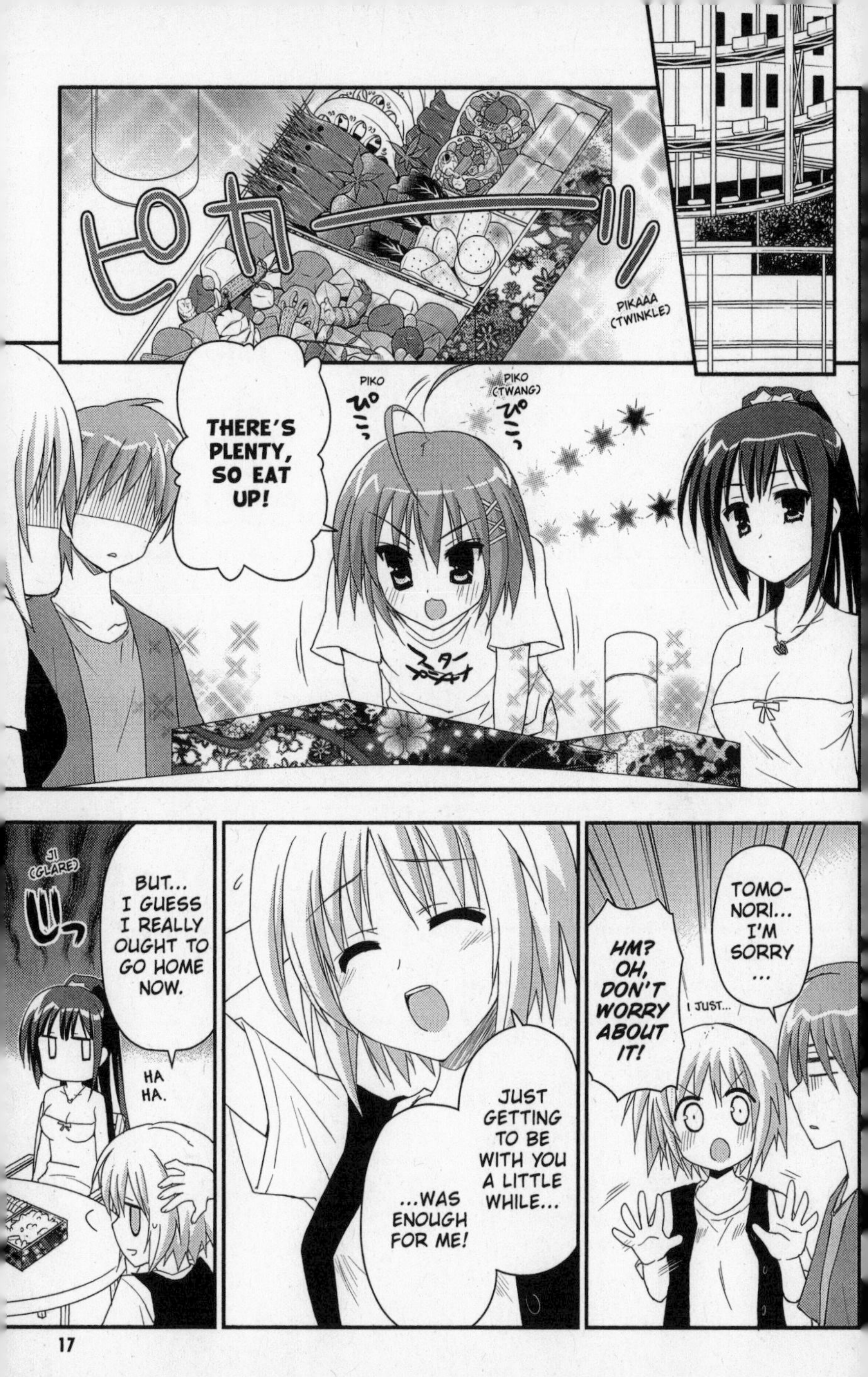
ピカーッ
PIKAAA (TWINKLE)
THERE'S PLENTY, SO EAT UP!
ぴこ
PIKO
ぴこ
PIKO (TWANG)
TOMONORI... I'M SORRY...
I JUST...
HM? OH, DON'T WORRY ABOUT IT!
JUST GETTING TO BE WITH YOU A LITTLE WHILE...
...WAS ENOUGH FOR ME!
BUT... I GUESS I REALLY OUGHT TO GO HOME NOW.
HA HA.
じっ
JI (GLARE)

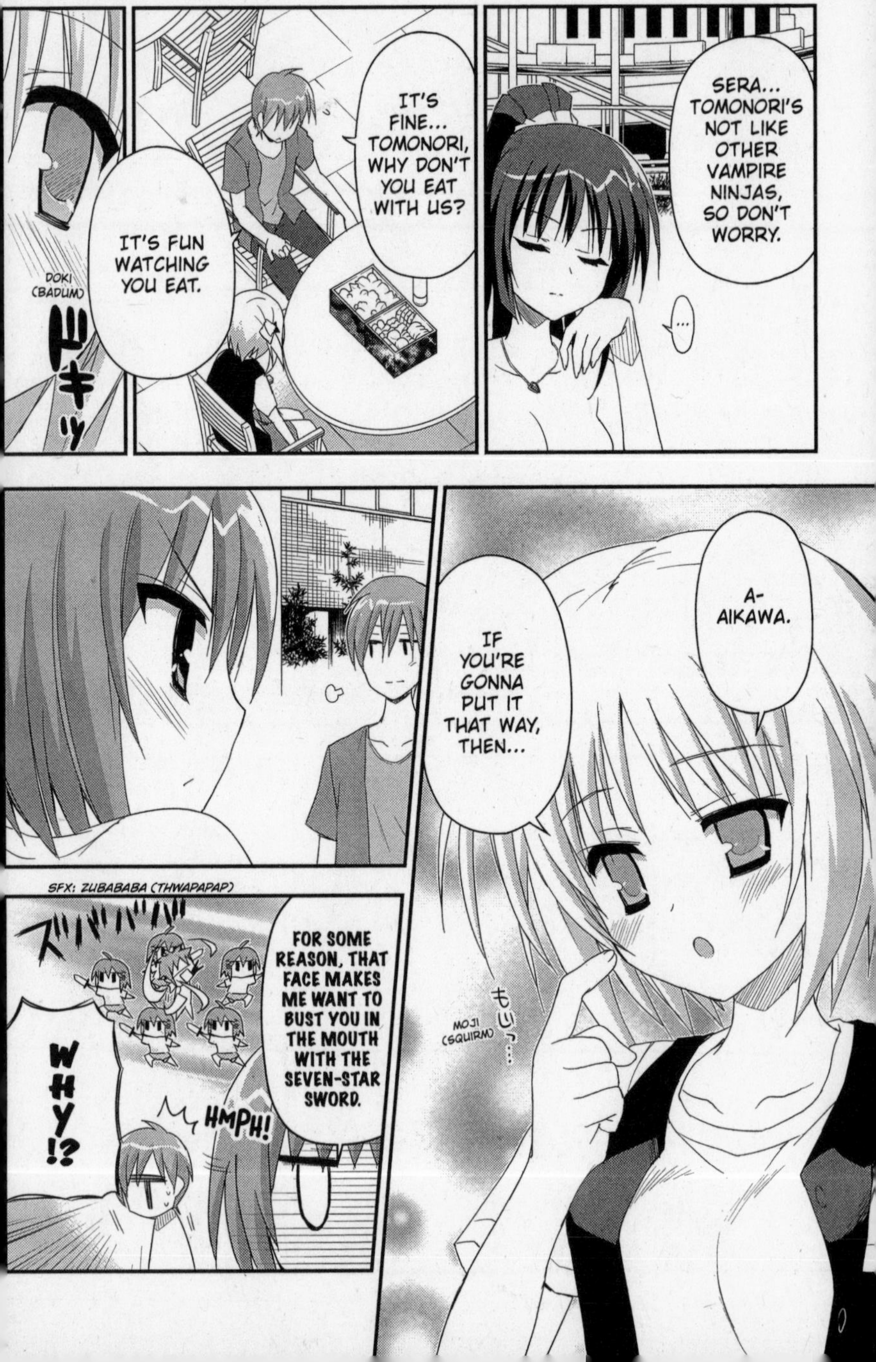
SERA... TOMONORI'S NOT LIKE OTHER VAMPIRE NINJAS, SO DON'T WORRY.
...
IT'S FINE... TOMONORI, WHY DON'T YOU EAT WITH US?
IT'S FUN WATCHING YOU EAT.
DOKI (BADUM)
A- AIKAWA.
IF YOU'RE GONNA PUT IT THAT WAY, THEN...
MOJI (SQUIRM)
SFX: ZUBABABA (THWAPAPAP)
FOR SOME REASON, THAT FACE MAKES ME WANT TO BUST YOU IN THE MOUTH WITH THE SEVEN-STAR SWORD.
HMPH!
WHY!?

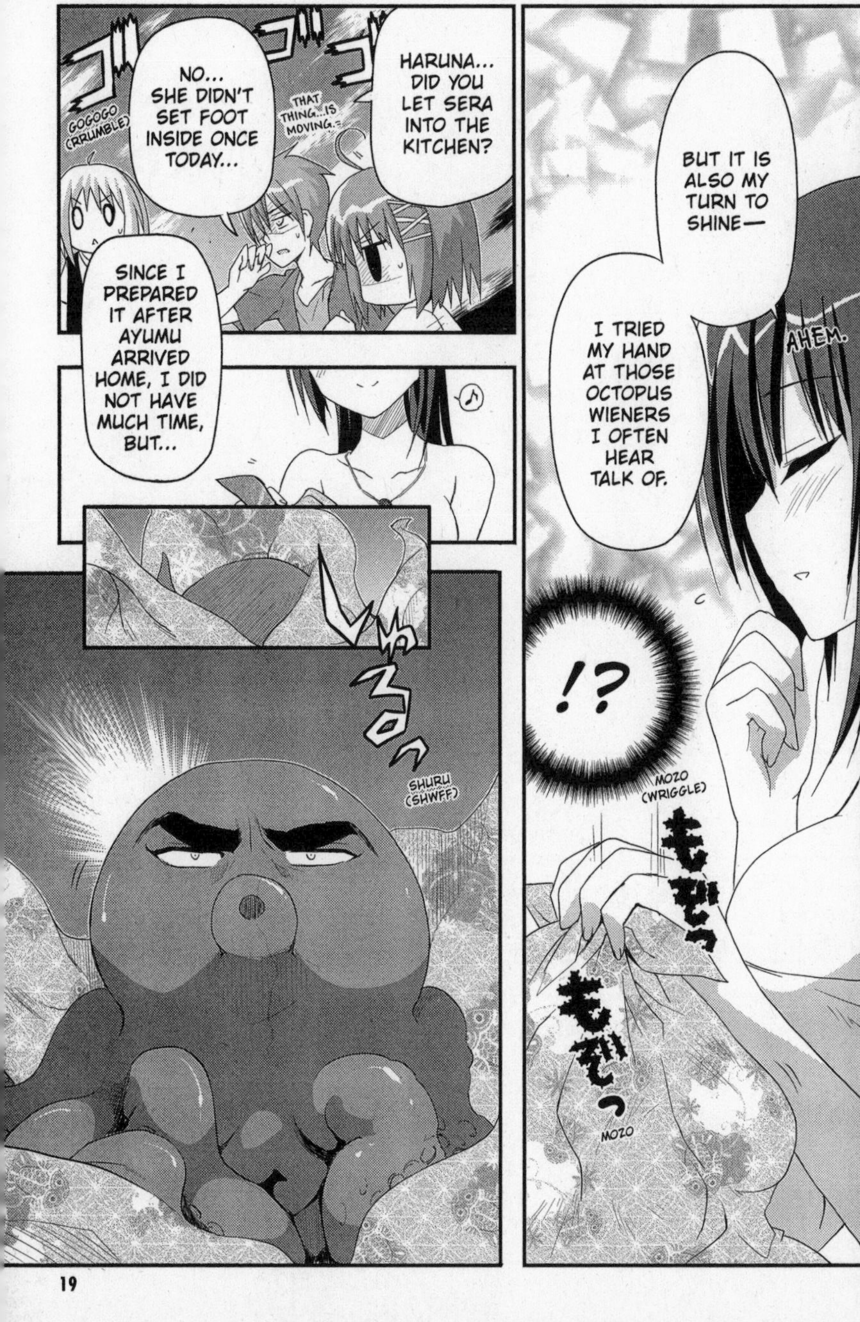
BUT IT IS ALSO MY TURN TO SHINE—
AHEM.
I TRIED MY HAND AT THOSE OCTOPUS WIENERS I OFTEN HEAR TALK OF.
!?
MOZO (WRIGGLE)
MOZO
HARUNA... DID YOU LET SERA INTO THE KITCHEN?
THAT THING...IS MOVING...
NO... SHE DIDN'T SET FOOT INSIDE ONCE TODAY...
GOGOGO (RRUMBLE)
SINCE I PREPARED IT AFTER AYUMU ARRIVED HOME, I DID NOT HAVE MUCH TIME, BUT...
♪
SHURU (SHWFF)

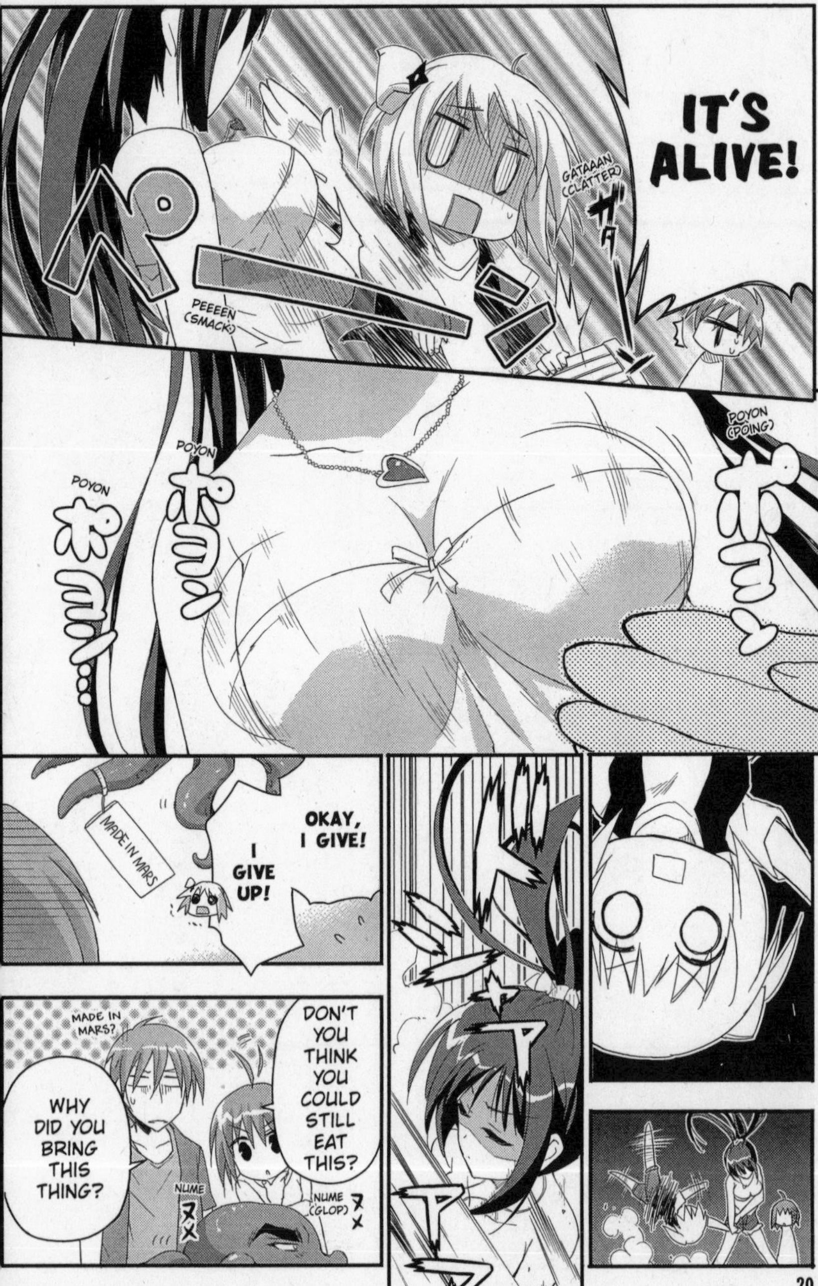

IT'S ALIVE!
GATAAAN (CLATTER)
PEEEEN (SMACK)
POYON (POING)
POYON
POYON
DOSHAAAA (SMASSSH)
OKAY, I GIVE!
I GIVE UP!
MADE IN MARS
DON'T YOU THINK YOU COULD STILL EAT THIS?
MADE IN MARS?
WHY DID YOU BRING THIS THING?
NUME (GLOP)
NUME

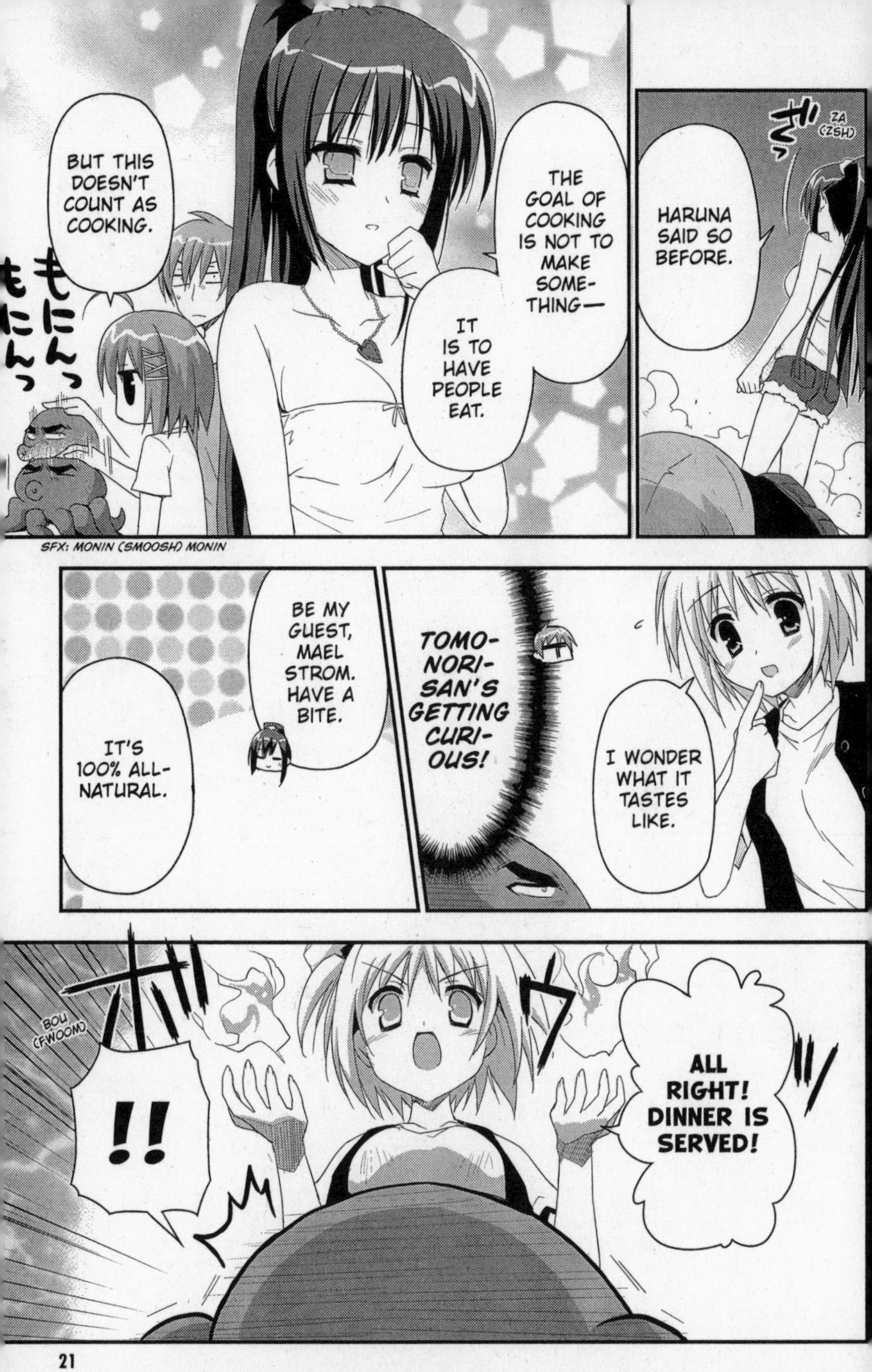
ざっ
ZA (ZSH)
HARUNA SAID SO BEFORE.
THE GOAL OF COOKING IS NOT TO MAKE SOME-THING—
IT IS TO HAVE PEOPLE EAT.
BUT THIS DOESN'T COUNT AS COOKING.
もにんっ もにんっ
SFX: MONIN (SMOOSH) MONIN
I WONDER WHAT IT TASTES LIKE.
TOMO-NORI-SAN'S GETTING CURI-OUS!
BE MY GUEST, MAEL STROM. HAVE A BITE.
IT'S 100% ALL-NATURAL.
ALL RIGHT! DINNER IS SERVED!
BOU (FWOOM)
!!

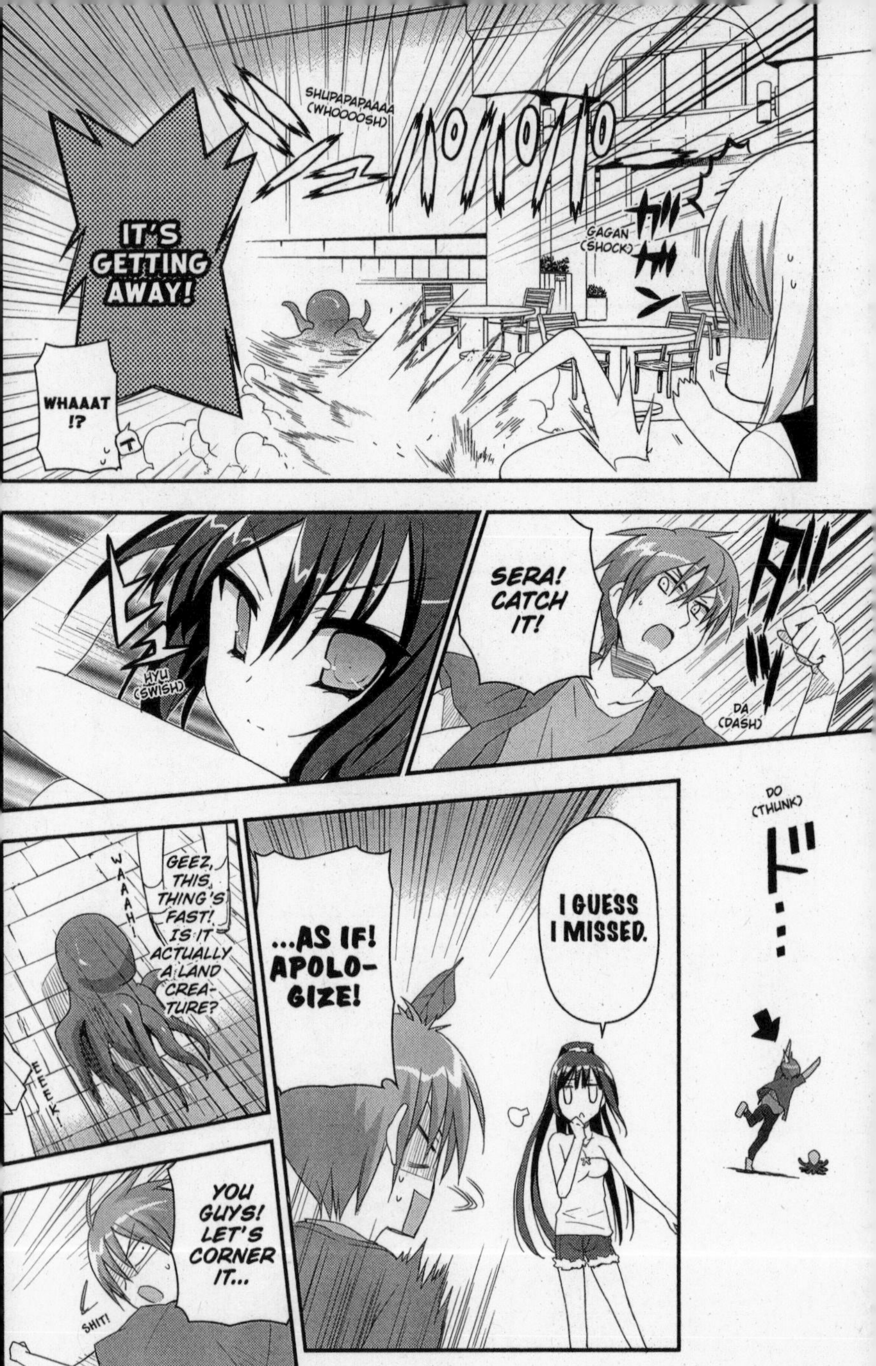
SHUPAPAPAAAA (WHOOOOSH)
GAGAN (SHOCK)
IT'S GETTING AWAY!
WHAAAT !?
DA (DASH)
SERA! CATCH IT!
HYU (SWISH)
DO (THUNK)
I GUESS I MISSED.
...AS IF! APOLO-GIZE!
WAAAH!
GEEZ, THIS THING'S FAST! IS IT ACTUALLY A LAND CREA-TURE?
EEEEK!
YOU GUYS! LET'S CORNER IT...
SHIT!

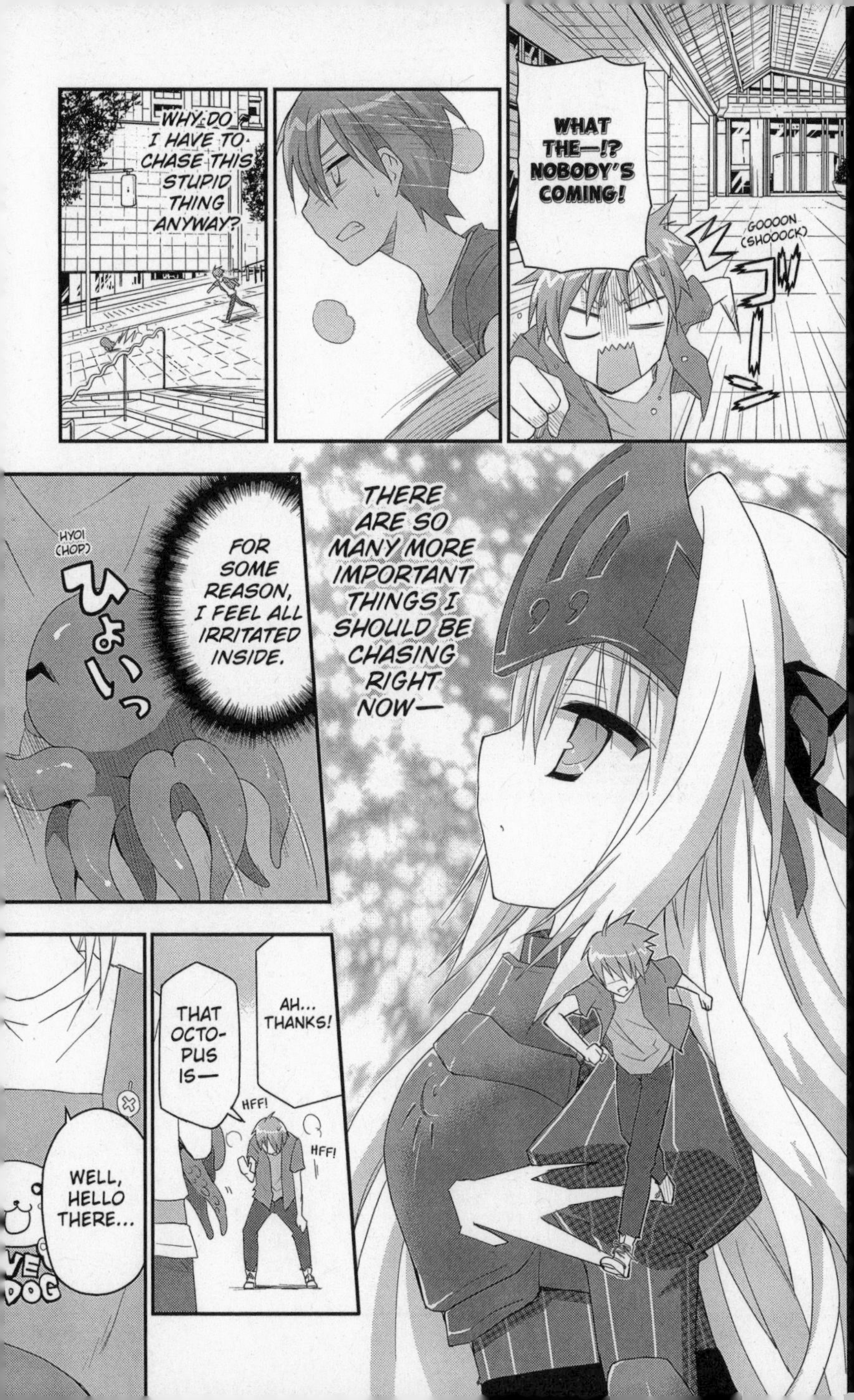
WHAT THE—!? NOBODY'S COMING!
GOOOON (SHOOOCK)
WHY DO I HAVE TO CHASE THIS STUPID THING ANYWAY?
THERE ARE SO MANY MORE IMPORTANT THINGS I SHOULD BE CHASING RIGHT NOW—
FOR SOME REASON, I FEEL ALL IRRITATED INSIDE.
HYOI (HOP)
ひょいっ
AH... THANKS!
THAT OCTOPUS IS—
HFF!
HFF!
WELL, HELLO THERE...
DOG

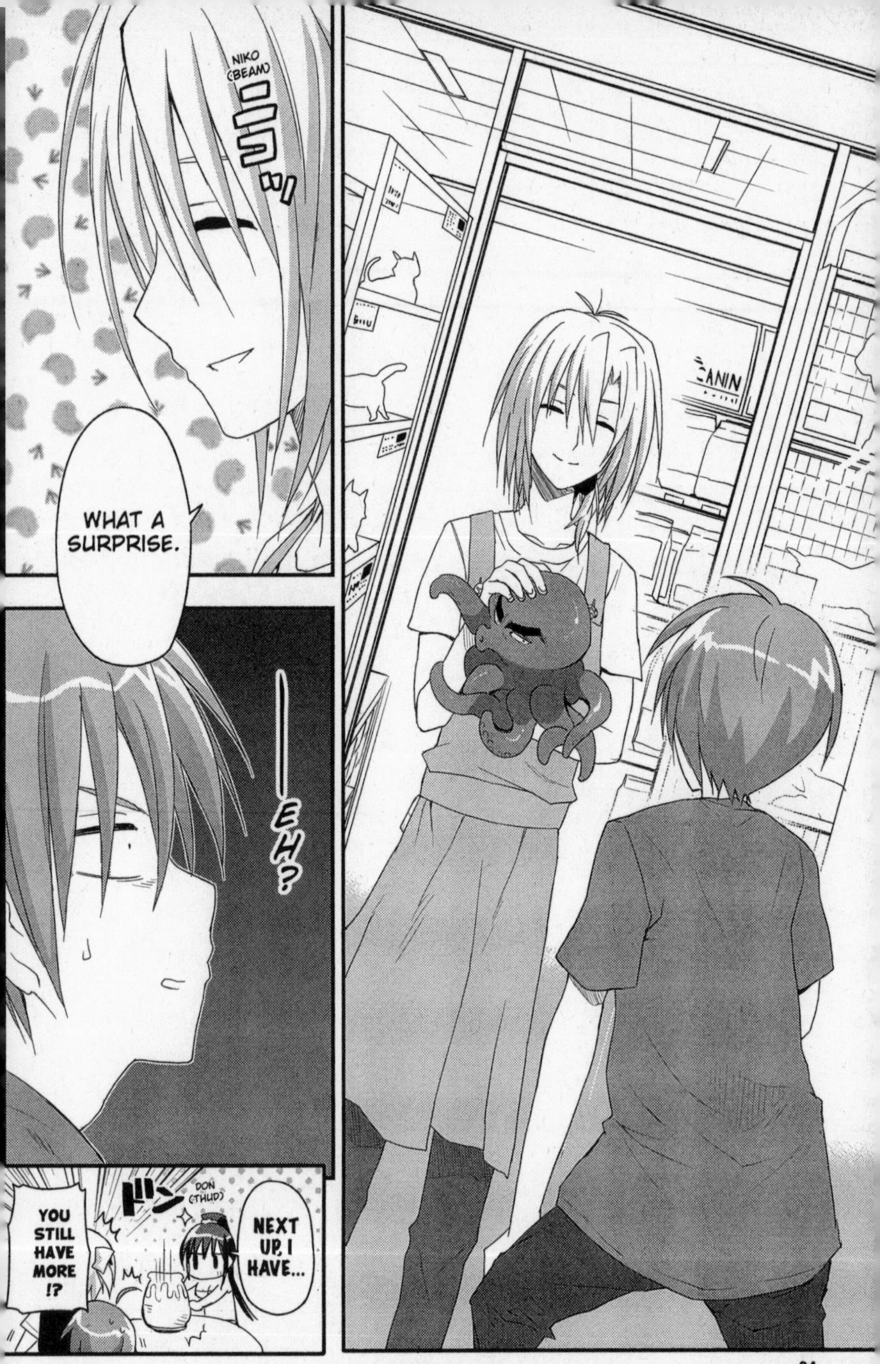
CANIN
NIKO (BEAM)
ニコッ
WHAT A SURPRISE.
EH?
NEXT UP, I HAVE...
DON (THUD)
YOU STILL HAVE MORE !?

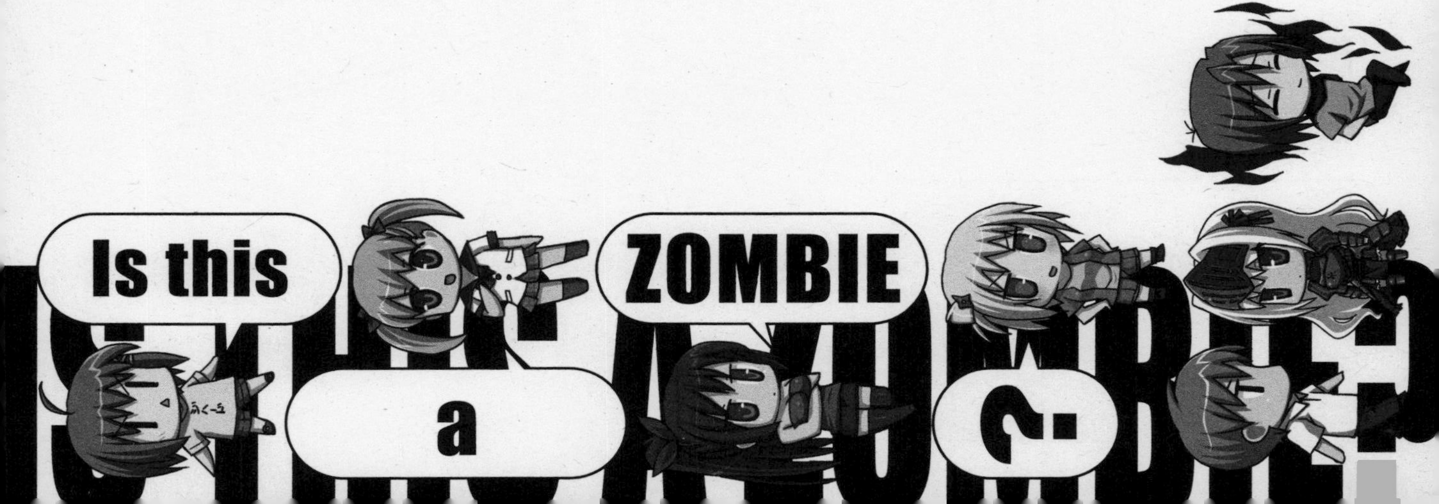
Is this
a
ZOMBIE
?

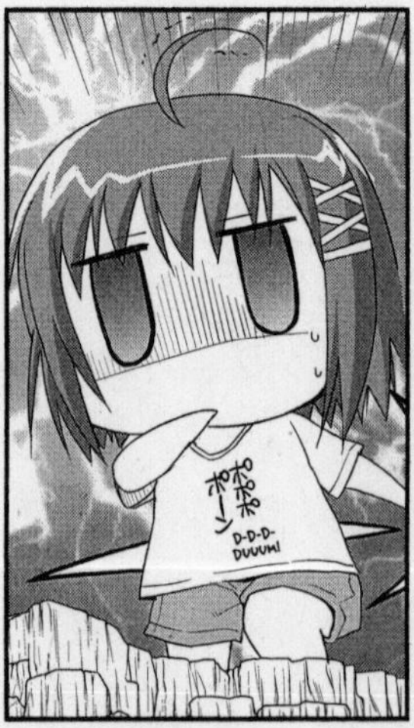
ポポポポーン
D-D-D-DUUUM!

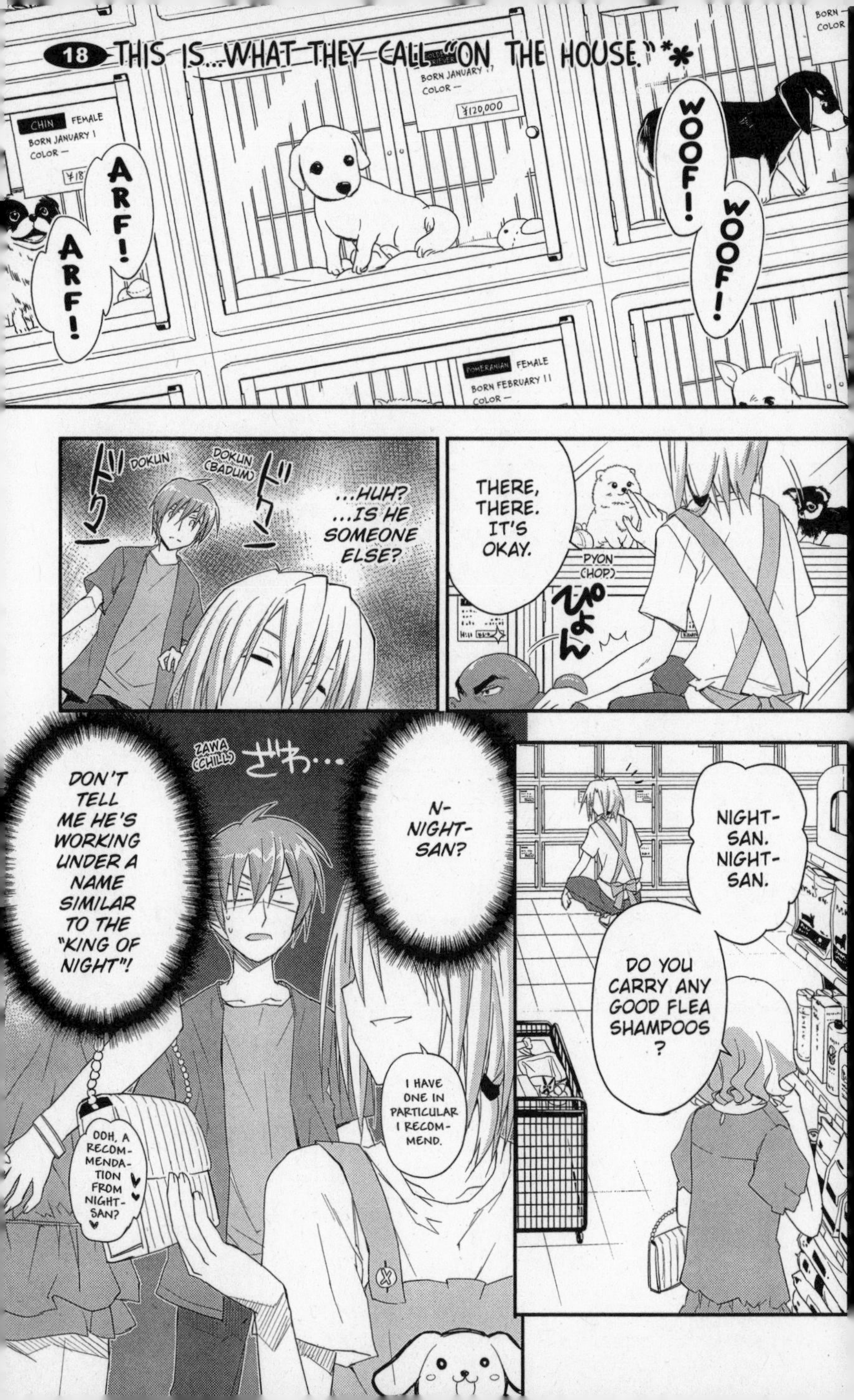
18 THIS IS...WHAT THEY CALL "ON THE HOUSE."*
BORN COLOR
BORN JANUARY 17
COLOR —
¥120,000
CHIN FEMALE
BORN JANUARY 1
COLOR —
WOOF! WOOF!
ARF! ARF!
POMERANIAN FEMALE
BORN FEBRUARY 11
COLOR —
THERE, THERE. IT'S OKAY.
PYON (HOP) ぴょん
DOKUN DOKUN (BADUM)
...HUH? ...IS HE SOMEONE ELSE?
NIGHT-SAN. NIGHT-SAN.
DO YOU CARRY ANY GOOD FLEA SHAMPOOS?
N-NIGHT-SAN?
ZAWA (CHILL) ざわ...
DON'T TELL ME HE'S WORKING UNDER A NAME SIMILAR TO THE "KING OF NIGHT"!
I HAVE ONE IN PARTICULAR I RECOMMEND.
OOH, A RECOMMENDATION FROM NIGHT-SAN?

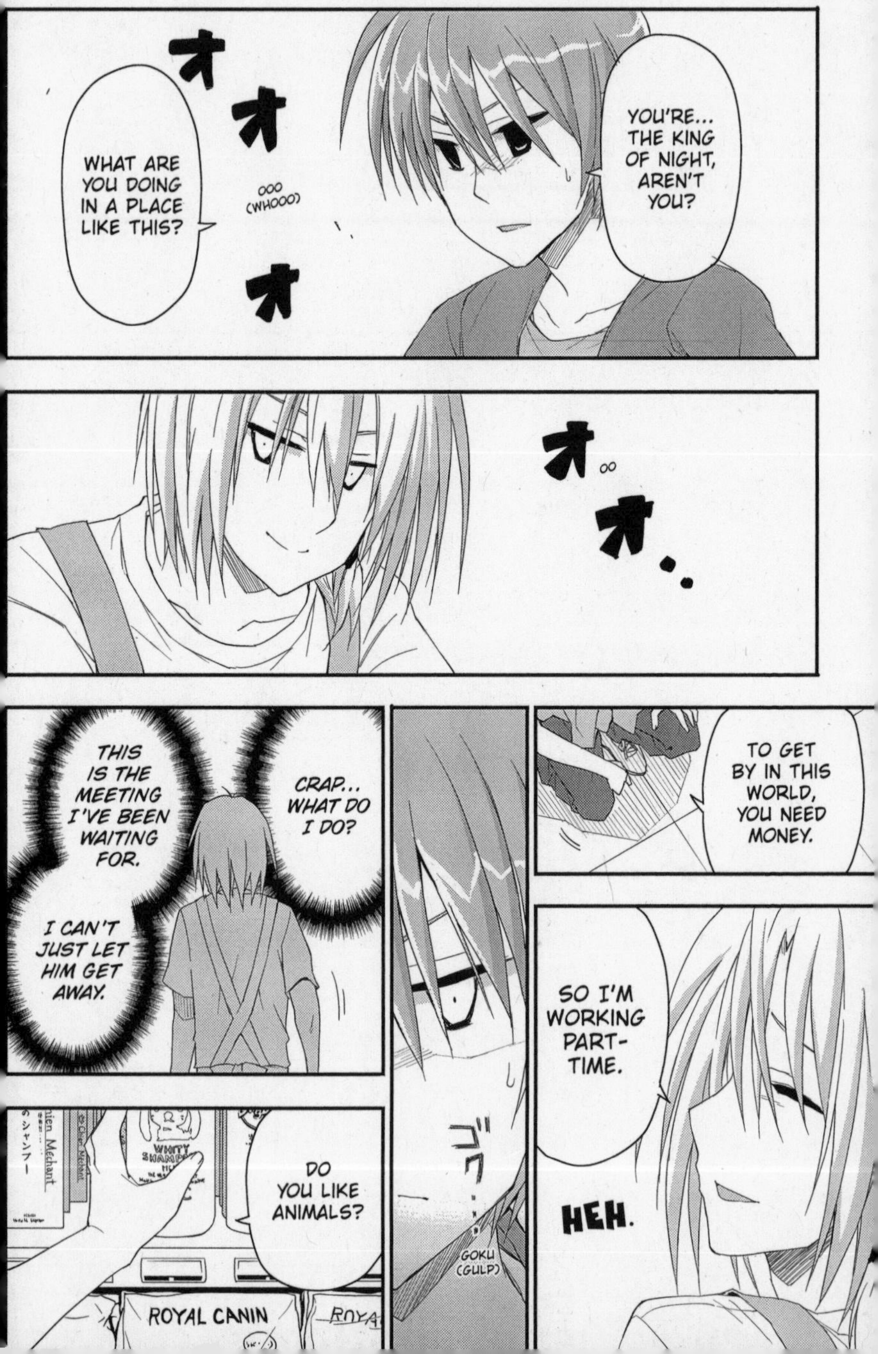

YOU'RE... THE KING OF NIGHT, AREN'T YOU?
オオオ
OOO (WHOOO)
WHAT ARE YOU DOING IN A PLACE LIKE THIS?
オオ..
TO GET BY IN THIS WORLD, YOU NEED MONEY.
SO I'M WORKING PART-TIME.
HEH.
ゴク..
GOKU (GULP)
CRAP... WHAT DO I DO?
THIS IS THE MEETING I'VE BEEN WAITING FOR.
I CAN'T JUST LET HIM GET AWAY.
DO YOU LIKE ANIMALS?
ROYAL CANIN

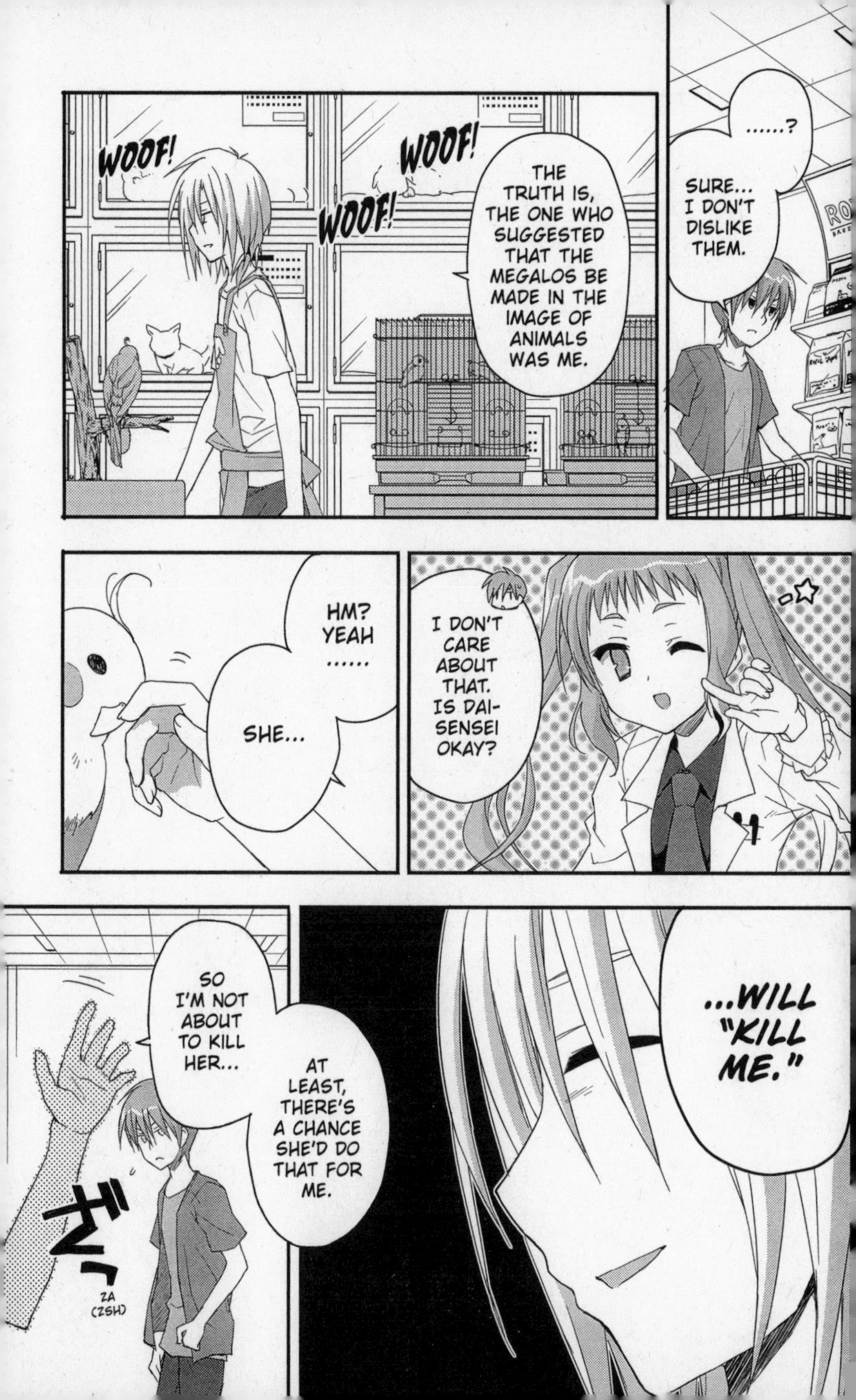
......?
SURE... I DON'T DISLIKE THEM.
WOOF!
WOOF!
WOOF!
THE TRUTH IS, THE ONE WHO SUGGESTED THAT THE MEGALOS BE MADE IN THE IMAGE OF ANIMALS WAS ME.
I DON'T CARE ABOUT THAT. IS DAI-SENSEI OKAY?
HM? YEAH ......
SHE...
...WILL "KILL ME."
SO I'M NOT ABOUT TO KILL HER...
AT LEAST, THERE'S A CHANCE SHE'D DO THAT FOR ME.
ZA (ZSH)

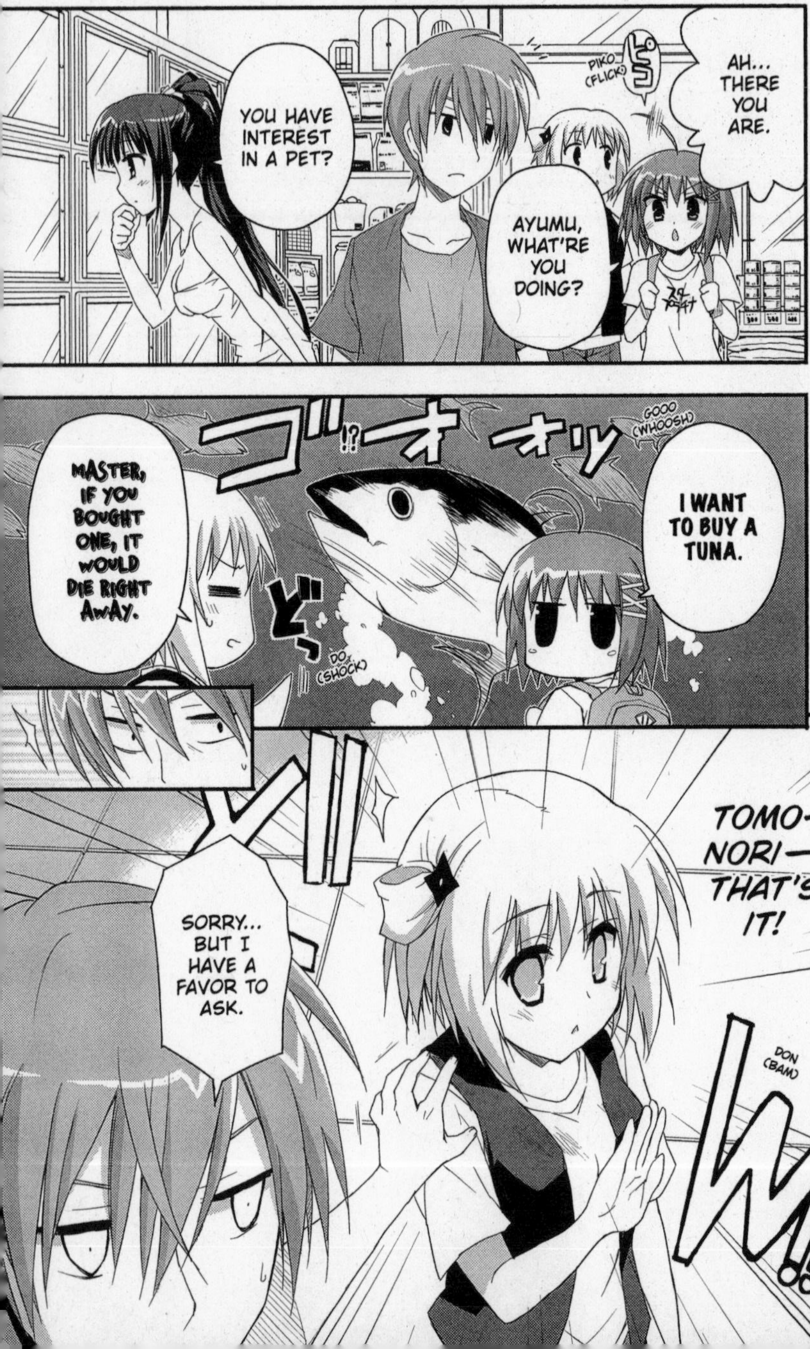
AH... THERE YOU ARE.
PIKO (FLICK)
AYUMU, WHAT'RE YOU DOING?
YOU HAVE INTEREST IN A PET?
GOOO (WHOOSH)
I WANT TO BUY A TUNA.
DO (SHOCK)
MASTER, IF YOU BOUGHT ONE, IT WOULD DIE RIGHT AWAY.
TOMO-NORI—THAT'S IT!
DON (BAM)
SORRY... BUT I HAVE A FAVOR TO ASK.

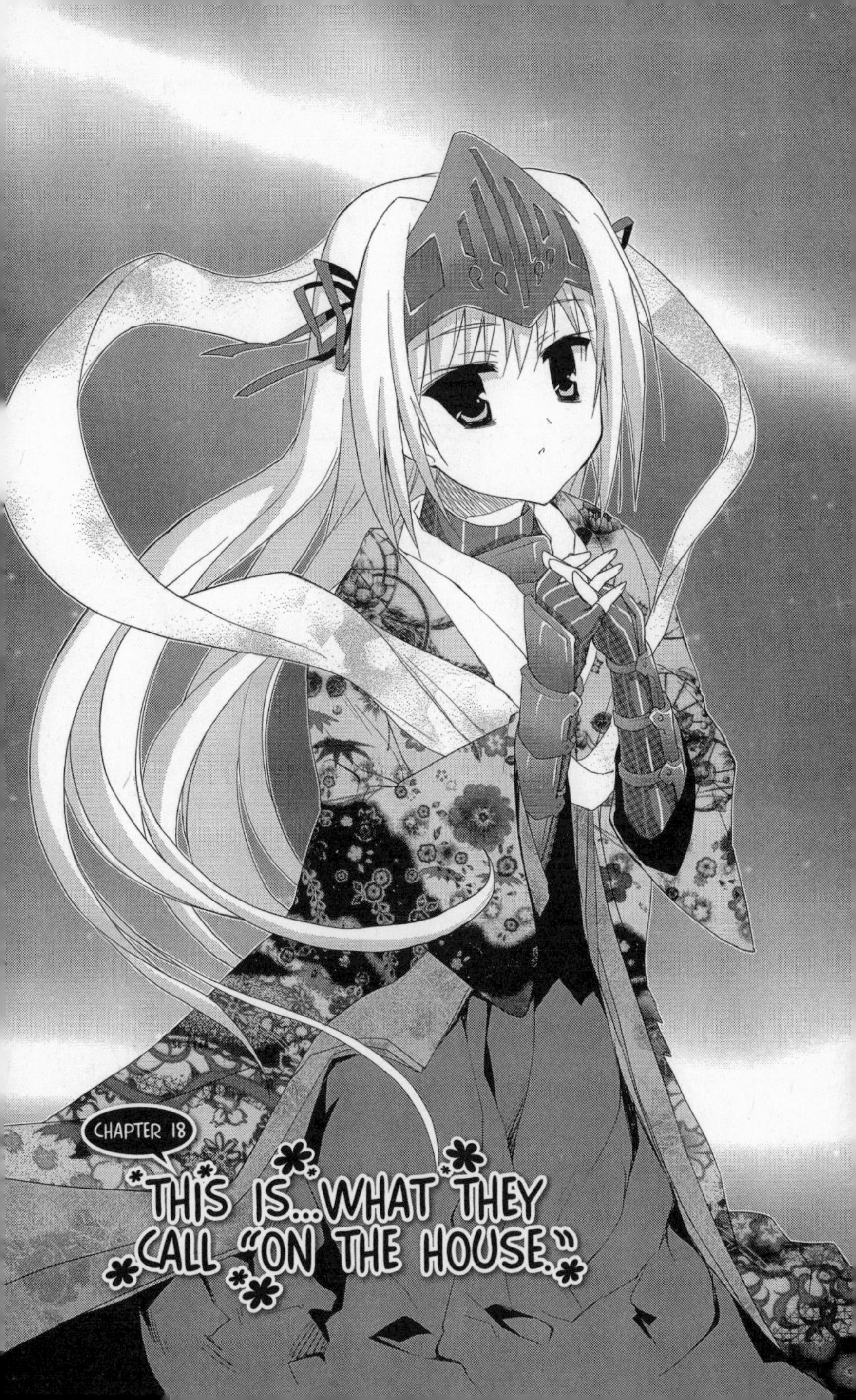
CHAPTER 18
"THIS IS...WHAT THEY CALL "ON THE HOUSE.""

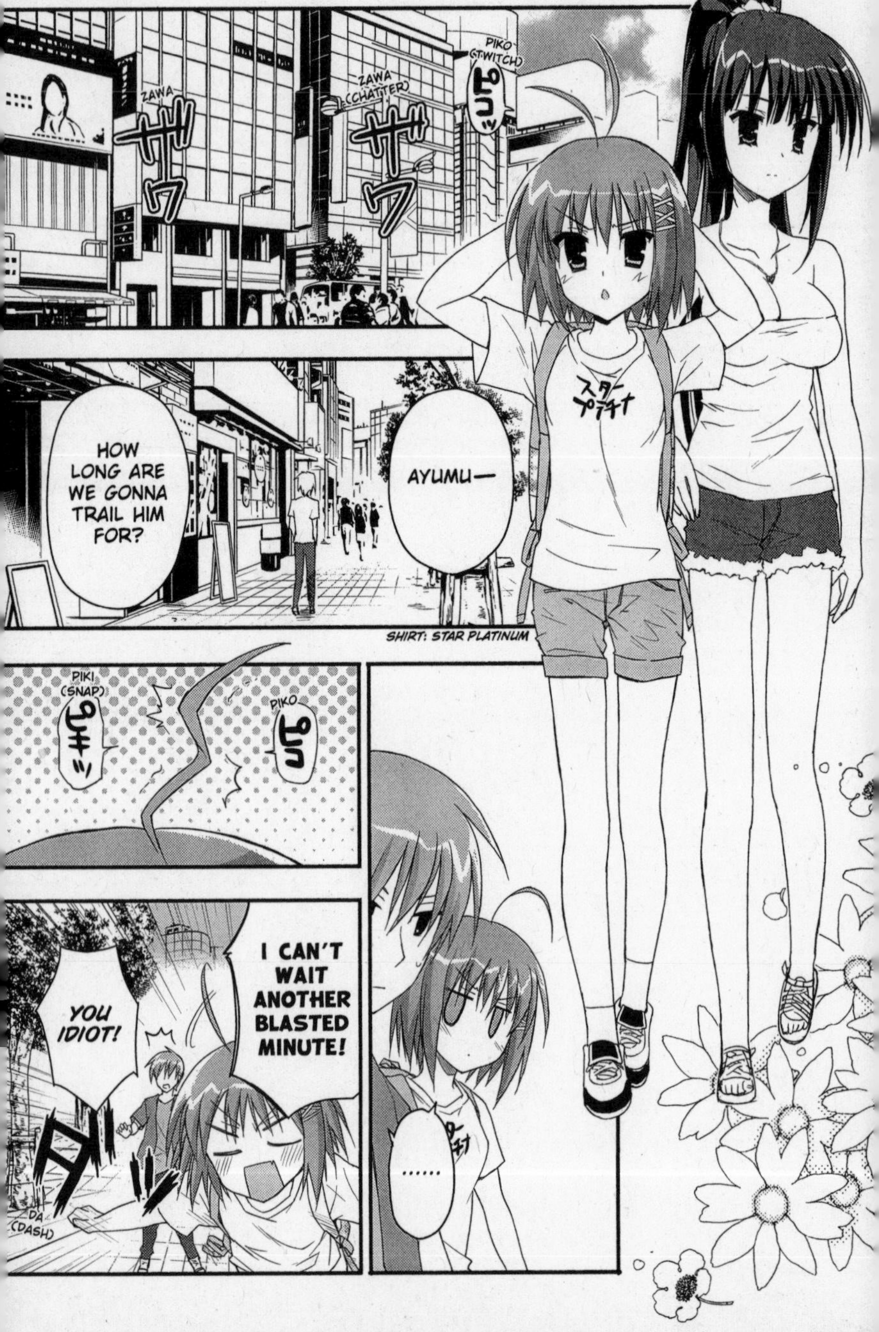

PIKO (TWITCH)
ピコッ
ZAWA (CHATTER)
ザワ
ZAWA
ザワ
AYUMU—
HOW LONG ARE WE GONNA TRAIL HIM FOR?
スタープラチナ
SHIRT: STAR PLATINUM
PIKO
ピコ
PIKI (SNAP)
ピキッ
……
I CAN'T WAIT ANOTHER BLASTED MINUTE!
YOU IDIOT!
DA (DASH)

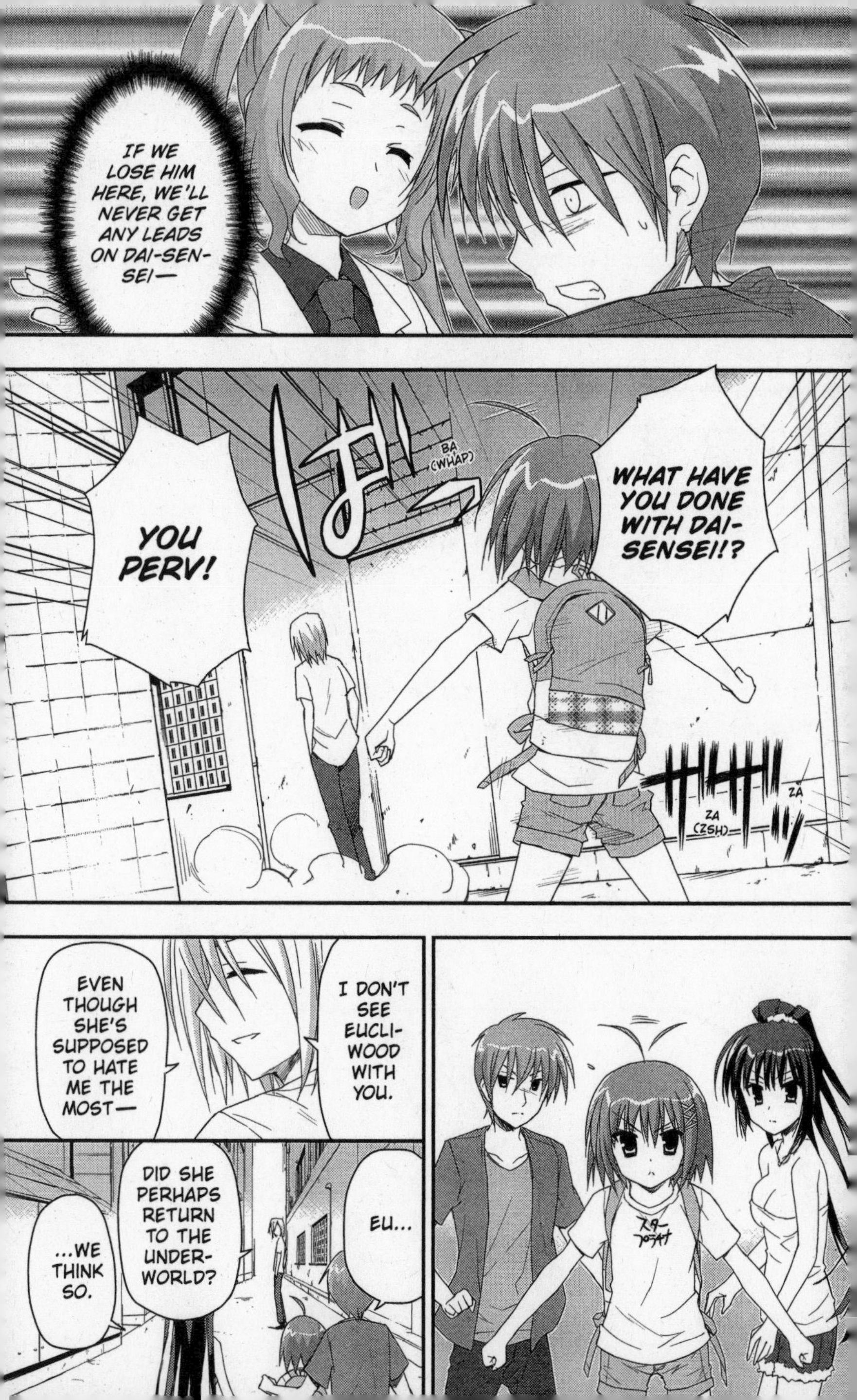
IF WE LOSE HIM HERE, WE'LL NEVER GET ANY LEADS ON DAI-SENSEI—
WHAT HAVE YOU DONE WITH DAI-SENSEI!?
ZA ZA (ZSH)
BA (WHAP)
YOU PERV!
I DON'T SEE EUCLIWOOD WITH YOU.
EVEN THOUGH SHE'S SUPPOSED TO HATE ME THE MOST—
EU...
DID SHE PERHAPS RETURN TO THE UNDERWORLD?
...WE THINK SO.

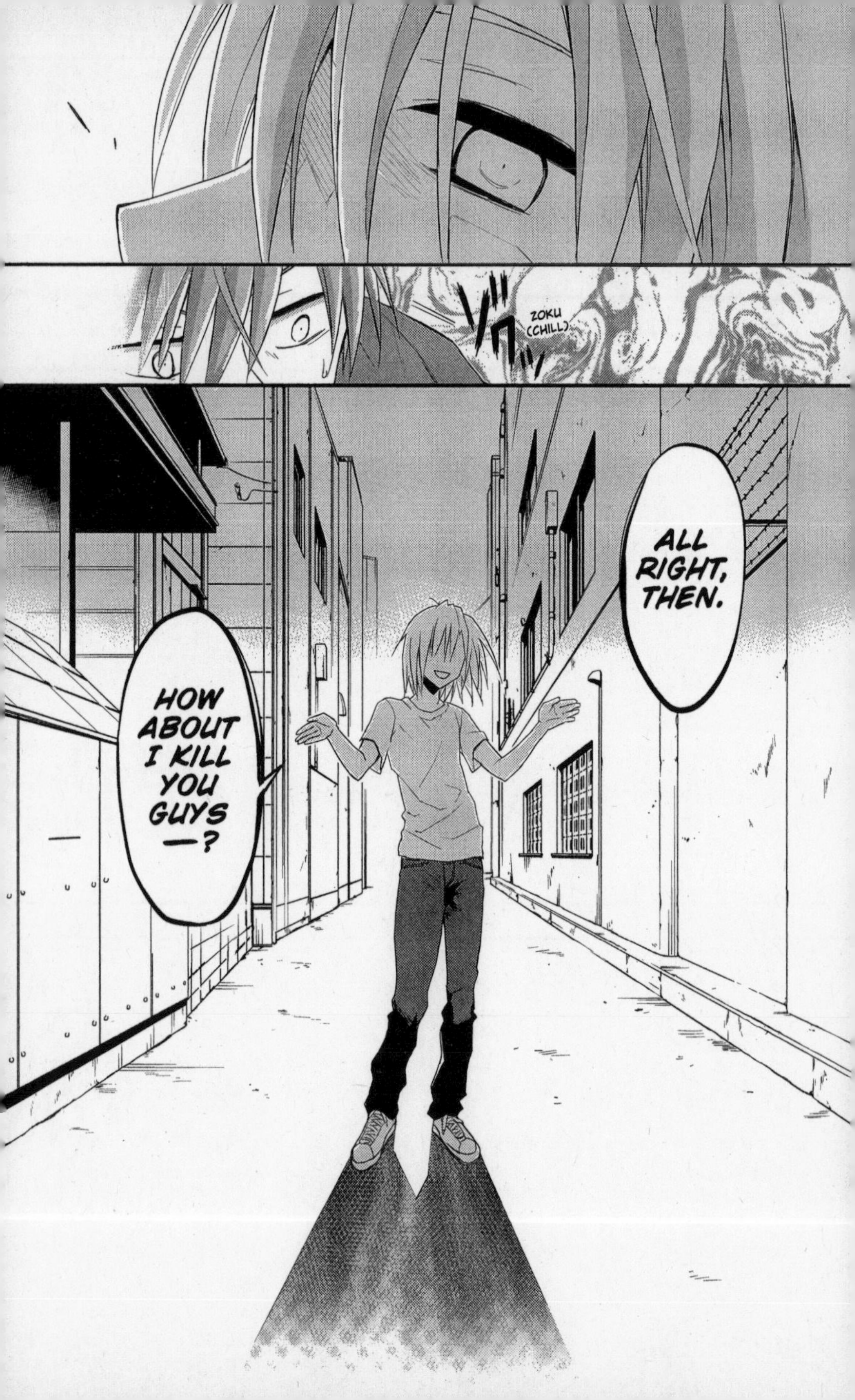
ZOKU (CHILL)
ALL RIGHT, THEN.
HOW ABOUT I KILL YOU GUYS—?

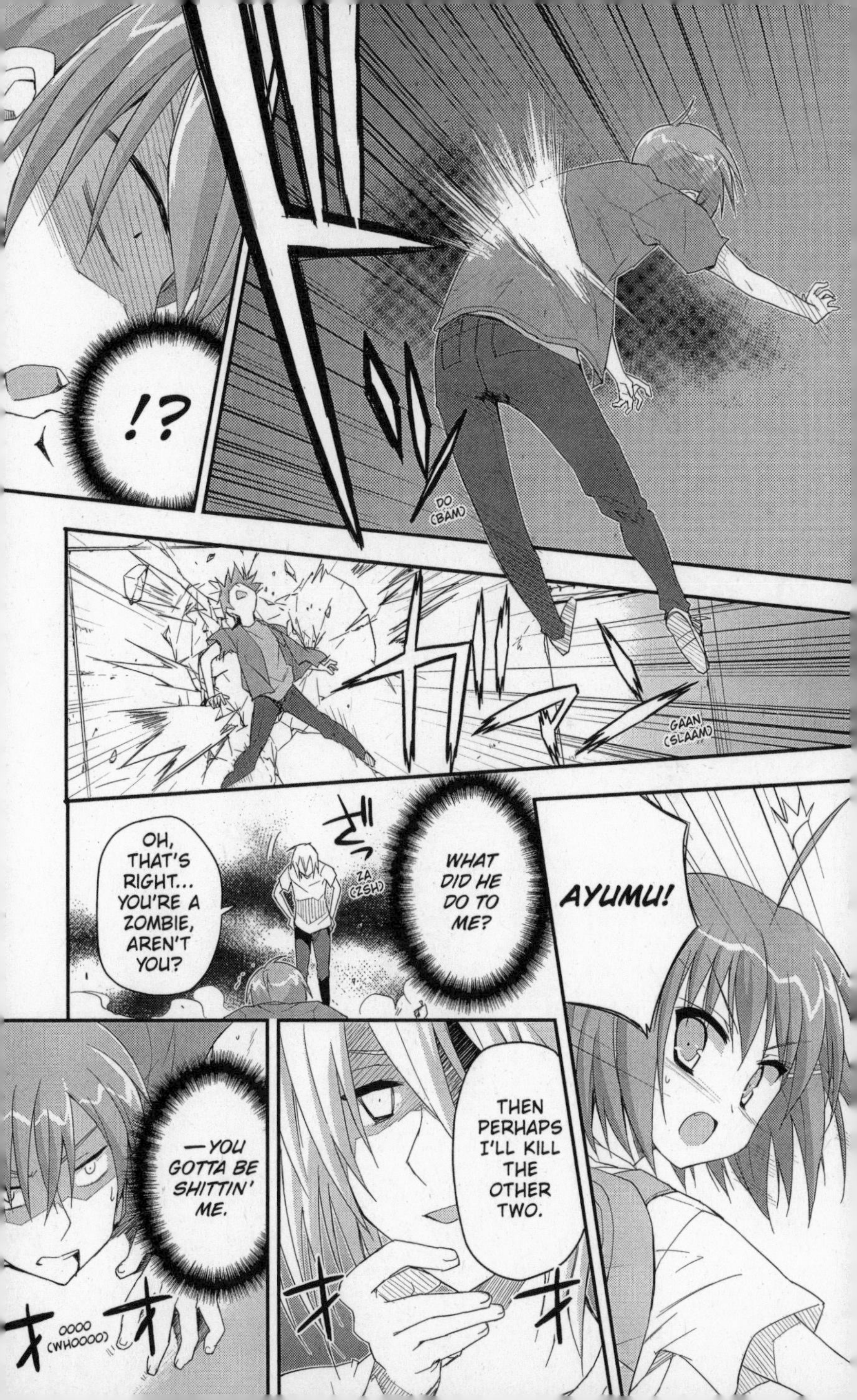
!?
DO (BAM)
GAAN (SLAAM)
AYUMU!
WHAT DID HE DO TO ME?
ZA (ZSH)
OH, THAT'S RIGHT... YOU'RE A ZOMBIE, AREN'T YOU?
THEN PERHAPS I'LL KILL THE OTHER TWO.
—YOU GOTTA BE SHITTIN' ME.
OOOO (WHOOOO)

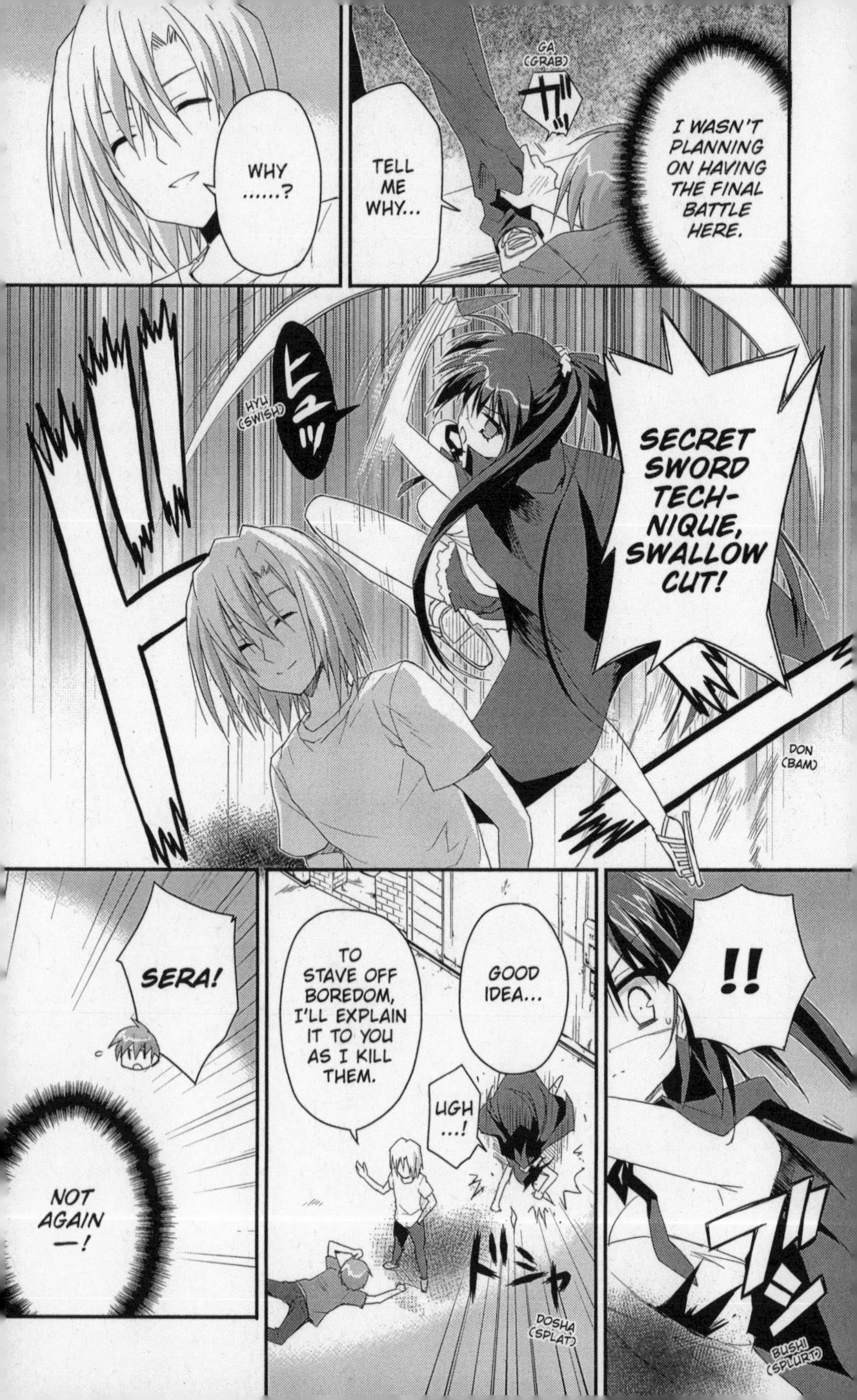
I WASN'T PLANNING ON HAVING THE FINAL BATTLE HERE.
GA (GRAB)
TELL ME WHY...
WHY ......?
SECRET SWORD TECH-NIQUE, SWALLOW CUT!
HYU (SWISH)
DON (BAM)
!!
BUSHI (SPLURT)
GOOD IDEA...
TO STAVE OFF BOREDOM, I'LL EXPLAIN IT TO YOU AS I KILL THEM.
UGH ...!
DOSHA (SPLAT)
SERA!
NOT AGAIN —!

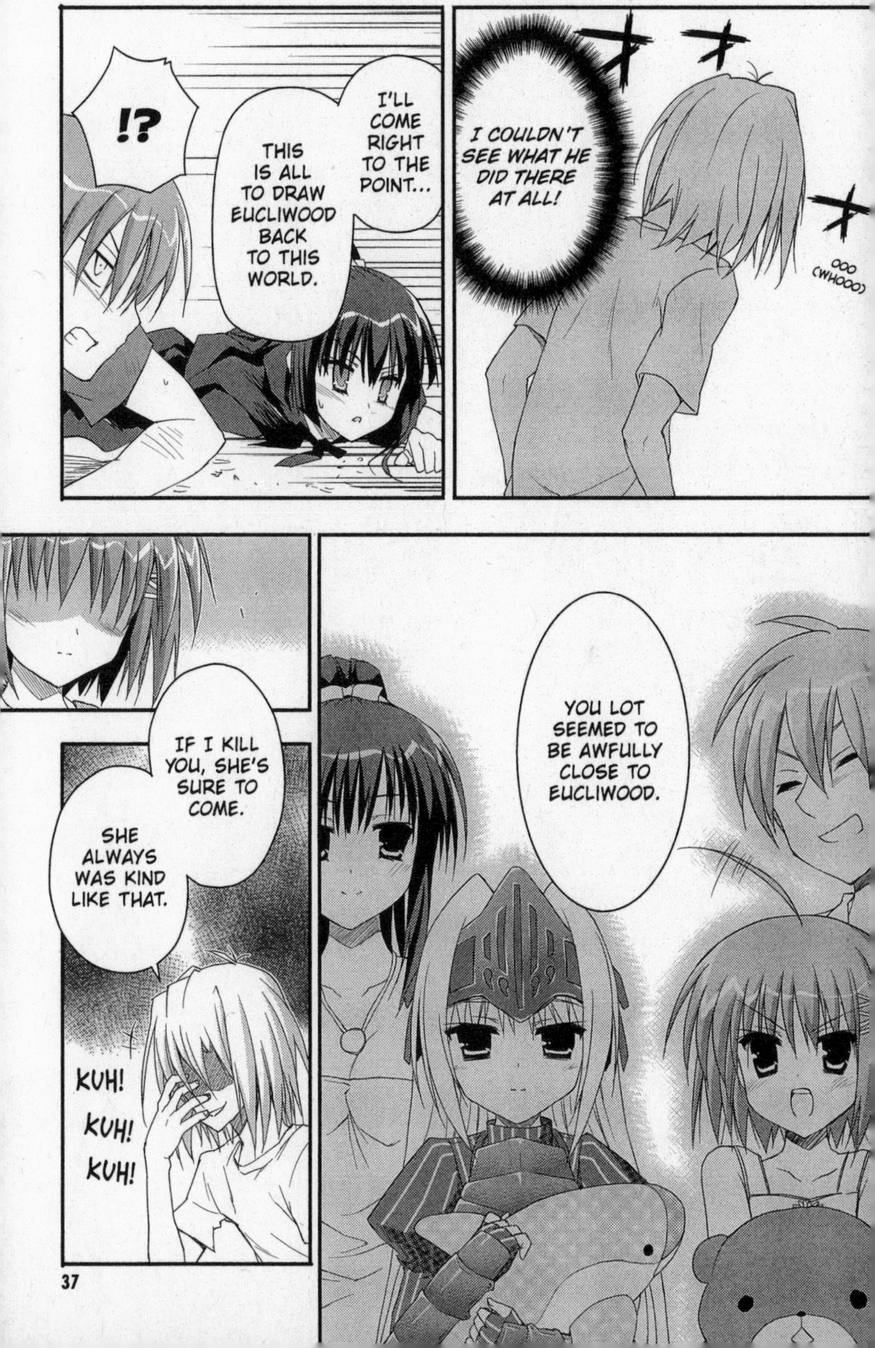
I COULDN'T SEE WHAT HE DID THERE AT ALL!
OOO (WHOOO)
I'LL COME RIGHT TO THE POINT...
THIS IS ALL TO DRAW EUCLIWOOD BACK TO THIS WORLD.
!?
YOU LOT SEEMED TO BE AWFULLY CLOSE TO EUCLIWOOD.
IF I KILL YOU, SHE'S SURE TO COME.
SHE ALWAYS WAS KIND LIKE THAT.
KUH! KUH! KUH!

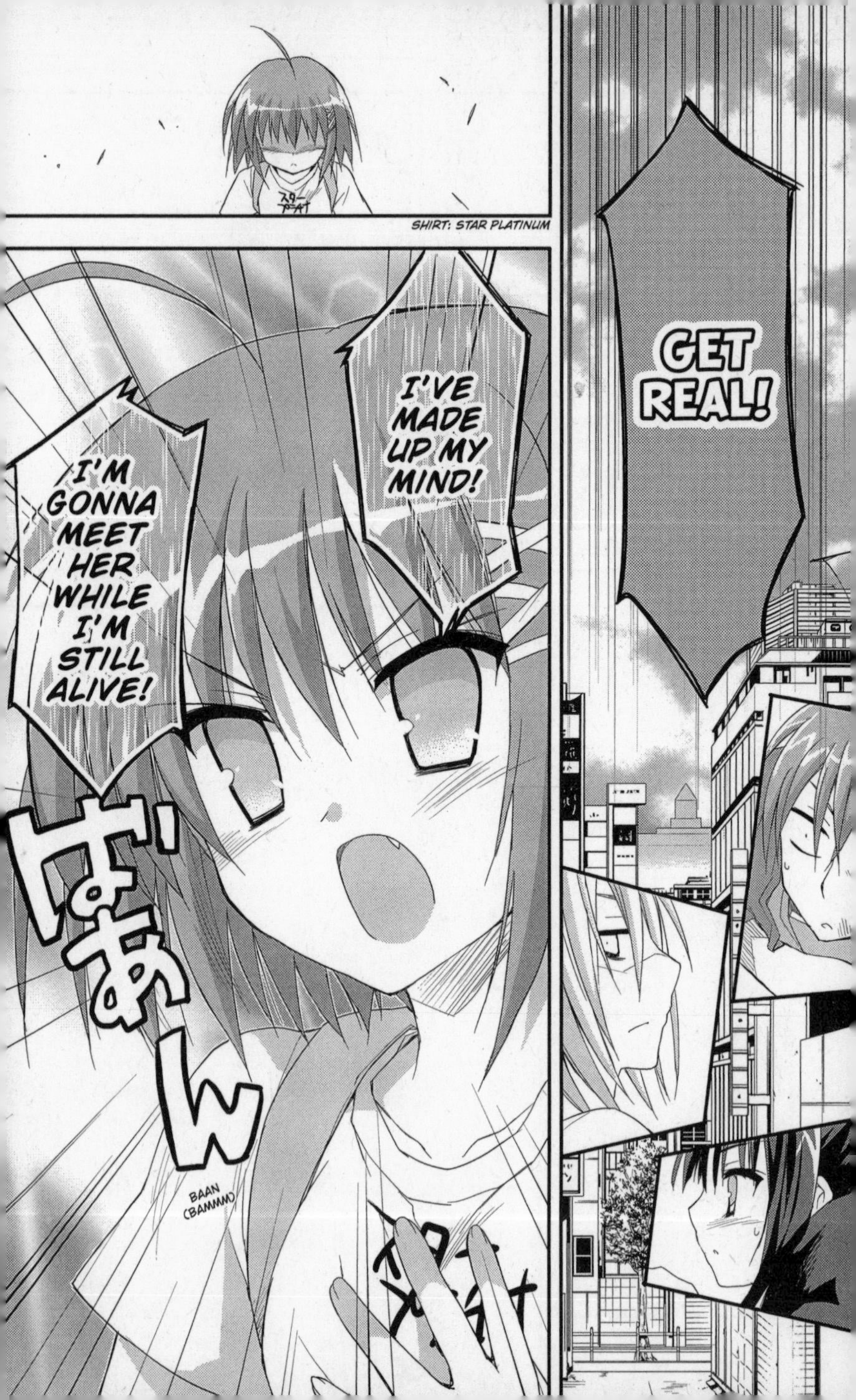
SHIRT: STAR PLATINUM
I'VE MADE UP MY MIND!
I'M GONNA MEET HER WHILE I'M STILL ALIVE!
ばあん
BAAN (BAMMM)
GET REAL!

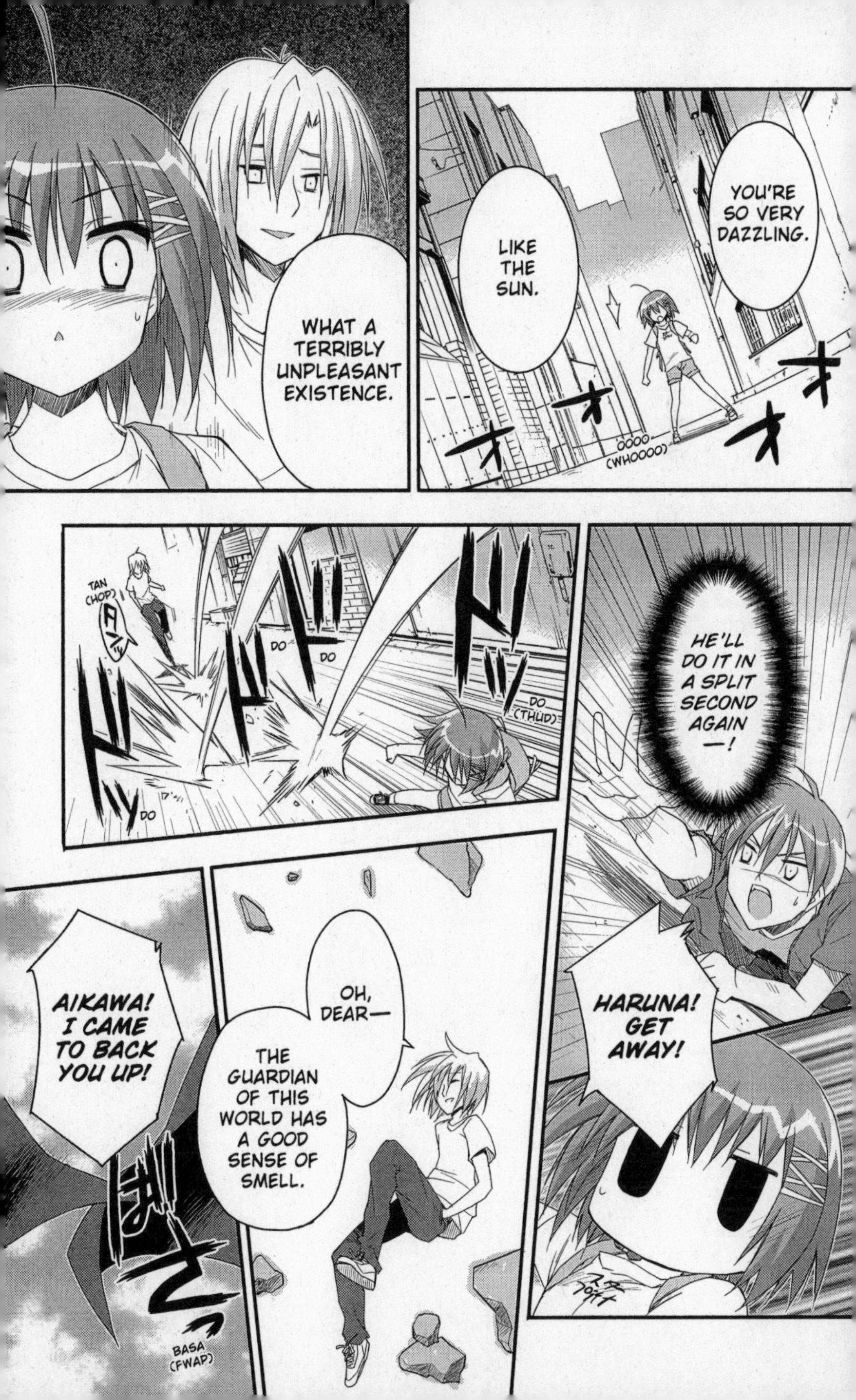
YOU'RE SO VERY DAZZLING.
LIKE THE SUN.
OOOO (WHOOOO)
WHAT A TERRIBLY UNPLEASANT EXISTENCE.
HE'LL DO IT IN A SPLIT SECOND AGAIN—!
DO
DO
DO (THUD)
DO
TAN (HOP)
HARUNA! GET AWAY!
OH, DEAR—
THE GUARDIAN OF THIS WORLD HAS A GOOD SENSE OF SMELL.
AIKAWA! I CAME TO BACK YOU UP!
BASA (FWAP)

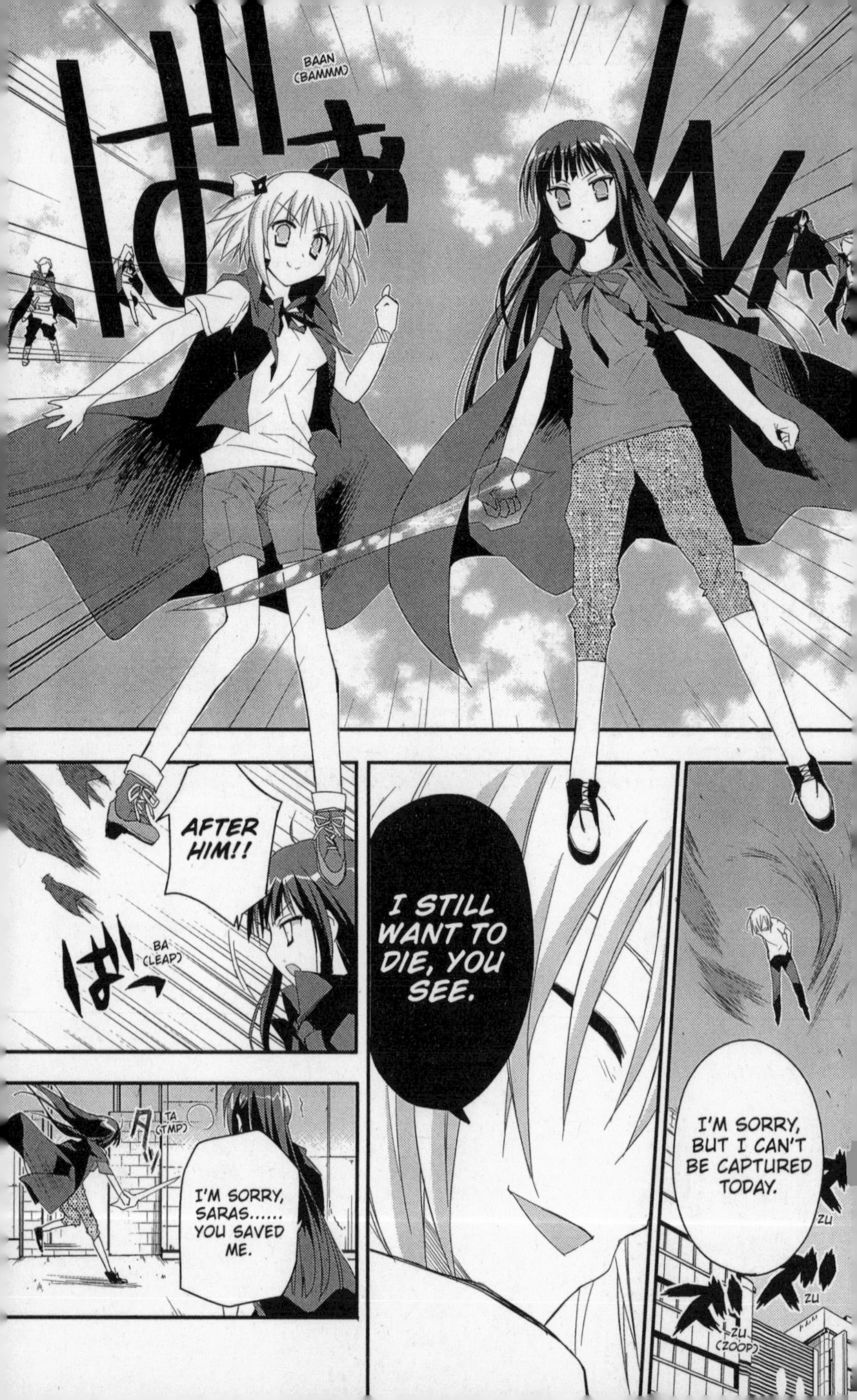
BAAN
(BAMMM)
I'M SORRY, BUT I CAN'T BE CAPTURED TODAY.
ZU
ZU
ZU
(ZOOP)
I STILL WANT TO DIE, YOU SEE.
AFTER HIM!!
BA
(LEAP)
TA
(TMP)
I'M SORRY, SARAS...... YOU SAVED ME.

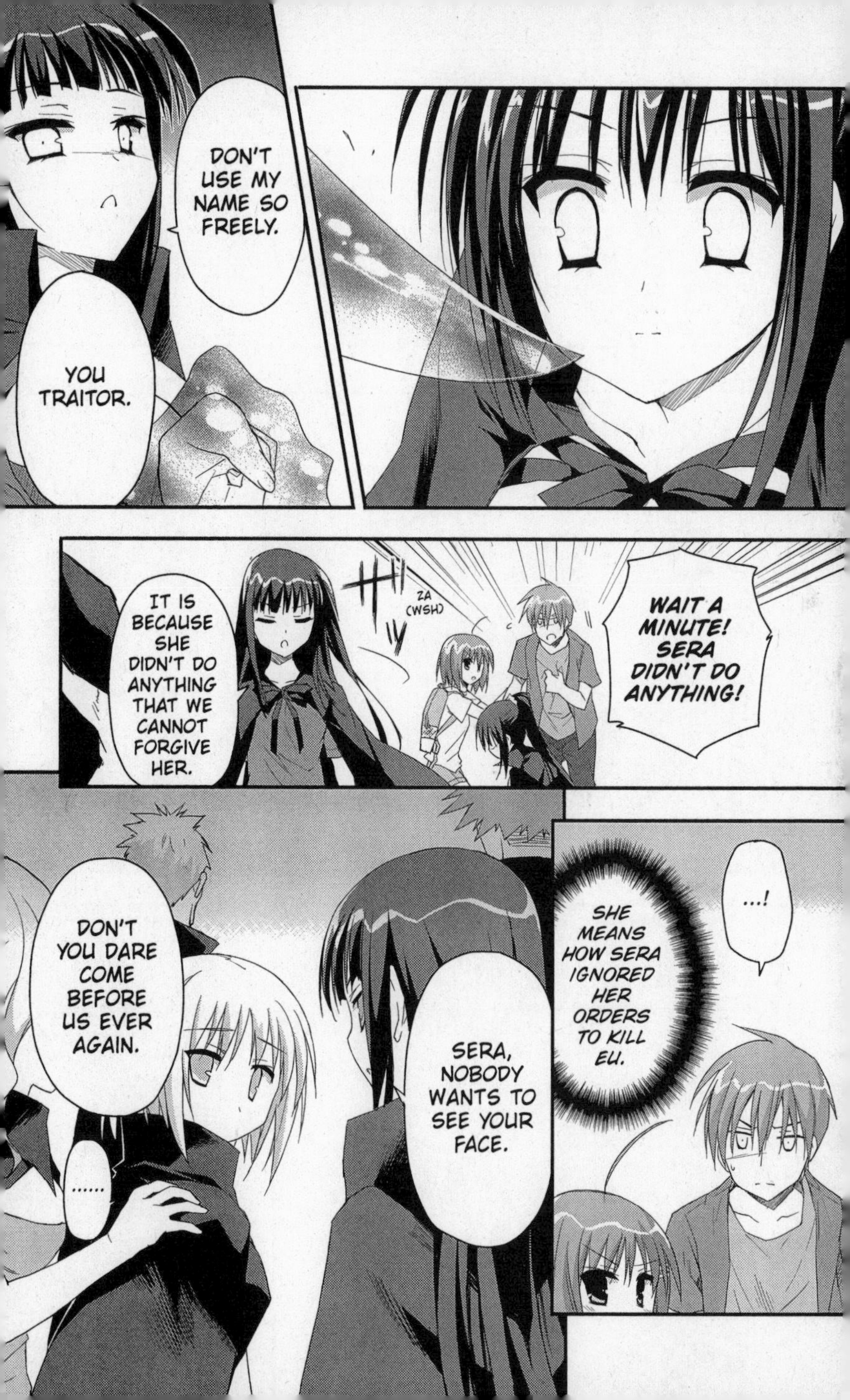
DON'T USE MY NAME SO FREELY.
YOU TRAITOR.
WAIT A MINUTE! SERA DIDN'T DO ANYTHING!
ZA (WSH)
IT IS BECAUSE SHE DIDN'T DO ANYTHING THAT WE CANNOT FORGIVE HER.
...!
SHE MEANS HOW SERA IGNORED HER ORDERS TO KILL EU.
SERA, NOBODY WANTS TO SEE YOUR FACE.
DON'T YOU DARE COME BEFORE US EVER AGAIN.
......

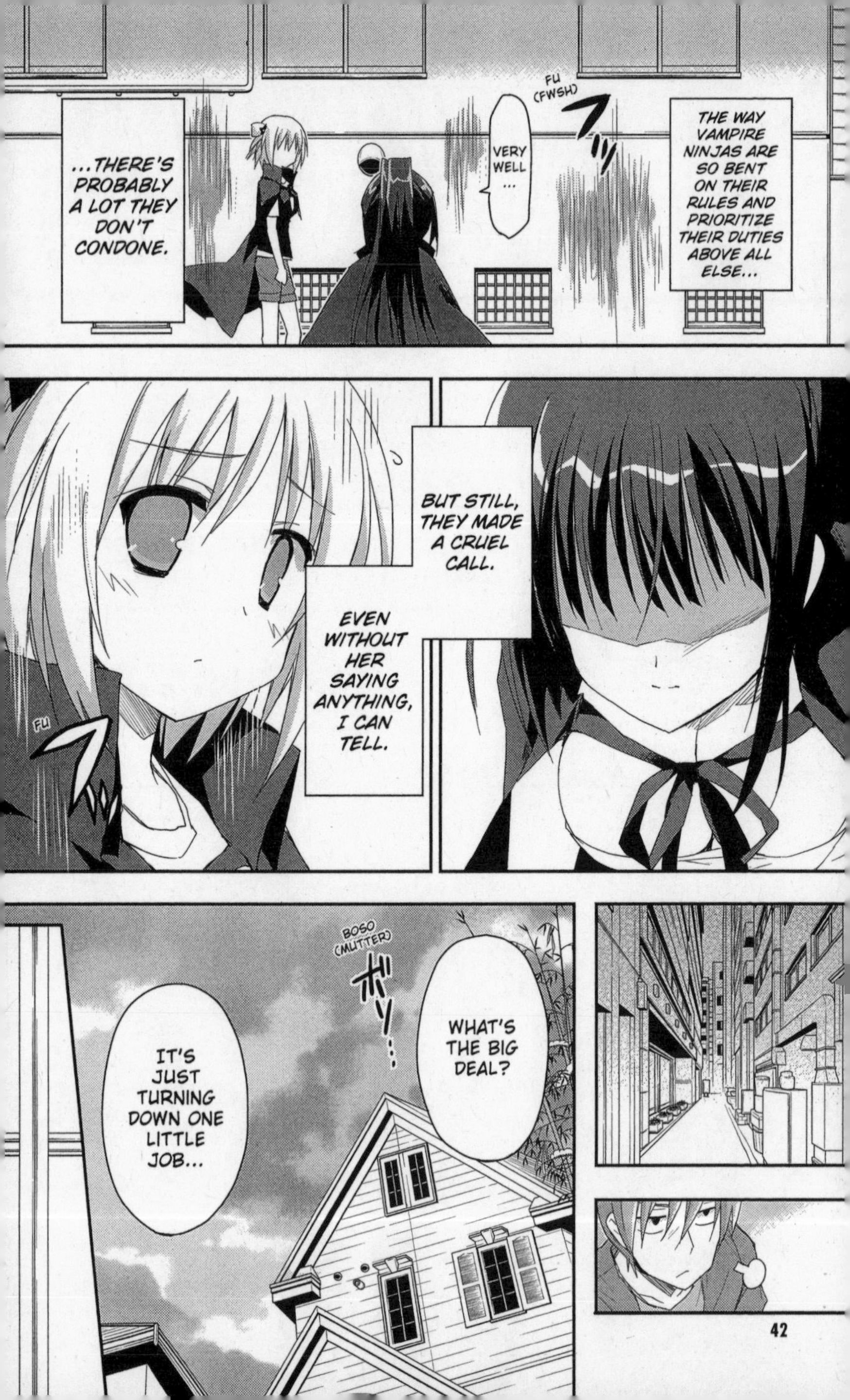
THE WAY VAMPIRE NINJAS ARE SO BENT ON THEIR RULES AND PRIORITIZE THEIR DUTIES ABOVE ALL ELSE...
FU (FWSH)
VERY WELL ...
...THERE'S PROBABLY A LOT THEY DON'T CONDONE.
BUT STILL, THEY MADE A CRUEL CALL.
EVEN WITHOUT HER SAYING ANYTHING, I CAN TELL.
FU
BOSO (MUTTER)
WHAT'S THE BIG DEAL?
IT'S JUST TURNING DOWN ONE LITTLE JOB...

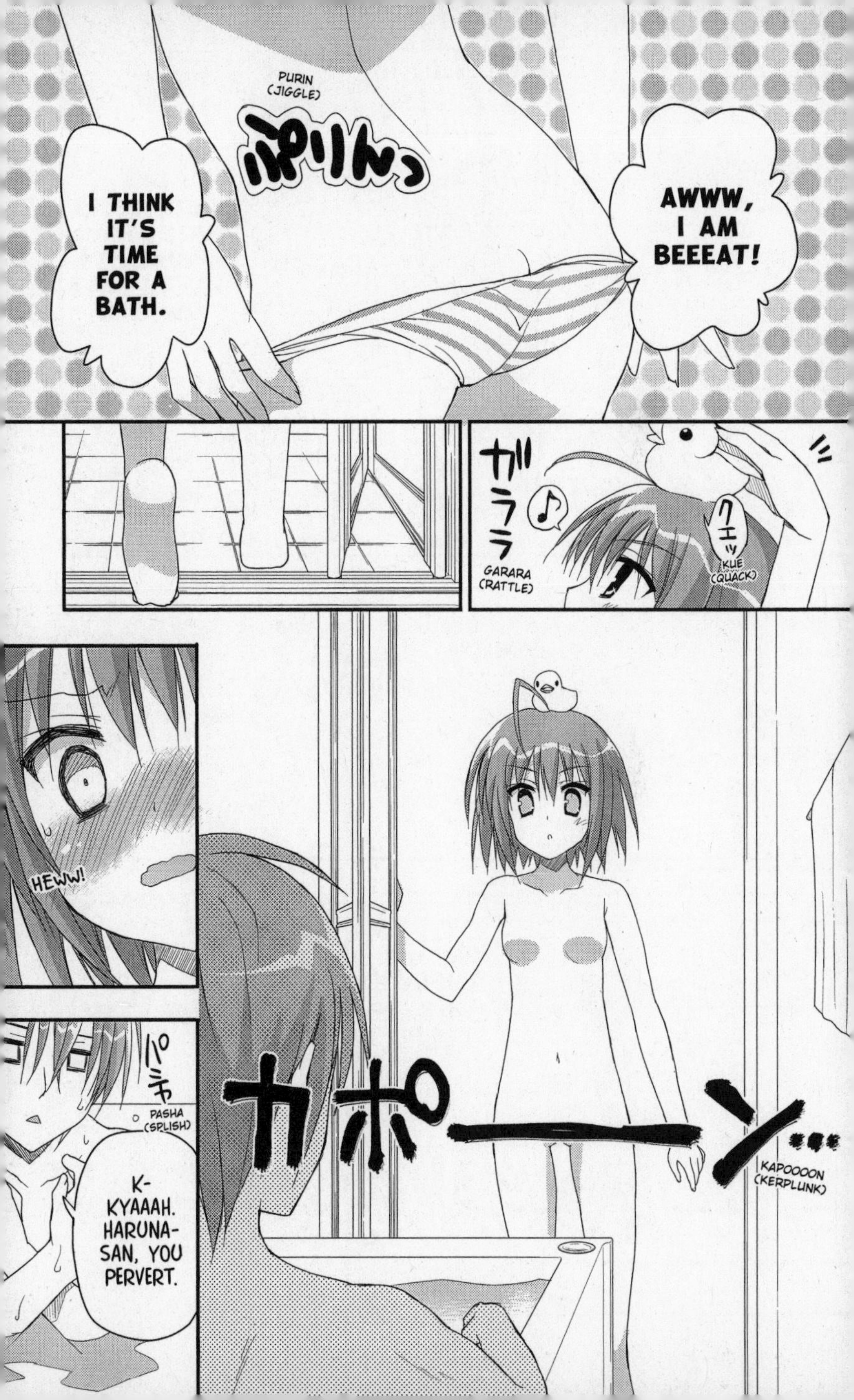

AWWW, I AM BEEEAT!
PURIN (JIGGLE)
ぷりんっ
I THINK IT'S TIME FOR A BATH.
クエッ
KUE (QUACK)
♪
ガララ
GARARA (RATTLE)
カポーーン…
KAPOOOON (KERPLUNK)
HEWW!
パシャ
PASHA (SPLISH)
K-KYAAAH. HARUNA-SAN, YOU PERVERT.

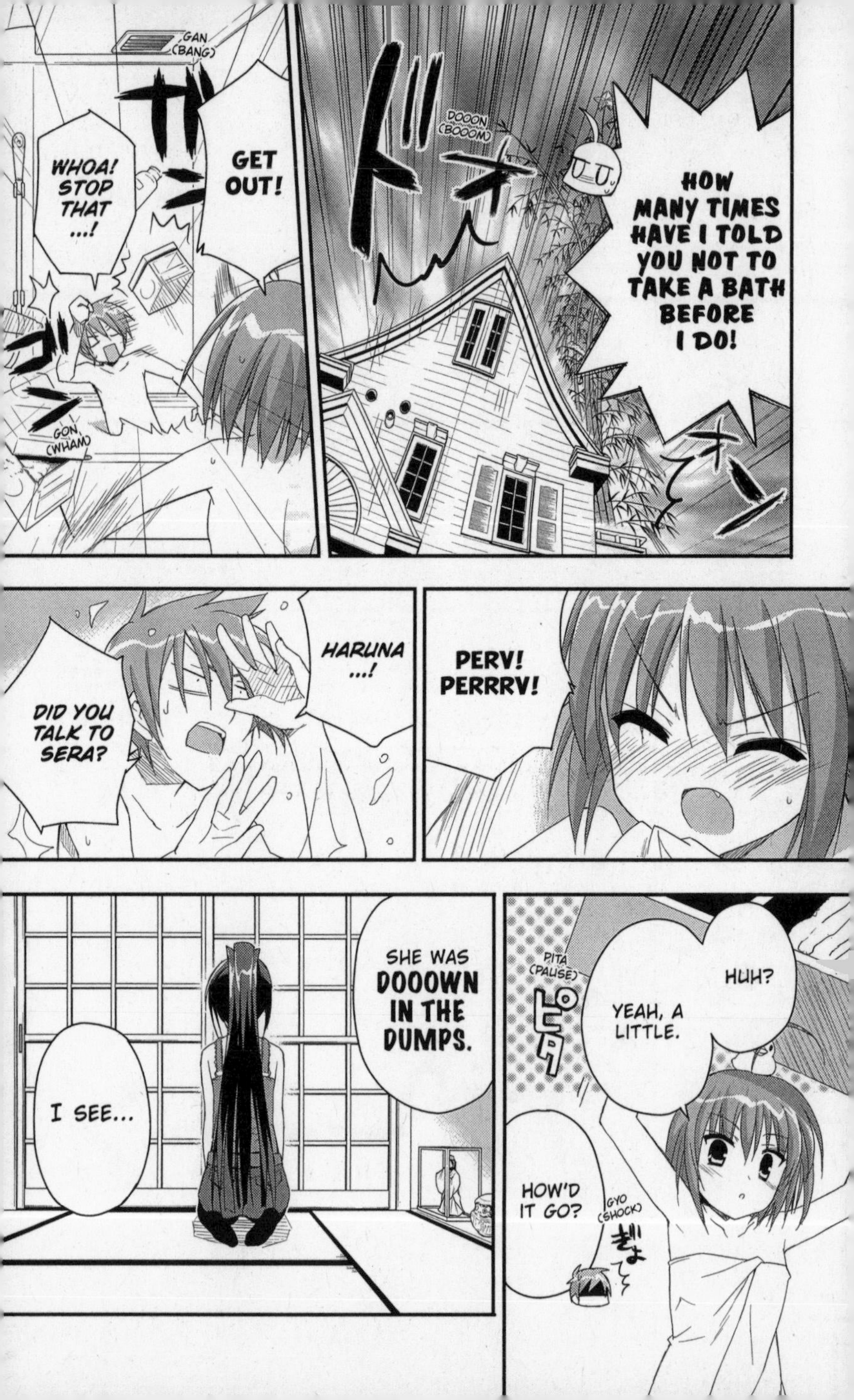
DOOON (BOOOM)
HOW MANY TIMES HAVE I TOLD YOU NOT TO TAKE A BATH BEFORE I DO!
GAN (BANG)
GET OUT!
WHOA! STOP THAT ...!
GON (WHAM)
PERV! PERRRV!
HARUNA ...!
DID YOU TALK TO SERA?
PITA (PAUSE)
HUH?
YEAH, A LITTLE.
HOW'D IT GO?
GYO (SHOCK)
SHE WAS DOOOWN IN THE DUMPS.
I SEE...

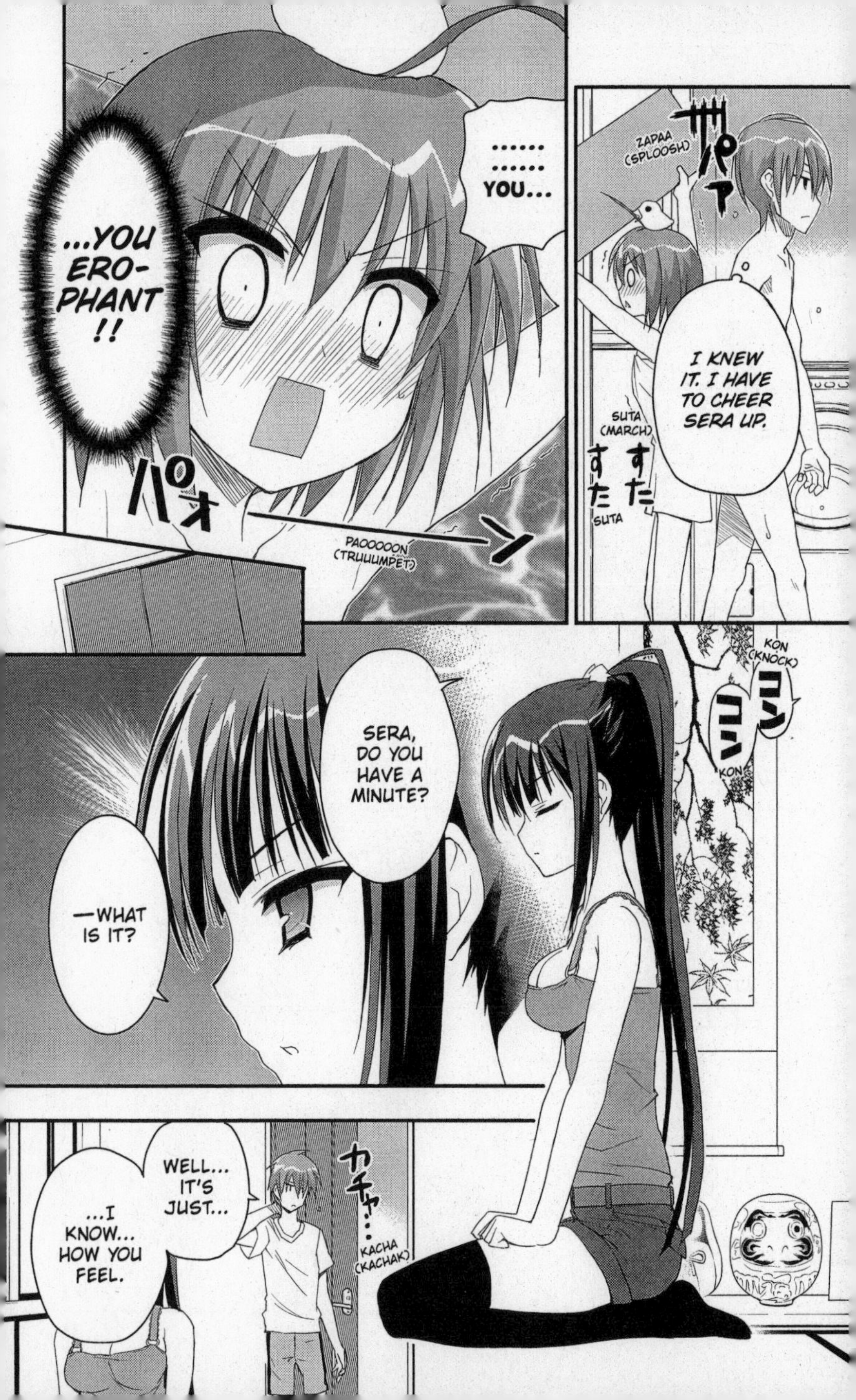
ザパァ
ZAPAA (SPLOOSH)
I KNEW IT. I HAVE TO CHEER SERA UP.
すたすた
SUTA (MARCH)
SUTA
.... YOU...
...YOU ERO-PHANT!!
パオーン
PAOOOOON (TRUUUMPET)
コンコン
KON (KNOCK)
KON
SERA, DO YOU HAVE A MINUTE?
—WHAT IS IT?
カチャ
KACHA (KACHAK)
WELL... IT'S JUST...
...I KNOW... HOW YOU FEEL.

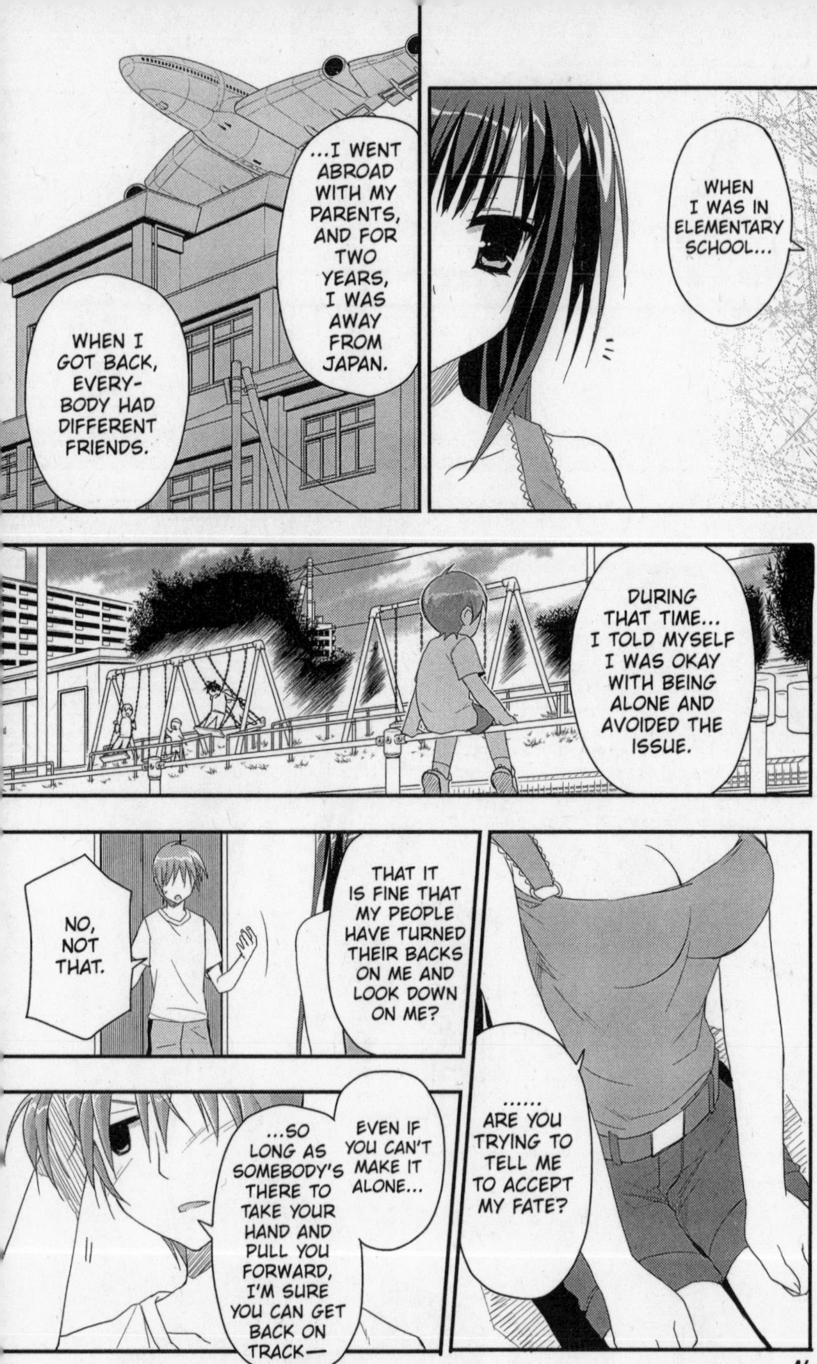

WHEN I WAS IN ELEMENTARY SCHOOL...
...I WENT ABROAD WITH MY PARENTS, AND FOR TWO YEARS, I WAS AWAY FROM JAPAN.
WHEN I GOT BACK, EVERY-BODY HAD DIFFERENT FRIENDS.
DURING THAT TIME... I TOLD MYSELF I WAS OKAY WITH BEING ALONE AND AVOIDED THE ISSUE.
THAT IT IS FINE THAT MY PEOPLE HAVE TURNED THEIR BACKS ON ME AND LOOK DOWN ON ME?
NO, NOT THAT.
......ARE YOU TRYING TO TELL ME TO ACCEPT MY FATE?
EVEN IF YOU CAN'T MAKE IT ALONE...
...SO LONG AS SOMEBODY'S THERE TO TAKE YOUR HAND AND PULL YOU FORWARD, I'M SURE YOU CAN GET BACK ON TRACK—

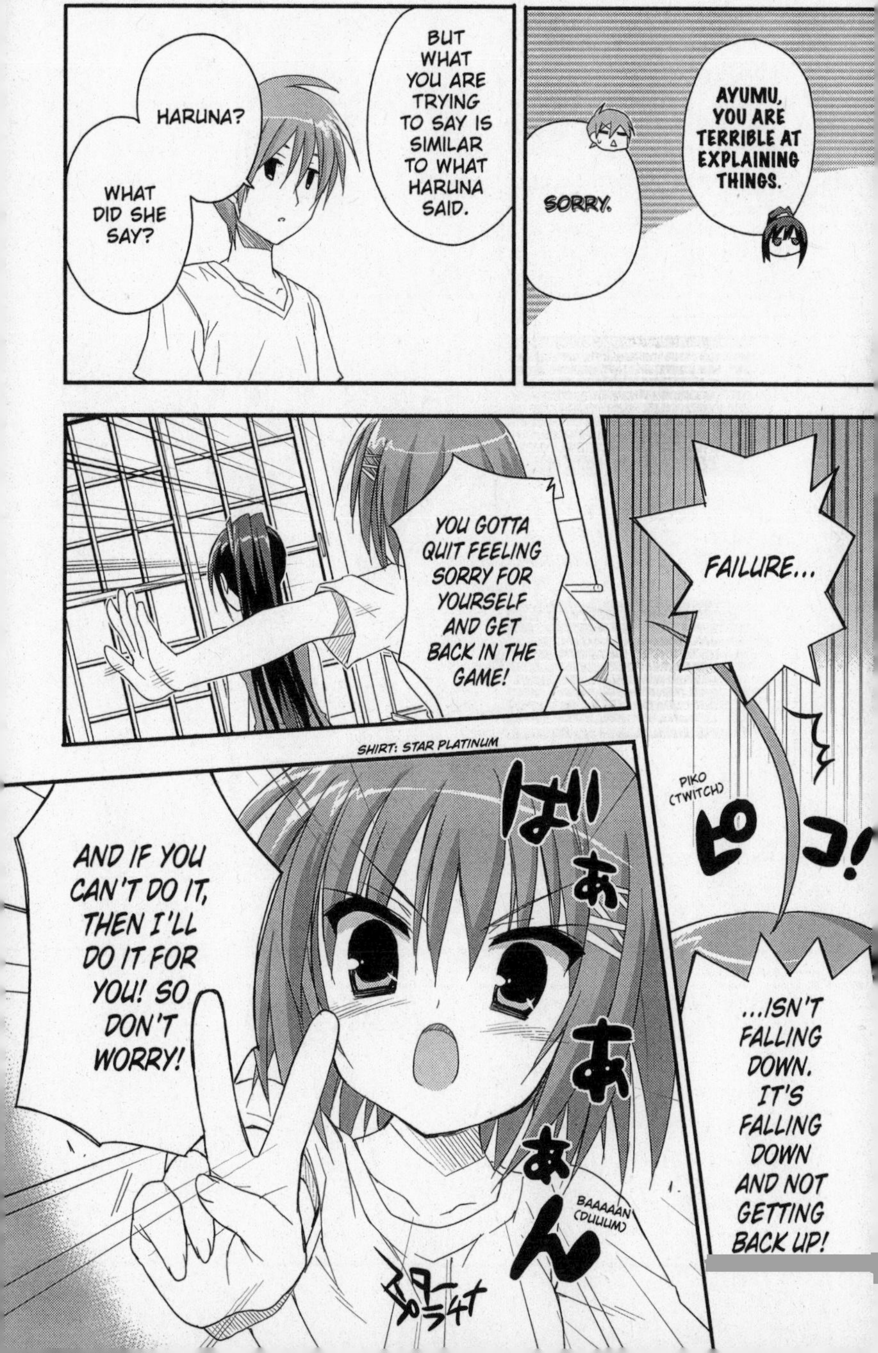

AYUMU, YOU ARE TERRIBLE AT EXPLAINING THINGS.
SORRY.
BUT WHAT YOU ARE TRYING TO SAY IS SIMILAR TO WHAT HARUNA SAID.
HARUNA?
WHAT DID SHE SAY?
FAILURE...
ピコ!
PIKO (TWITCH)
...ISN'T FALLING DOWN. IT'S FALLING DOWN AND NOT GETTING BACK UP!
YOU GOTTA QUIT FEELING SORRY FOR YOURSELF AND GET BACK IN THE GAME!
SHIRT: STAR PLATINUM
AND IF YOU CAN'T DO IT, THEN I'LL DO IT FOR YOU! SO DON'T WORRY!
ばぁぁぁん
BAAAAAN (DUUUM)

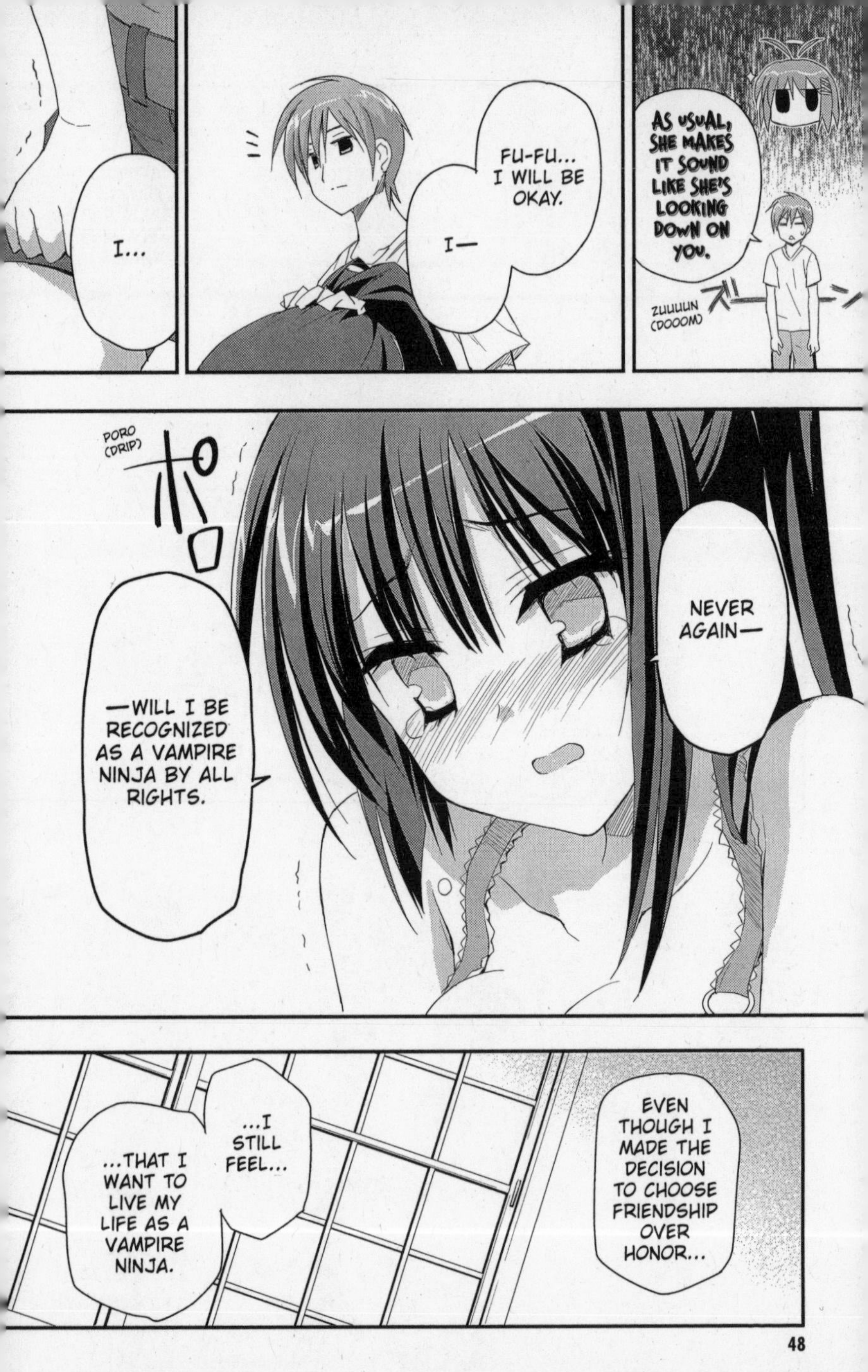

AS USUAL, SHE MAKES IT SOUND LIKE SHE'S LOOKING DOWN ON YOU.
ZUUUUN (DOOOM)
FU-FU... I WILL BE OKAY.
I—
I...
NEVER AGAIN—
—WILL I BE RECOGNIZED AS A VAMPIRE NINJA BY ALL RIGHTS.
PORO (DRIP)
EVEN THOUGH I MADE THE DECISION TO CHOOSE FRIENDSHIP OVER HONOR...
...I STILL FEEL...
...THAT I WANT TO LIVE MY LIFE AS A VAMPIRE NINJA.

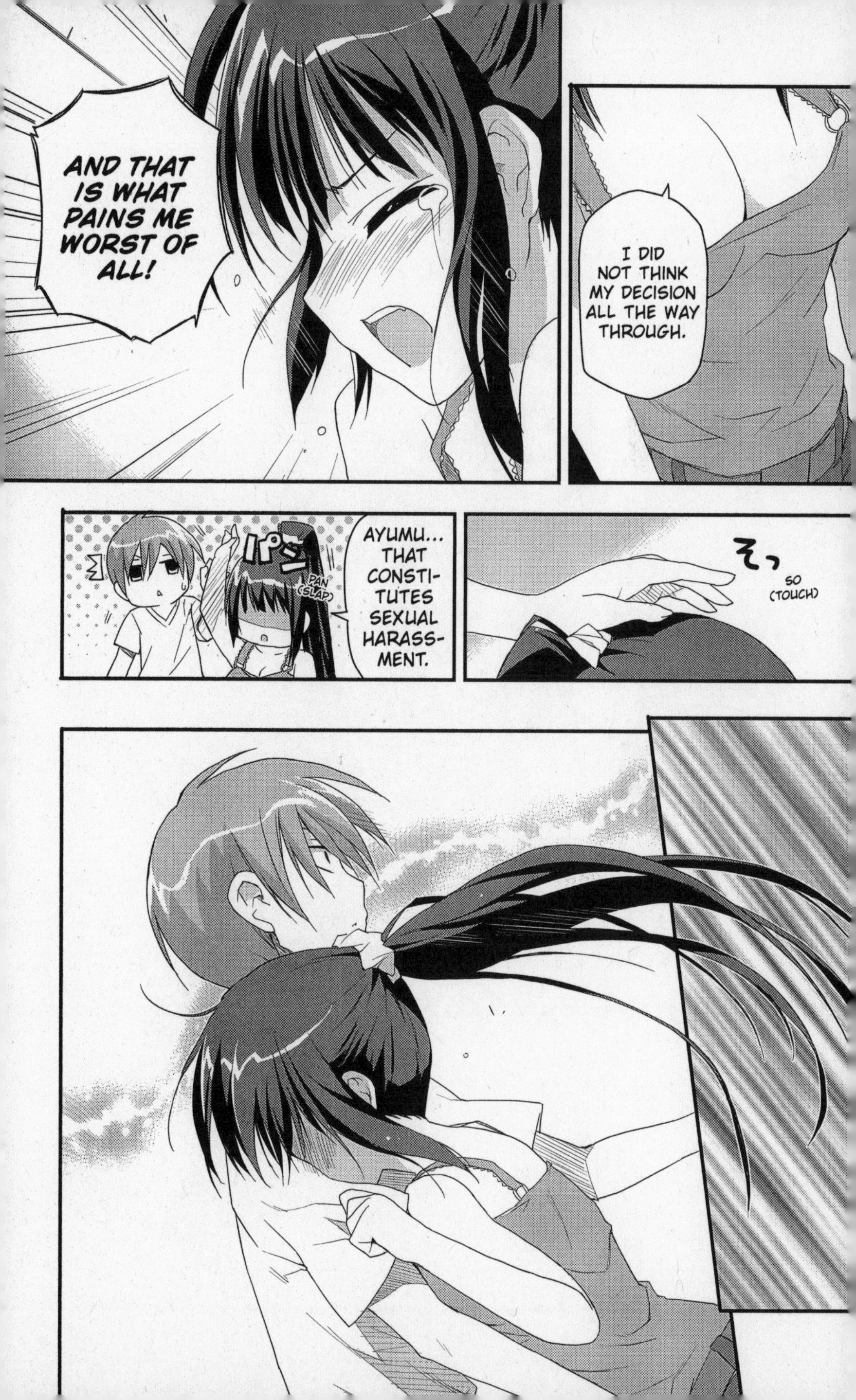
I DID NOT THINK MY DECISION ALL THE WAY THROUGH.
AND THAT IS WHAT PAINS ME WORST OF ALL!
SO (TOUCH)
PAN (SLAP)
AYUMU... THAT CONSTI-TUTES SEXUAL HARASS-MENT.

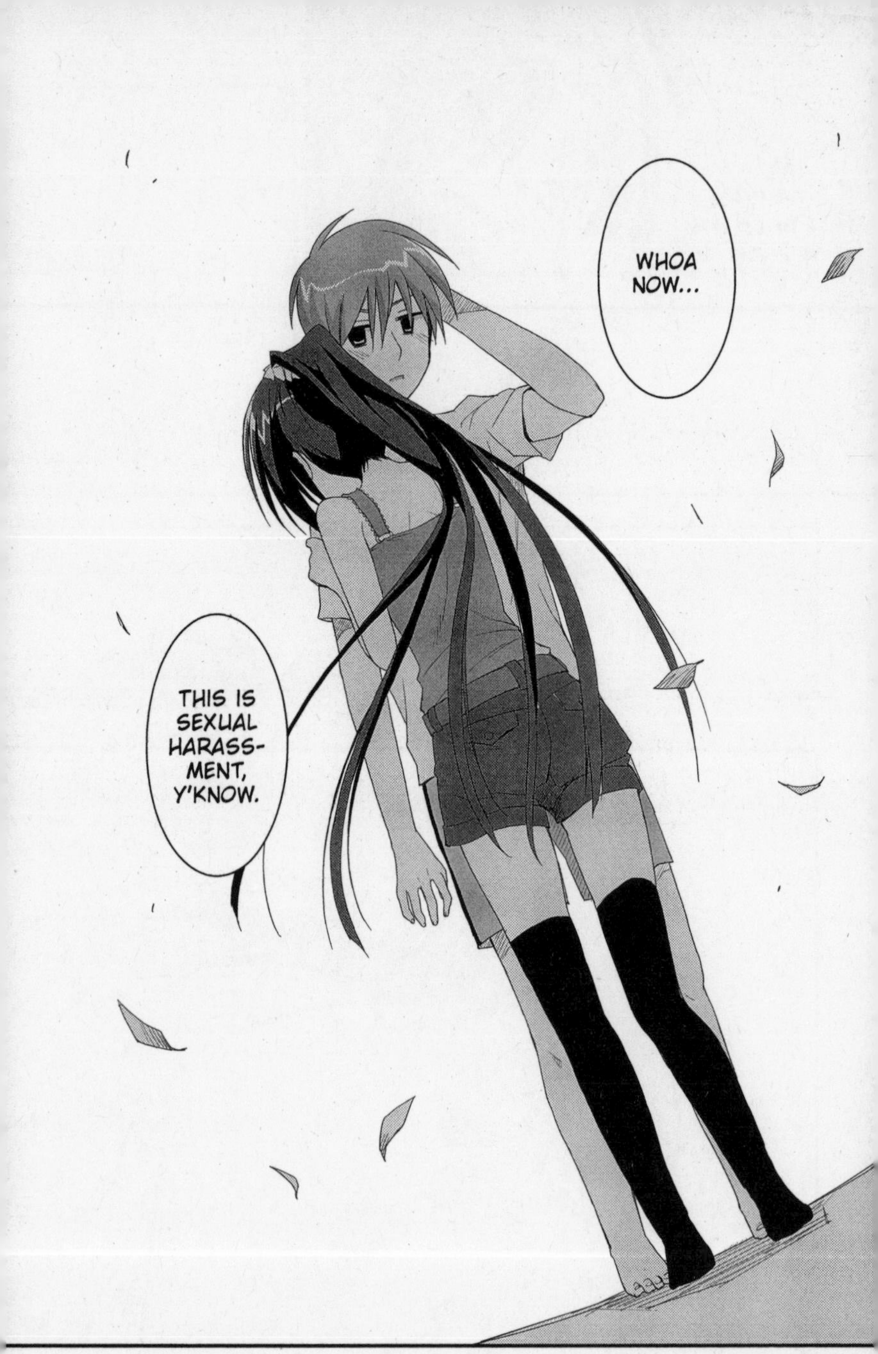
WHOA NOW...
THIS IS SEXUAL HARASS-MENT, Y'KNOW.

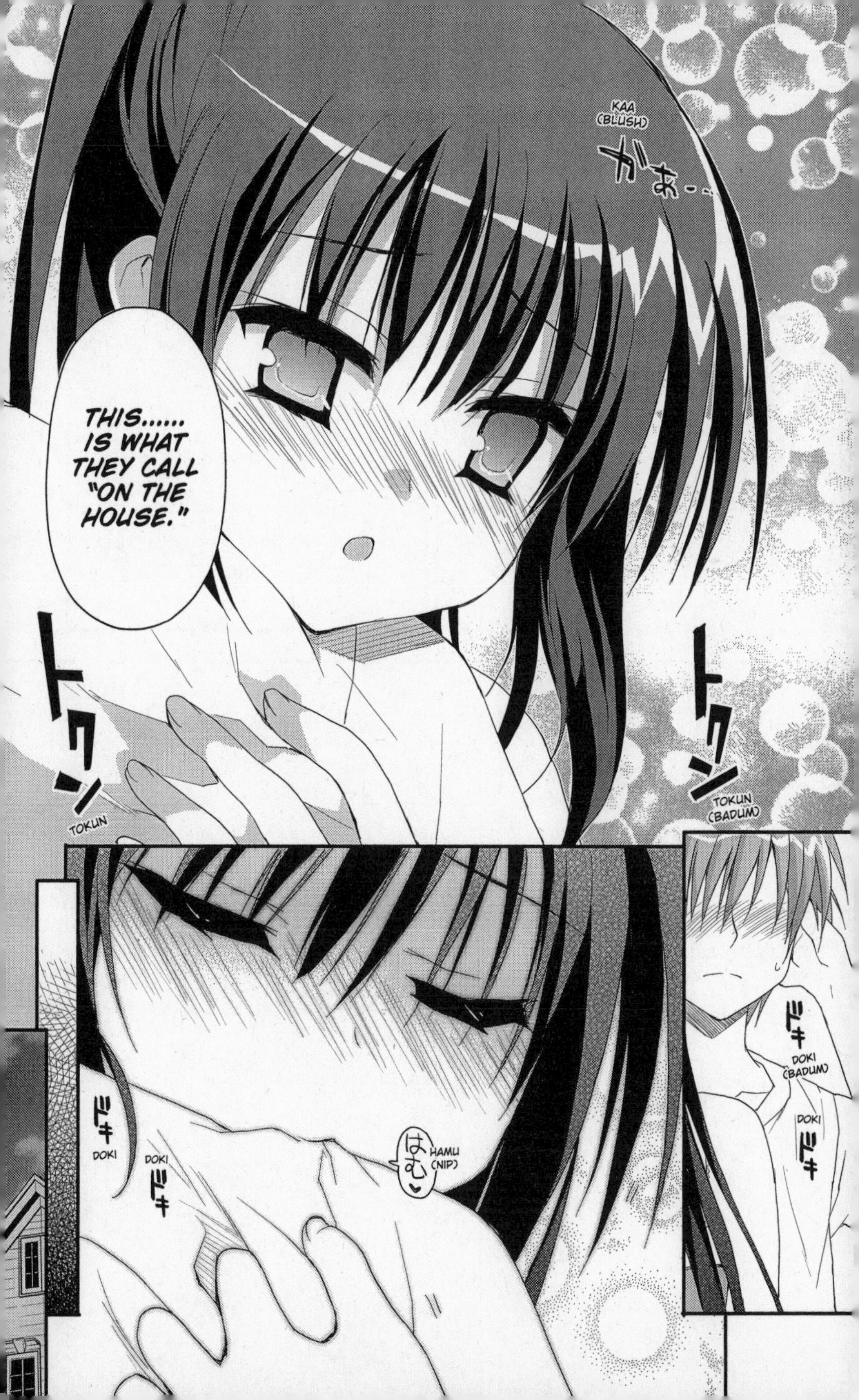

かぁ…
KAA (BLUSH)
THIS...... IS WHAT THEY CALL "ON THE HOUSE."
トクン
TOKUN (BADUM)
トクン
TOKUN
ドキ
DOKI (BADUM)
ドキ
DOKI
はむ♥
HAMU (NIP)
ドキ
DOKI
ドキ
DOKI

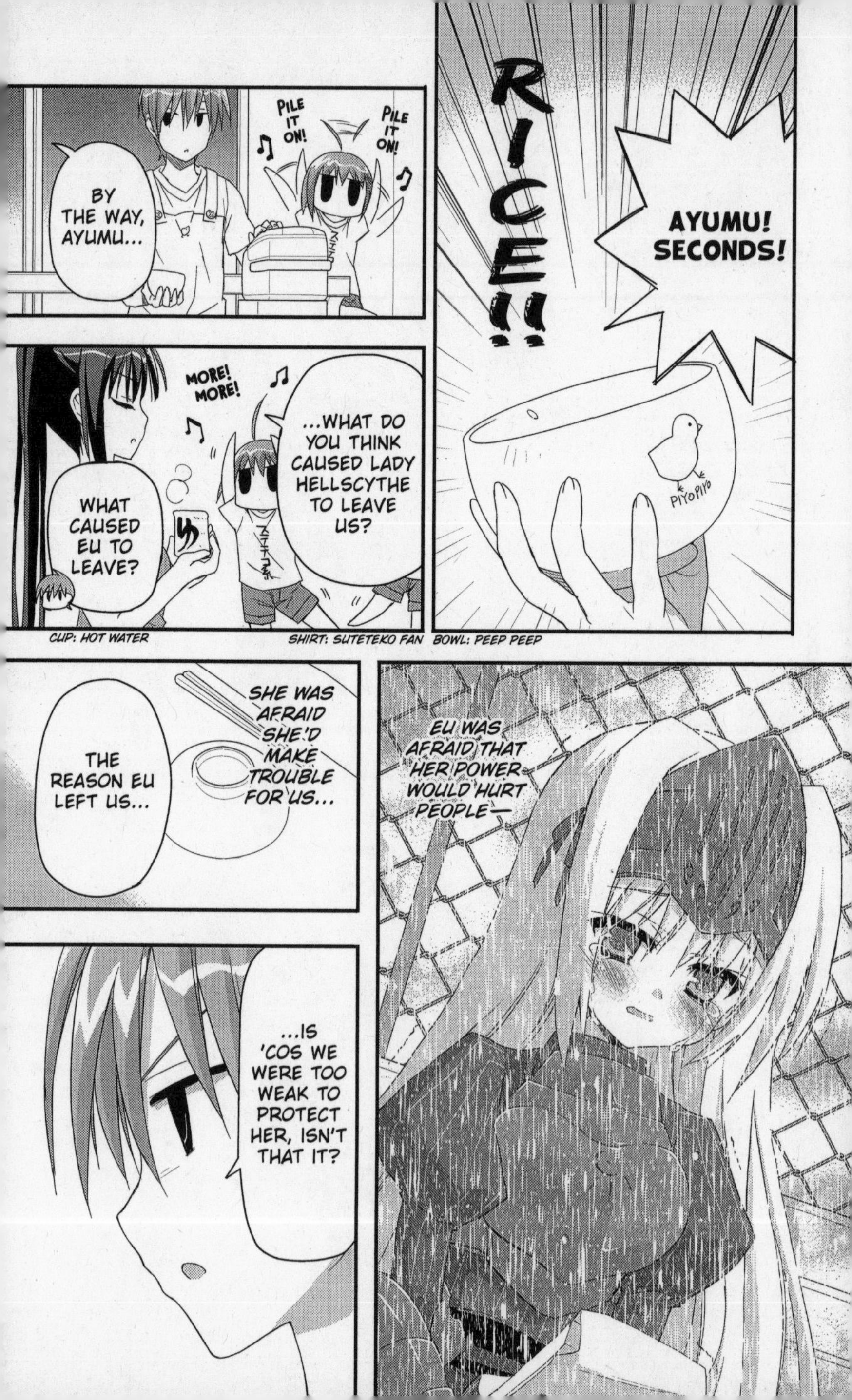
RICE!!
AYUMU! SECONDS!
PIYOPIYO
PILE IT ON!
PILE IT ON!
BY THE WAY, AYUMU...
MORE! MORE!
...WHAT DO YOU THINK CAUSED LADY HELLSCYTHE TO LEAVE US?
WHAT CAUSED EU TO LEAVE?
BOWL: PEEP PEEP
SHIRT: SUTETEKO FAN
CUP: HOT WATER
EU WAS AFRAID THAT HER POWER WOULD HURT PEOPLE—
SHE WAS AFRAID SHE'D MAKE TROUBLE FOR US...
THE REASON EU LEFT US...
...IS 'COS WE WERE TOO WEAK TO PROTECT HER, ISN'T THAT IT?

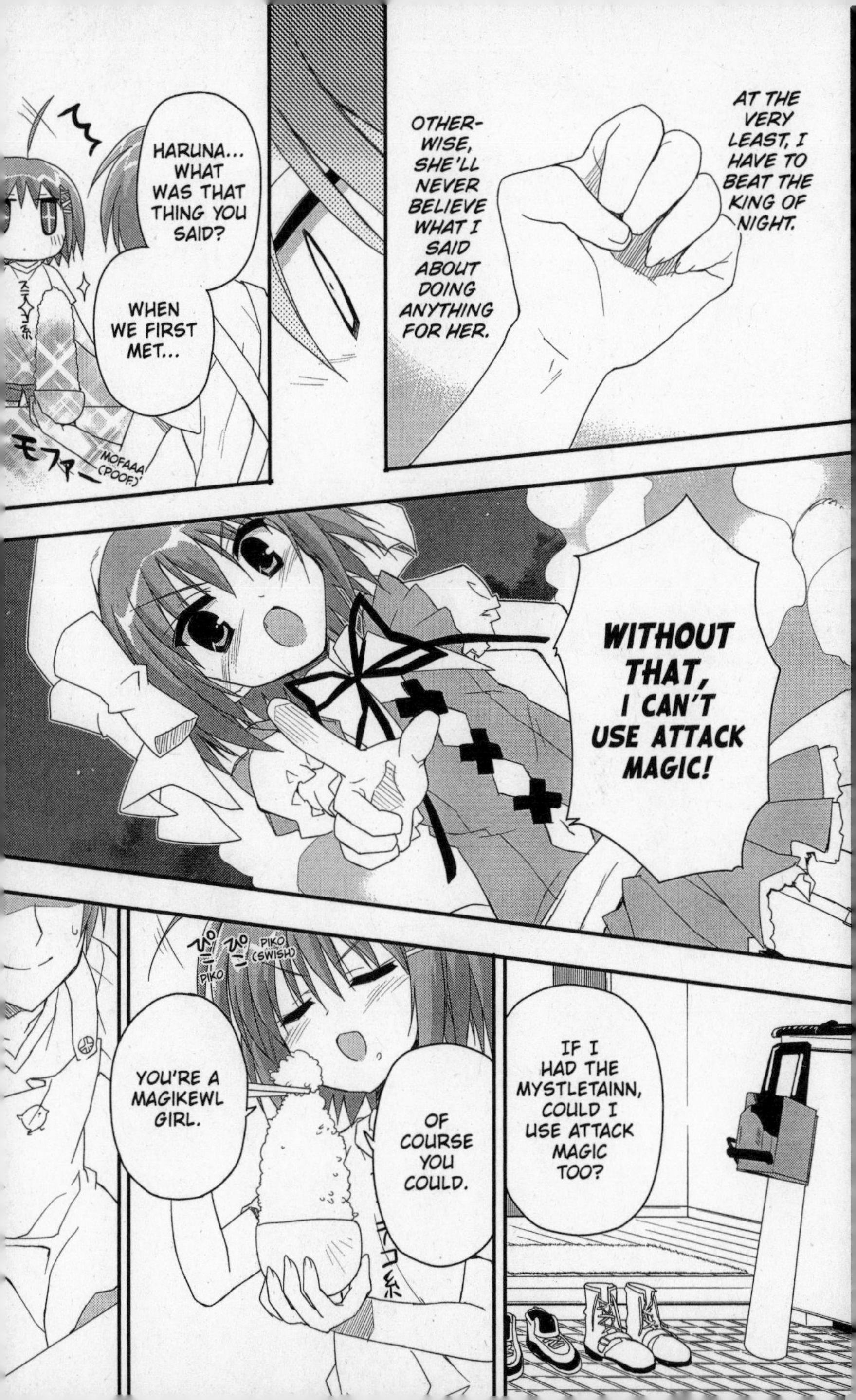
AT THE VERY LEAST, I HAVE TO BEAT THE KING OF NIGHT.
OTHER-WISE, SHE'LL NEVER BELIEVE WHAT I SAID ABOUT DOING ANYTHING FOR HER.
HARUNA... WHAT WAS THAT THING YOU SAID?
WHEN WE FIRST MET...
モファー
MOFAAA (POOF)
WITHOUT THAT, I CAN'T USE ATTACK MAGIC!
IF I HAD THE MYSTLETAINN, COULD I USE ATTACK MAGIC TOO?
OF COURSE YOU COULD.
PIKO PIKO (SWISH)
YOU'RE A MAGIKEWL GIRL.

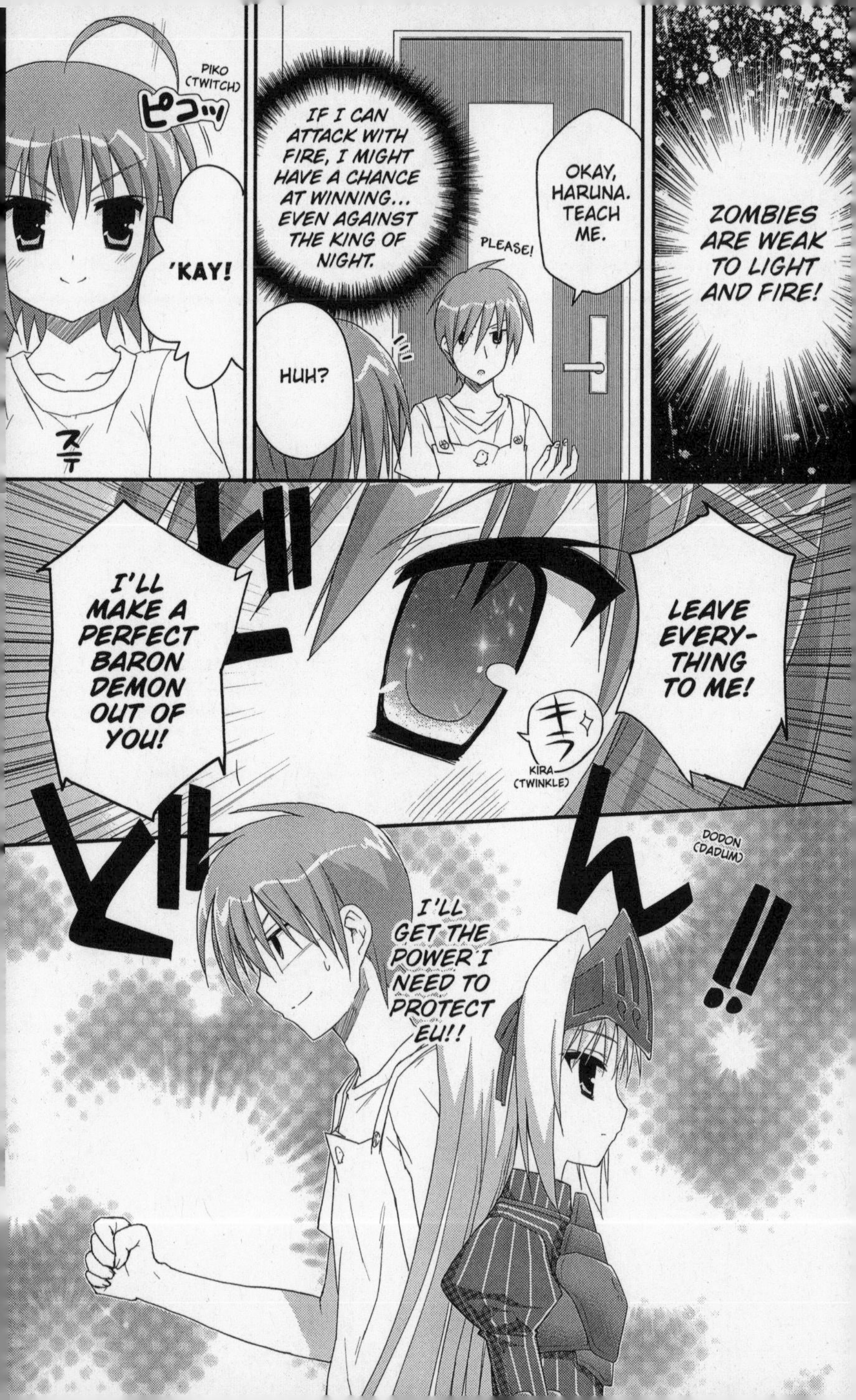
ZOMBIES ARE WEAK TO LIGHT AND FIRE!
OKAY, HARUNA. TEACH ME.
PLEASE!
IF I CAN ATTACK WITH FIRE, I MIGHT HAVE A CHANCE AT WINNING… EVEN AGAINST THE KING OF NIGHT.
HUH?
PIKO (TWITCH)
ピコッ
'KAY!
LEAVE EVERY-THING TO ME!
キラ
KIRA (TWINKLE)
I'LL MAKE A PERFECT BARON DEMON OUT OF YOU!
DODON (DADUM)
I'LL GET THE POWER I NEED TO PROTECT EU!!

IS THIS A ZOMBIE?

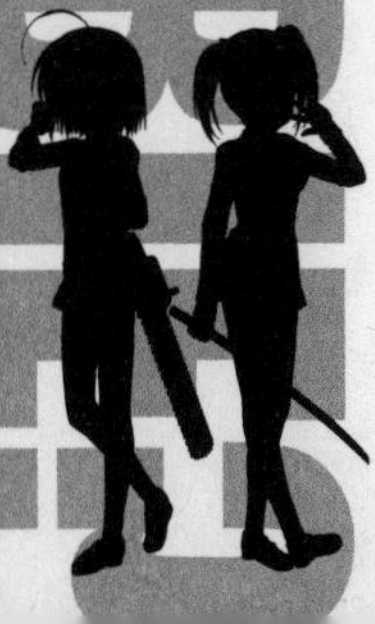

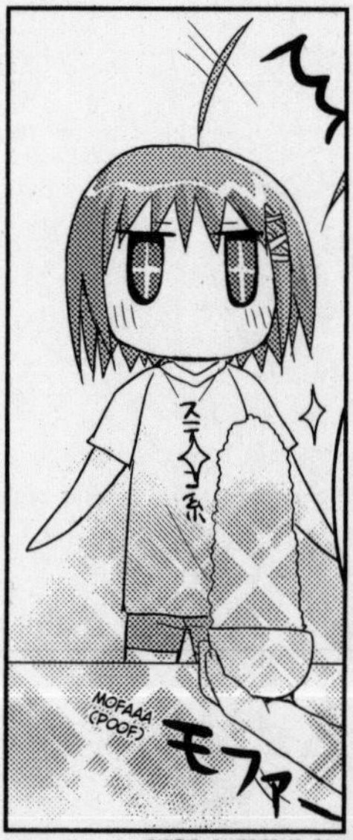
MOFAAA (POOF)
モファー

SHIRT: SUTETEKO FAN

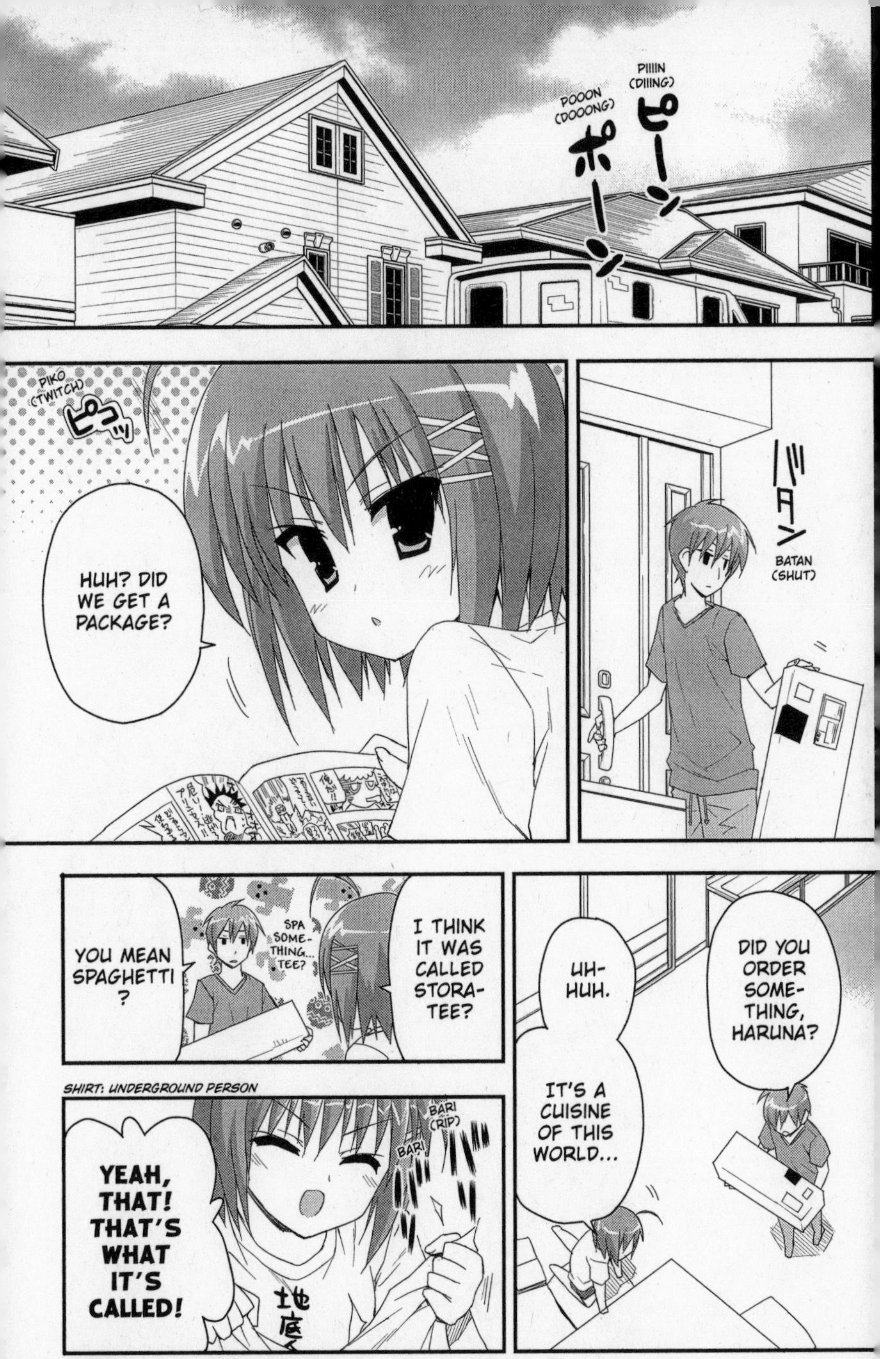
PIIIN (DIIING)
ピーン
POOON (DOOONG)
ポーン
BATAN (SHUT)
バタン
PIKO (TWITCH)
ぴこっ
HUH? DID WE GET A PACKAGE?
DID YOU ORDER SOMETHING, HARUNA?
UH-HUH.
IT'S A CUISINE OF THIS WORLD...
I THINK IT WAS CALLED STORA-TEE?
SPA SOME-THING... TEE?
YOU MEAN SPAGHETTI?
SHIRT: UNDERGROUND PERSON
BARI (RIP)
BARI
YEAH, THAT! THAT'S WHAT IT'S CALLED!

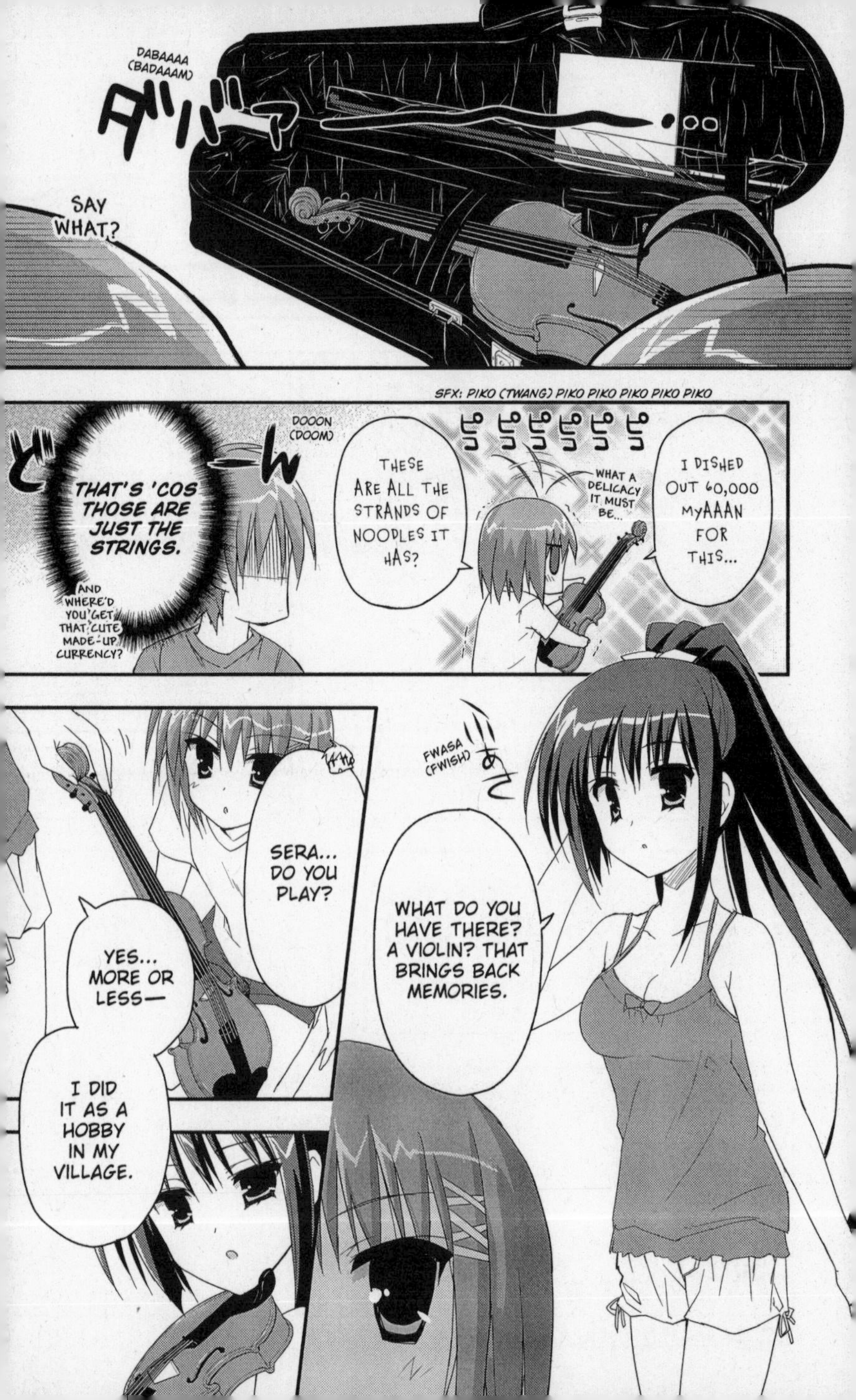
DABAAAA (BADAAAM)
ダバァ
SAY WHAT?
SFX: PIKO (TWANG) PIKO PIKO PIKO PIKO PIKO
ピピピピピピ
I DISHED OUT 60,000 MYAAAN FOR THIS...
WHAT A DELICACY IT MUST BE...
THESE ARE ALL THE STRANDS OF NOODLES IT HAS?
DOOON (DOOM)
THAT'S 'COS THOSE ARE JUST THE STRINGS.
AND WHERE'D YOU GET THAT CUTE MADE-UP CURRENCY?
FWASA (FWISH)
WHAT DO YOU HAVE THERE? A VIOLIN? THAT BRINGS BACK MEMORIES.
SERA... DO YOU PLAY?
YES... MORE OR LESS—
I DID IT AS A HOBBY IN MY VILLAGE.

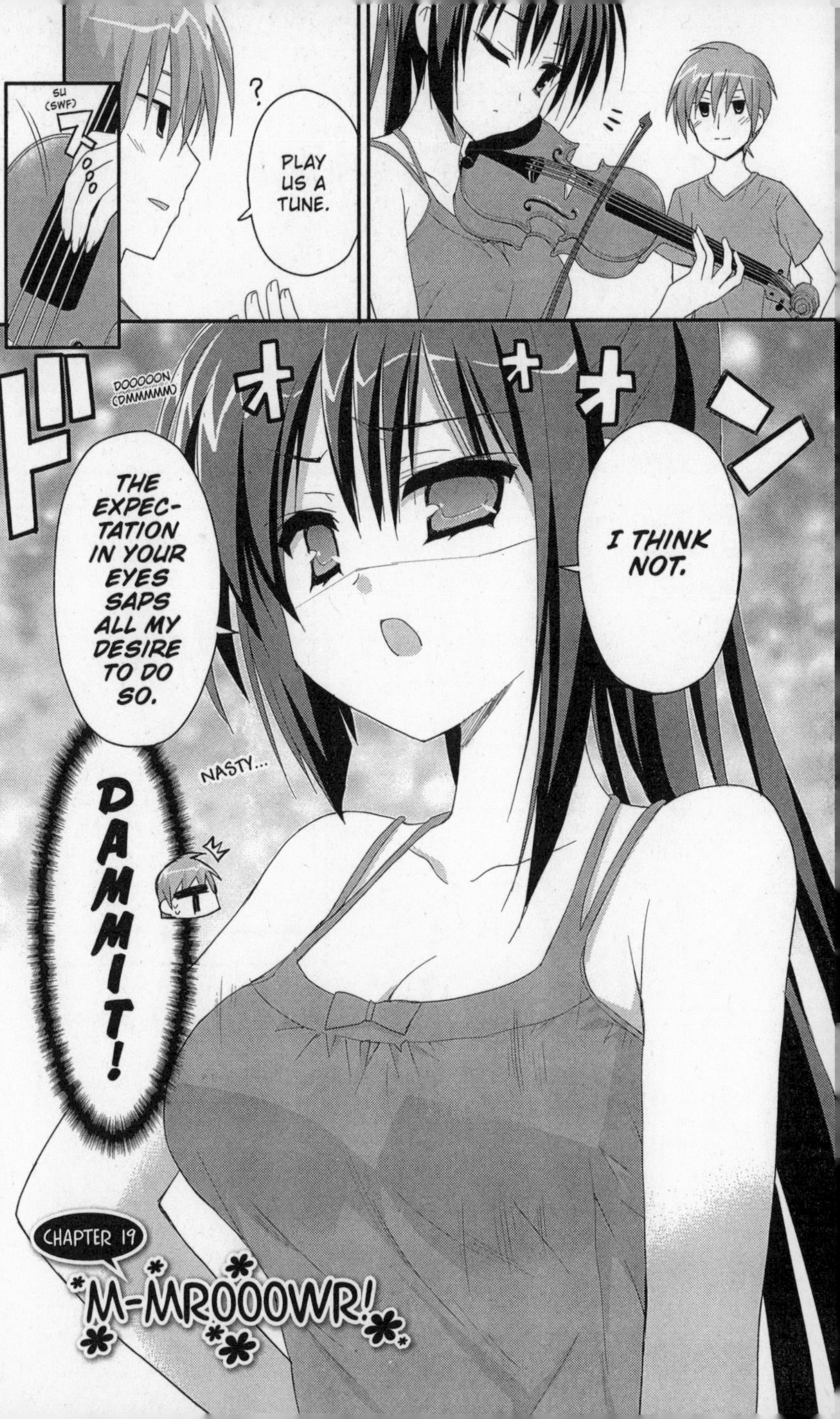
?
PLAY US A TUNE.
SU (SWF)
DOOOOON (DMMMMM)
I THINK NOT.
THE EXPECTATION IN YOUR EYES SAPS ALL MY DESIRE TO DO SO.
NASTY...
DAMMIT!
CHAPTER 19
M-MROOOWR!

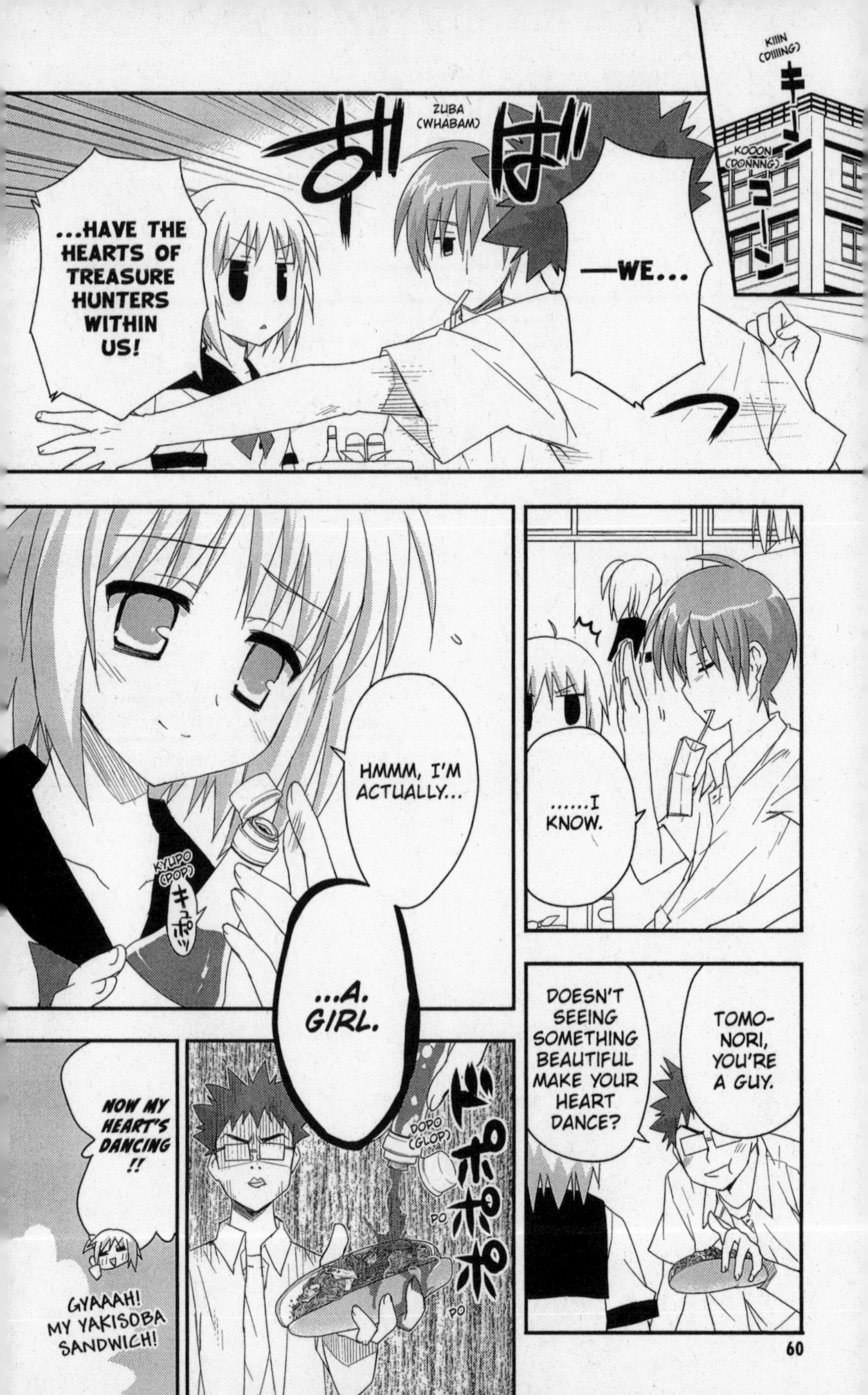
KIIN (DIIIING)
KOOON (DONNNG)
—WE...
ZUBA (WHABAM)
...HAVE THE HEARTS OF TREASURE HUNTERS WITHIN US!
......I KNOW.
HMMM, I'M ACTUALLY...
KYUPO (POP)
キュポッ
...A. GIRL.
TOMO-NORI, YOU'RE A GUY.
DOESN'T SEEING SOMETHING BEAUTIFUL MAKE YOUR HEART DANCE?
DOPO (GLOP)
PO
PO
NOW MY HEART'S DANCING!!
GYAAAH! MY YAKISOBA SANDWICH!

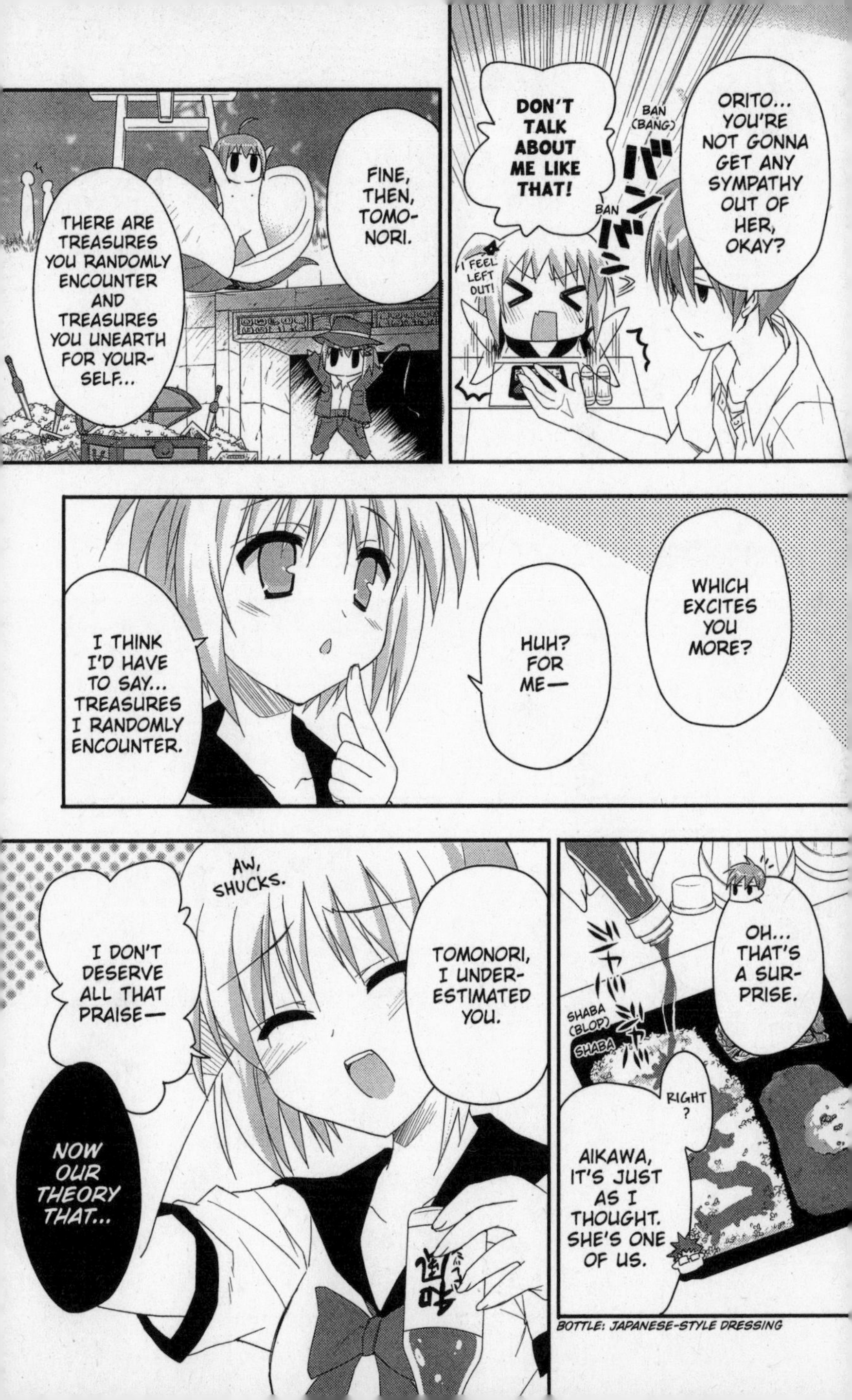

ORITO... YOU'RE NOT GONNA GET ANY SYMPATHY OUT OF HER, OKAY?
BAN (BANG)
BAN
DON'T TALK ABOUT ME LIKE THAT!
I FEEL LEFT OUT!
FINE, THEN, TOMO-NORI.
THERE ARE TREASURES YOU RANDOMLY ENCOUNTER AND TREASURES YOU UNEARTH FOR YOUR-SELF...
WHICH EXCITES YOU MORE?
HUH? FOR ME—
I THINK I'D HAVE TO SAY... TREASURES I RANDOMLY ENCOUNTER.
OH... THAT'S A SUR-PRISE.
SHABA (BLOP)
SHABA
RIGHT ?
AIKAWA, IT'S JUST AS I THOUGHT. SHE'S ONE OF US.
BOTTLE: JAPANESE-STYLE DRESSING
TOMONORI, I UNDER-ESTIMATED YOU.
AW, SHUCKS.
I DON'T DESERVE ALL THAT PRAISE—
NOW OUR THEORY THAT...

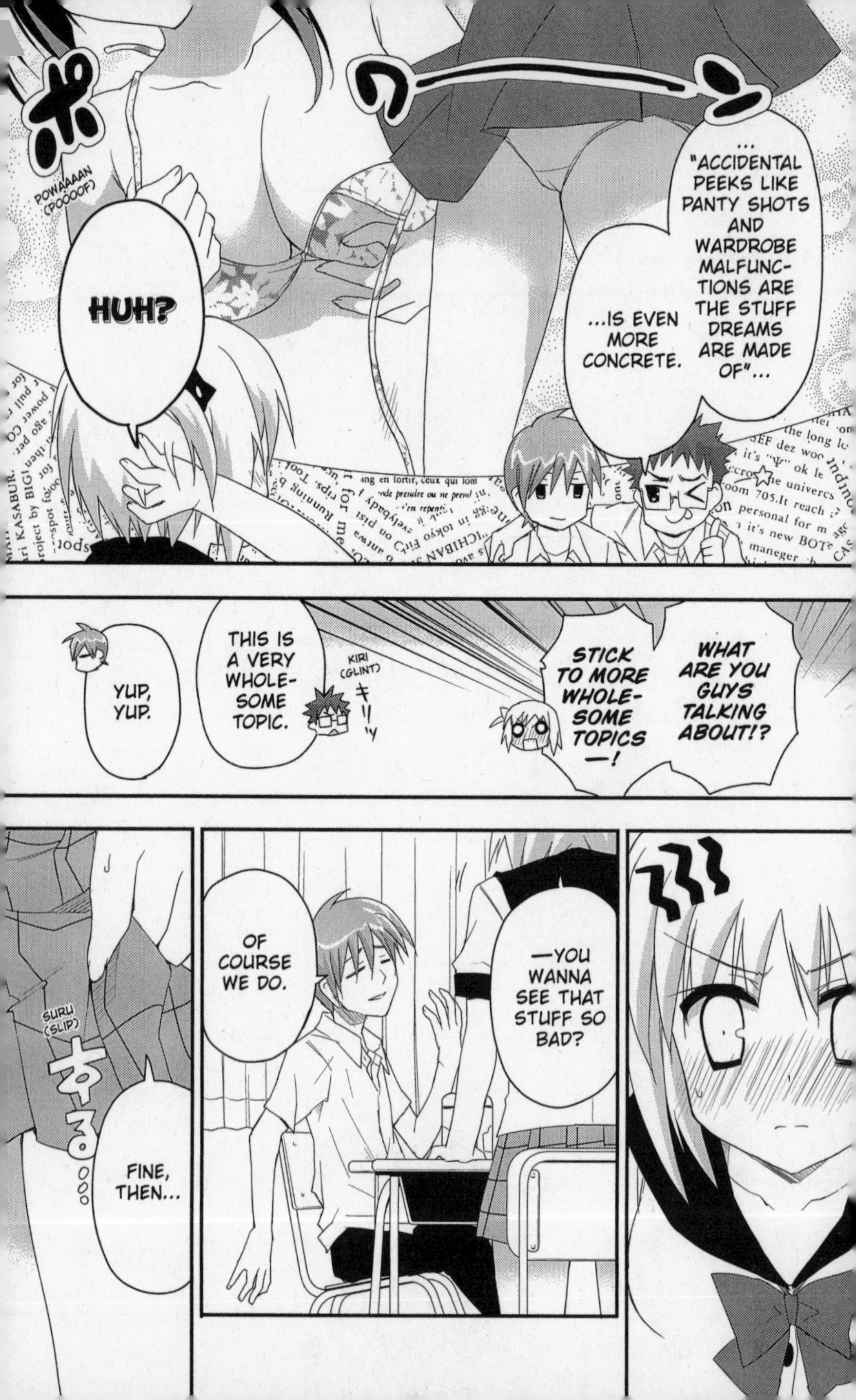
... "ACCIDENTAL PEEKS LIKE PANTY SHOTS AND WARDROBE MALFUNCTIONS ARE THE STUFF DREAMS ARE MADE OF"...
...IS EVEN MORE CONCRETE.
POWAAAAN (POOOOF)
HUH?
WHAT ARE YOU GUYS TALKING ABOUT!?
STICK TO MORE WHOLE-SOME TOPICS —!
KIRI (GLINT)
THIS IS A VERY WHOLE-SOME TOPIC.
YUP, YUP.
—YOU WANNA SEE THAT STUFF SO BAD?
OF COURSE WE DO.
SURU (SLIP)
FINE, THEN...

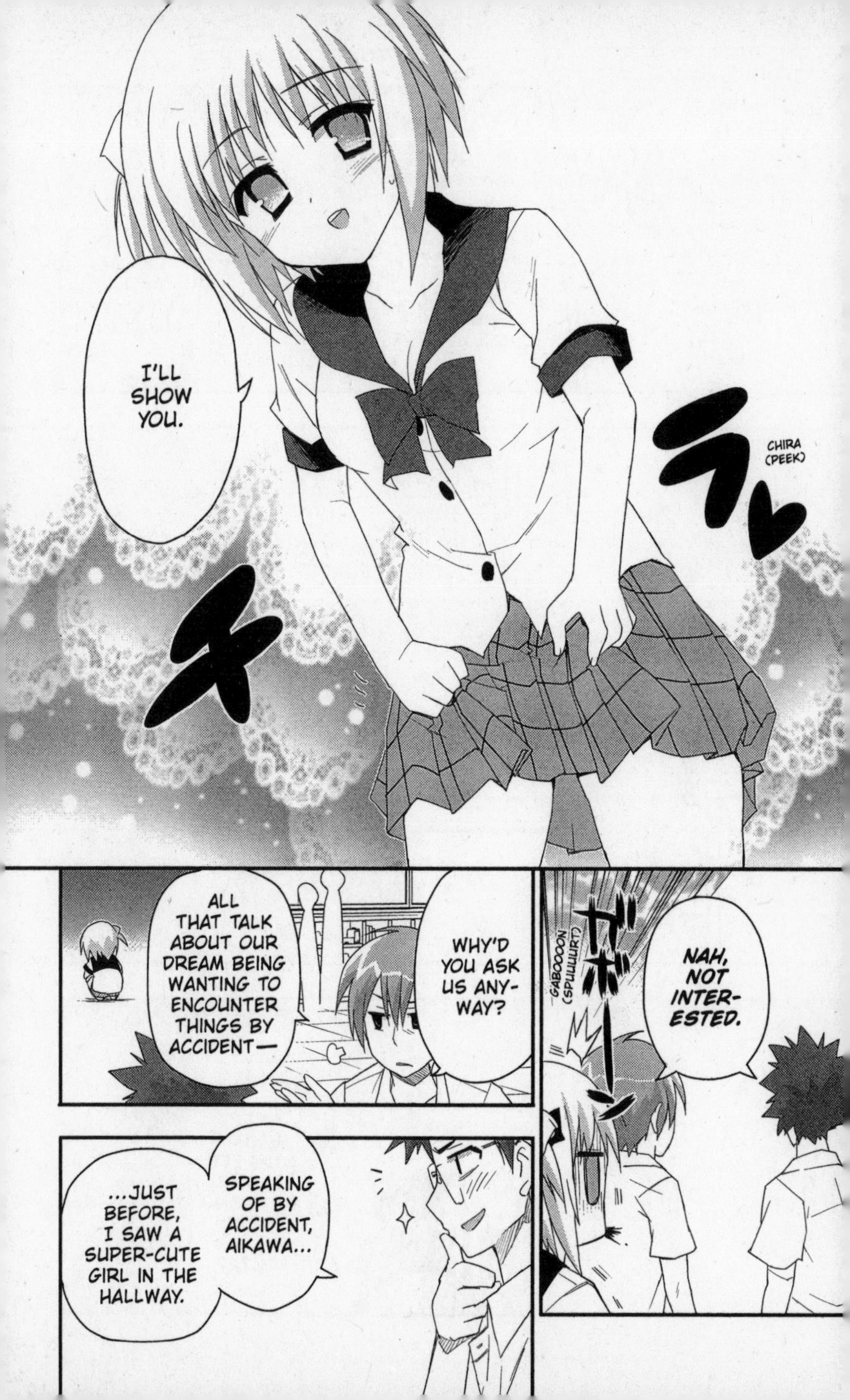
I'LL SHOW YOU.
CHIRA (PEEK)
NAH, NOT INTER-ESTED.
GABOOOOON (SPLUUUURT)
WHY'D YOU ASK US ANY-WAY?
ALL THAT TALK ABOUT OUR DREAM BEING WANTING TO ENCOUNTER THINGS BY ACCIDENT—
SPEAKING OF BY ACCIDENT, AIKAWA...
...JUST BEFORE, I SAW A SUPER-CUTE GIRL IN THE HALLWAY.

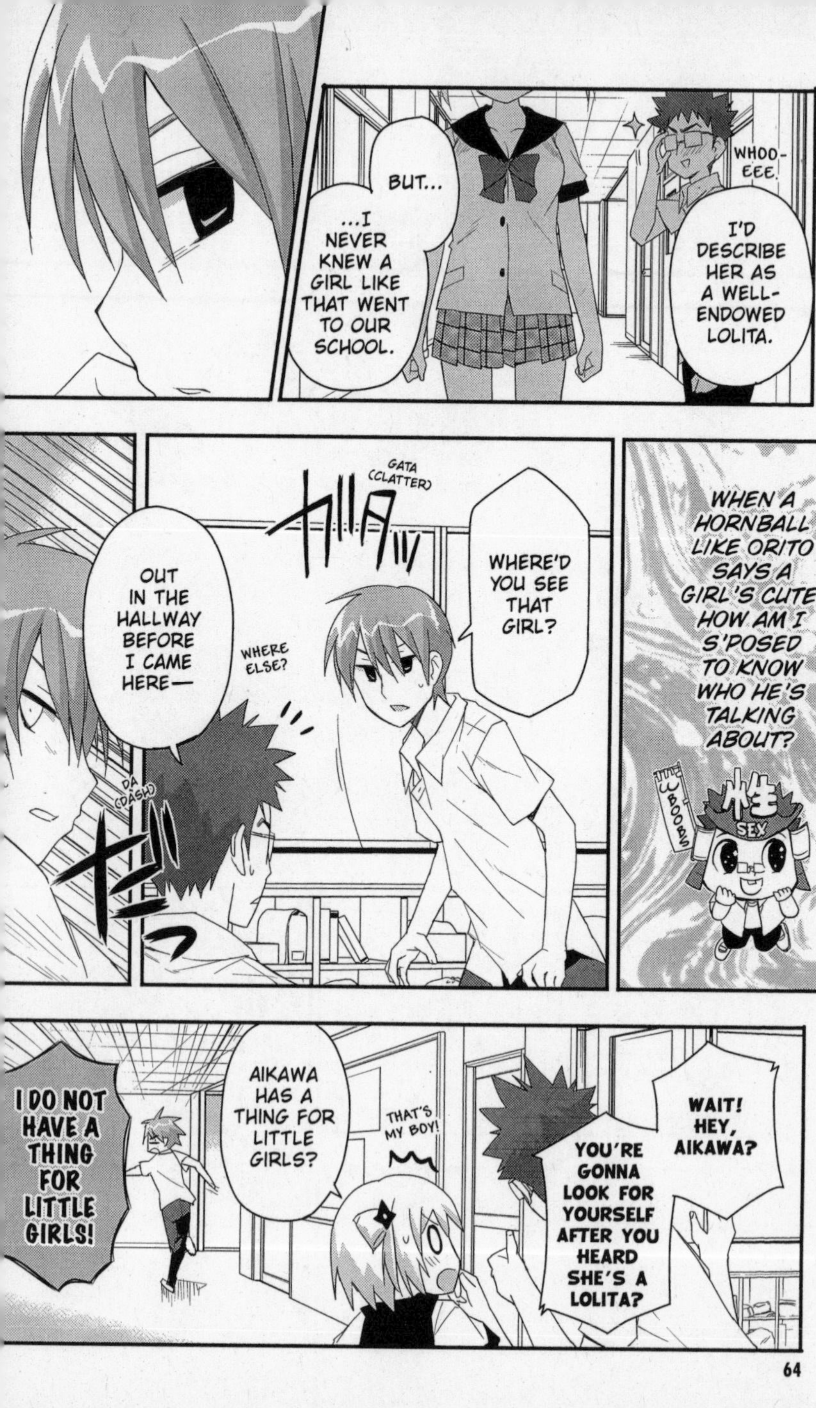
WHOO-EEE.
I'D DESCRIBE HER AS A WELL-ENDOWED LOLITA.
BUT...
...I NEVER KNEW A GIRL LIKE THAT WENT TO OUR SCHOOL.
WHEN A HORNBALL LIKE ORITO SAYS A GIRL'S CUTE, HOW AM I S'POSED TO KNOW WHO HE'S TALKING ABOUT?
BOOBS
SEX
GATA (CLATTER)
WHERE'D YOU SEE THAT GIRL?
OUT IN THE HALLWAY BEFORE I CAME HERE—
WHERE ELSE?
DA (DASH)
WAIT! HEY, AIKAWA?
YOU'RE GONNA LOOK FOR YOURSELF AFTER YOU HEARD SHE'S A LOLITA?
THAT'S MY BOY!
AIKAWA HAS A THING FOR LITTLE GIRLS?
I DO NOT HAVE A THING FOR LITTLE GIRLS!

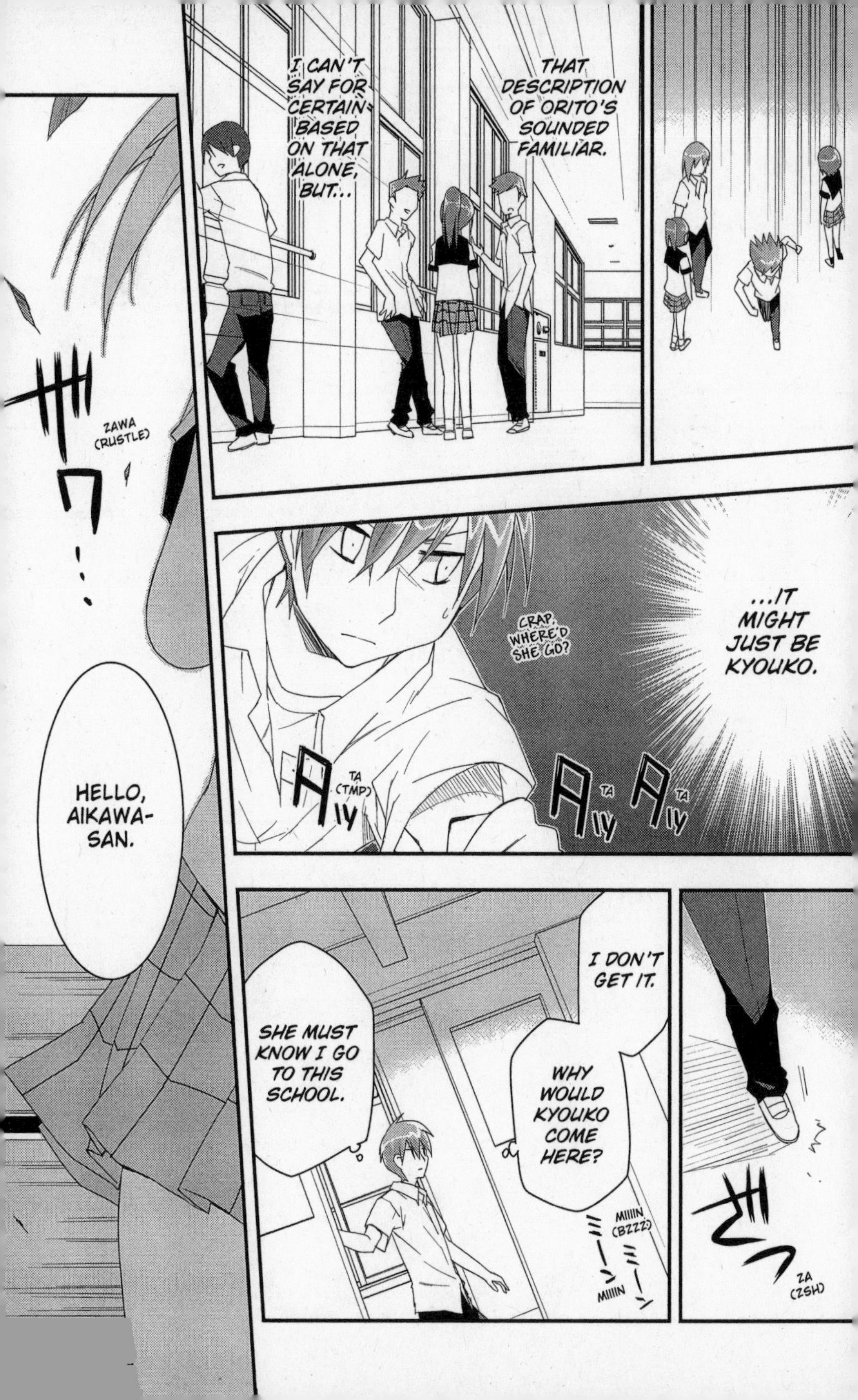
THAT DESCRIPTION OF ORITO'S SOUNDED FAMILIAR.
I CAN'T SAY FOR CERTAIN BASED ON THAT ALONE, BUT...
...IT MIGHT JUST BE KYOUKO.
CRAP, WHERE'D SHE GO?
TA
TA
TA (TMP)
ZA (ZSH)
I DON'T GET IT.
WHY WOULD KYOUKO COME HERE?
SHE MUST KNOW I GO TO THIS SCHOOL.
MIIIIN (BZZZ)
MIIIIN
ZAWA (RUSTLE)
HELLO, AIKAWA-SAN.

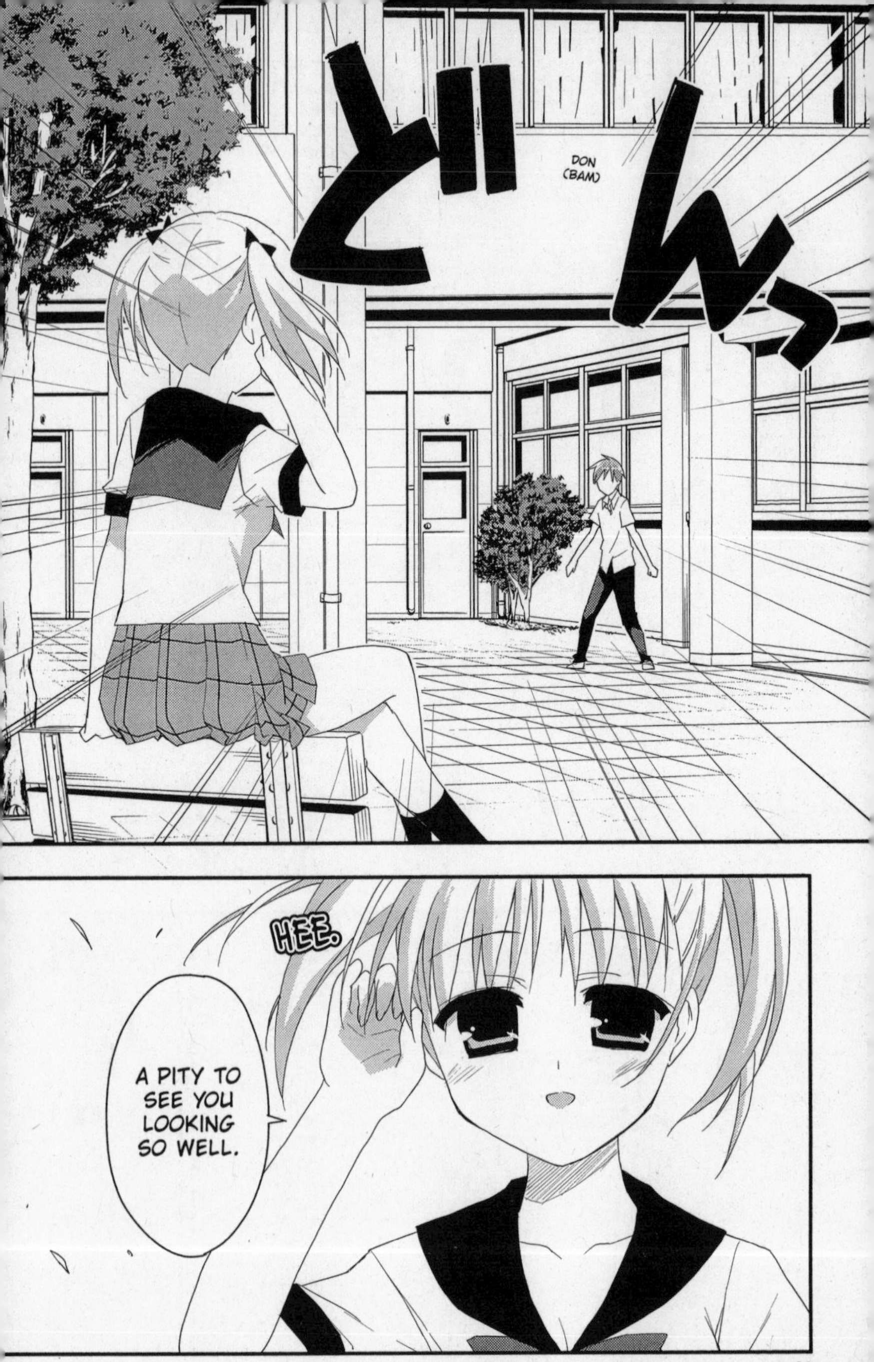
どんっ
DON (BAM)
HEE.
A PITY TO SEE YOU LOOKING SO WELL.

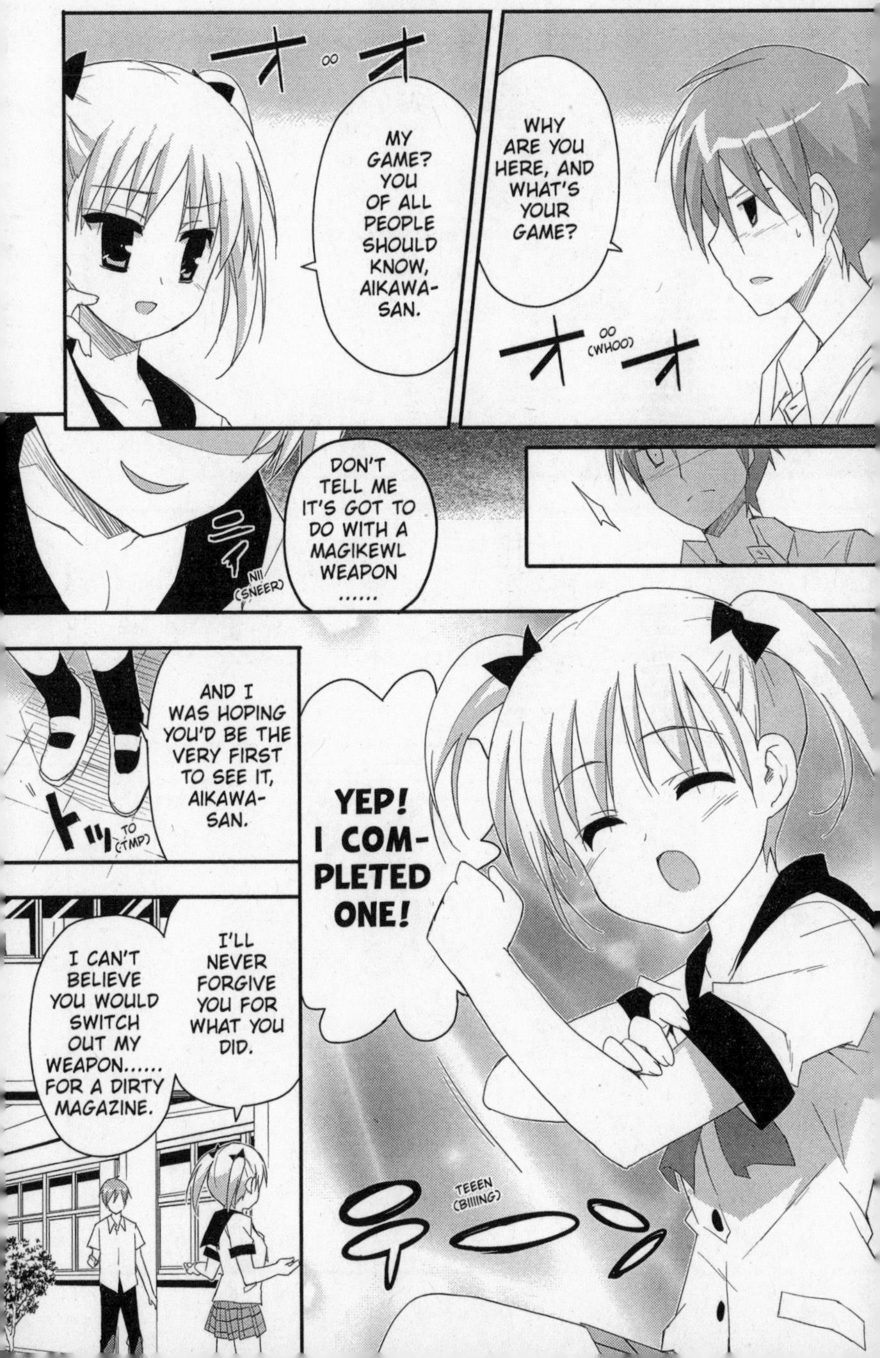
WHY ARE YOU HERE, AND WHAT'S YOUR GAME?
OO (WHOO)
MY GAME? YOU OF ALL PEOPLE SHOULD KNOW, AIKAWA-SAN.
DON'T TELL ME IT'S GOT TO DO WITH A MAGIKEWL WEAPON ......
NII (SNEER)
YEP! I COM-PLETED ONE!
TEEEN (BIIIING)
AND I WAS HOPING YOU'D BE THE VERY FIRST TO SEE IT, AIKAWA-SAN.
TO (TMP)
I'LL NEVER FORGIVE YOU FOR WHAT YOU DID.
I CAN'T BELIEVE YOU WOULD SWITCH OUT MY WEAPON...... FOR A DIRTY MAGAZINE.

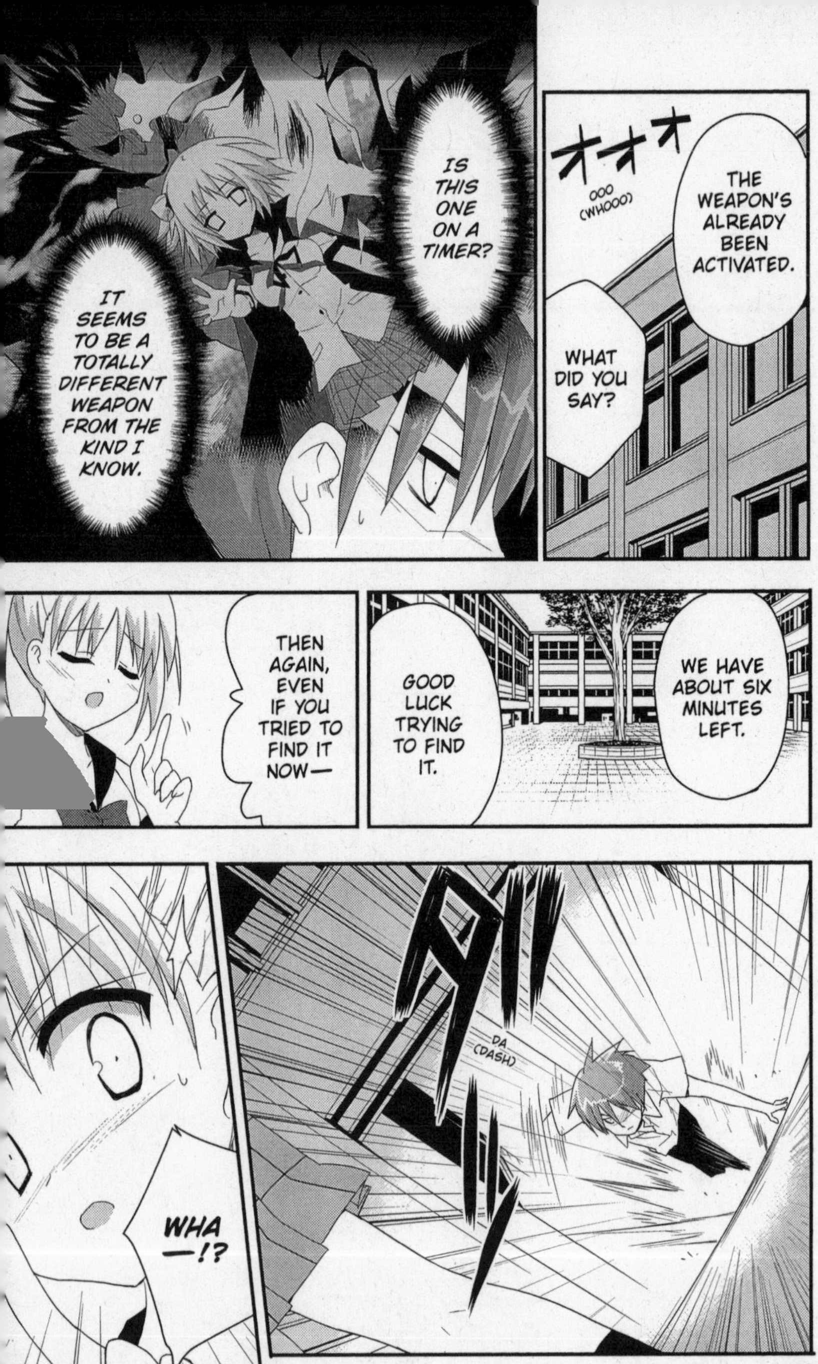
オオオ
OOO (WHOOO)
THE WEAPON'S ALREADY BEEN ACTIVATED.
WHAT DID YOU SAY?
IS THIS ONE ON A TIMER?
IT SEEMS TO BE A TOTALLY DIFFERENT WEAPON FROM THE KIND I KNOW.
WE HAVE ABOUT SIX MINUTES LEFT.
GOOD LUCK TRYING TO FIND IT.
THEN AGAIN, EVEN IF YOU TRIED TO FIND IT NOW—
ダ
DA (DASH)
WHA—!?

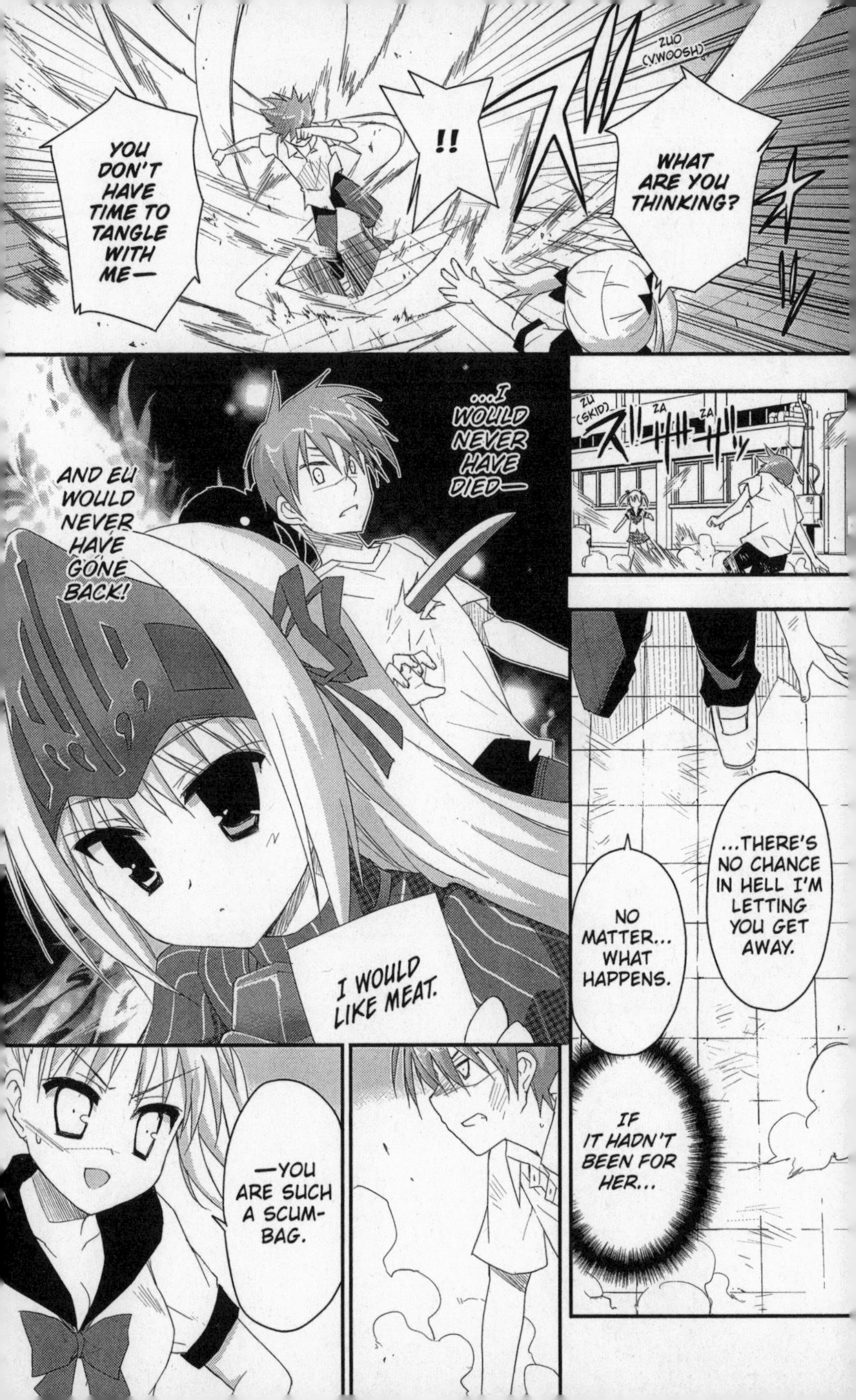
ZUO (V.WOOSH)
WHAT ARE YOU THINKING?
!!
YOU DON'T HAVE TIME TO TANGLE WITH ME—
ZU (SKID)
ZA
ZA
...THERE'S NO CHANCE IN HELL I'M LETTING YOU GET AWAY.
NO MATTER... WHAT HAPPENS.
...I WOULD NEVER HAVE DIED—
AND EU WOULD NEVER HAVE GONE BACK!
I WOULD LIKE MEAT.
IF IT HADN'T BEEN FOR HER...
—YOU ARE SUCH A SCUM-BAG.

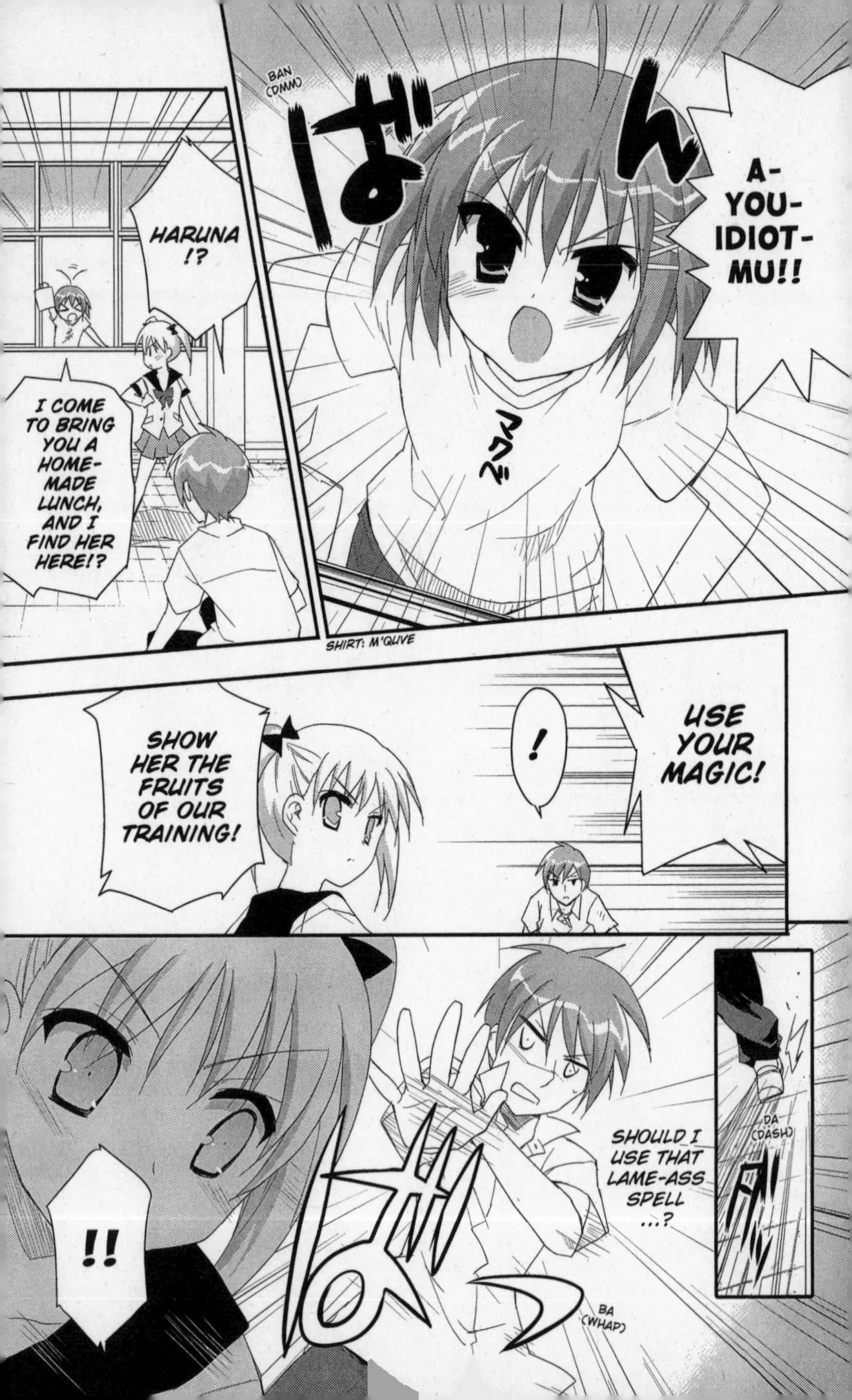
BAN (DMM)
ばん
A-YOU-IDIOT-MU!!
マクベ
SHIRT: M'QUVE
HARUNA!?
I COME TO BRING YOU A HOME-MADE LUNCH, AND I FIND HER HERE!?
USE YOUR MAGIC!
!
SHOW HER THE FRUITS OF OUR TRAINING!
DA (DASH)
SHOULD I USE THAT LAME-ASS SPELL ...?
BA (WHAP)
!!

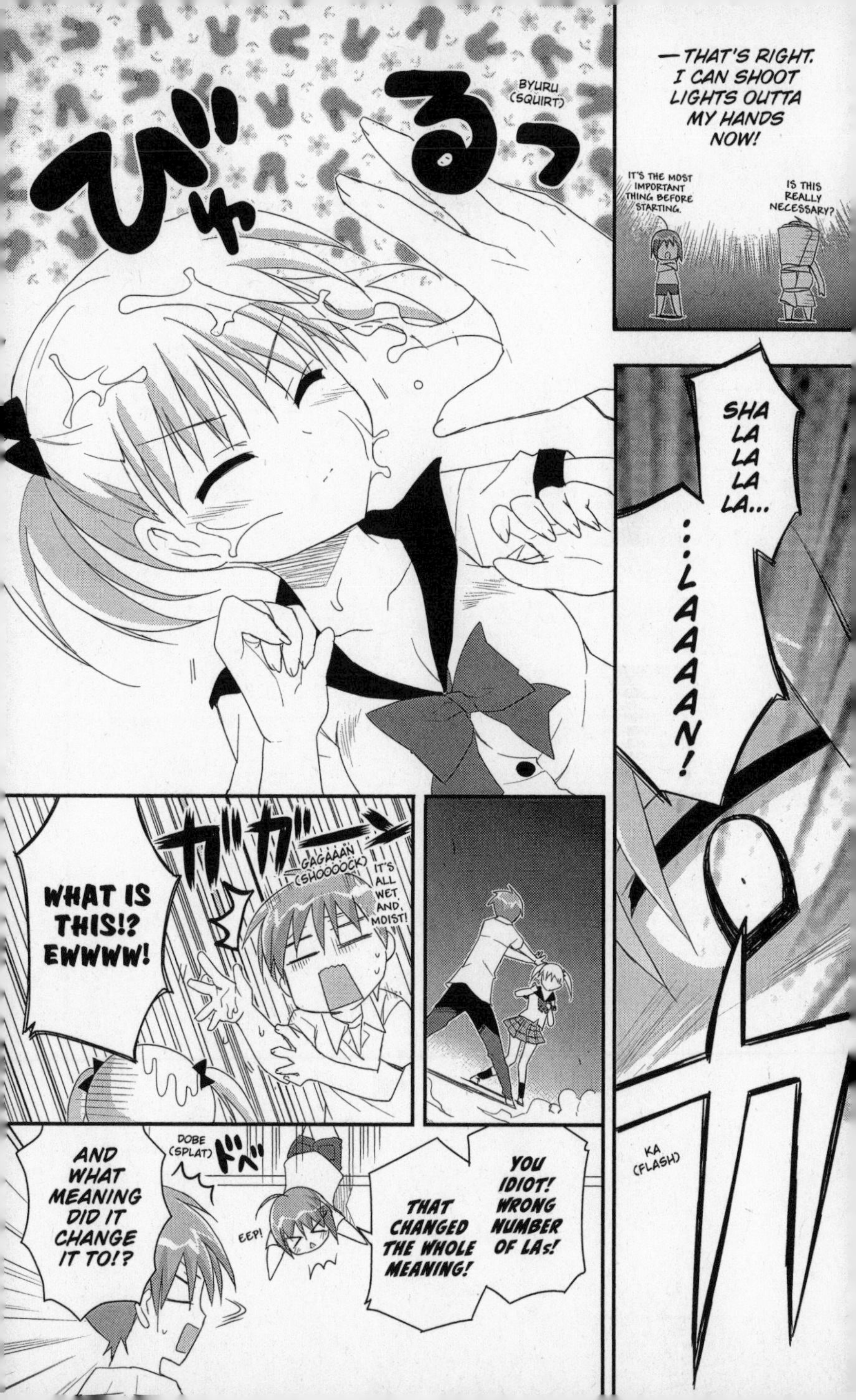
—THAT'S RIGHT. I CAN SHOOT LIGHTS OUTTA MY HANDS NOW!
IS THIS REALLY NECESSARY?
IT'S THE MOST IMPORTANT THING BEFORE STARTING.
SHA LA LA LA LA...
...LAAAAAN!
KA (FLASH)
びゅるっ
BYURU (SQUIRT)
ガガーン
GAGAAAN (SHOOOOCK)
IT'S ALL WET AND MOIST!
WHAT IS THIS!? EWWWW!
YOU IDIOT! WRONG NUMBER OF LAs!
THAT CHANGED THE WHOLE MEANING!
EEP!
ドベ
DOBE (SPLAT)
AND WHAT MEANING DID IT CHANGE IT TO!?

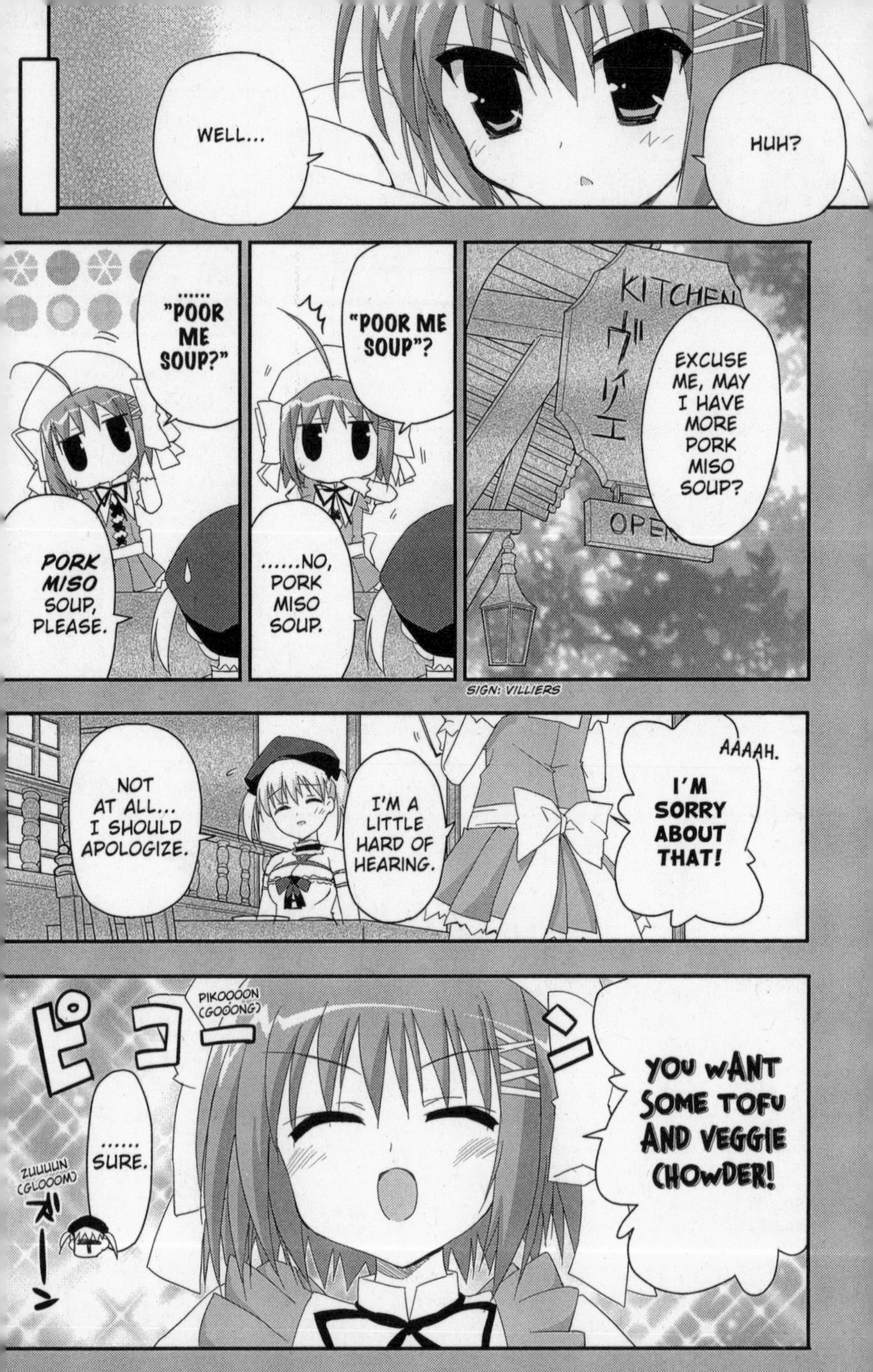
HUH?
WELL...
KITCHEN ヴィリエ
OPEN
EXCUSE ME, MAY I HAVE MORE PORK MISO SOUP?
SIGN: VILLIERS
"POOR ME SOUP"?
......NO, PORK MISO SOUP.
......"POOR ME SOUP?"
PORK MISO SOUP, PLEASE.
AAAAH. I'M SORRY ABOUT THAT!
I'M A LITTLE HARD OF HEARING.
NOT AT ALL... I SHOULD APOLOGIZE.
ピコーン
PIKOOOON (GOOONG)
YOU WANT SOME TOFU AND VEGGIE CHOWDER!
......SURE.
ズーン
ZUUUUN (GLOOOM)

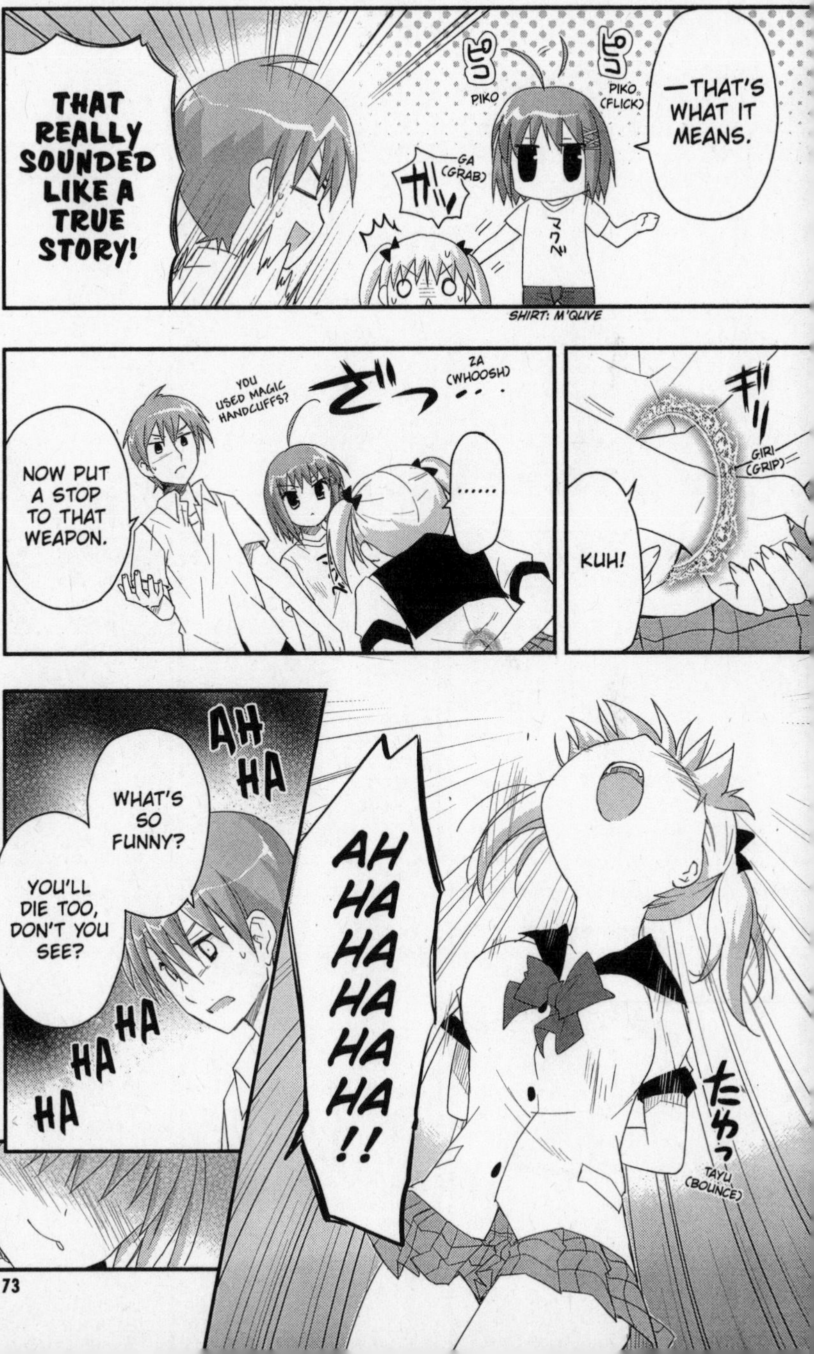
—THAT'S WHAT IT MEANS.
PIKO (FLICK)
PIKO
GA (GRAB)
THAT REALLY SOUNDED LIKE A TRUE STORY!
SHIRT: M'QUVE
GIRI (GRIP)
KUH!
ZA (WHOOSH)
......
YOU USED MAGIC HANDCUFFS?
NOW PUT A STOP TO THAT WEAPON.
AH HA HA HA HA HA HA HA!!
TAYU (BOUNCE)
AH HA
WHAT'S SO FUNNY?
YOU'LL DIE TOO, DON'T YOU SEE?
HA HA HA

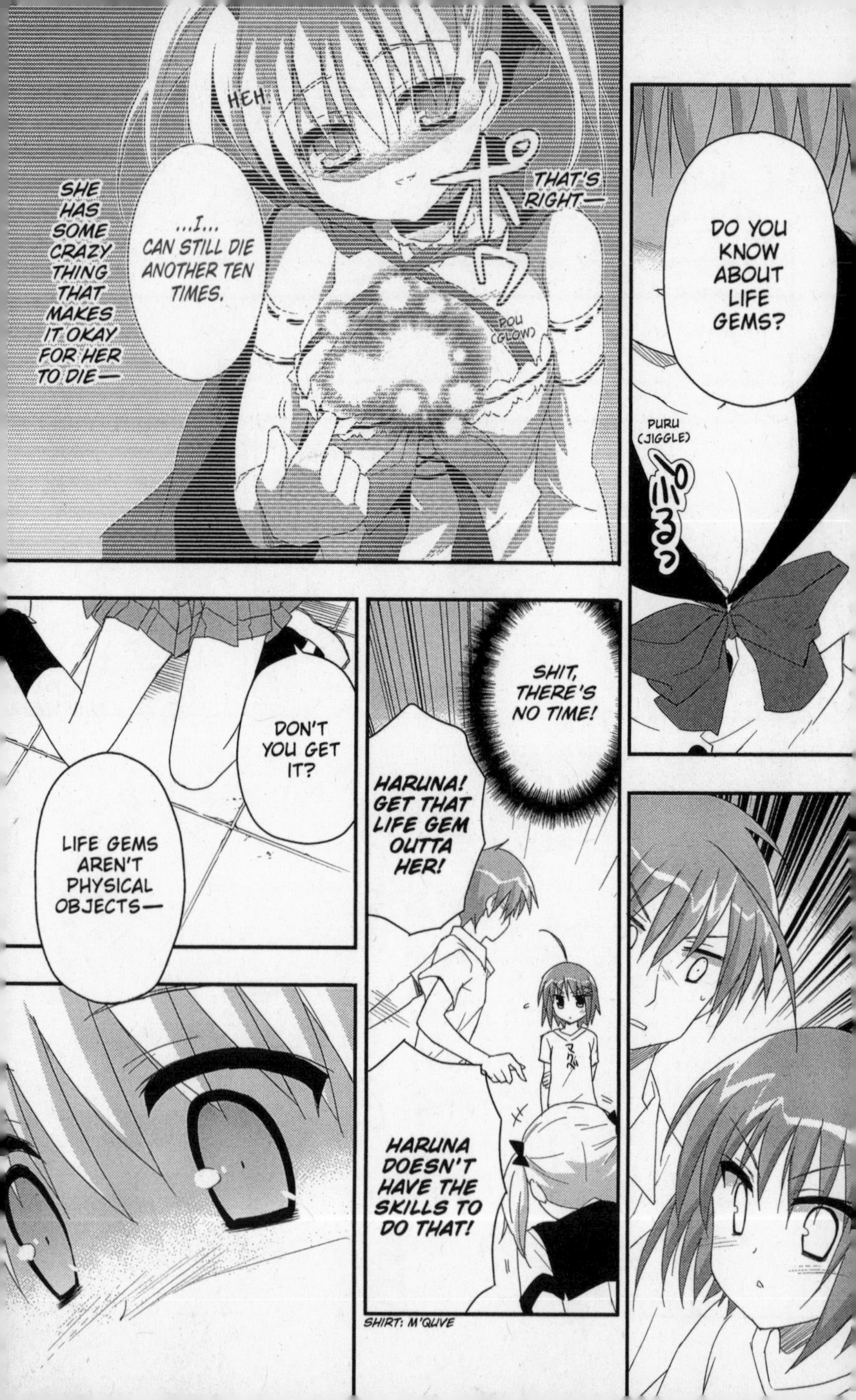
DO YOU KNOW ABOUT LIFE GEMS?
PURU (JIGGLE)
HEH
THAT'S RIGHT—
...I... CAN STILL DIE ANOTHER TEN TIMES.
POU (GLOW)
SHE HAS SOME CRAZY THING THAT MAKES IT OKAY FOR HER TO DIE—
SHIT, THERE'S NO TIME!
HARUNA! GET THAT LIFE GEM OUTTA HER!
HARUNA DOESN'T HAVE THE SKILLS TO DO THAT!
SHIRT: M'QUVE
DON'T YOU GET IT?
LIFE GEMS AREN'T PHYSICAL OBJECTS—

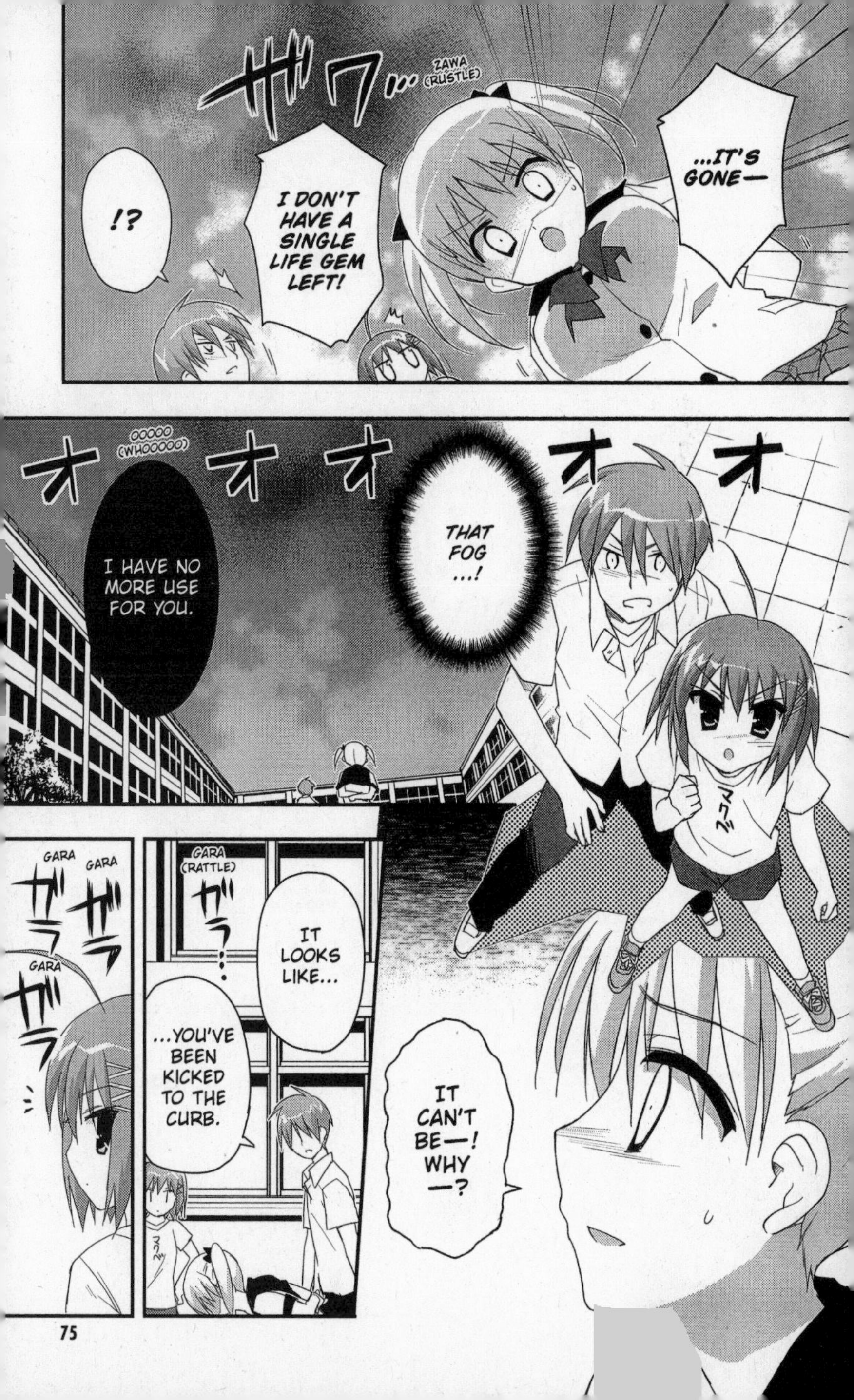
ZAWA (RUSTLE)
...IT'S GONE—
I DON'T HAVE A SINGLE LIFE GEM LEFT!
!?
OOOOO (WHOOOOO)
THAT FOG ...!
I HAVE NO MORE USE FOR YOU.
IT CAN'T BE—! WHY—?
GARA (RATTLE)
IT LOOKS LIKE...
...YOU'VE BEEN KICKED TO THE CURB.
GARA
GARA
GARA

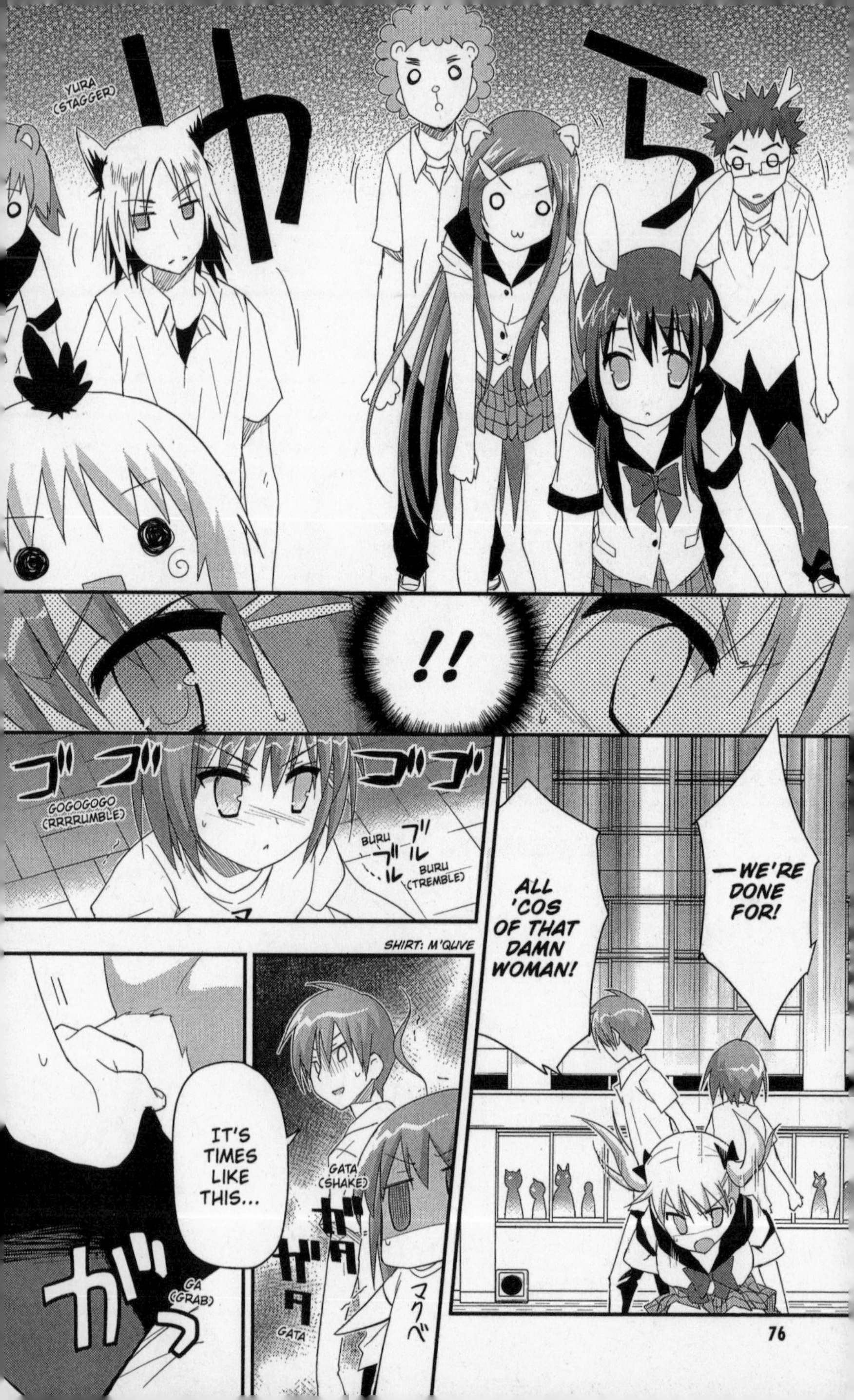
ゆら
YURA
(STAGGER)
!!
—WE'RE DONE FOR!
ALL 'COS OF THAT DAMN WOMAN!
ゴゴゴゴ
GOGOGOGO
(RRRRUMBLE)
ブルブル
BURU
BURU
(TREMBLE)
SHIRT: M'QUVE
マクベ
ガタガタ
GATA
(SHAKE)
GATA
IT'S TIMES LIKE THIS...
ガッ
GA
(GRAB)

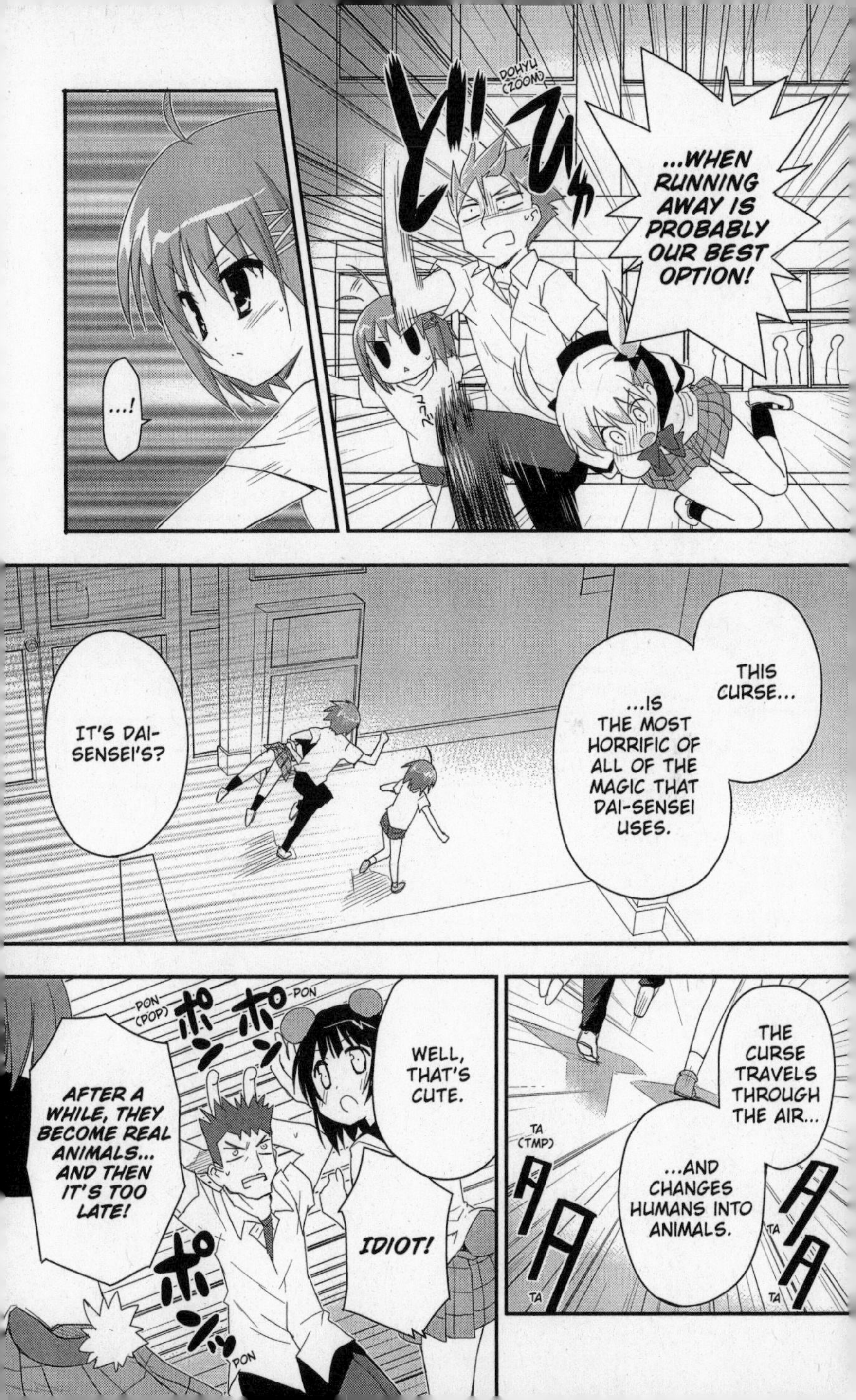
DOHYU (ZOOM)
...WHEN RUNNING AWAY IS PROBABLY OUR BEST OPTION!
...!
THIS CURSE...
...IS THE MOST HORRIFIC OF ALL OF THE MAGIC THAT DAI-SENSEI USES.
IT'S DAI-SENSEI'S?
THE CURSE TRAVELS THROUGH THE AIR...
...AND CHANGES HUMANS INTO ANIMALS.
TA (TMP)
TA
TA
TA
PON
PON (POP)
WELL, THAT'S CUTE.
IDIOT!
AFTER A WHILE, THEY BECOME REAL ANIMALS... AND THEN IT'S TOO LATE!
PON

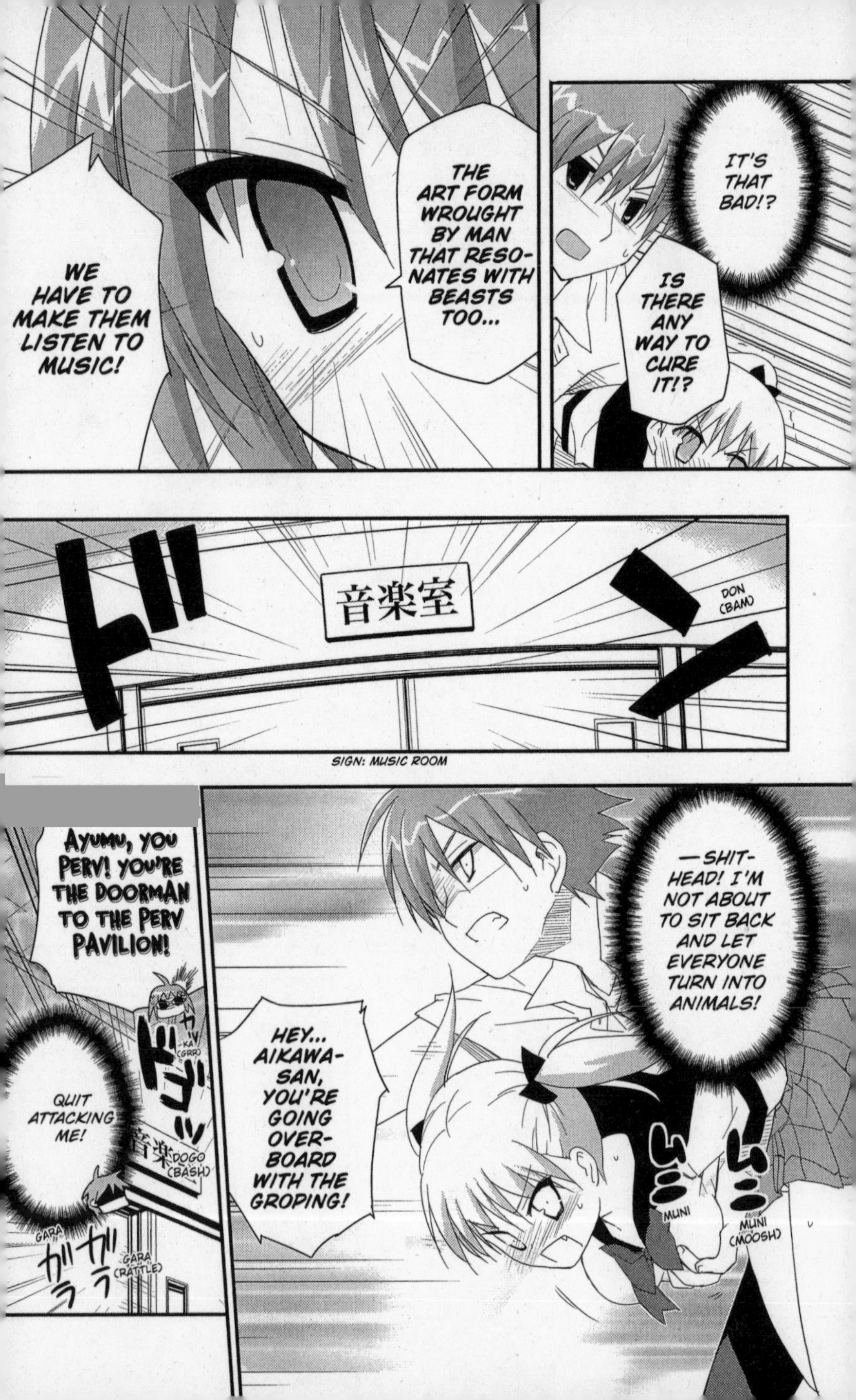
IT'S THAT BAD!?
IS THERE ANY WAY TO CURE IT!?
THE ART FORM WROUGHT BY MAN THAT RESONATES WITH BEASTS TOO...
WE HAVE TO MAKE THEM LISTEN TO MUSIC!
DON (BAM)
音楽室
SIGN: MUSIC ROOM
—SHIT-HEAD! I'M NOT ABOUT TO SIT BACK AND LET EVERYONE TURN INTO ANIMALS!
MUNI
MUNI (MOOSH)
HEY... AIKAWA-SAN, YOU'RE GOING OVERBOARD WITH THE GROPING!
AYUMU, YOU PERV! YOU'RE THE DOORMAN TO THE PERV PAVILION!
KA (GRR)
QUIT ATTACKING ME!
DOGO (BASH)
GARA
GARA (RATTLE)

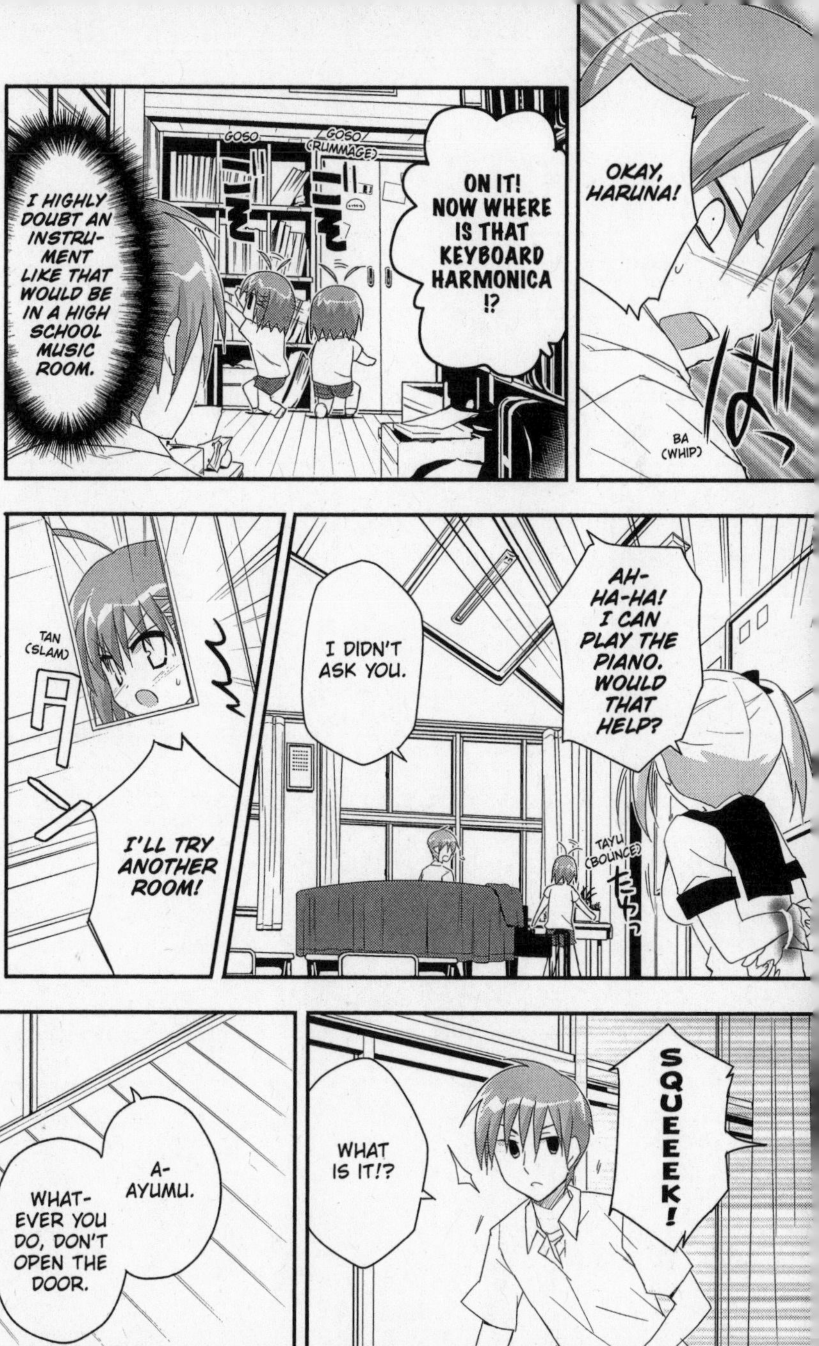

OKAY, HARUNA!
BA (WHIP)
ON IT! NOW WHERE IS THAT KEYBOARD HARMONICA!?
GOSO (RUMMAGE)
GOSO
I HIGHLY DOUBT AN INSTRU-MENT LIKE THAT WOULD BE IN A HIGH SCHOOL MUSIC ROOM.
AH-HA-HA! I CAN PLAY THE PIANO. WOULD THAT HELP?
TAYU (BOUNCE)
I DIDN'T ASK YOU.
TAN (SLAM)
I'LL TRY ANOTHER ROOM!
SQUEEEK!
WHAT IS IT!?
A-AYUMU.
WHAT-EVER YOU DO, DON'T OPEN THE DOOR.

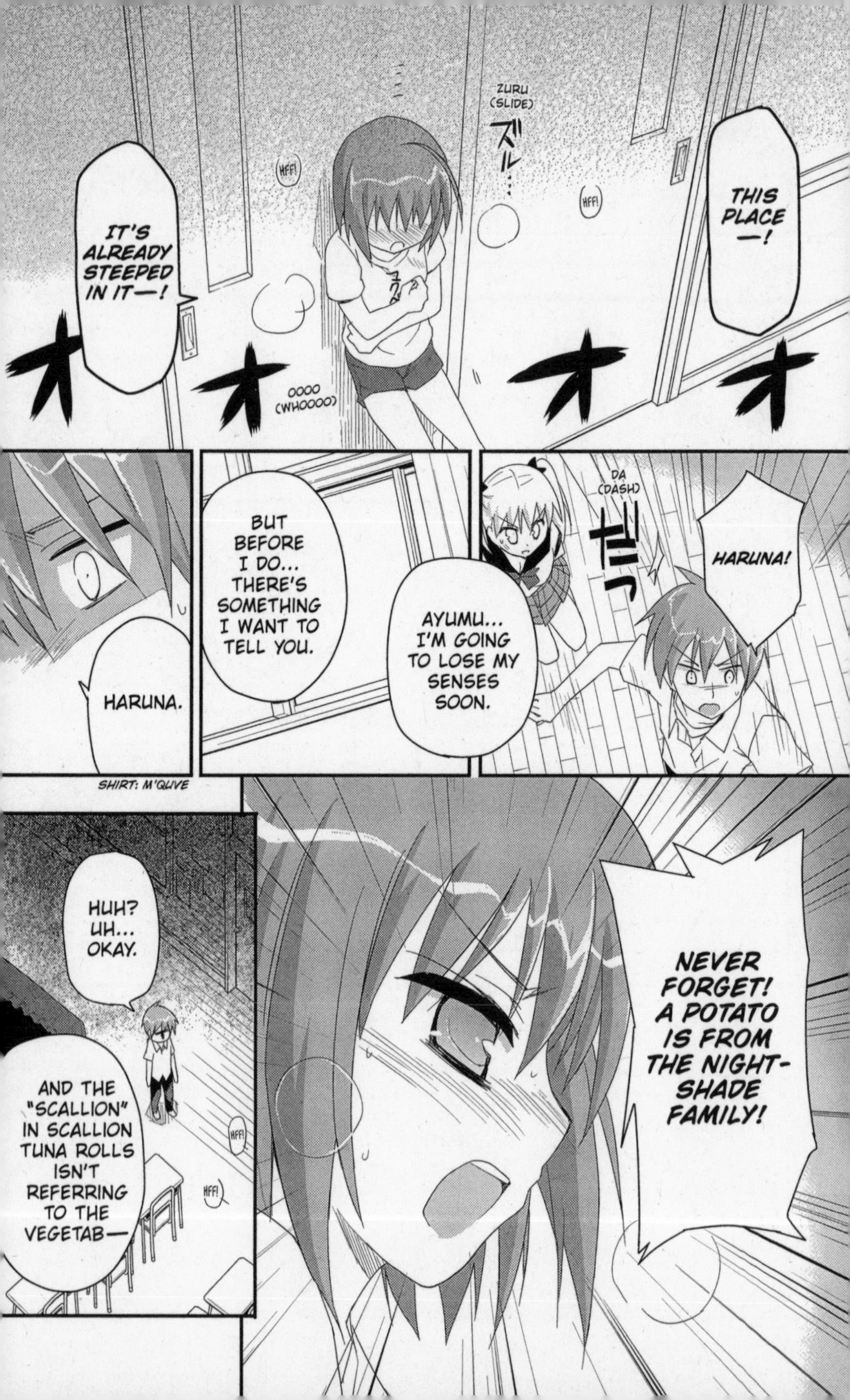
THIS PLACE—!
HFF!
ZURU (SLIDE)
HFF!
IT'S ALREADY STEEPED IN IT—!
OOOO (WHOOOO)
DA (DASH)
HARUNA!
AYUMU... I'M GOING TO LOSE MY SENSES SOON.
BUT BEFORE I DO... THERE'S SOMETHING I WANT TO TELL YOU.
HARUNA.
SHIRT: M'QUVE
NEVER FORGET! A POTATO IS FROM THE NIGHT-SHADE FAMILY!
HUH? UH... OKAY.
HFF!
HFF!
AND THE "SCALLION" IN SCALLION TUNA ROLLS ISN'T REFERRING TO THE VEGETAB—

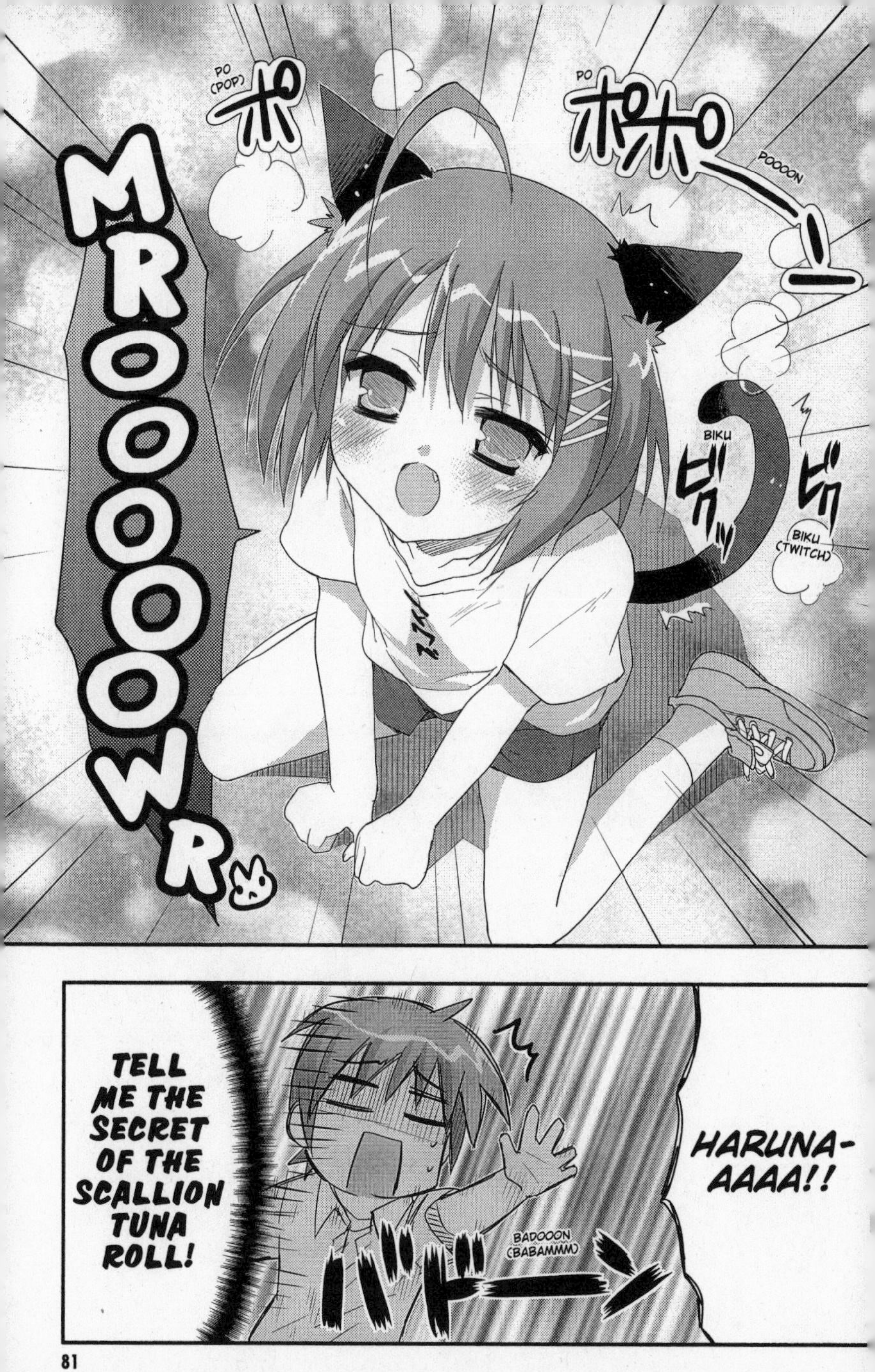
PO
POOOON
PO (POP)
MROOOOOOWR
BIKU
BIKU (TWITCH)
HARUNA-AAAA!!
BADOOON (BABAMMM)
TELL ME THE SECRET OF THE SCALLION TUNA ROLL!

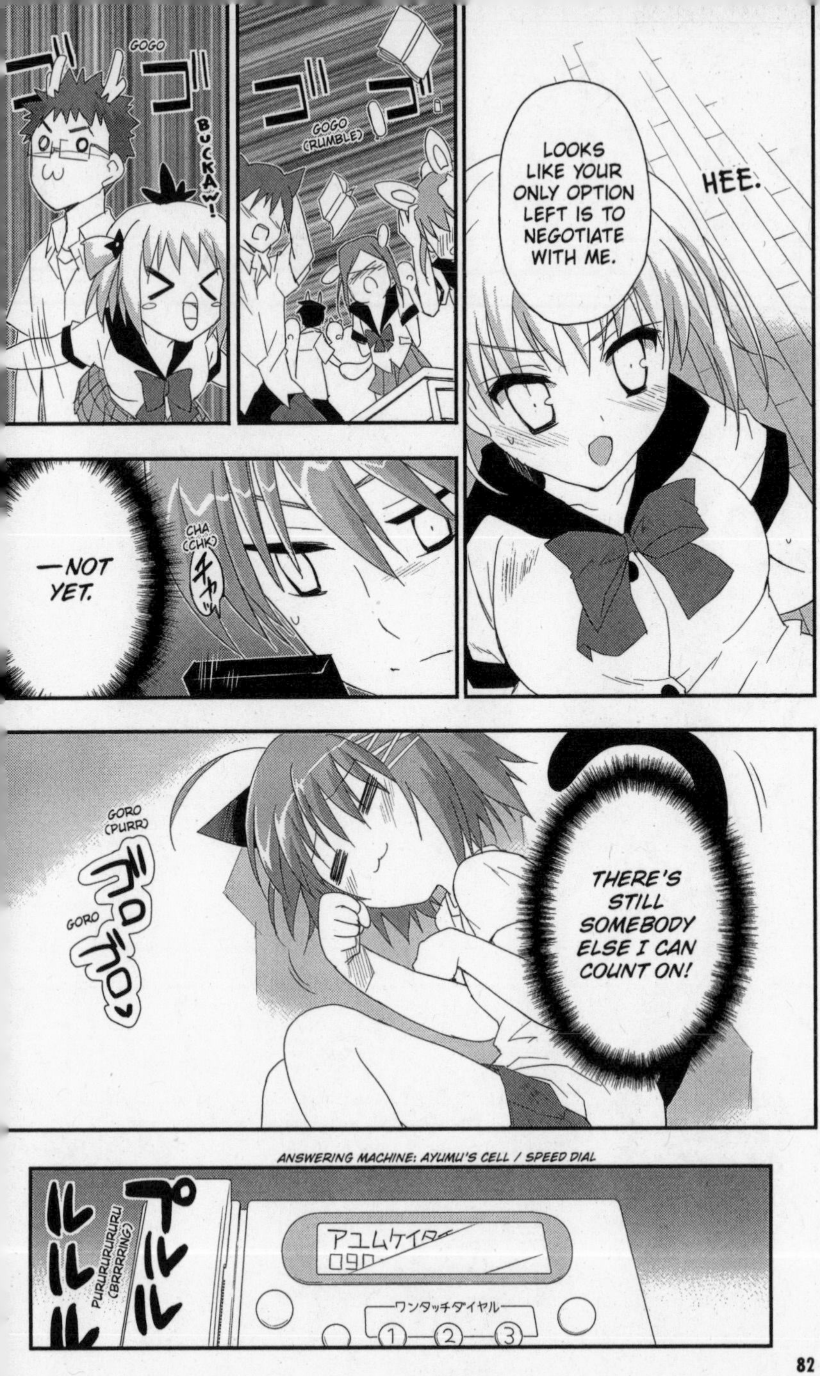

LOOKS LIKE YOUR ONLY OPTION LEFT IS TO NEGOTIATE WITH ME.
HEE.
GOGO (RUMBLE)
GOGO
BUCKAW!
CHA (CHK)
—NOT YET.
THERE'S STILL SOMEBODY ELSE I CAN COUNT ON!
GORO (PURR)
GORO
ANSWERING MACHINE: AYUMU'S CELL / SPEED DIAL
PURURURURU (BRRRRING)
ワンタッチダイヤル
1 2 3

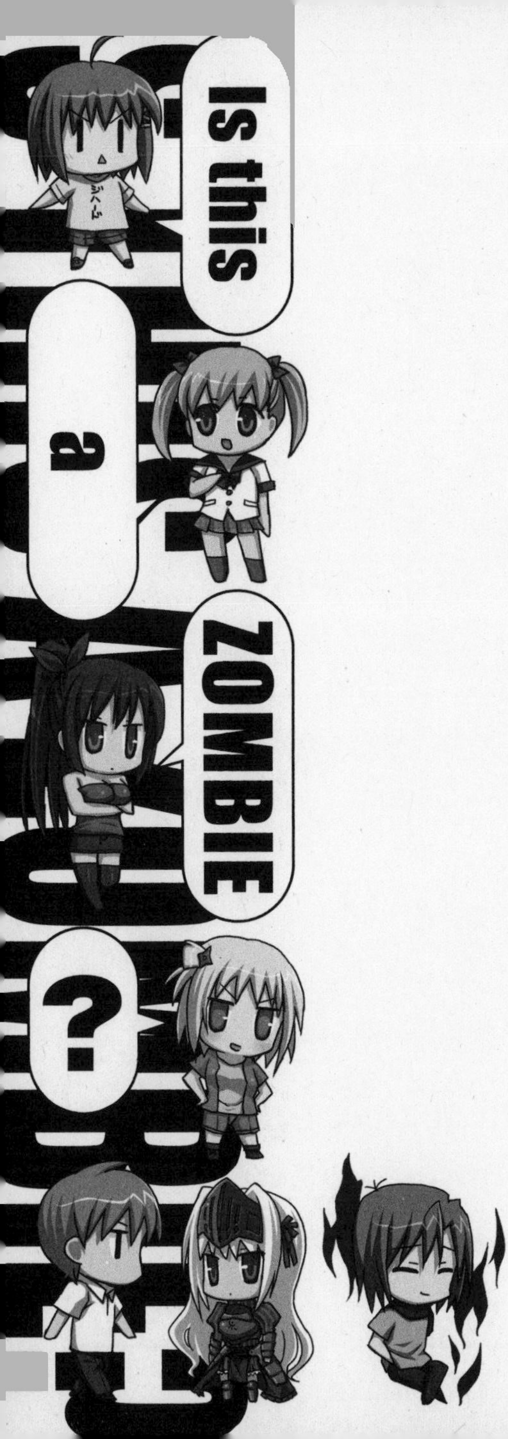

Is this
a
ZOMBIE
?

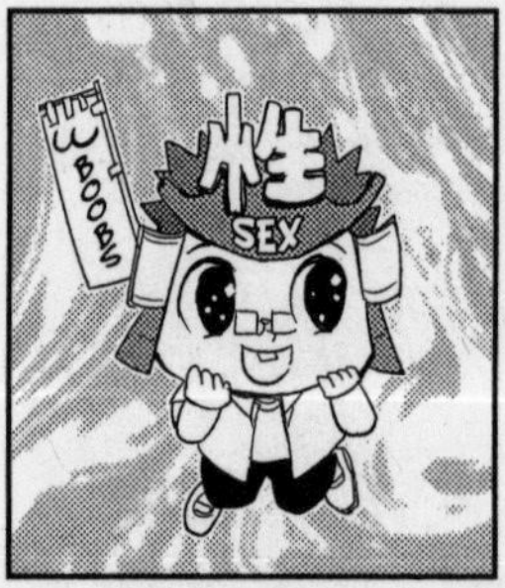
性
SEX
BOOBS

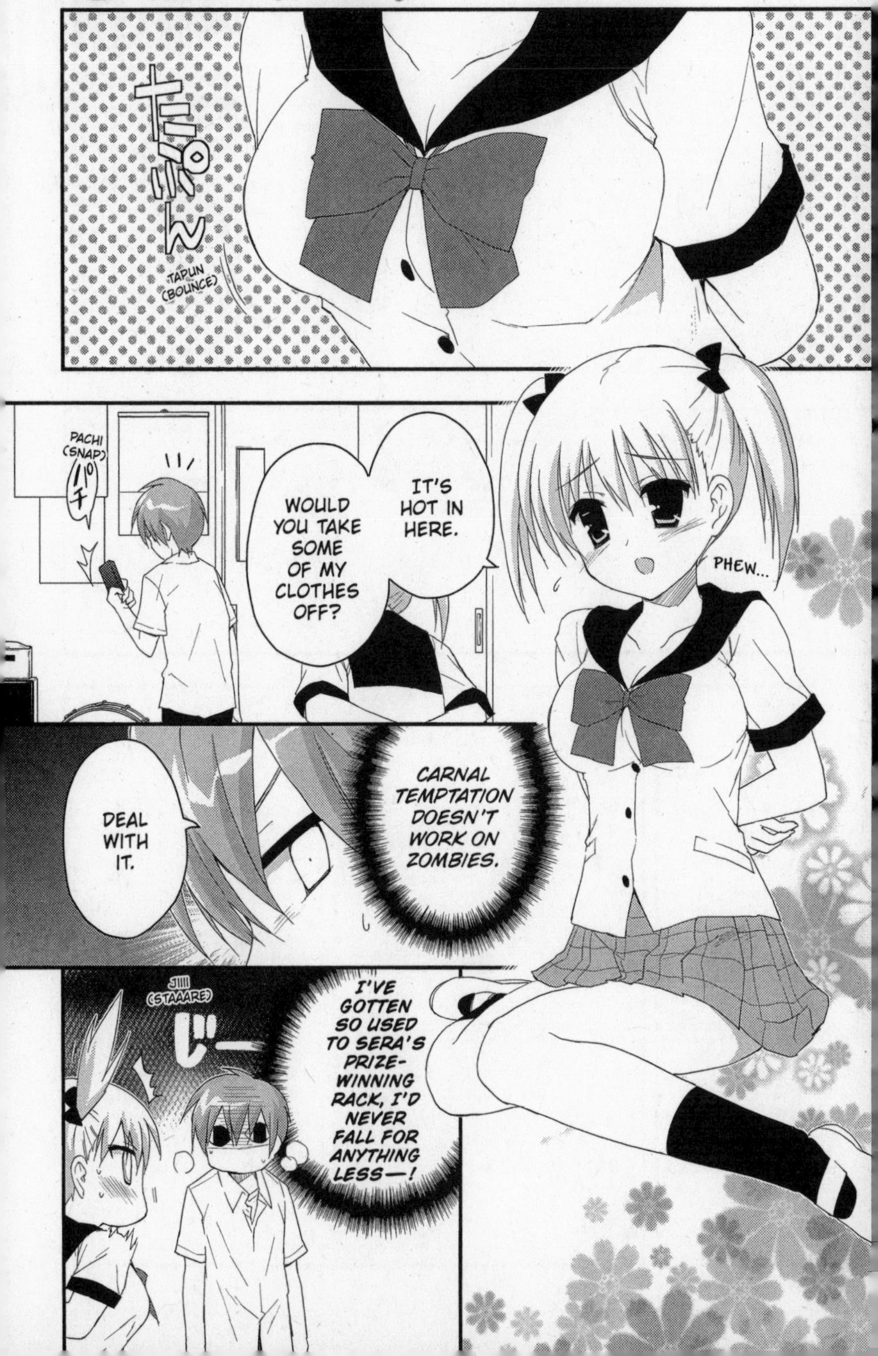
たぷん
TAPUN (BOUNCE)
PHEW...
IT'S HOT IN HERE.
WOULD YOU TAKE SOME OF MY CLOTHES OFF?
パチ
PACHI (SNAP)
CARNAL TEMPTATION DOESN'T WORK ON ZOMBIES.
DEAL WITH IT.
I'VE GOTTEN SO USED TO SERA'S PRIZE-WINNING RACK, I'D NEVER FALL FOR ANYTHING LESS—!
ジー
JIIII (STAAARE)

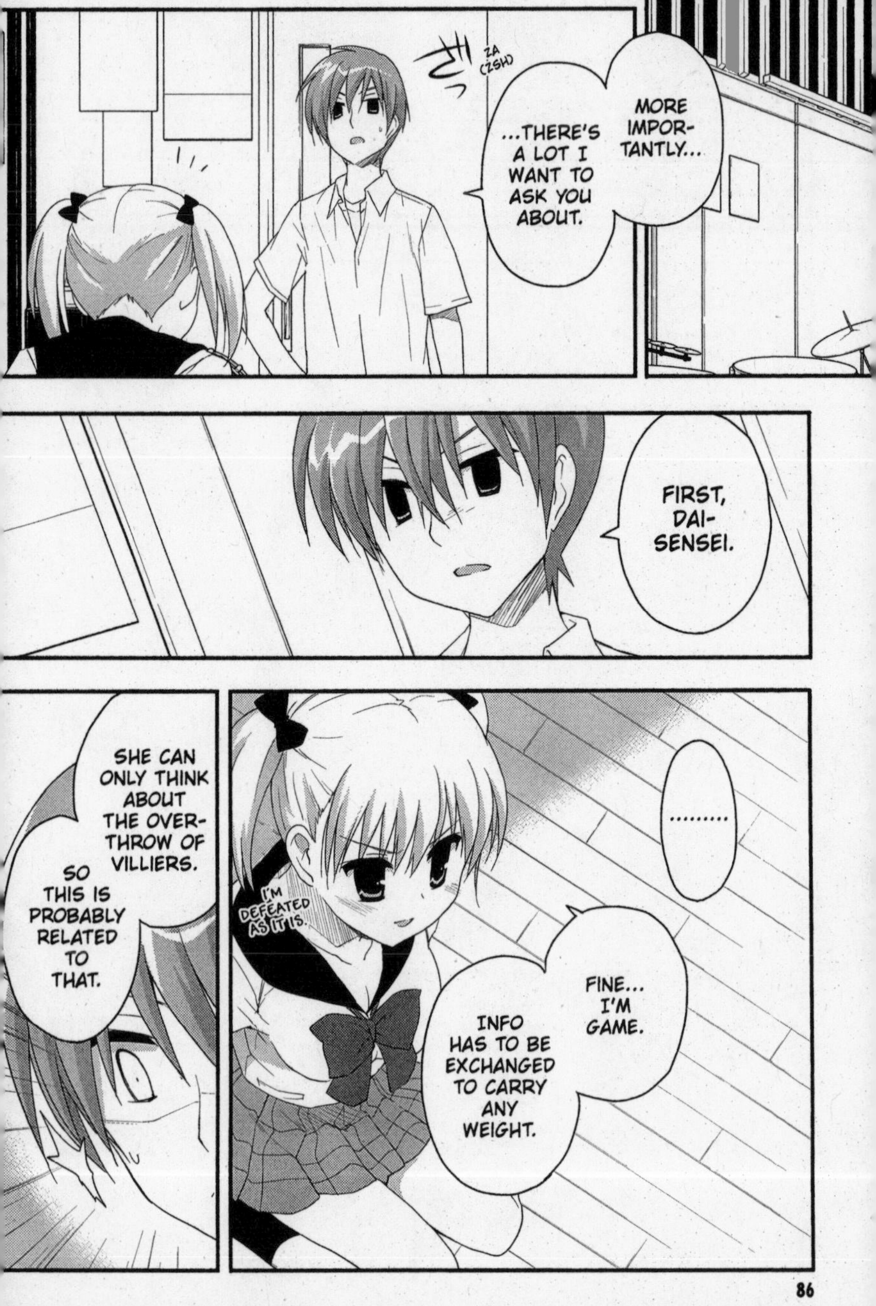
MORE IMPOR-TANTLY...
...THERE'S A LOT I WANT TO ASK YOU ABOUT.
ZA (ZSH)
FIRST, DAI-SENSEI.
....
FINE... I'M GAME.
INFO HAS TO BE EXCHANGED TO CARRY ANY WEIGHT.
I'M DEFEATED AS IT IS.
SHE CAN ONLY THINK ABOUT THE OVER-THROW OF VILLIERS.
SO THIS IS PROBABLY RELATED TO THAT.

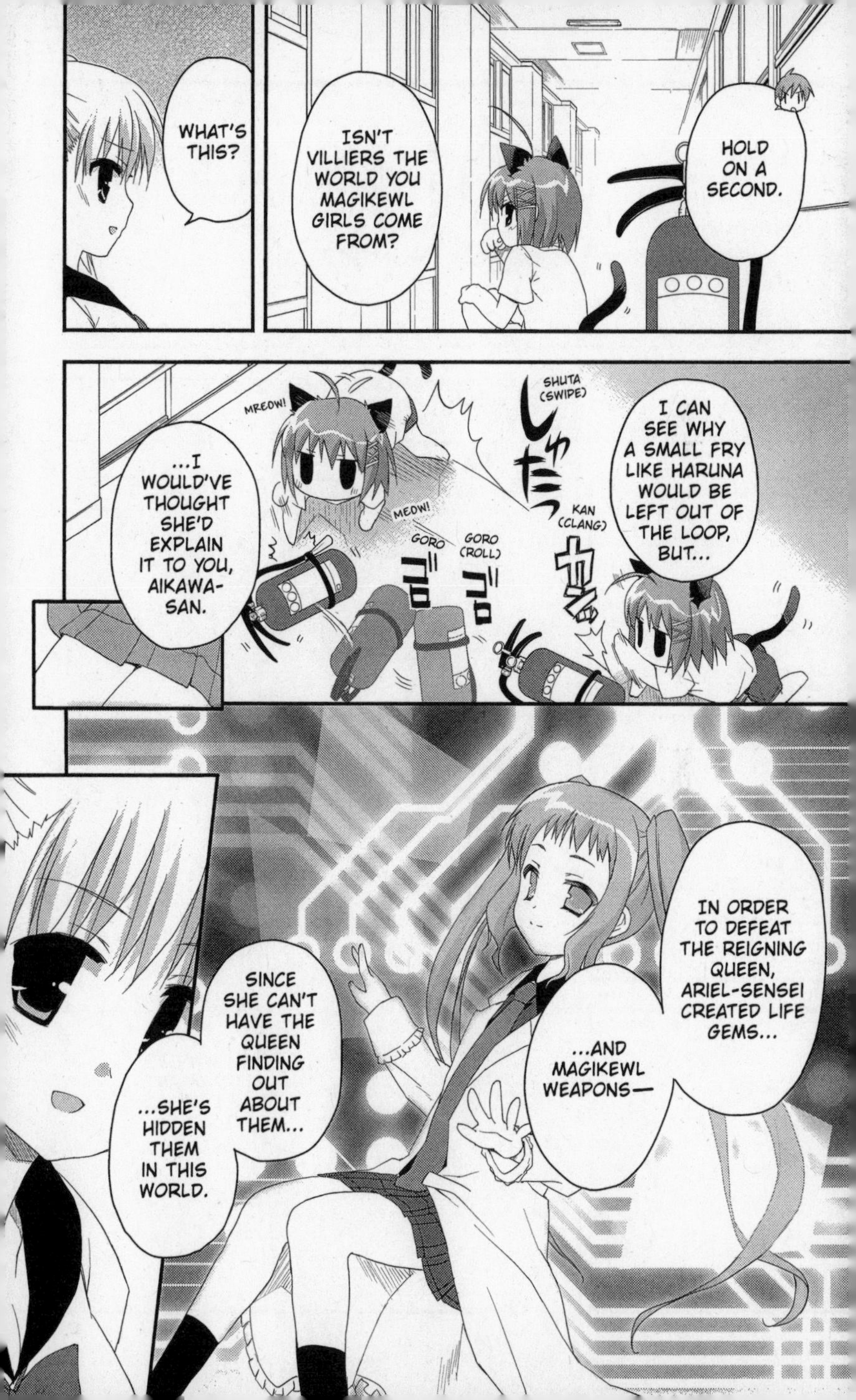

HOLD ON A SECOND.
ISN'T VILLIERS THE WORLD YOU MAGIKEWL GIRLS COME FROM?
WHAT'S THIS?
SHUTA (SWIPE)
I CAN SEE WHY A SMALL FRY LIKE HARUNA WOULD BE LEFT OUT OF THE LOOP, BUT...
KAN (CLANG)
MREOW!
MEOW!
GORO
GORO (ROLL)
...I WOULD'VE THOUGHT SHE'D EXPLAIN IT TO YOU, AIKAWA-SAN.
IN ORDER TO DEFEAT THE REIGNING QUEEN, ARIEL-SENSEI CREATED LIFE GEMS...
...AND MAGIKEWL WEAPONS—
SINCE SHE CAN'T HAVE THE QUEEN FINDING OUT ABOUT THEM...
...SHE'S HIDDEN THEM IN THIS WORLD.

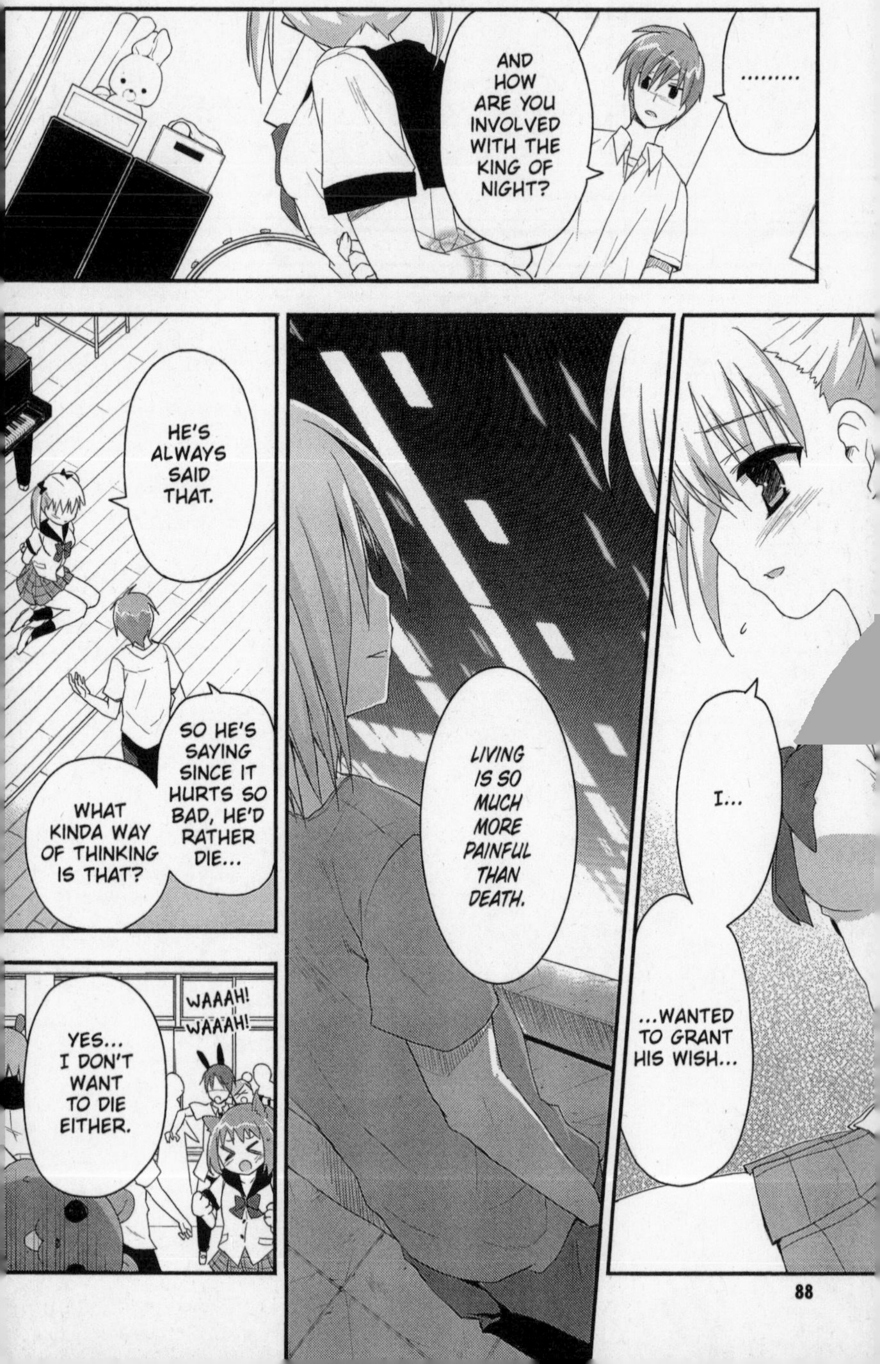
....
AND HOW ARE YOU INVOLVED WITH THE KING OF NIGHT?
I...
...WANTED TO GRANT HIS WISH...
LIVING IS SO MUCH MORE PAINFUL THAN DEATH.
HE'S ALWAYS SAID THAT.
SO HE'S SAYING SINCE IT HURTS SO BAD, HE'D RATHER DIE...
WHAT KINDA WAY OF THINKING IS THAT?
WAAAH! WAAAH!
YES... I DON'T WANT TO DIE EITHER.

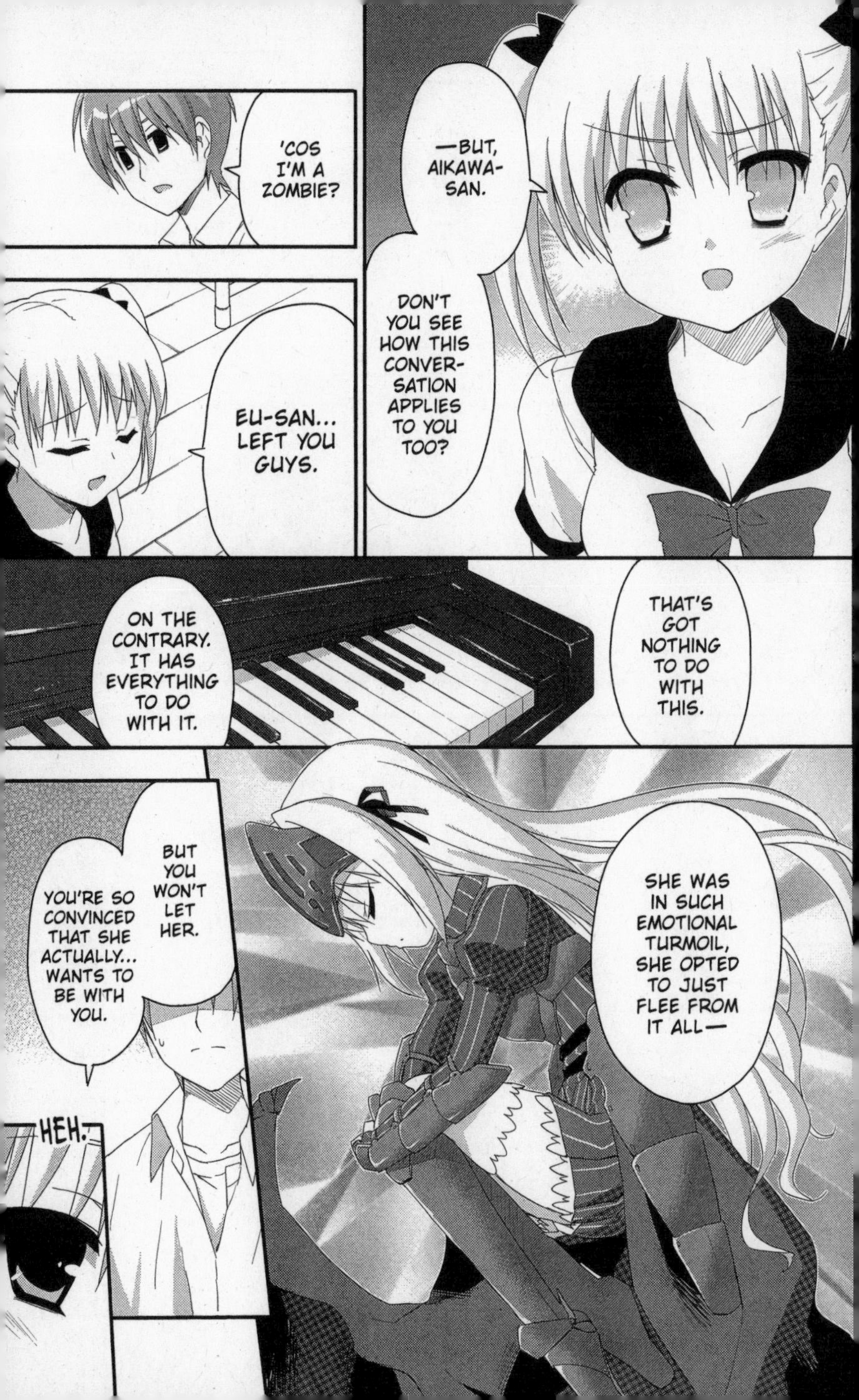
—BUT, AIKAWA-SAN.
DON'T YOU SEE HOW THIS CONVERSATION APPLIES TO YOU TOO?
'COS I'M A ZOMBIE?
EU-SAN... LEFT YOU GUYS.
THAT'S GOT NOTHING TO DO WITH THIS.
ON THE CONTRARY. IT HAS EVERYTHING TO DO WITH IT.
SHE WAS IN SUCH EMOTIONAL TURMOIL, SHE OPTED TO JUST FLEE FROM IT ALL—
BUT YOU WON'T LET HER.
YOU'RE SO CONVINCED THAT SHE ACTUALLY... WANTS TO BE WITH YOU.
HEH.

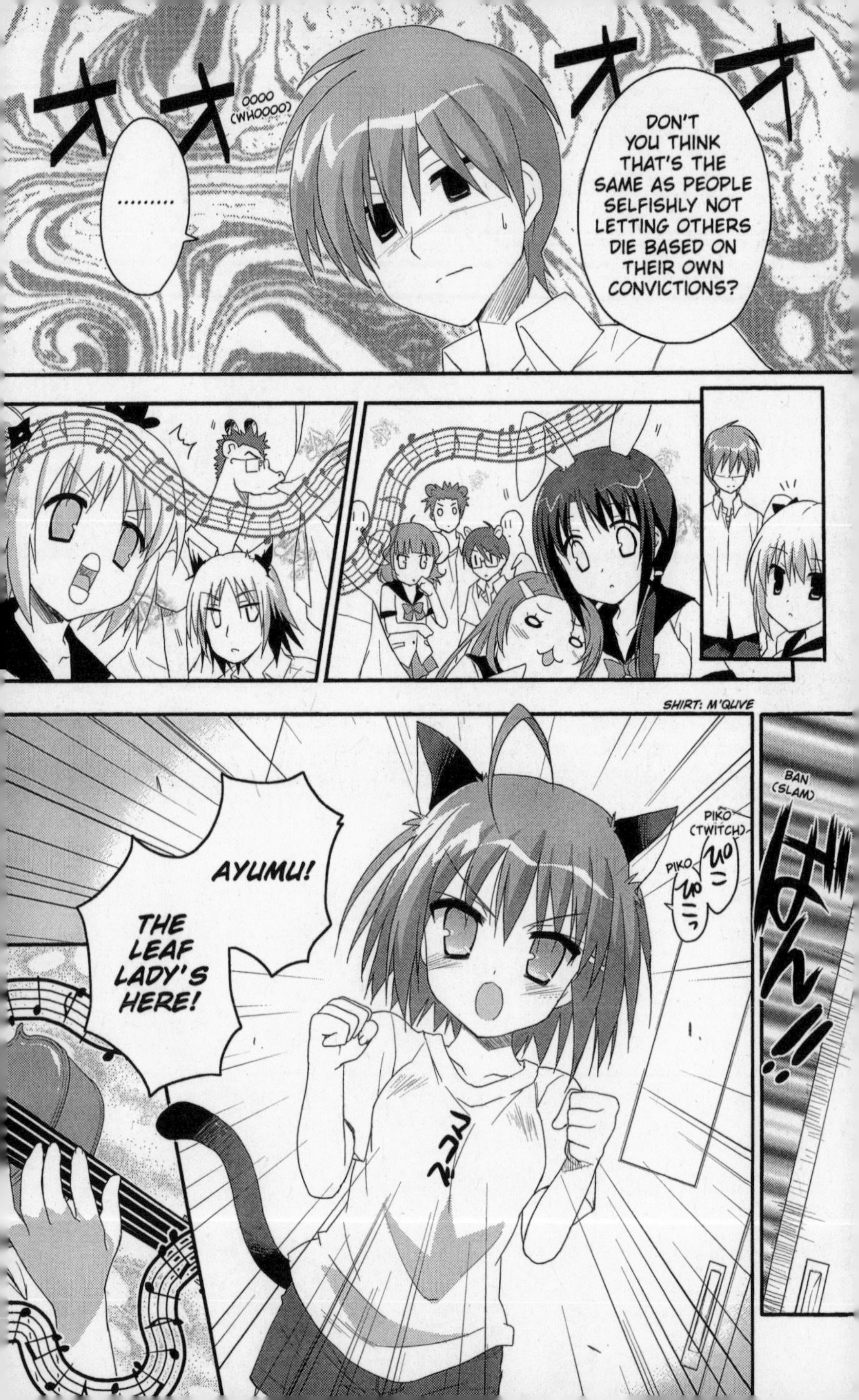
OOOO (WHOOOO)
DON'T YOU THINK THAT'S THE SAME AS PEOPLE SELFISHLY NOT LETTING OTHERS DIE BASED ON THEIR OWN CONVICTIONS?
....
SHIRT: M'QUVE
BAN (SLAM)
PIKO (TWITCH)
PIKO
AYUMU!
THE LEAF LADY'S HERE!

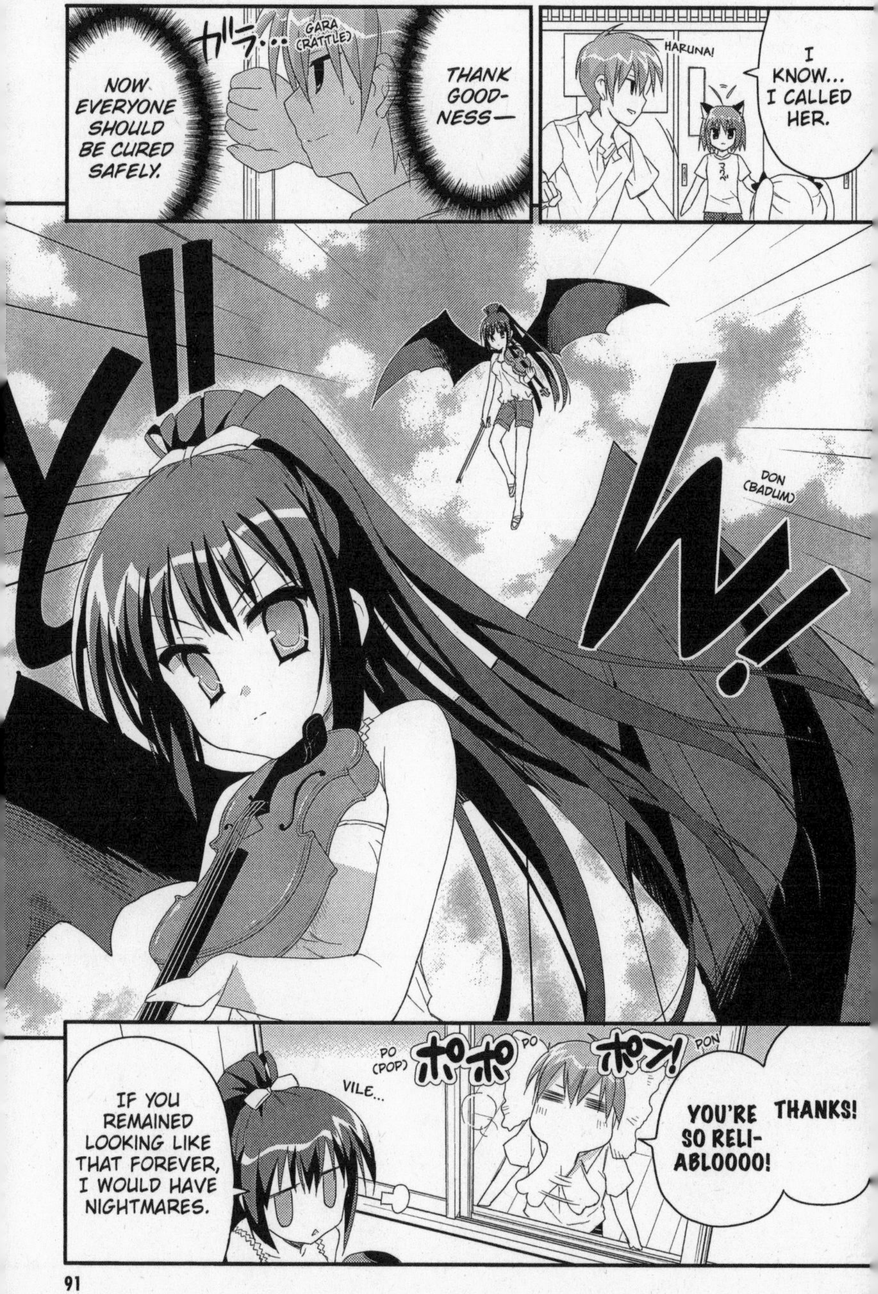
HARUNA!
I KNOW... I CALLED HER.
ガラ...
GARA (RATTLE)
THANK GOODNESS—
NOW EVERYONE SHOULD BE CURED SAFELY.
DON (BADUM)
PON
THANKS!
YOU'RE SO RELI-ABLOOOO!
ポポポン!
PO
PO (POP)
VILE...
IF YOU REMAINED LOOKING LIKE THAT FOREVER, I WOULD HAVE NIGHTMARES.

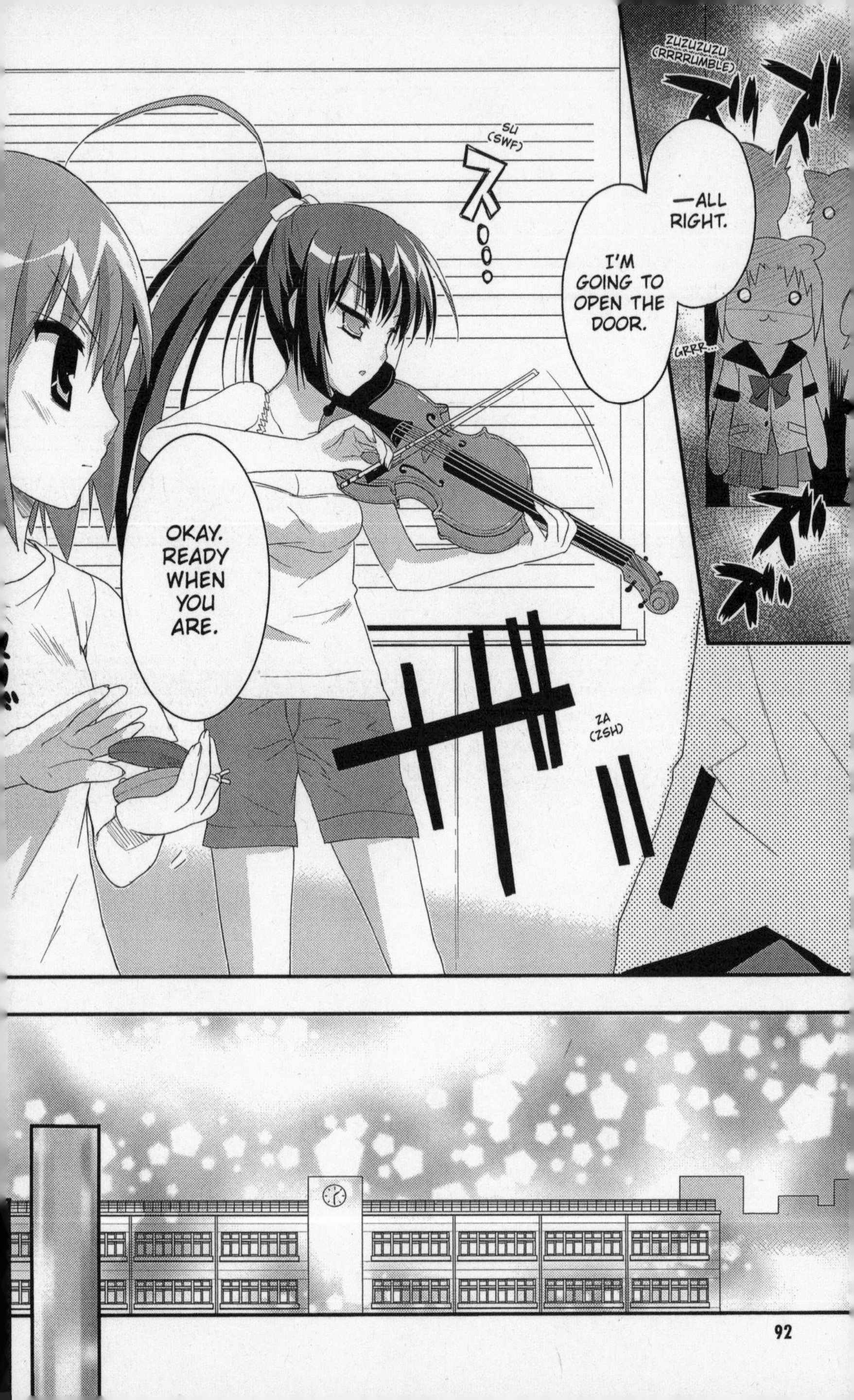
ZUZUZUZU (RRRRUMBLE)
—ALL RIGHT.
I'M GOING TO OPEN THE DOOR.
GRRR...
SU (SWF)
OKAY. READY WHEN YOU ARE.
ZA (ZSH)

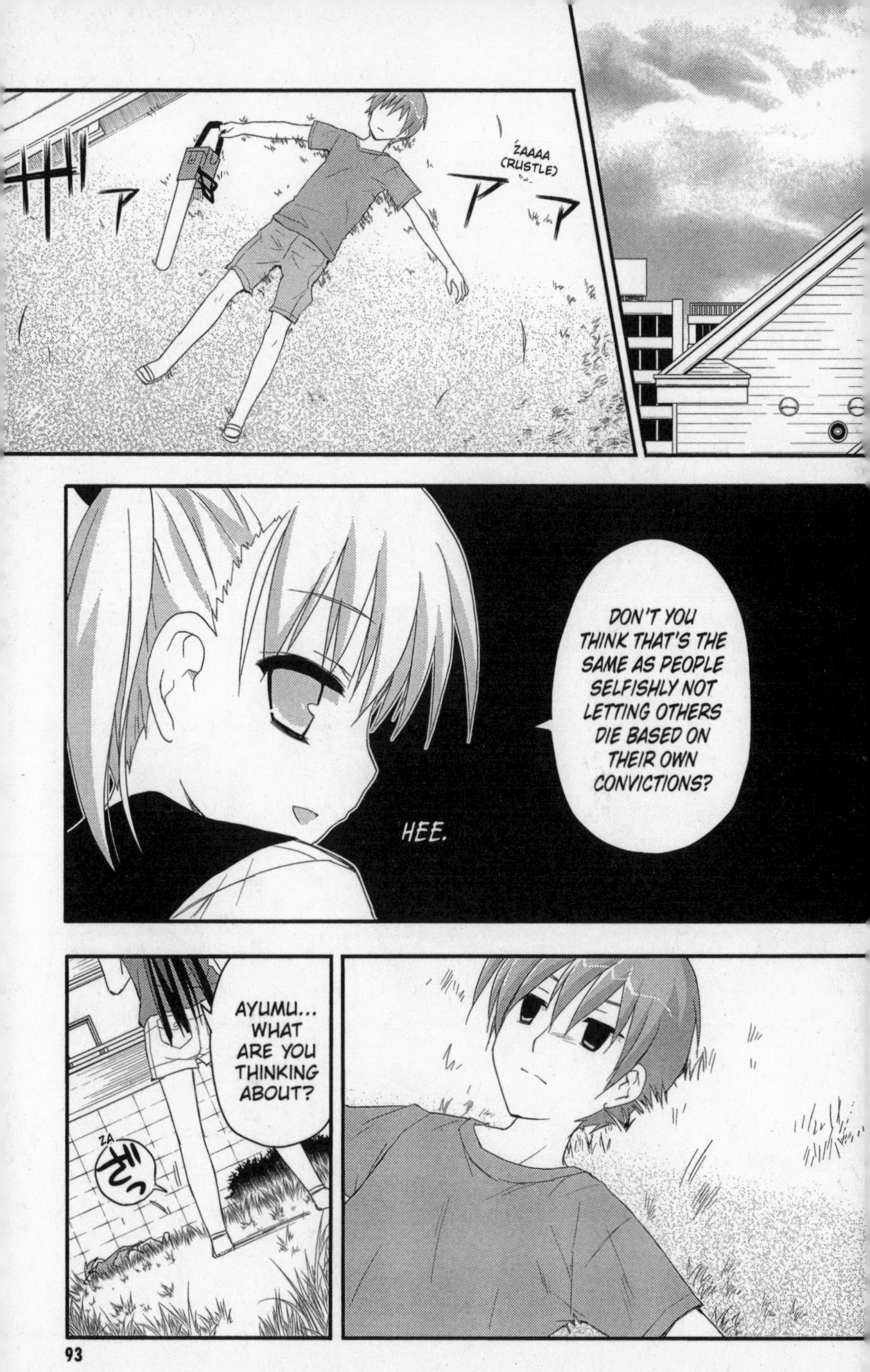
ZAAAA (RUSTLE)
DON'T YOU THINK THAT'S THE SAME AS PEOPLE SELFISHLY NOT LETTING OTHERS DIE BASED ON THEIR OWN CONVICTIONS?
HEE.
AYUMU... WHAT ARE YOU THINKING ABOUT?
ZA

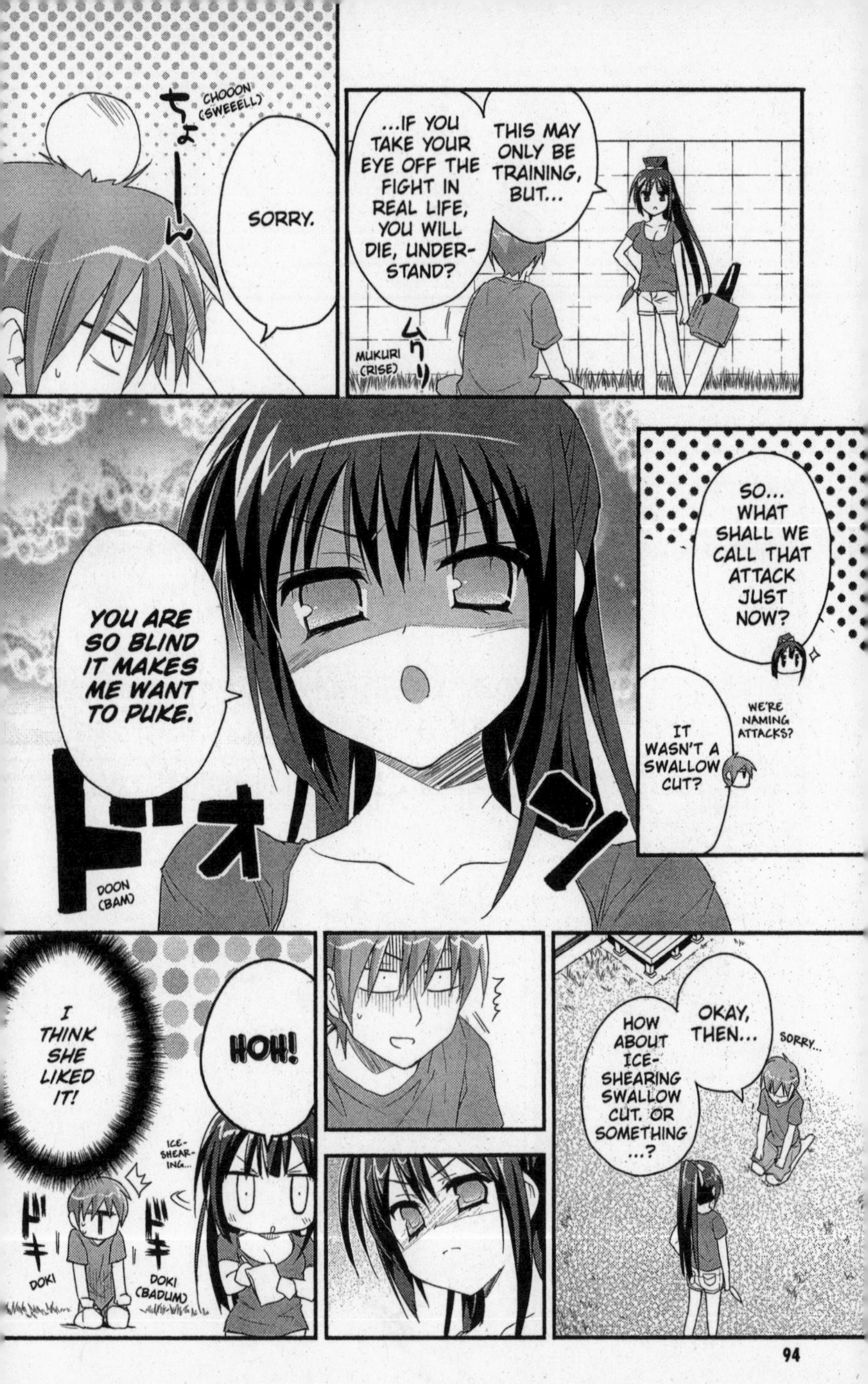
THIS MAY ONLY BE TRAINING, BUT...
...IF YOU TAKE YOUR EYE OFF THE FIGHT IN REAL LIFE, YOU WILL DIE, UNDERSTAND?
ムクリ
MUKURI (RISE)
ちょーん
CHOOON (SWEEELL)
SORRY.
SO... WHAT SHALL WE CALL THAT ATTACK JUST NOW?
WE'RE NAMING ATTACKS?
IT WASN'T A SWALLOW CUT?
YOU ARE SO BLIND IT MAKES ME WANT TO PUKE.
ドオン
DOON (BAM)
OKAY, THEN...
HOW ABOUT ICE-SHEARING SWALLOW CUT. OR SOMETHING ...?
SORRY...
HOH!
ICE-SHEARING...
I THINK SHE LIKED IT!
ドキ
DOKI
ドキ
DOKI (BADUM)

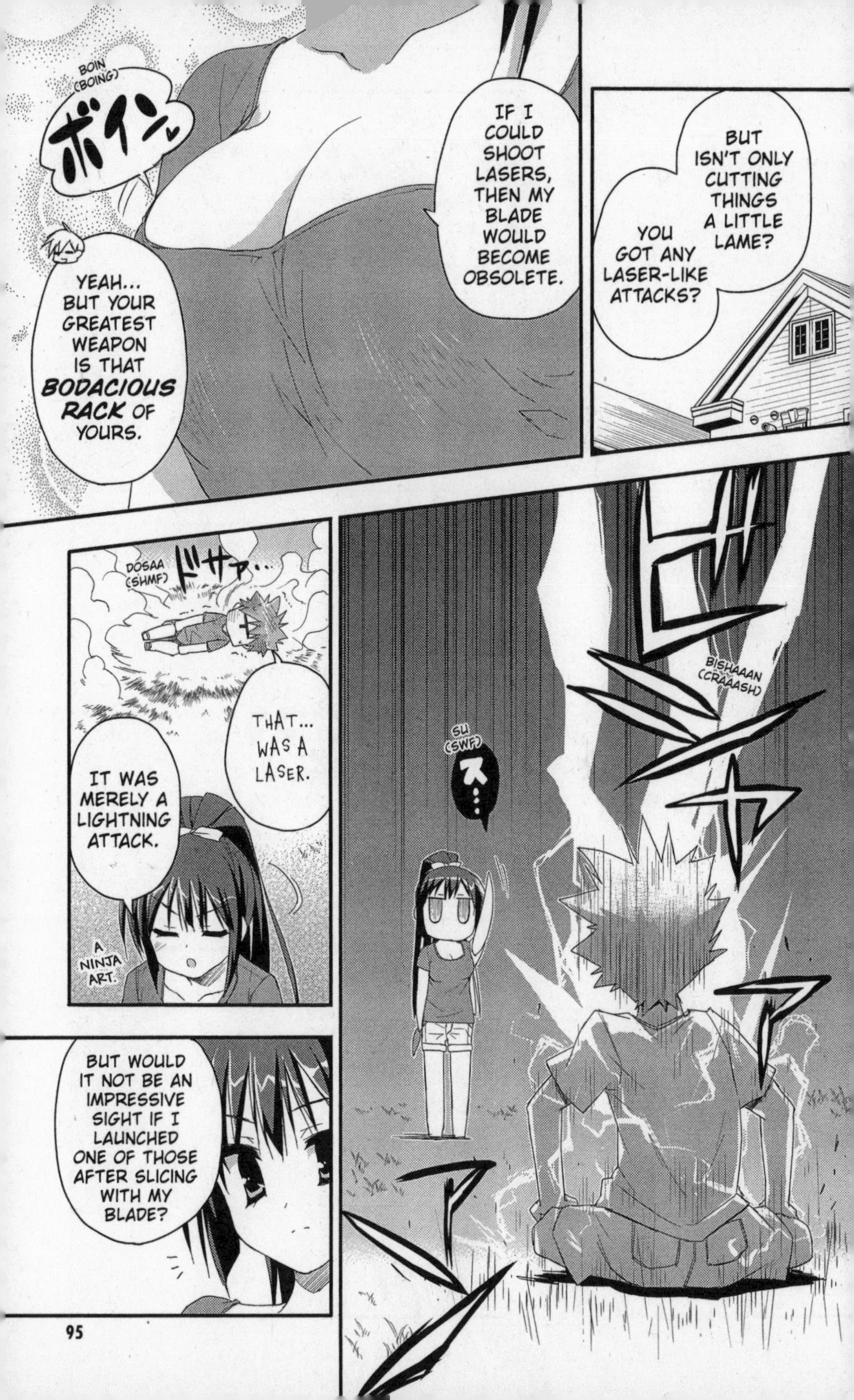

BUT ISN'T ONLY CUTTING THINGS A LITTLE LAME?
YOU GOT ANY LASER-LIKE ATTACKS?
IF I COULD SHOOT LASERS, THEN MY BLADE WOULD BECOME OBSOLETE.
BOIN (BOING)
ボイン
YEAH... BUT YOUR GREATEST WEAPON IS THAT **BODACIOUS RACK** OF YOURS.
BISHAAAN (CRAAASH)
ビシャアア
SU (SWF)
ス…
DOSAA (SHMF)
ドサァ…
THAT... WAS A LASER.
IT WAS MERELY A LIGHTNING ATTACK.
A NINJA ART.
BUT WOULD IT NOT BE AN IMPRESSIVE SIGHT IF I LAUNCHED ONE OF THOSE AFTER SLICING WITH MY BLADE?

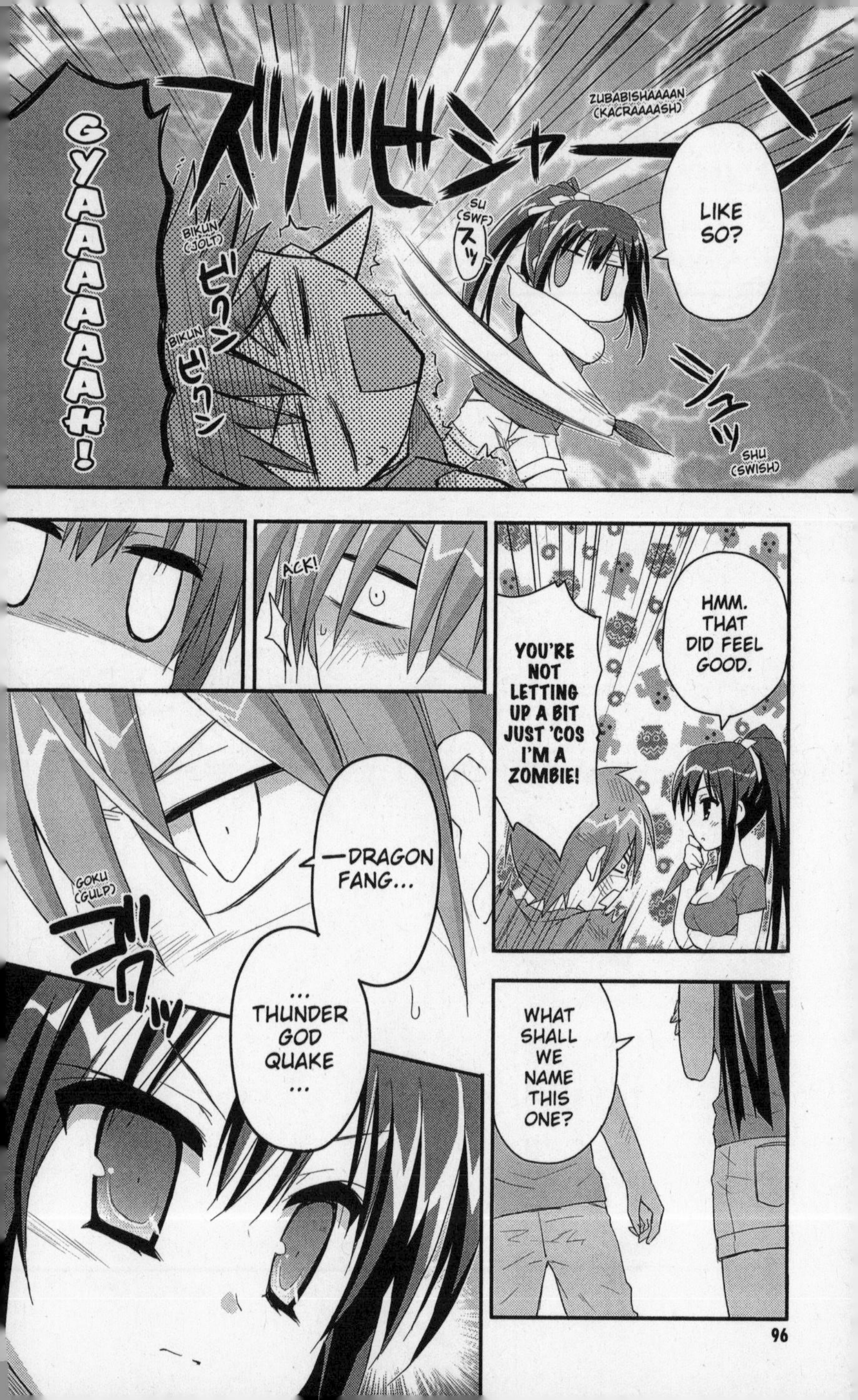
ZUBABISHAAAAN (KACRAAAASH)
LIKE SO?
SU (SWF)
SHU (SWISH)
BIKUN (JOLT)
BIKUN
GYAAAAAAAAH!
HMM. THAT DID FEEL GOOD.
YOU'RE NOT LETTING UP A BIT JUST 'COS I'M A ZOMBIE!
ACK!
WHAT SHALL WE NAME THIS ONE?
—DRAGON FANG...
... THUNDER GOD QUAKE ...
GOKU (GULP)

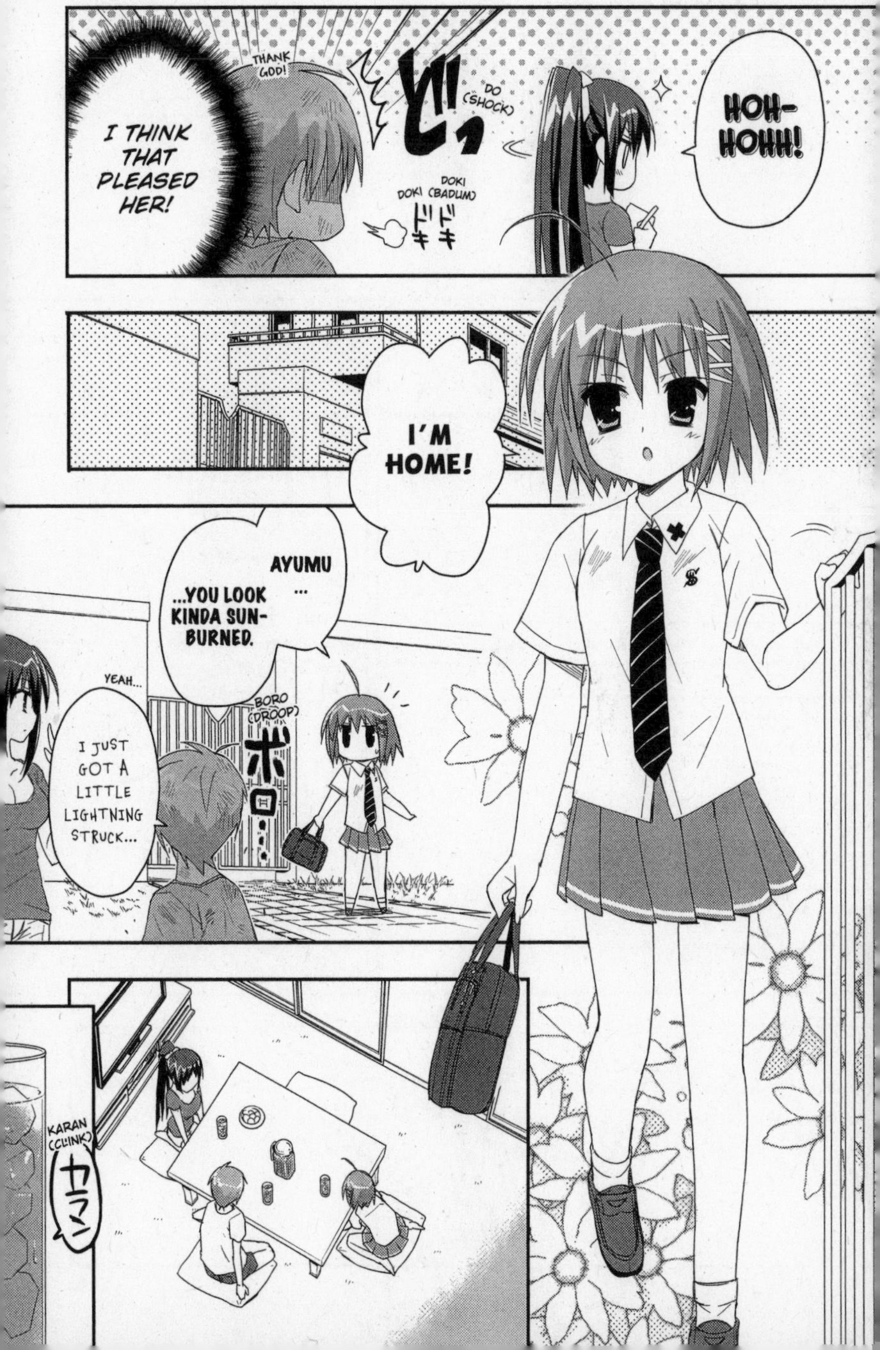
HOH-HOHH!
DO (SHOCK)
DOKI DOKI (BADUM)
THANK GOD!
I THINK THAT PLEASED HER!
I'M HOME!
AYUMU ...
...YOU LOOK KINDA SUN-BURNED.
BORO (DROOP)
YEAH...
I JUST GOT A LITTLE LIGHTNING STRUCK...
KARAN (CLINK)
カラン

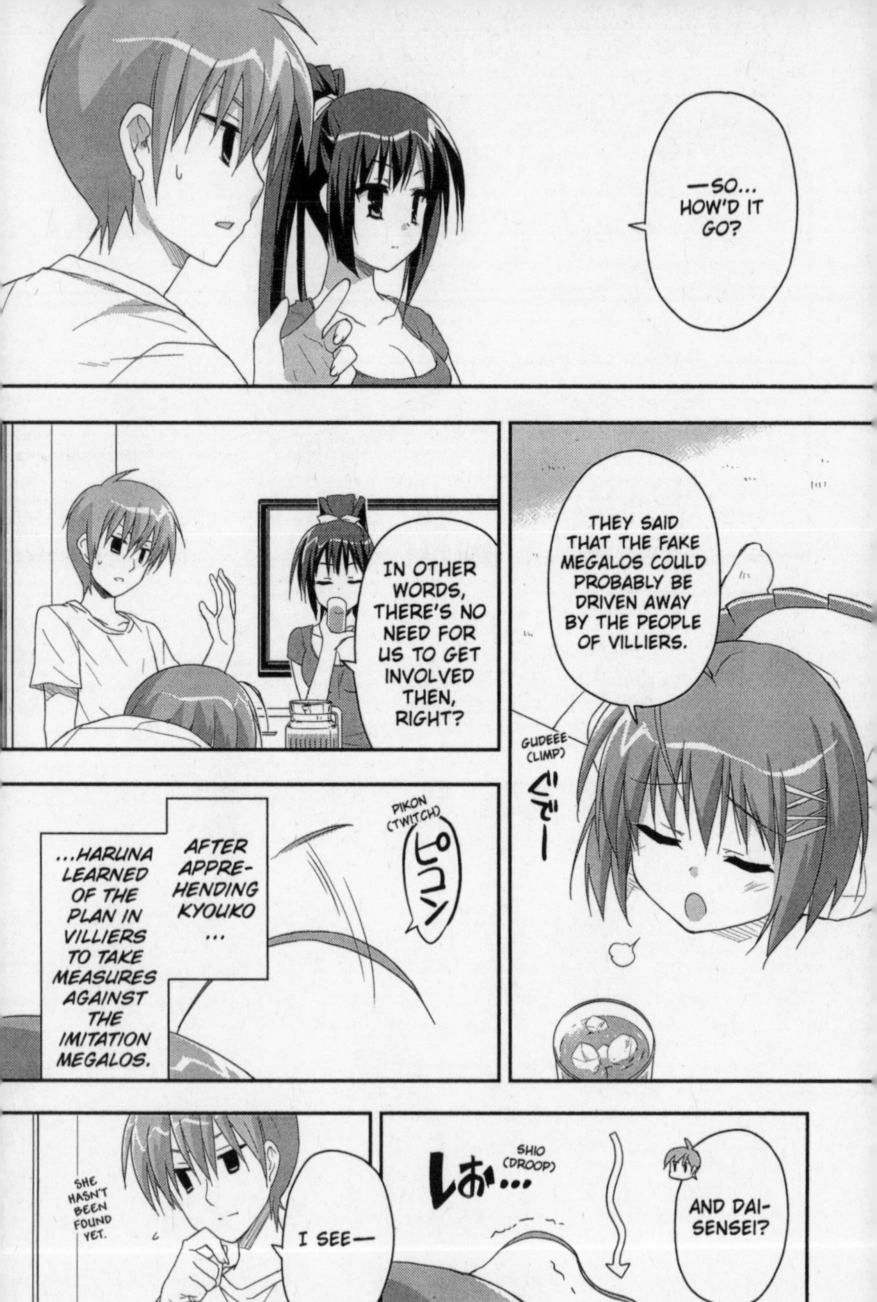
—SO... HOW'D IT GO?
THEY SAID THAT THE FAKE MEGALOS COULD PROBABLY BE DRIVEN AWAY BY THE PEOPLE OF VILLIERS.
GUDEEE (LIMP)
ぐでー
IN OTHER WORDS, THERE'S NO NEED FOR US TO GET INVOLVED THEN, RIGHT?
PIKON (TWITCH)
ピコン
AFTER APPREHENDING KYOUKO...
...HARUNA LEARNED OF THE PLAN IN VILLIERS TO TAKE MEASURES AGAINST THE IMITATION MEGALOS.
AND DAI-SENSEI?
SHIO (DROOP)
しお...
I SEE—
SHE HASN'T BEEN FOUND YET.

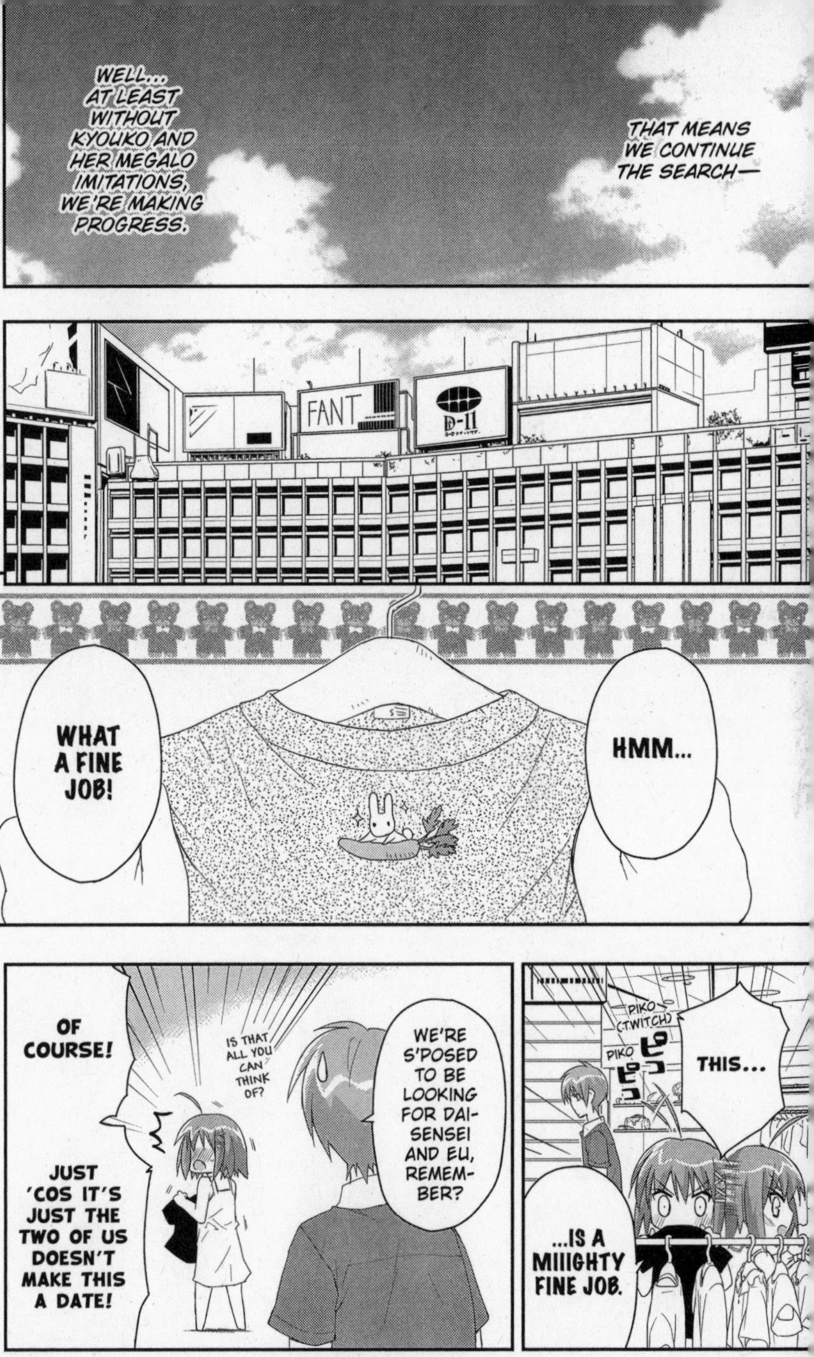
WELL... AT LEAST WITHOUT KYOUKO AND HER MEGALO IMITATIONS, WE'RE MAKING PROGRESS.
THAT MEANS WE CONTINUE THE SEARCH—
FANT
D-11
HMM...
WHAT A FINE JOB!
PIKO (TWITCH)
PIKO
ピコ ピコ
THIS...
...IS A MIIIGHTY FINE JOB.
WE'RE S'POSED TO BE LOOKING FOR DAI-SENSEI AND ELI, REMEMBER?
IS THAT ALL YOU CAN THINK OF?
OF COURSE!
JUST 'COS IT'S JUST THE TWO OF US DOESN'T MAKE THIS A DATE!

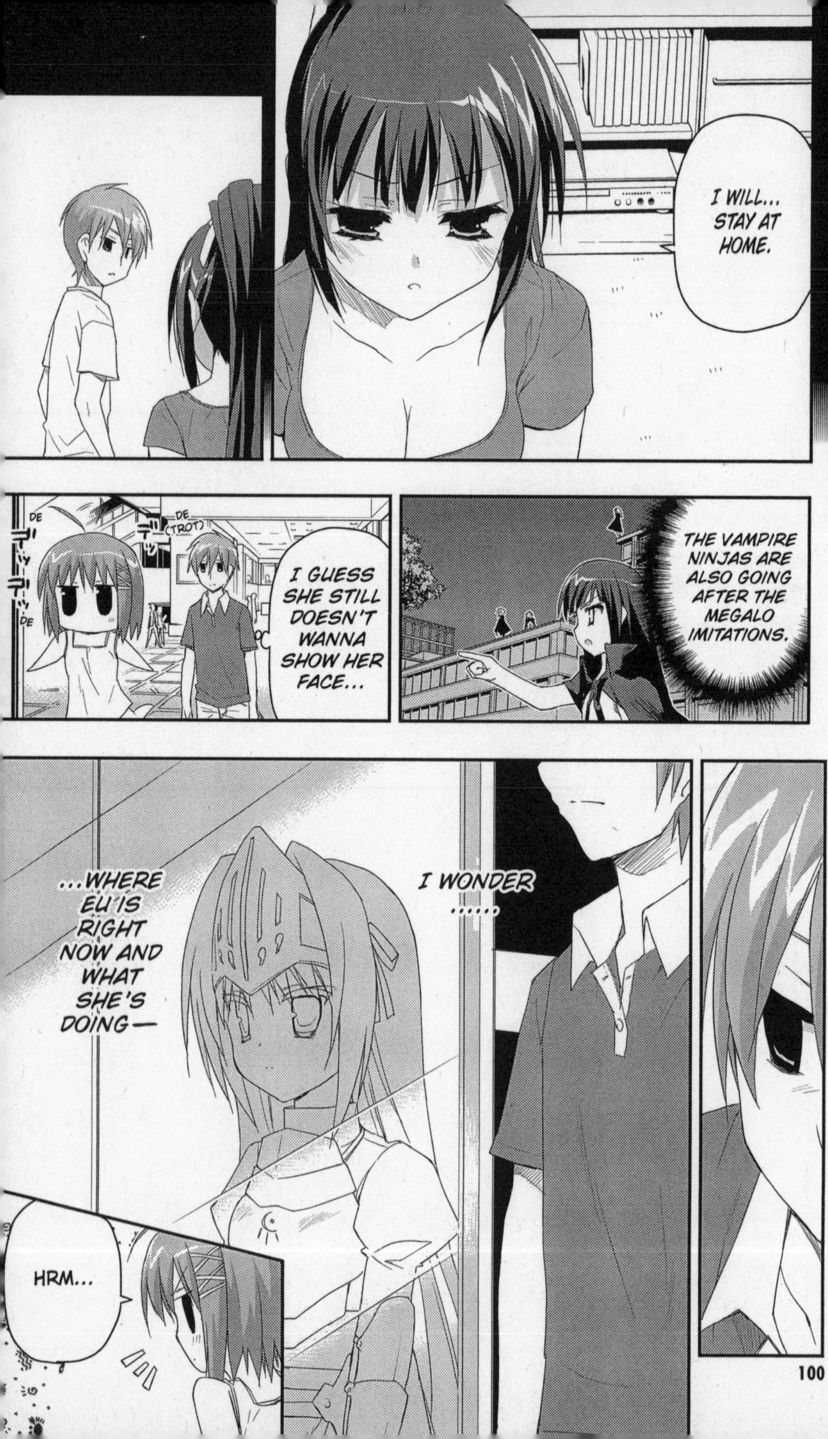
I WILL... STAY AT HOME.
THE VAMPIRE NINJAS ARE ALSO GOING AFTER THE MEGALO IMITATIONS.
DE DE (TROT)
DE DE
I GUESS SHE STILL DOESN'T WANNA SHOW HER FACE...
I WONDER ......
...WHERE EU IS RIGHT NOW AND WHAT SHE'S DOING—
HRM...

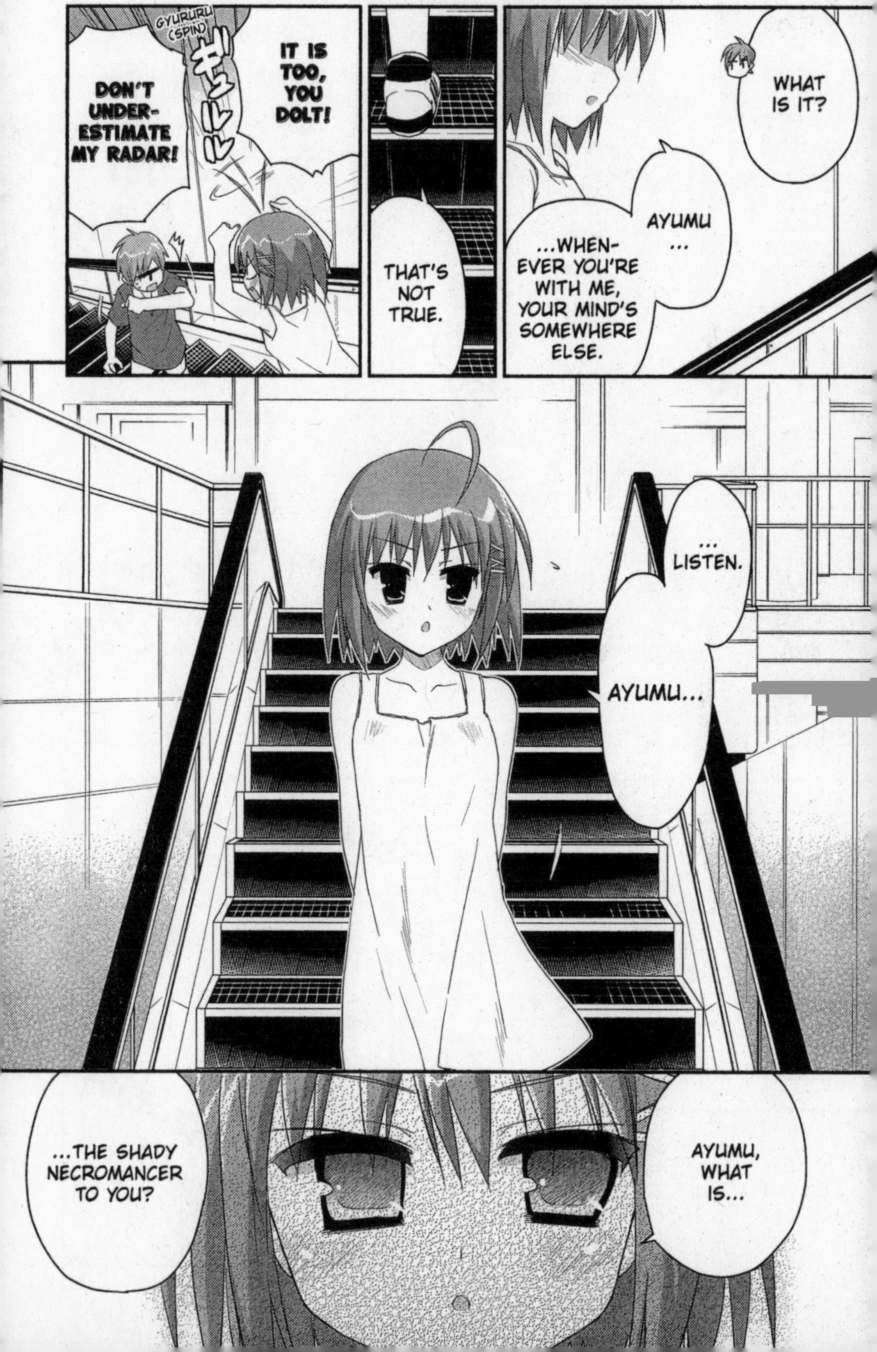
WHAT IS IT?
AYUMU ...
...WHEN-EVER YOU'RE WITH ME, YOUR MIND'S SOMEWHERE ELSE.
THAT'S NOT TRUE.
IT IS TOO, YOU DOLT!
GYURURU (SPIN)
ギュルル
DON'T UNDER-ESTIMATE MY RADAR!
... LISTEN.
AYUMU...
AYUMU, WHAT IS...
...THE SHADY NECROMANCER TO YOU?

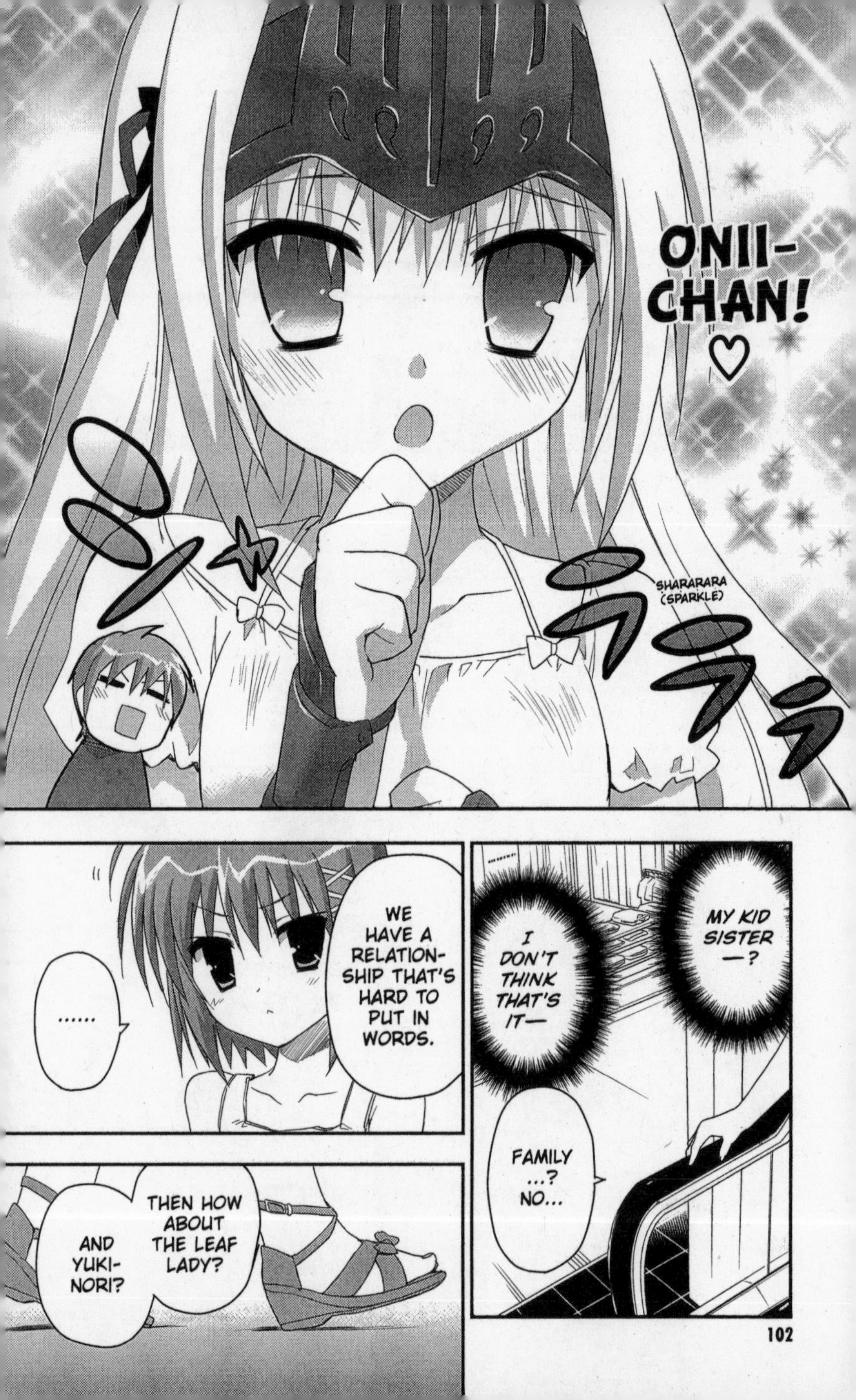
ONII-CHAN! ♡
SHARARARA (SPARKLE)
MY KID SISTER—?
I DON'T THINK THAT'S IT—
FAMILY...? NO...
WE HAVE A RELATIONSHIP THAT'S HARD TO PUT IN WORDS.
......
THEN HOW ABOUT THE LEAF LADY?
AND YUKI-NORI?

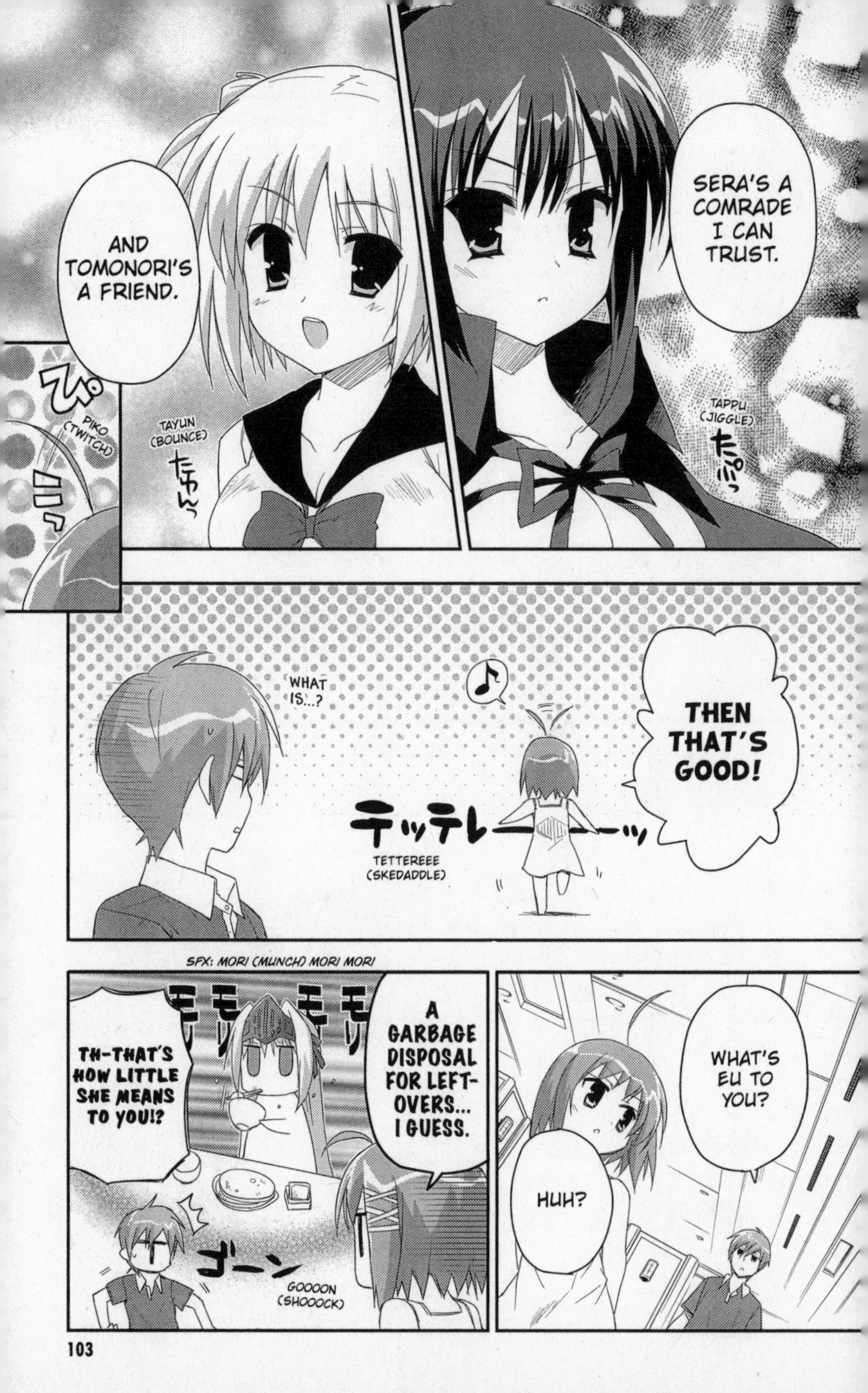
SERA'S A COMRADE I CAN TRUST.
TAPPU (JIGGLE)
AND TOMONORI'S A FRIEND.
TAYUN (BOUNCE)
PIKO (TWITCH)
THEN THAT'S GOOD!
テッテレーーーッ
TETTEREEE (SKEDADDLE)
WHAT IS...?
WHAT'S EU TO YOU?
HUH?
SFX: MORI (MUNCH) MORI MORI
A GARBAGE DISPOSAL FOR LEFT-OVERS... I GUESS.
TH-THAT'S HOW LITTLE SHE MEANS TO YOU!?
GOOOON (SHOOOCK)

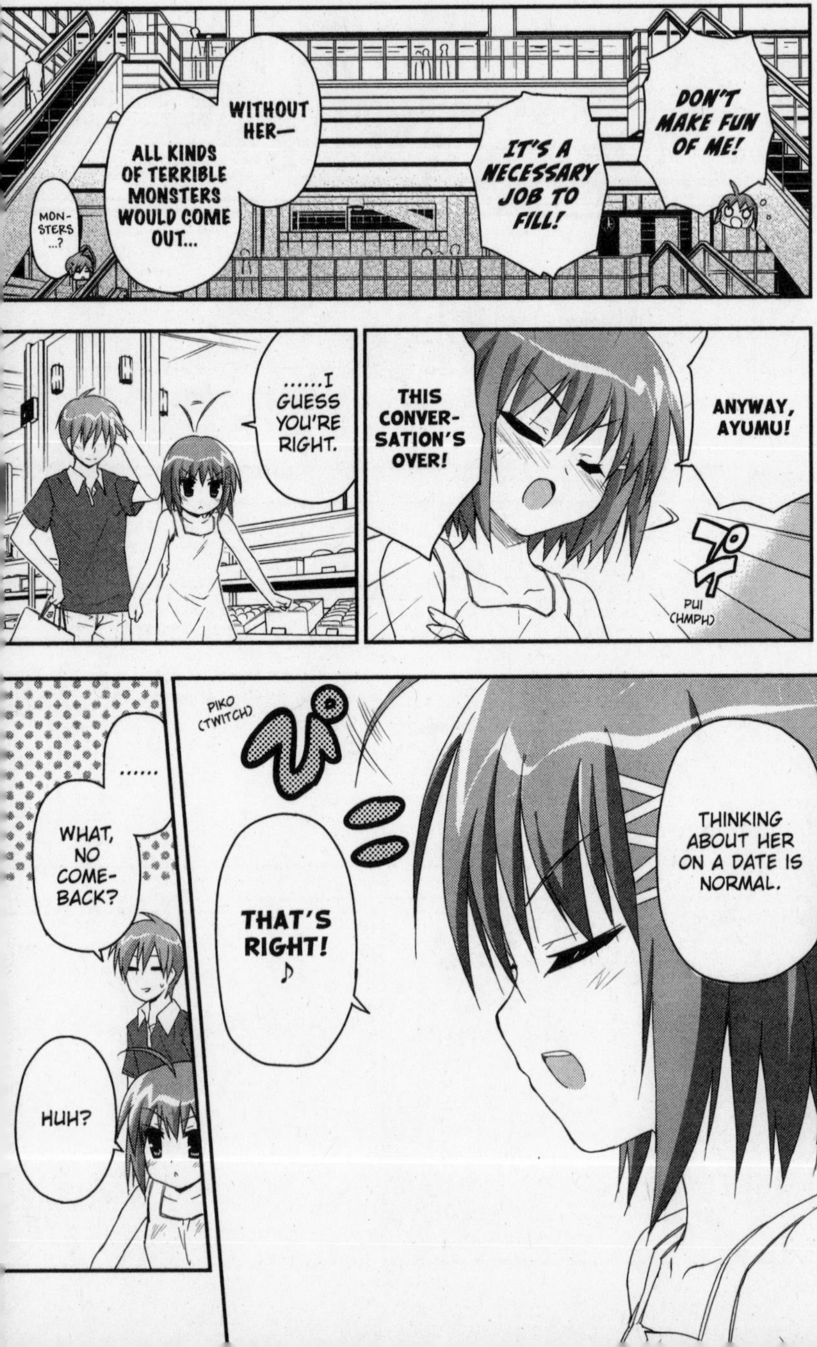
DON'T MAKE FUN OF ME!
IT'S A NECESSARY JOB TO FILL!
WITHOUT HER—
ALL KINDS OF TERRIBLE MONSTERS WOULD COME OUT...
MON-STERS ...?
ANYWAY, AYUMU!
THIS CONVER-SATION'S OVER!
PUI (HMPH)
......I GUESS YOU'RE RIGHT.
THINKING ABOUT HER ON A DATE IS NORMAL.
THAT'S RIGHT! ♪
PIKO (TWITCH)
......
WHAT, NO COME-BACK?
HUH?

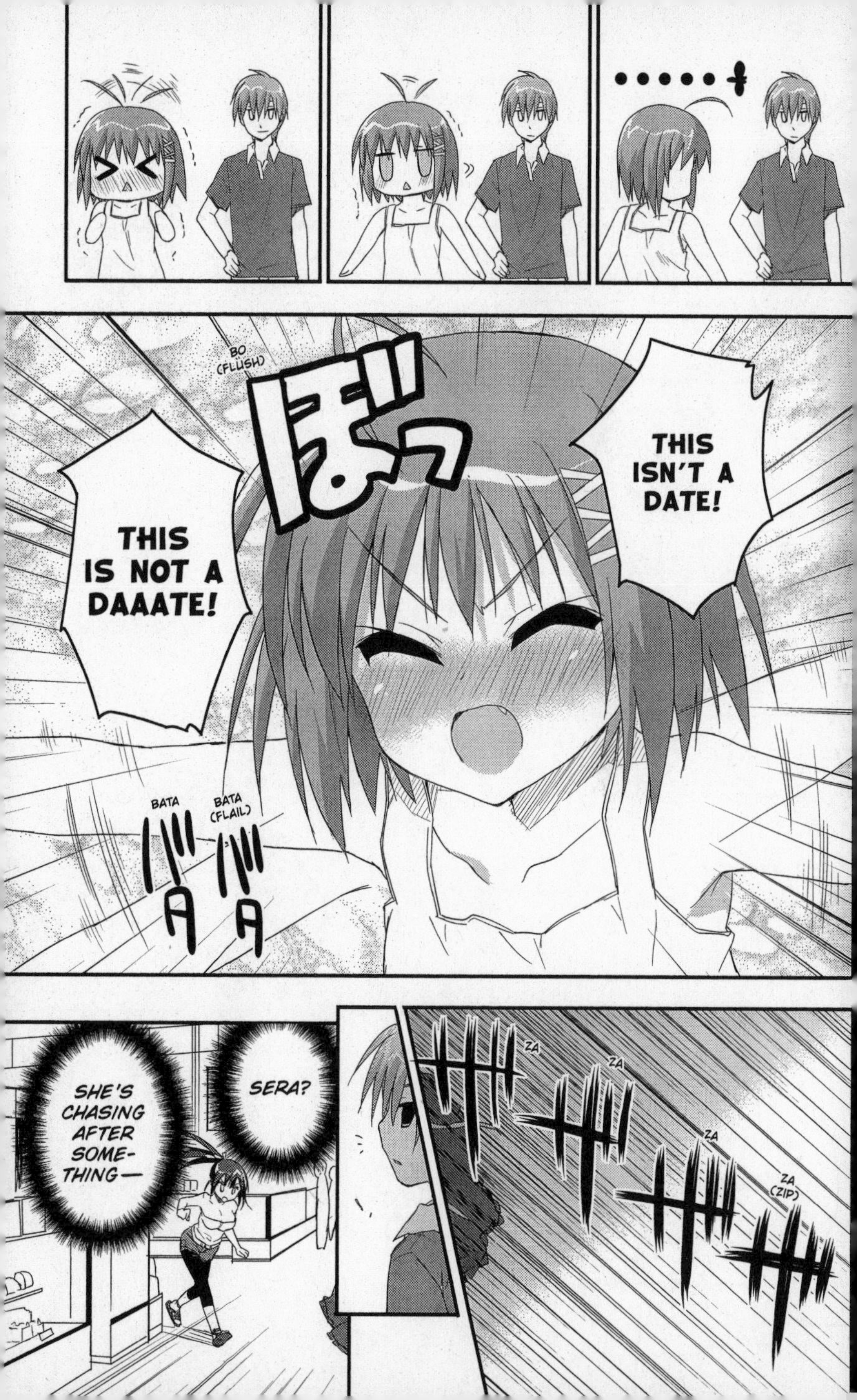
BO (FLUSH)
ぼっ
THIS ISN'T A DATE!
THIS IS NOT A DAAATE!
BATA BATA (FLAIL)
ZA ZA ZA ZA (ZIP)
SERA?
SHE'S CHASING AFTER SOME-THING—

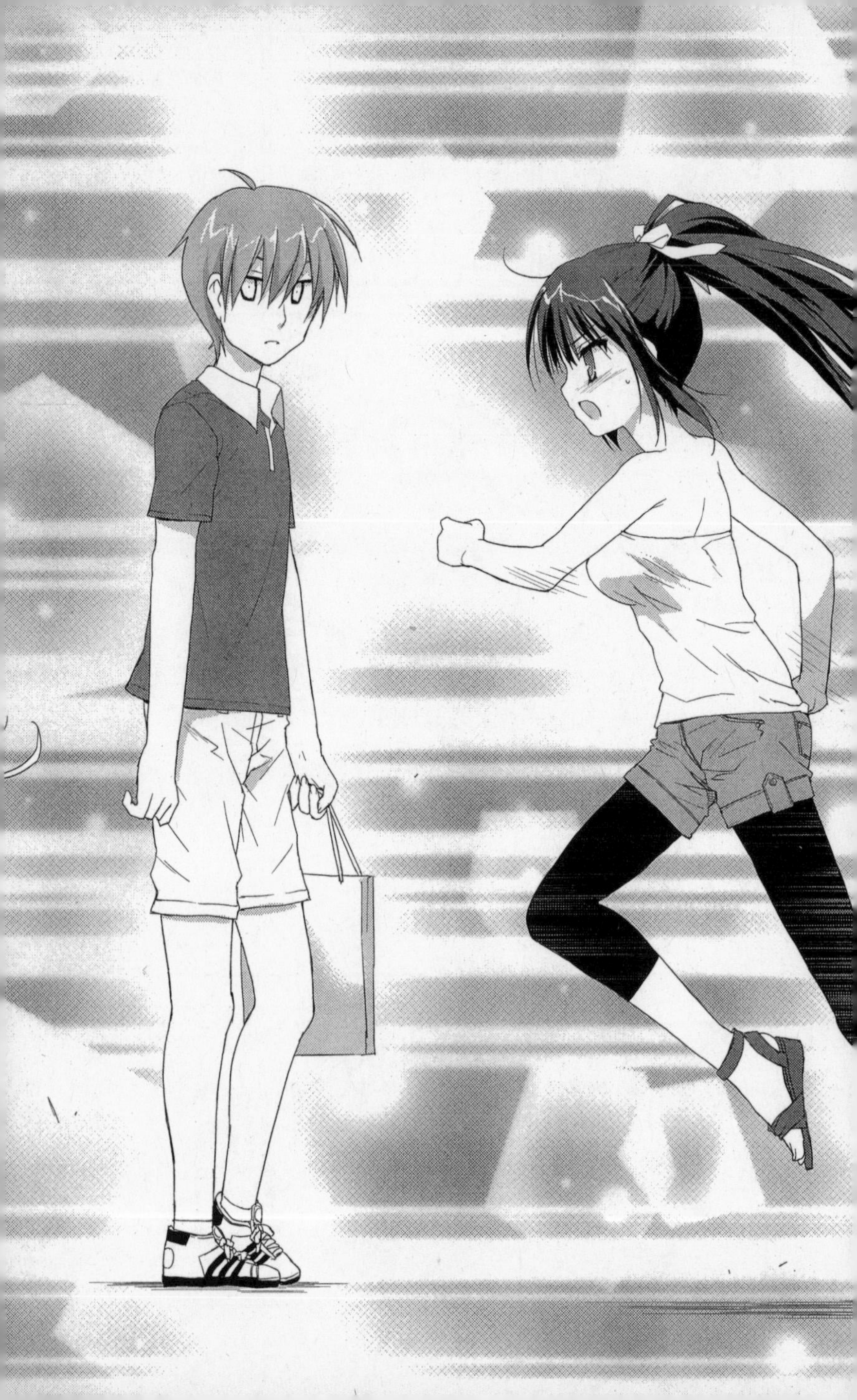

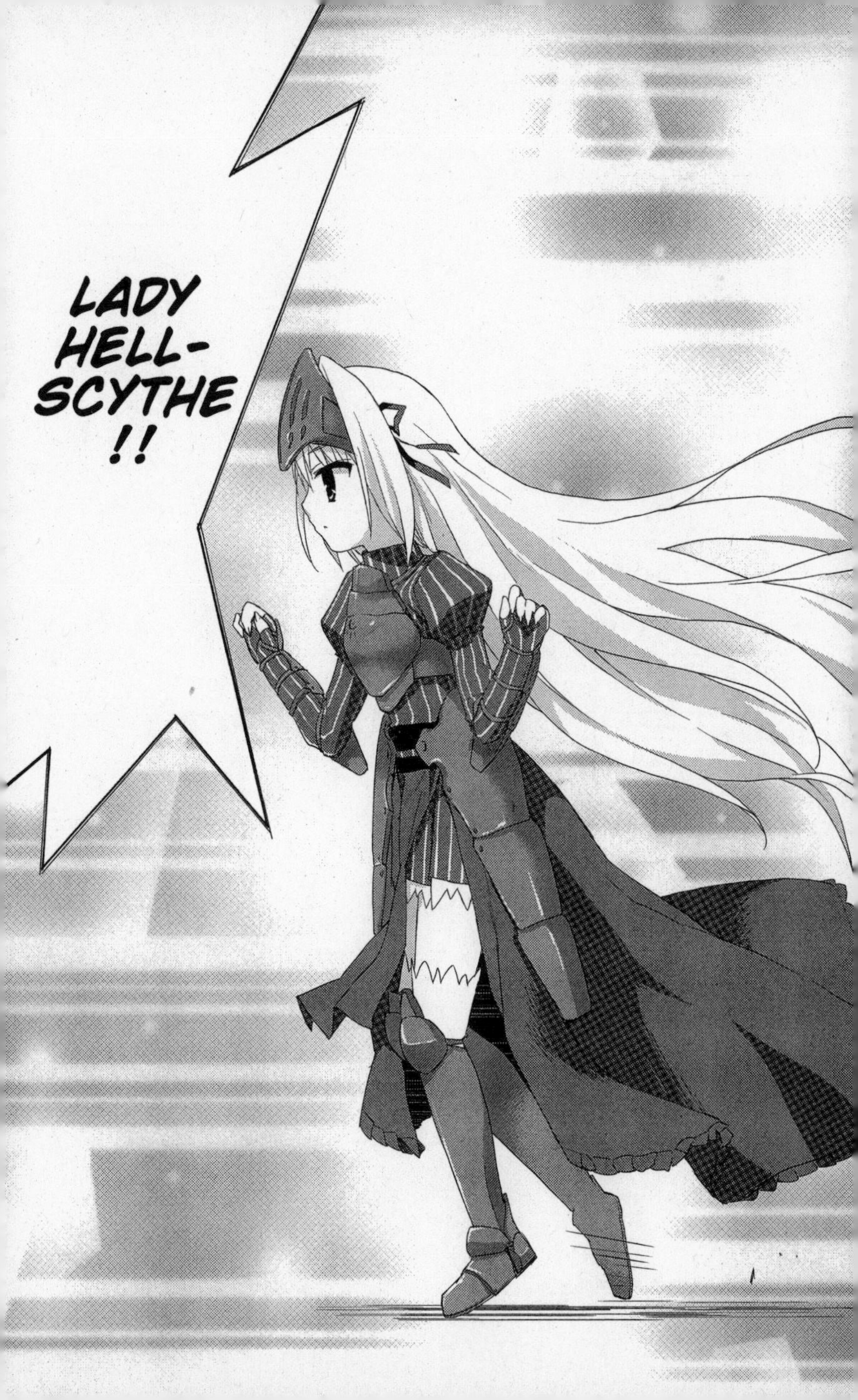
LADY HELL-SCYTHE !!

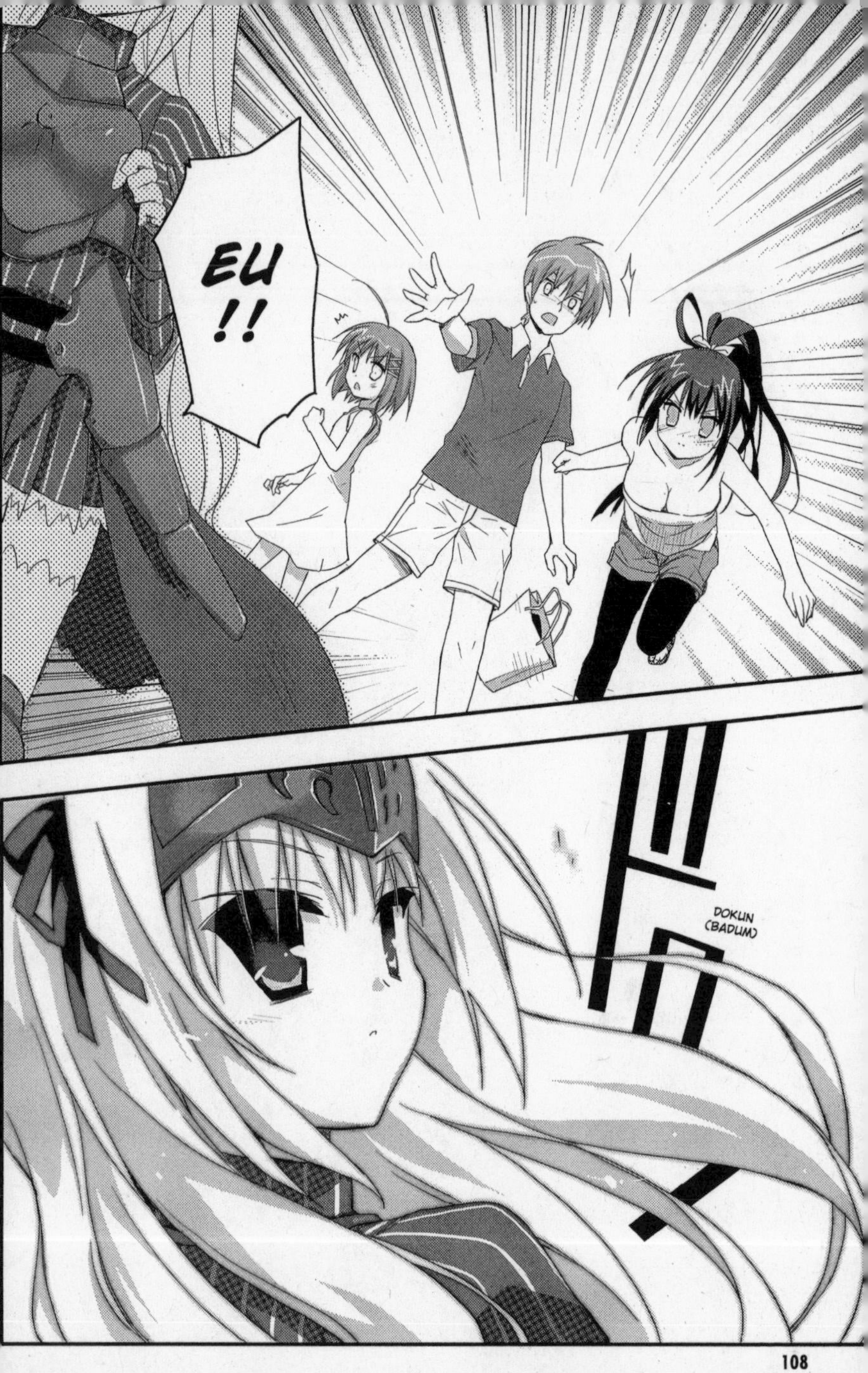
EU!!
DOKUN
(BADUM)

IS THIS A ZOMBIE?

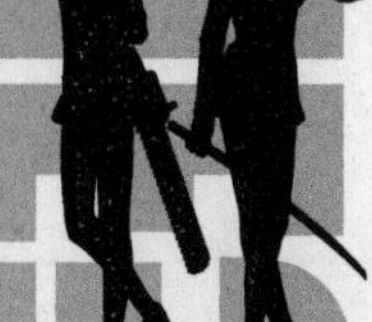

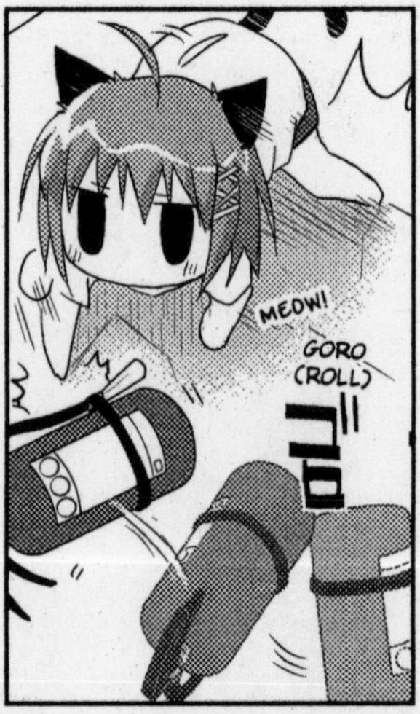
MEOW!
GORO (ROLL)
ゴロ

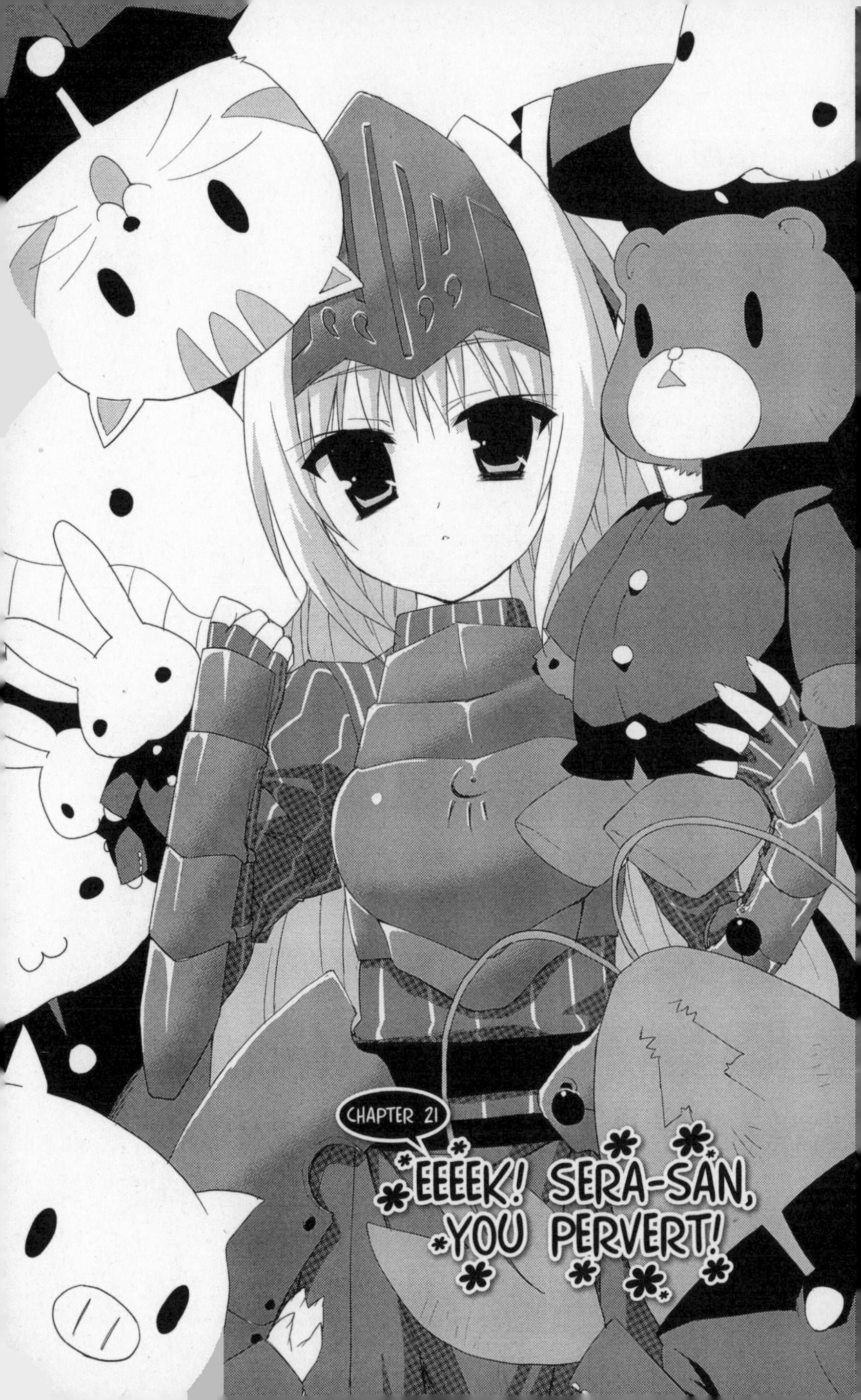
CHAPTER 21
EEEEK! SERA-SAN, YOU PERVERT!

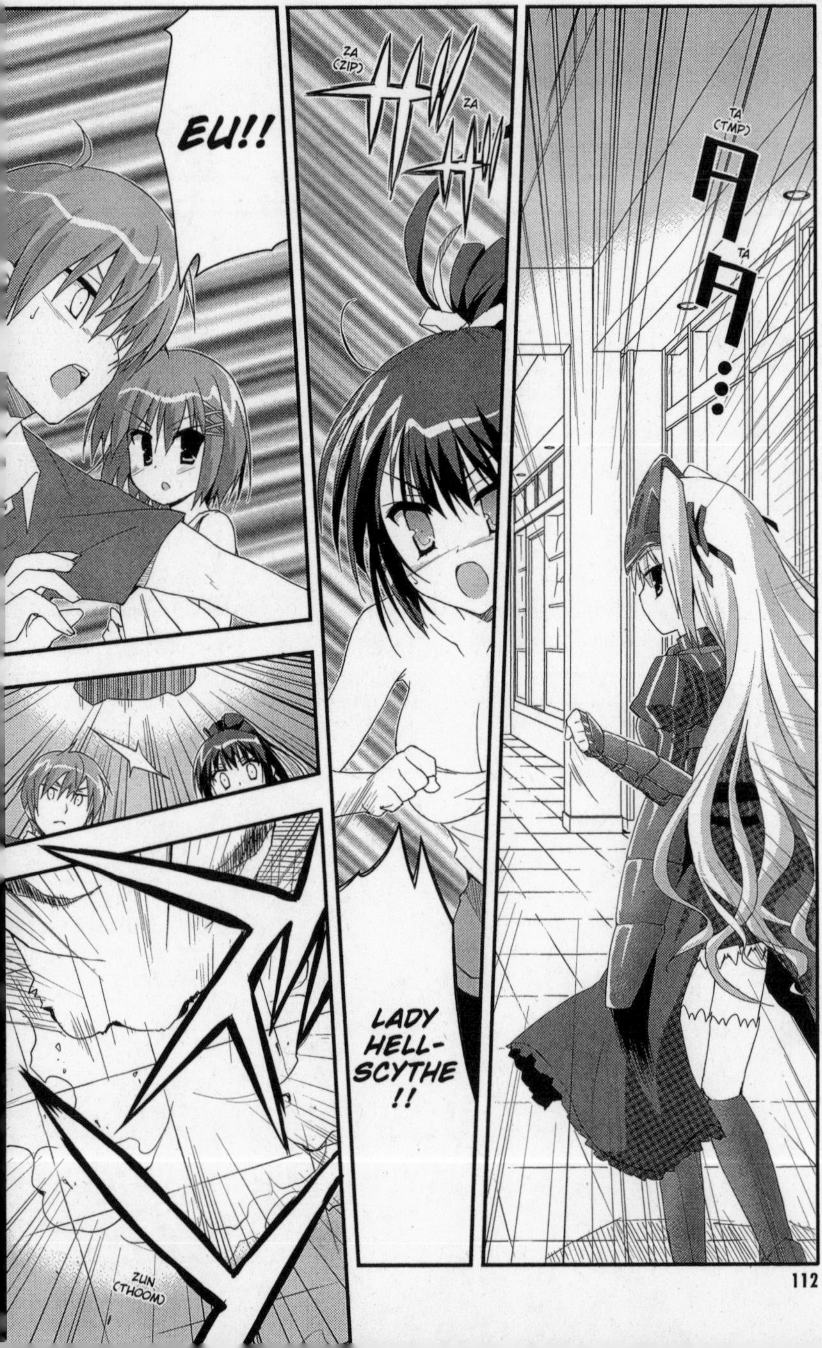
TA
(TMP)
TA
...
ZA
(ZIP)
ZA
LADY HELL-SCYTHE!!
EU!!
ZUN
(THOOM)

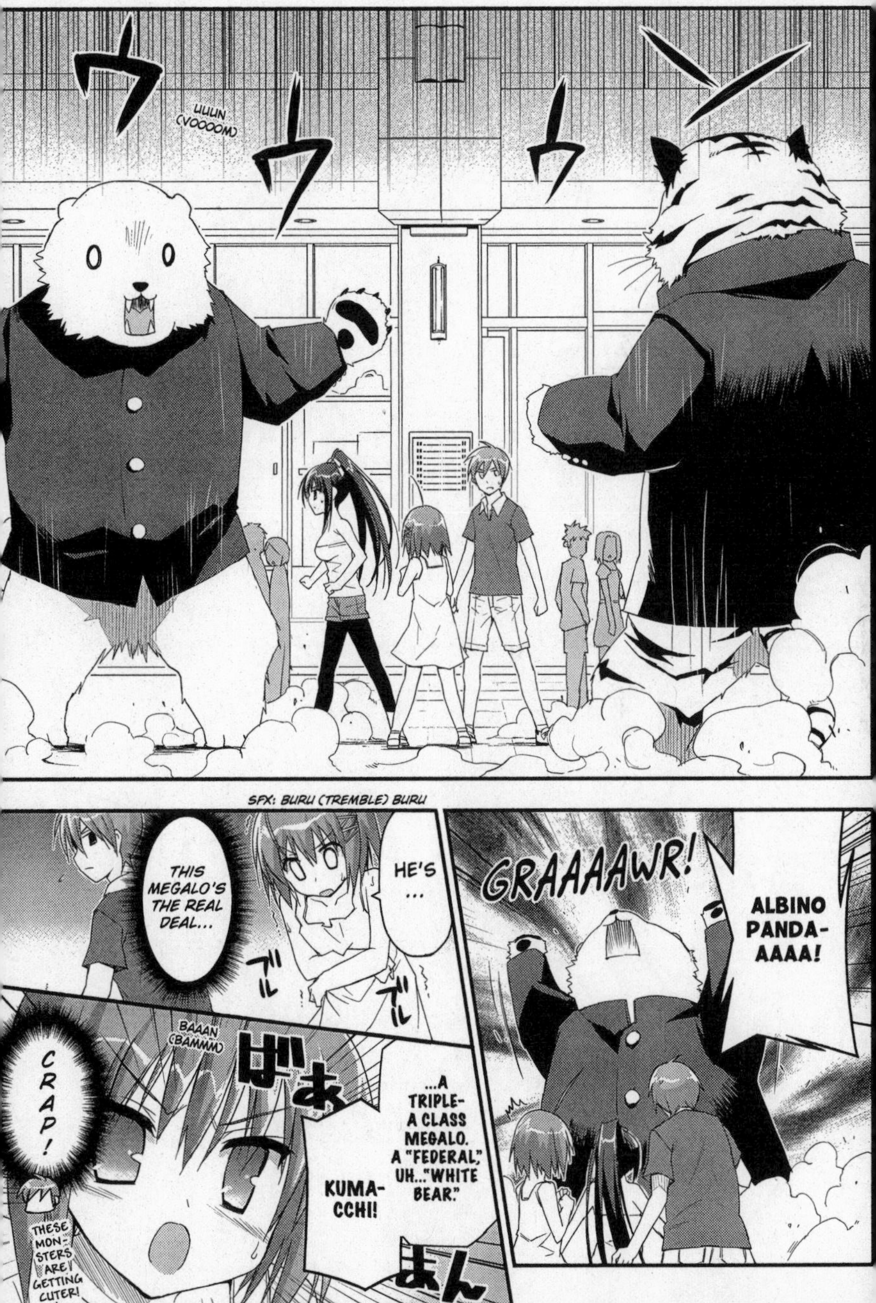
UUUN (VOOOOM)
SFX: BURU (TREMBLE) BURU
GRAAAAWR!
ALBINO PANDA-AAAA!
HE'S ...
THIS MEGALO'S THE REAL DEAL...
BAAAN (BAMMM)
...A TRIPLE-A CLASS MEGALO. A "FEDERAL," UH..."WHITE BEAR."
KUMA-CCHI!
CRAP!
THESE MONSTERS ARE GETTING CUTER!

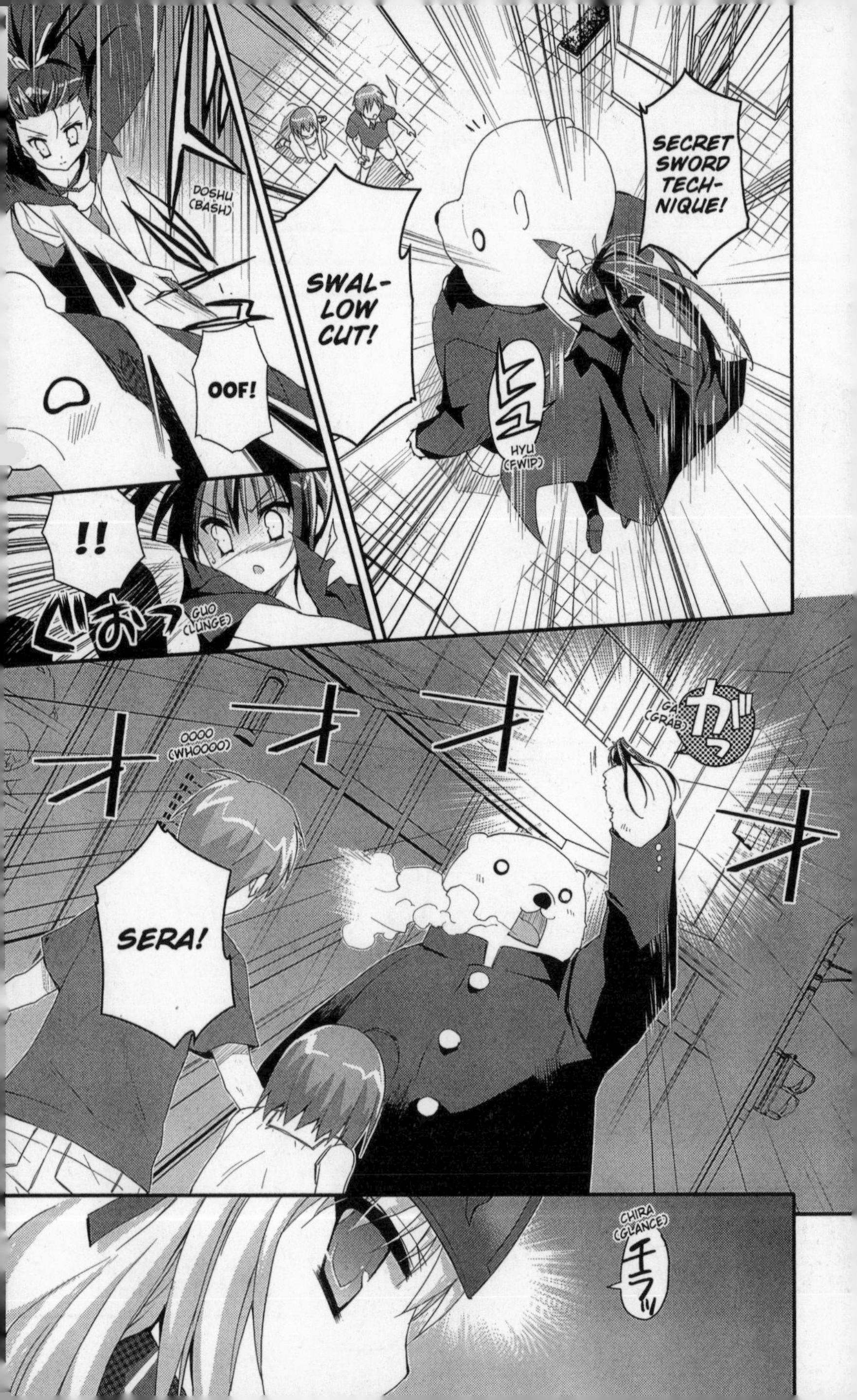
SECRET SWORD TECH-NIQUE!
SWAL-LOW CUT!
HYU (FWIP)
DOSHU (BASH)
OOF!
!!
GUO (LUNGE)
GA (GRAB)
OOOO (WHOOOO)
SERA!
CHIRA (GLANCE)

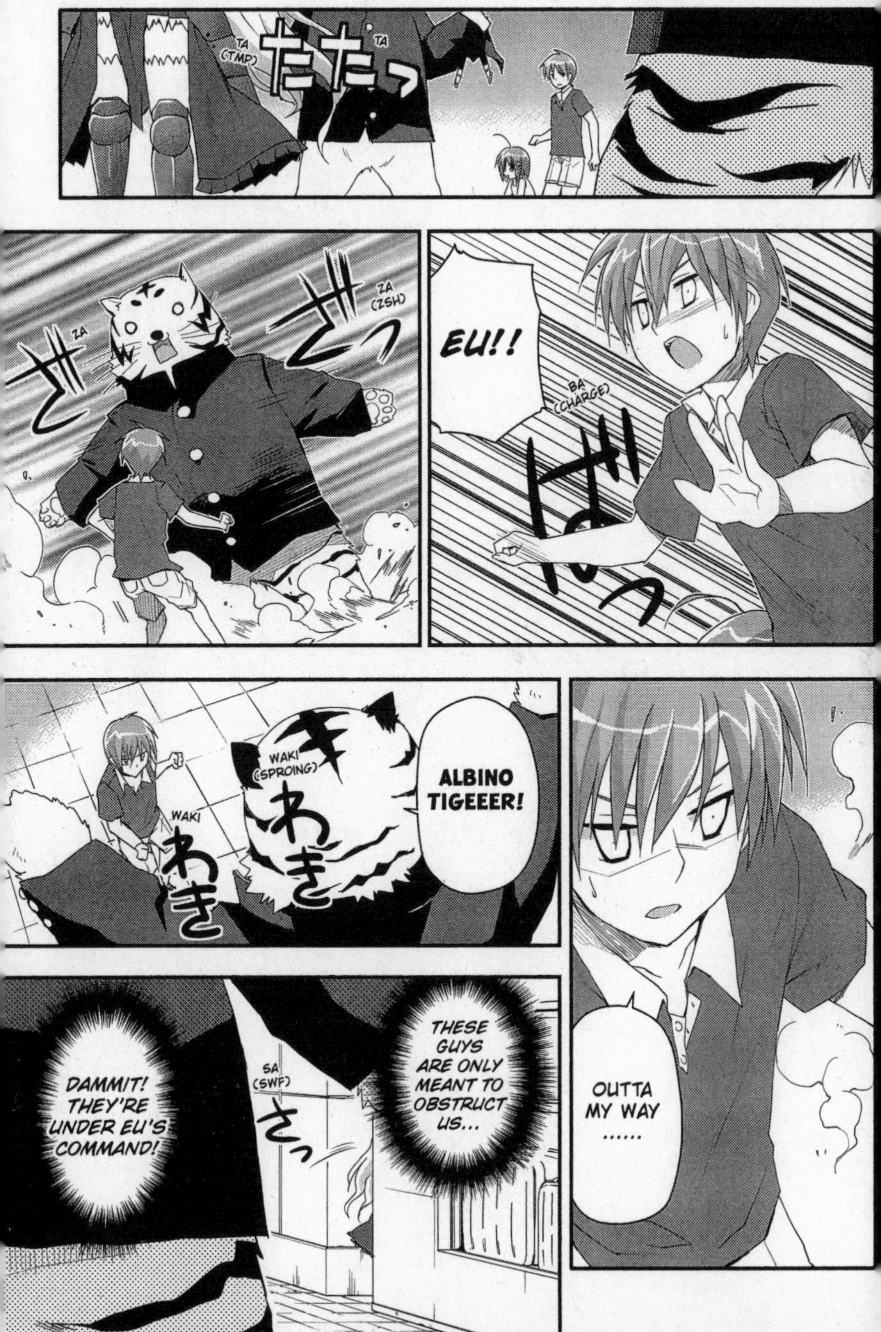
TA
TA
(TMP)
たたっ
EU!!
BA
(CHARGE)
ばっ
ZA
(ZSH)
ざっ
ZA
ざ
ALBINO TIGEEER!
WAKI
(SPROING)
わき
WAKI
わき
OUTTA MY WAY ......
THESE GUYS ARE ONLY MEANT TO OBSTRUCT US...
SA
(SWF)
さっ
DAMMIT! THEY'RE UNDER EU'S COMMAND!

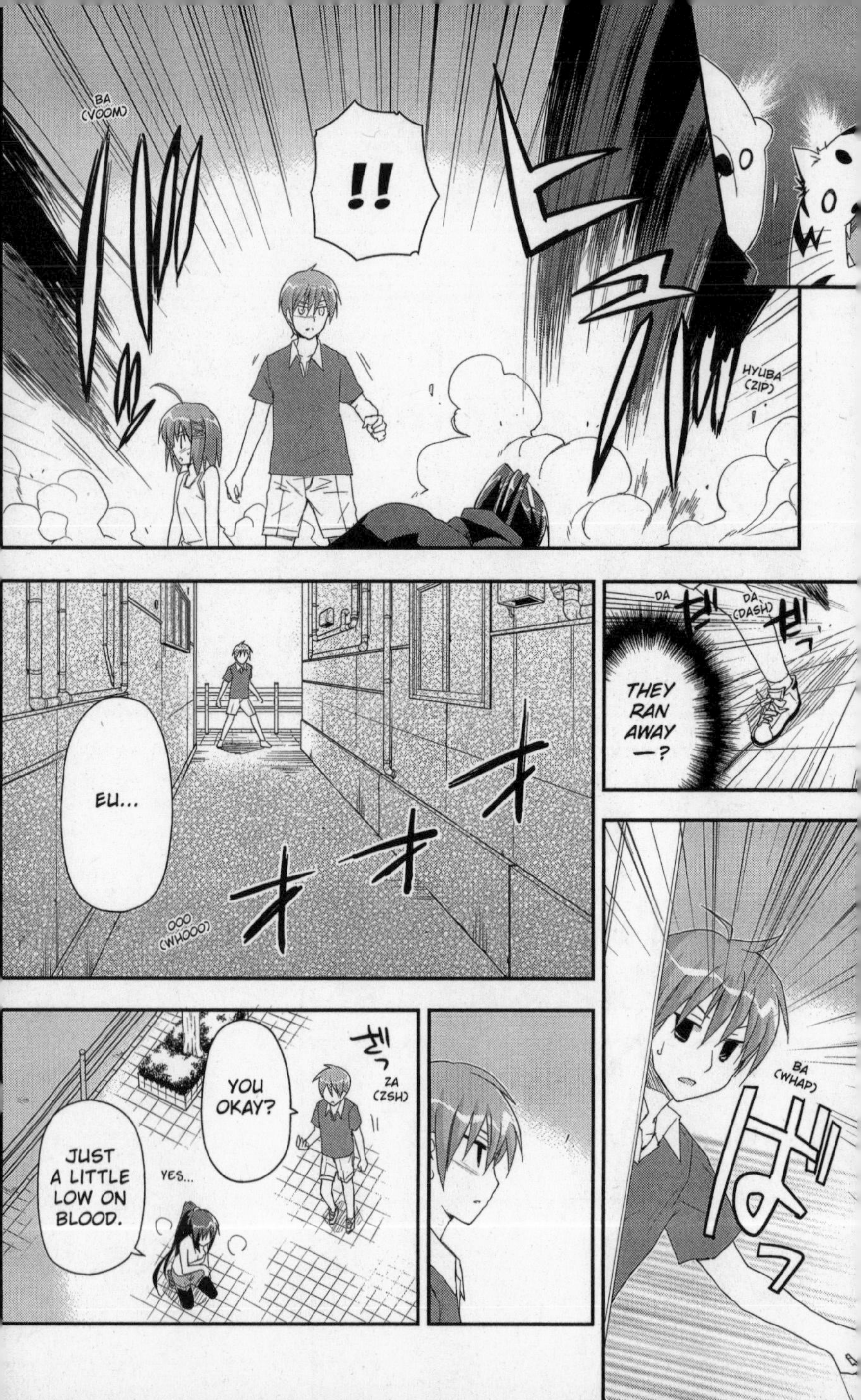
HYUBA (ZIP)
!!
BA (VOOM)
DA
DA (DASH)
THEY RAN AWAY—?
EU...
OOO (WHOOO)
BA (WHAP)
ZA (ZSH)
YOU OKAY?
YES...
JUST A LITTLE LOW ON BLOOD.

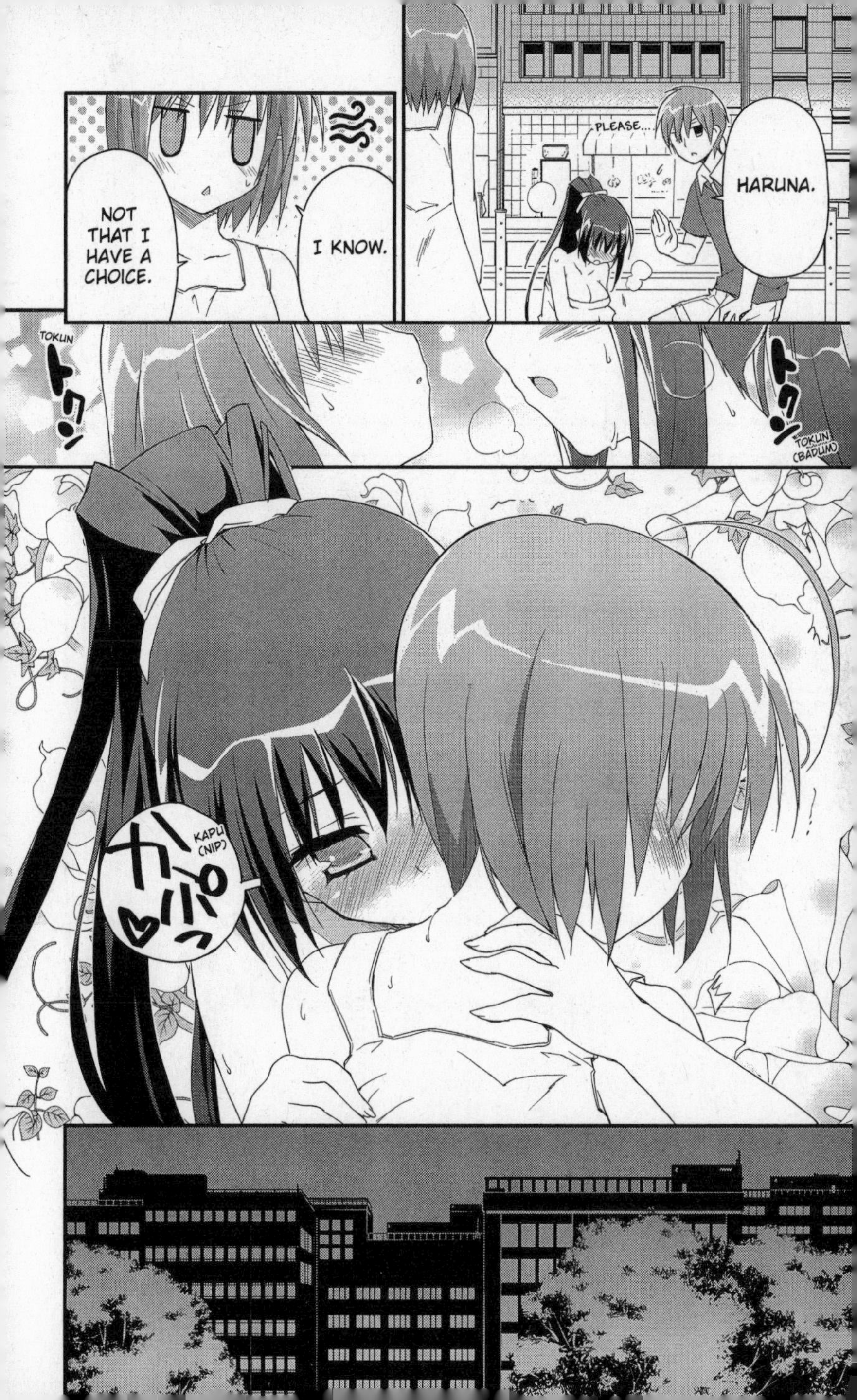
HARUNA.
PLEASE...
I KNOW.
NOT THAT I HAVE A CHOICE.
TOKUN (BADUM)
TOKUN
KAPU (NIP)

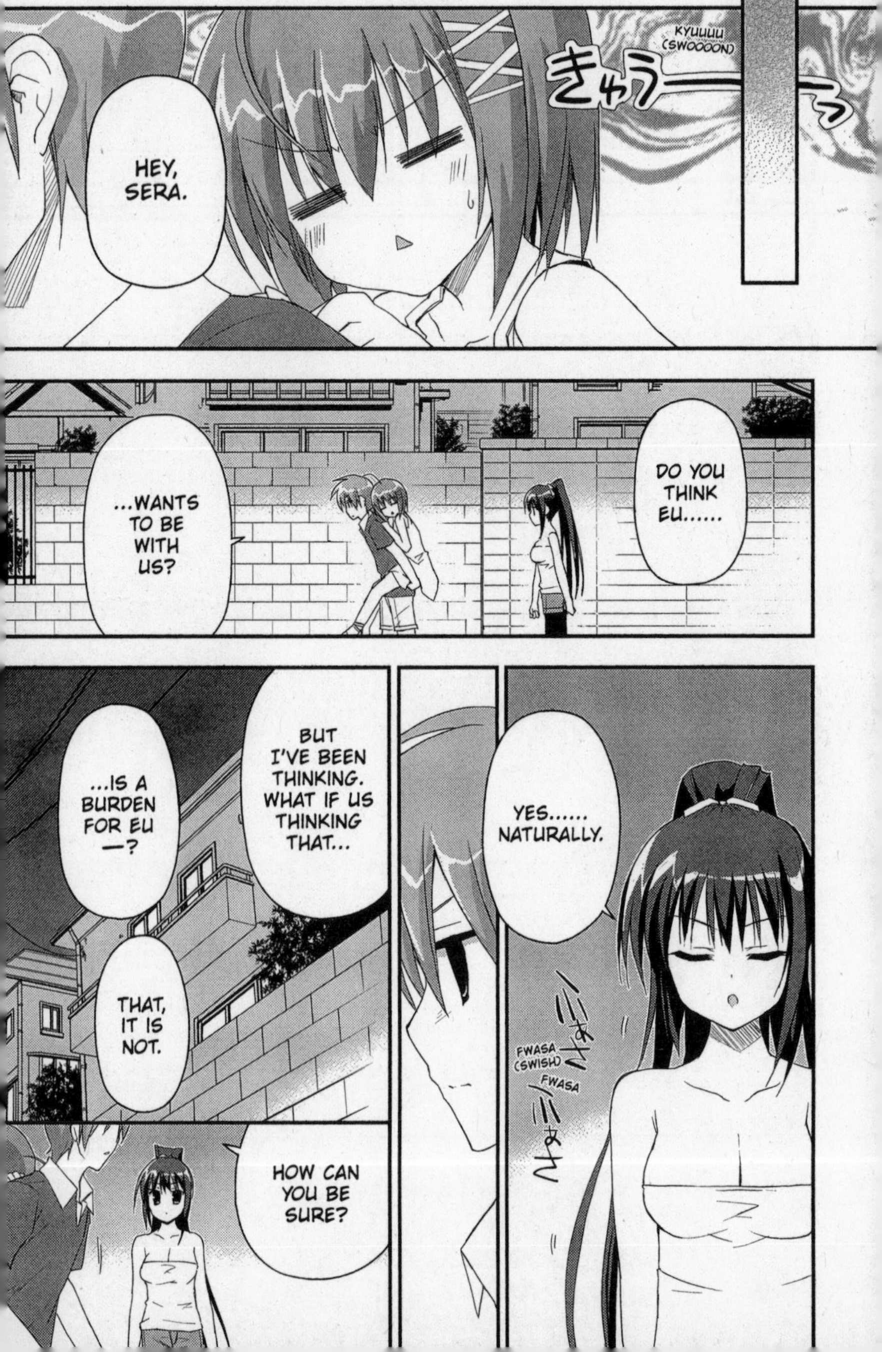

KYUUUU (SWOOOON)
きゅう――っ
HEY, SERA.
DO YOU THINK EU......
...WANTS TO BE WITH US?
YES...... NATURALLY.
BUT I'VE BEEN THINKING. WHAT IF US THINKING THAT...
...IS A BURDEN FOR EU—?
FWASA (SWISH)
FWASA
THAT, IT IS NOT.
HOW CAN YOU BE SURE?

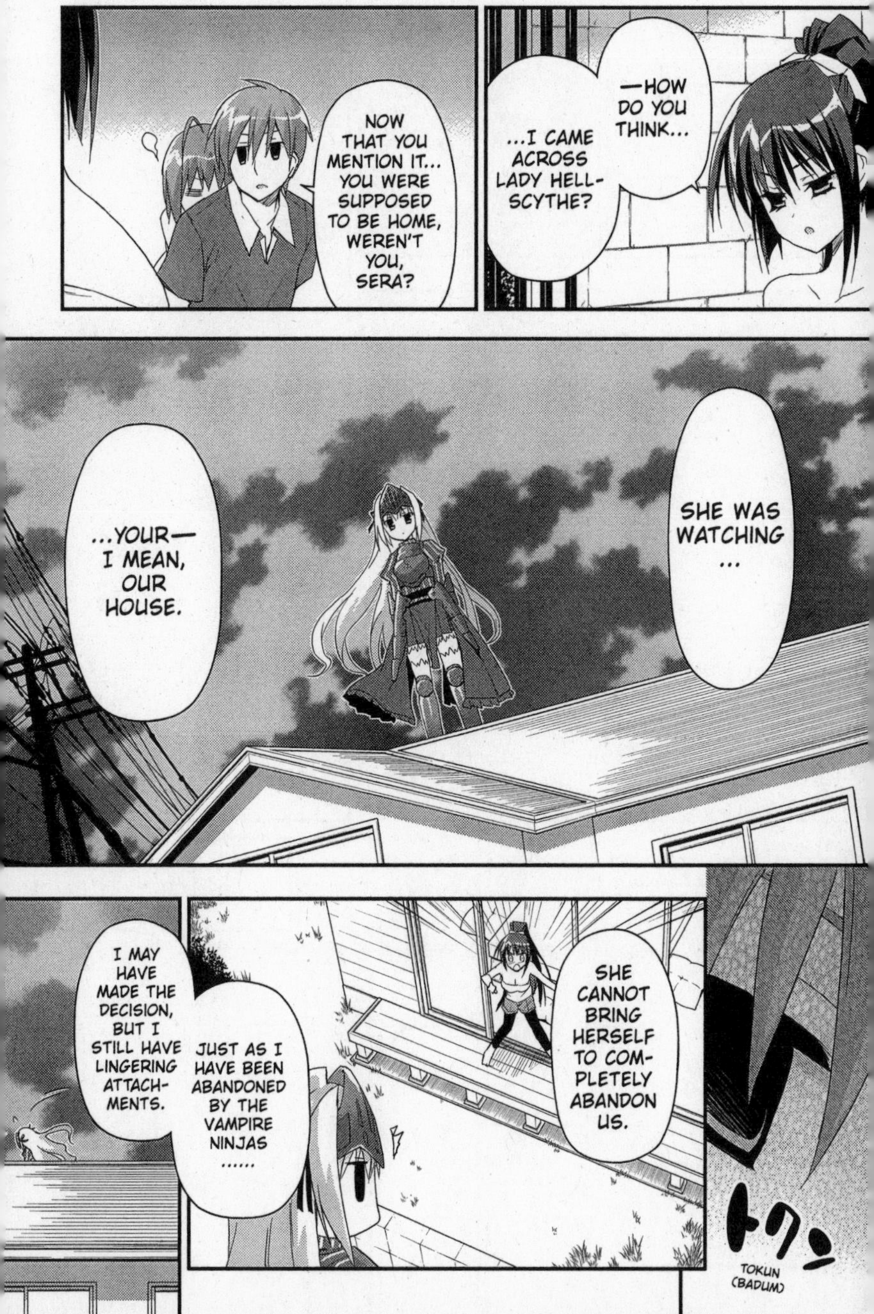
—HOW DO YOU THINK...
...I CAME ACROSS LADY HELL-SCYTHE?
NOW THAT YOU MENTION IT... YOU WERE SUPPOSED TO BE HOME, WEREN'T YOU, SERA?
SHE WAS WATCHING ...
...YOUR— I MEAN, OUR HOUSE.
SHE CANNOT BRING HERSELF TO COM-PLETELY ABANDON US.
TOKUN (BADUM)
JUST AS I HAVE BEEN ABANDONED BY THE VAMPIRE NINJAS ......
I MAY HAVE MADE THE DECISION, BUT I STILL HAVE LINGERING ATTACH-MENTS.

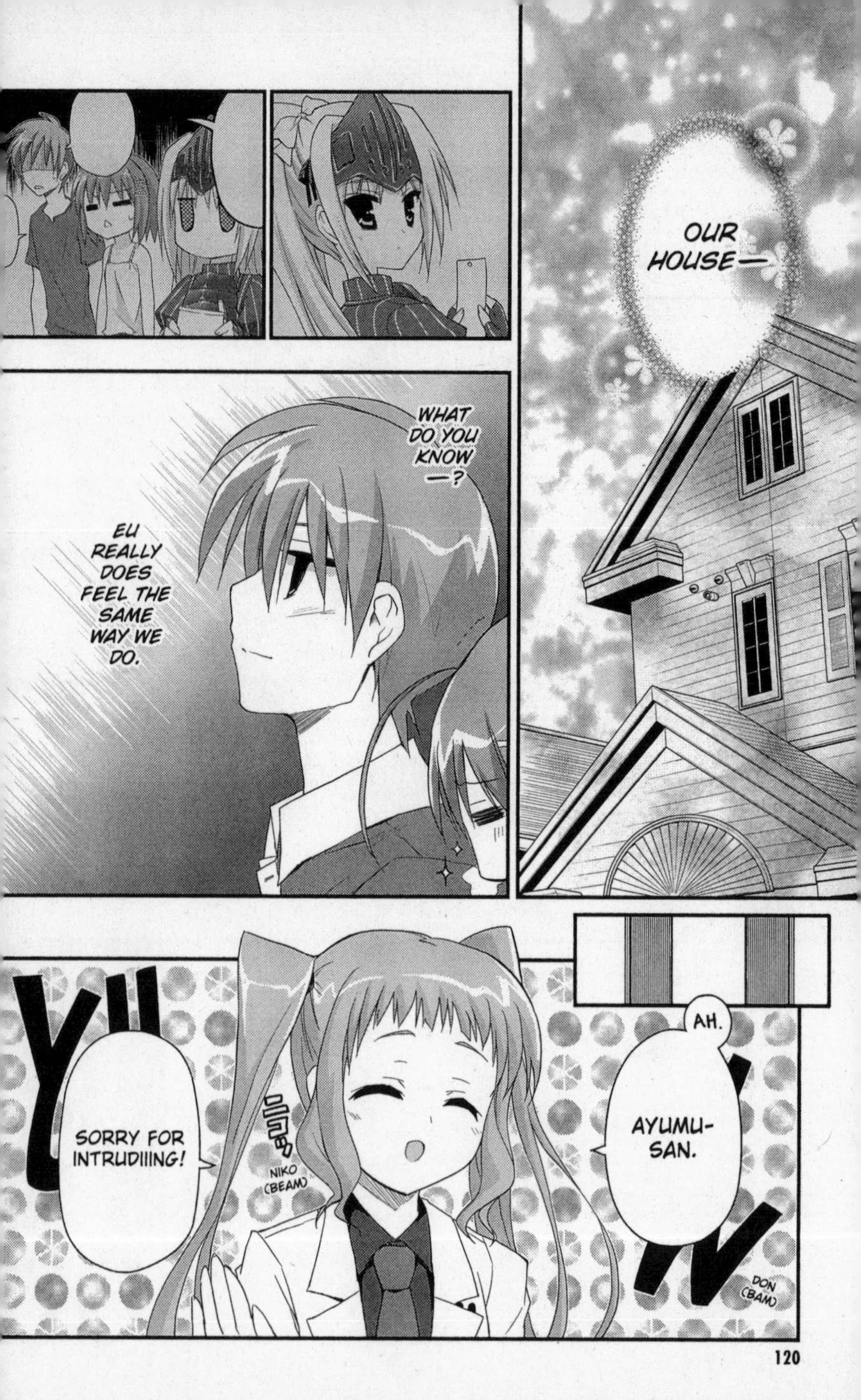
OUR HOUSE—
WHAT DO YOU KNOW—?
EU REALLY DOES FEEL THE SAME WAY WE DO.
AH.
AYUMU-SAN.
DON (BAM)
SORRY FOR INTRUDIIING!
NIKO (BEAM)

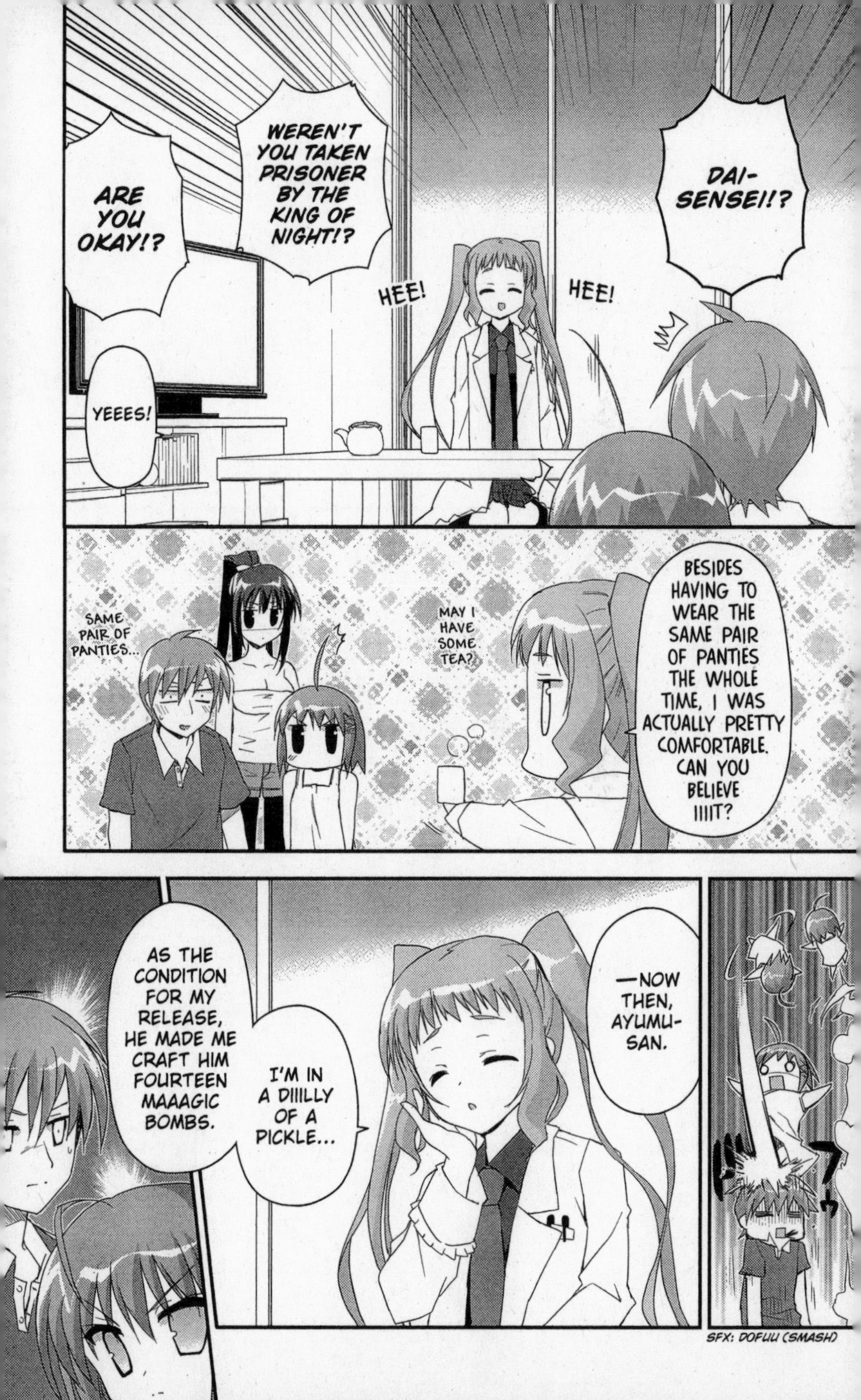
DAI-SENSEI!?
WEREN'T YOU TAKEN PRISONER BY THE KING OF NIGHT!?
ARE YOU OKAY!?
HEE!
HEE!
YEEES!
BESIDES HAVING TO WEAR THE SAME PAIR OF PANTIES THE WHOLE TIME, I WAS ACTUALLY PRETTY COMFORTABLE. CAN YOU BELIEVE IIIIT?
MAY I HAVE SOME TEA?
SAME PAIR OF PANTIES...
—NOW THEN, AYUMU-SAN.
I'M IN A DIIILLY OF A PICKLE...
AS THE CONDITION FOR MY RELEASE, HE MADE ME CRAFT HIM FOURTEEN MAAAGIC BOMBS.
SFX: DOFUU (SMASH)

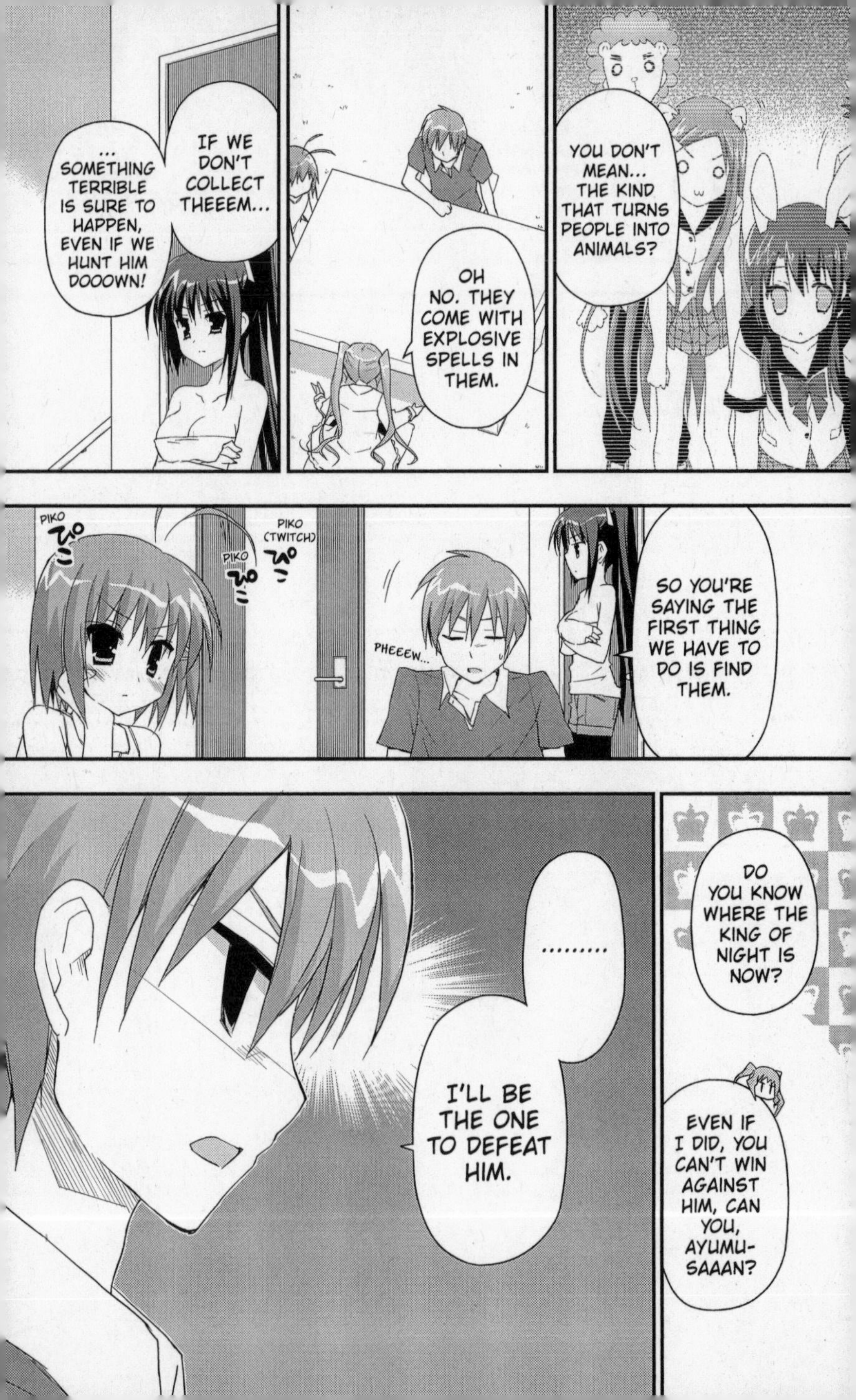
YOU DON'T MEAN... THE KIND THAT TURNS PEOPLE INTO ANIMALS?
OH NO. THEY COME WITH EXPLOSIVE SPELLS IN THEM.
IF WE DON'T COLLECT THEEEM...
... SOMETHING TERRIBLE IS SURE TO HAPPEN, EVEN IF WE HUNT HIM DOOOWN!
SO YOU'RE SAYING THE FIRST THING WE HAVE TO DO IS FIND THEM.
PHEEEW...
PIKO (TWITCH)
PIKO
PIKO
DO YOU KNOW WHERE THE KING OF NIGHT IS NOW?
EVEN IF I DID, YOU CAN'T WIN AGAINST HIM, CAN YOU, AYUMU-SAAAN?
....
I'LL BE THE ONE TO DEFEAT HIM.

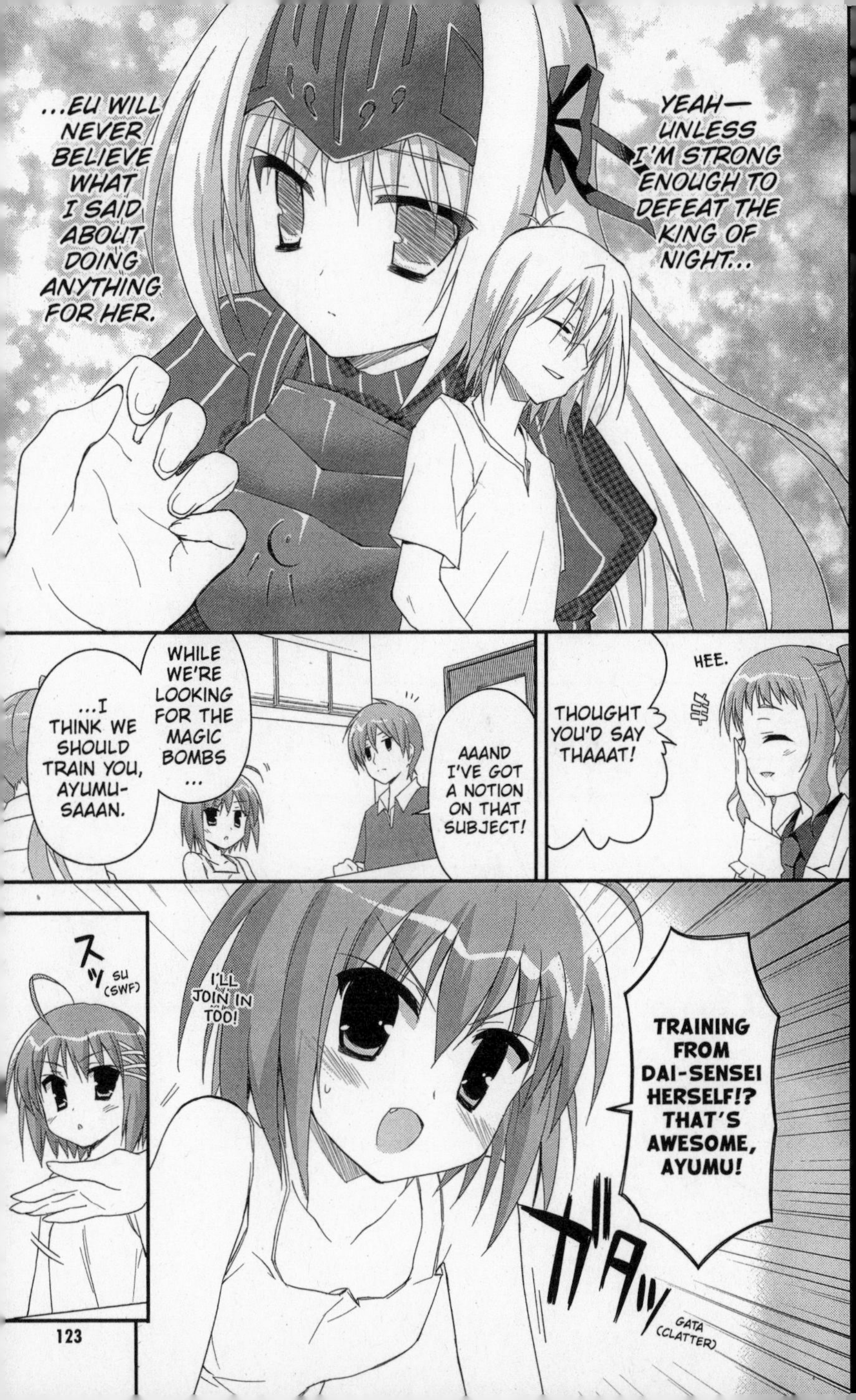
YEAH— UNLESS I'M STRONG ENOUGH TO DEFEAT THE KING OF NIGHT...
...EU WILL NEVER BELIEVE WHAT I SAID ABOUT DOING ANYTHING FOR HER.
HEE.
THOUGHT YOU'D SAY THAAAT!
AAAND I'VE GOT A NOTION ON THAT SUBJECT!
WHILE WE'RE LOOKING FOR THE MAGIC BOMBS...
...I THINK WE SHOULD TRAIN YOU, AYUMU-SAAAN.
TRAINING FROM DAI-SENSEI HERSELF!? THAT'S AWESOME, AYUMU!
ガタッ
GATA (CLATTER)
I'LL JOIN IN TOO!
スッ
SU (SWF)

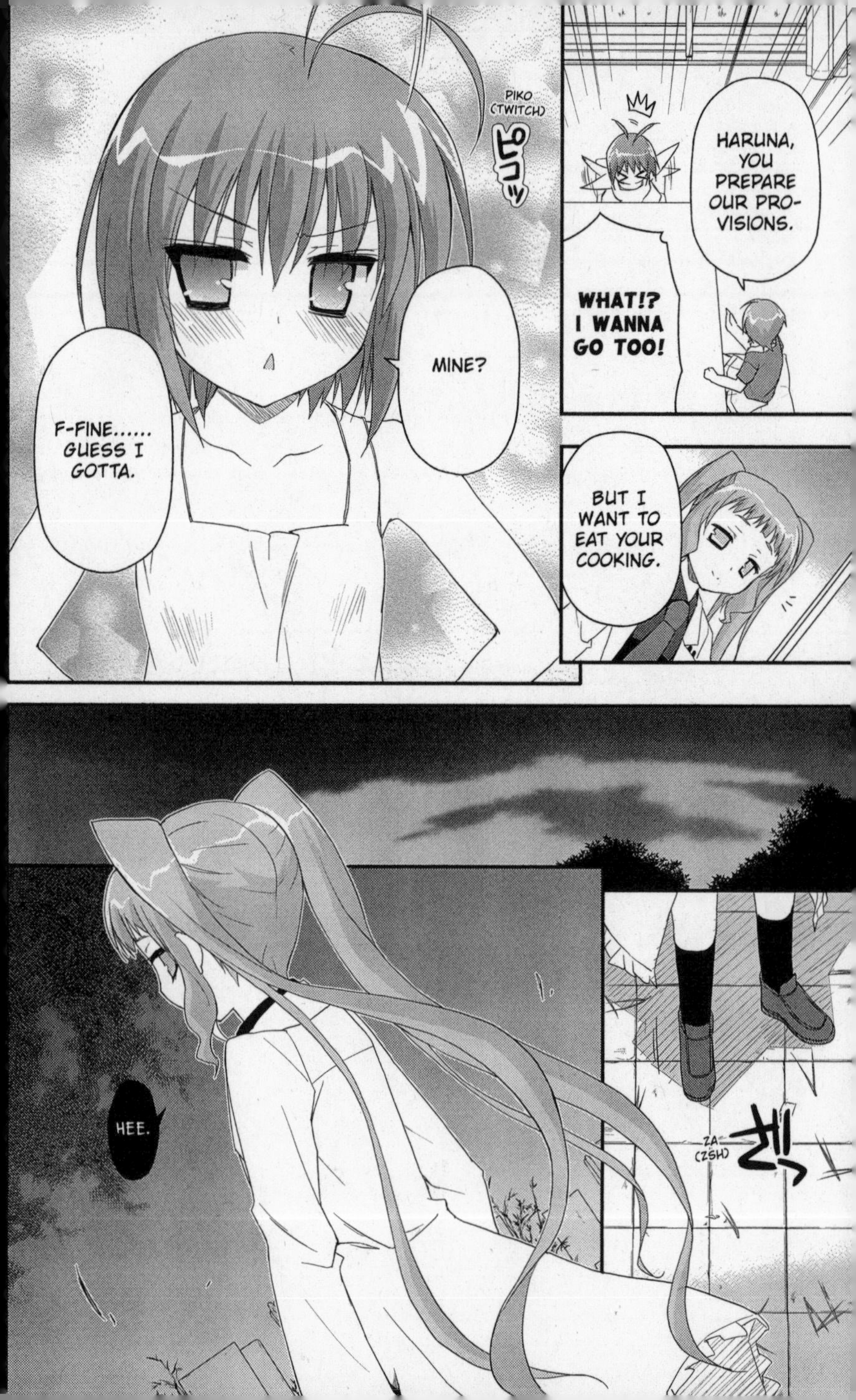
HARUNA, YOU PREPARE OUR PRO-VISIONS.
WHAT!? I WANNA GO TOO!
BUT I WANT TO EAT YOUR COOKING.
PIKO (TWITCH)
ピコッ
MINE?
F-FINE...... GUESS I GOTTA.
ZA (ZSH)
HEE.

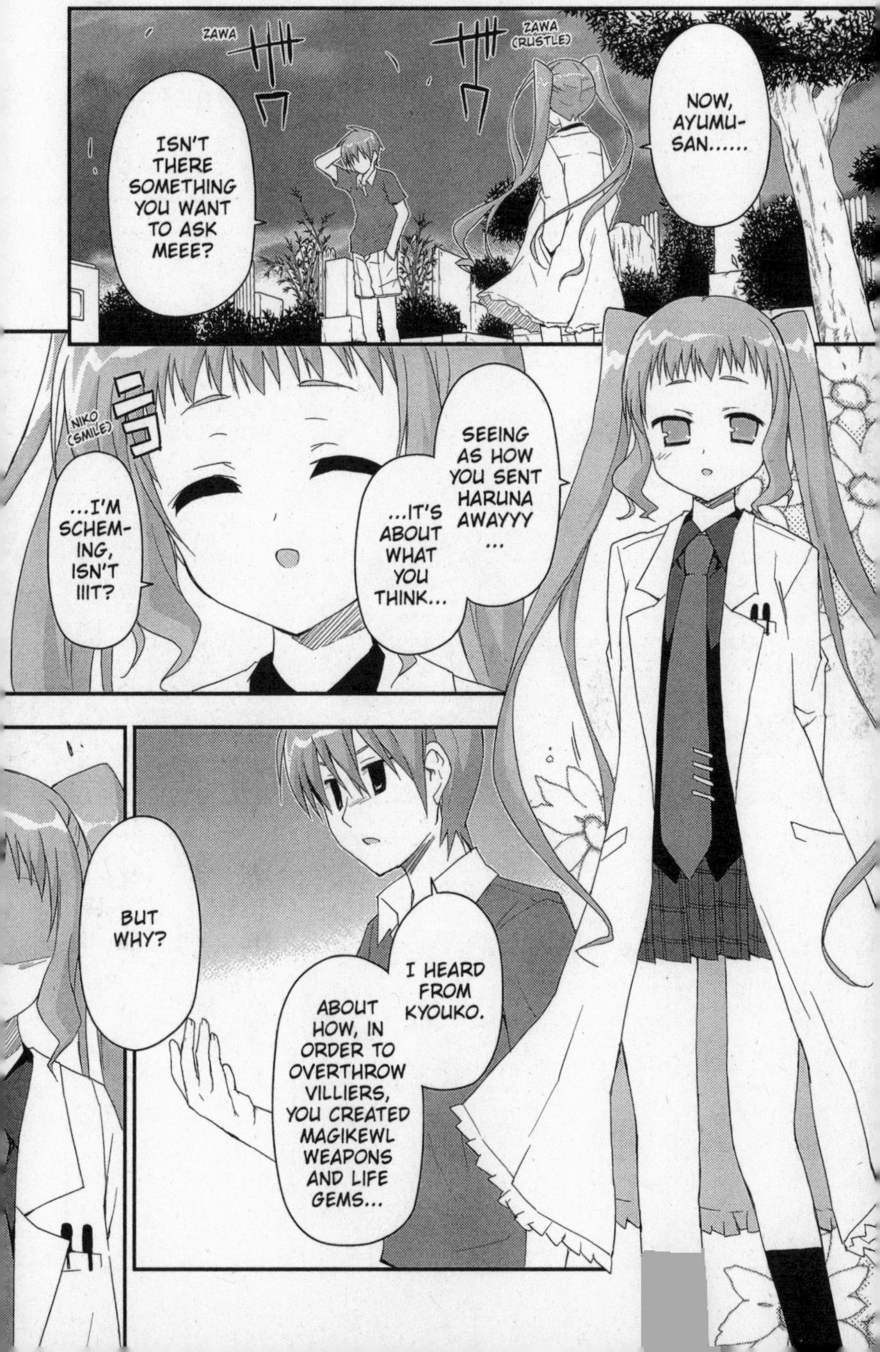
ZAWA (RUSTLE)
ZAWA
NOW, AYUMU-SAN......
ISN'T THERE SOMETHING YOU WANT TO ASK MEEE?
SEEING AS HOW YOU SENT HARUNA AWAYYY ...
...IT'S ABOUT WHAT YOU THINK...
NIKO (SMILE)
...I'M SCHEM-ING, ISN'T IIIT?
I HEARD FROM KYOUKO.
ABOUT HOW, IN ORDER TO OVERTHROW VILLIERS, YOU CREATED MAGIKEWL WEAPONS AND LIFE GEMS...
BUT WHY?

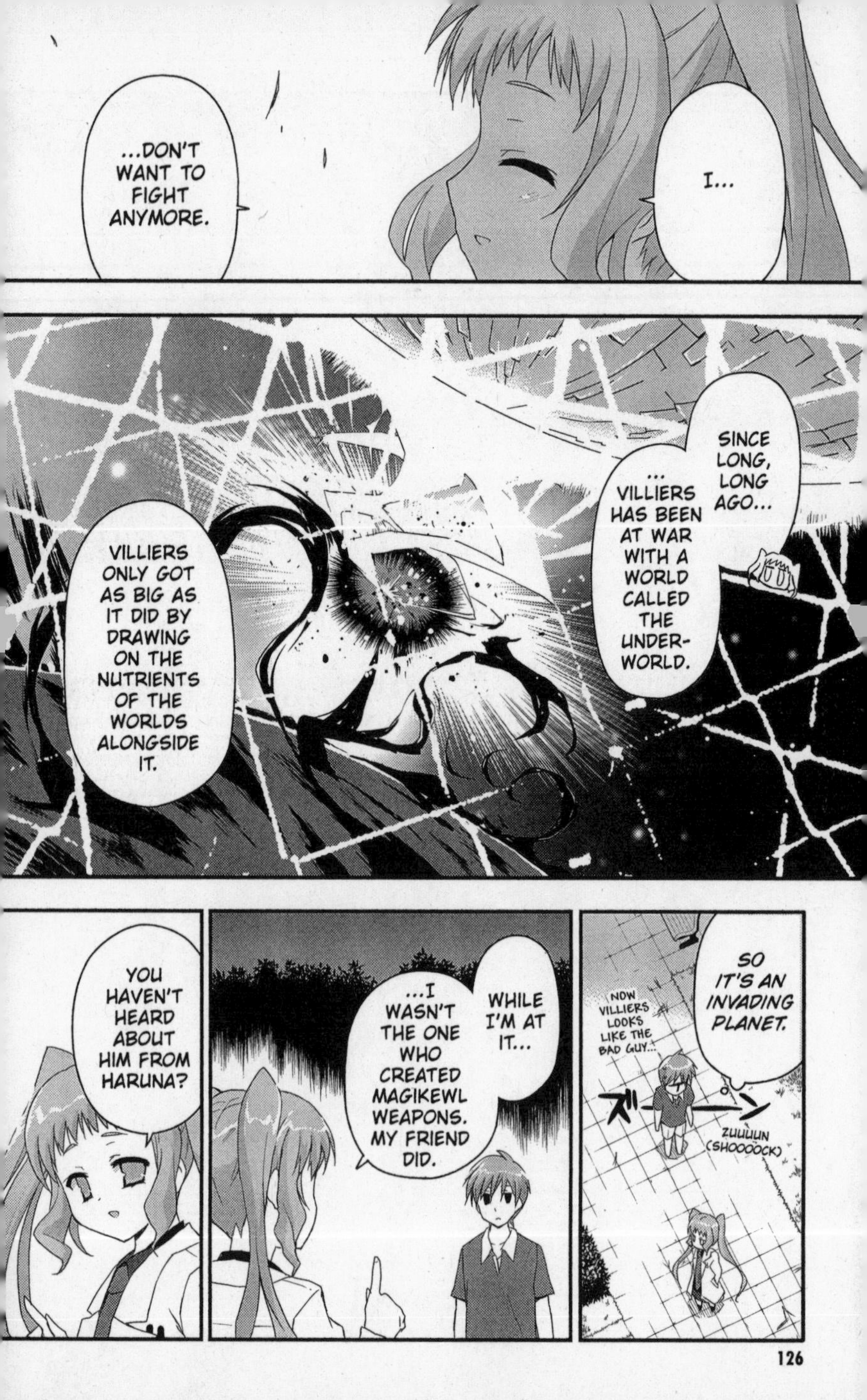
I...
...DON'T WANT TO FIGHT ANYMORE.
SINCE LONG, LONG AGO...
...VILLIERS HAS BEEN AT WAR WITH A WORLD CALLED THE UNDER-WORLD.
VILLIERS ONLY GOT AS BIG AS IT DID BY DRAWING ON THE NUTRIENTS OF THE WORLDS ALONGSIDE IT.
SO IT'S AN INVADING PLANET.
NOW VILLIERS LOOKS LIKE THE BAD GUY...
ZUUUUN (SHOOOOCK)
WHILE I'M AT IT...
...I WASN'T THE ONE WHO CREATED MAGIKEWL WEAPONS. MY FRIEND DID.
YOU HAVEN'T HEARD ABOUT HIM FROM HARUNA?

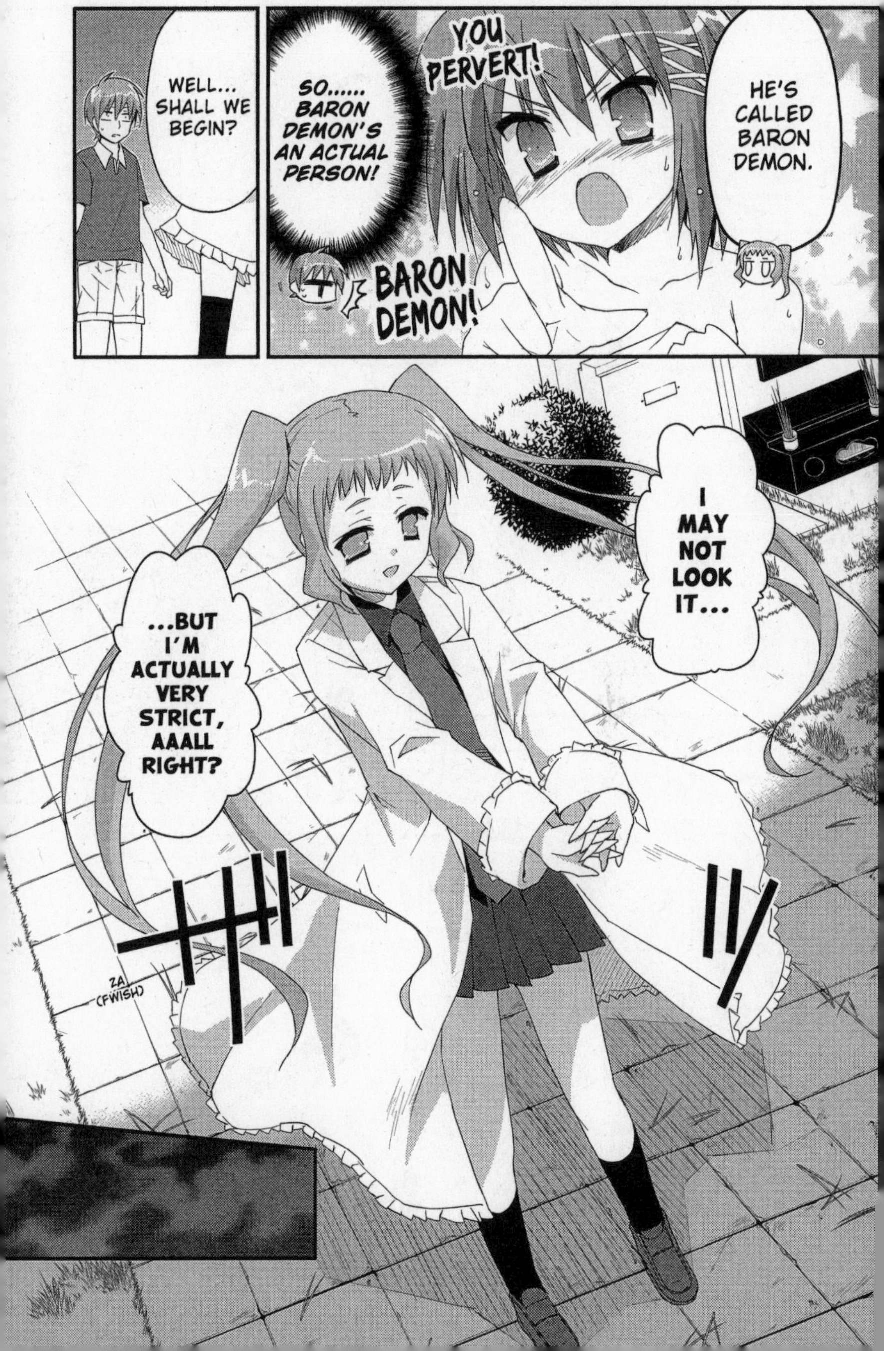
HE'S CALLED BARON DEMON.
YOU PERVERT!
SO...... BARON DEMON'S AN ACTUAL PERSON!
BARON DEMON!
WELL... SHALL WE BEGIN?
I MAY NOT LOOK IT...
...BUT I'M ACTUALLY VERY STRICT, AAALL RIGHT?
ZA (FWISH)

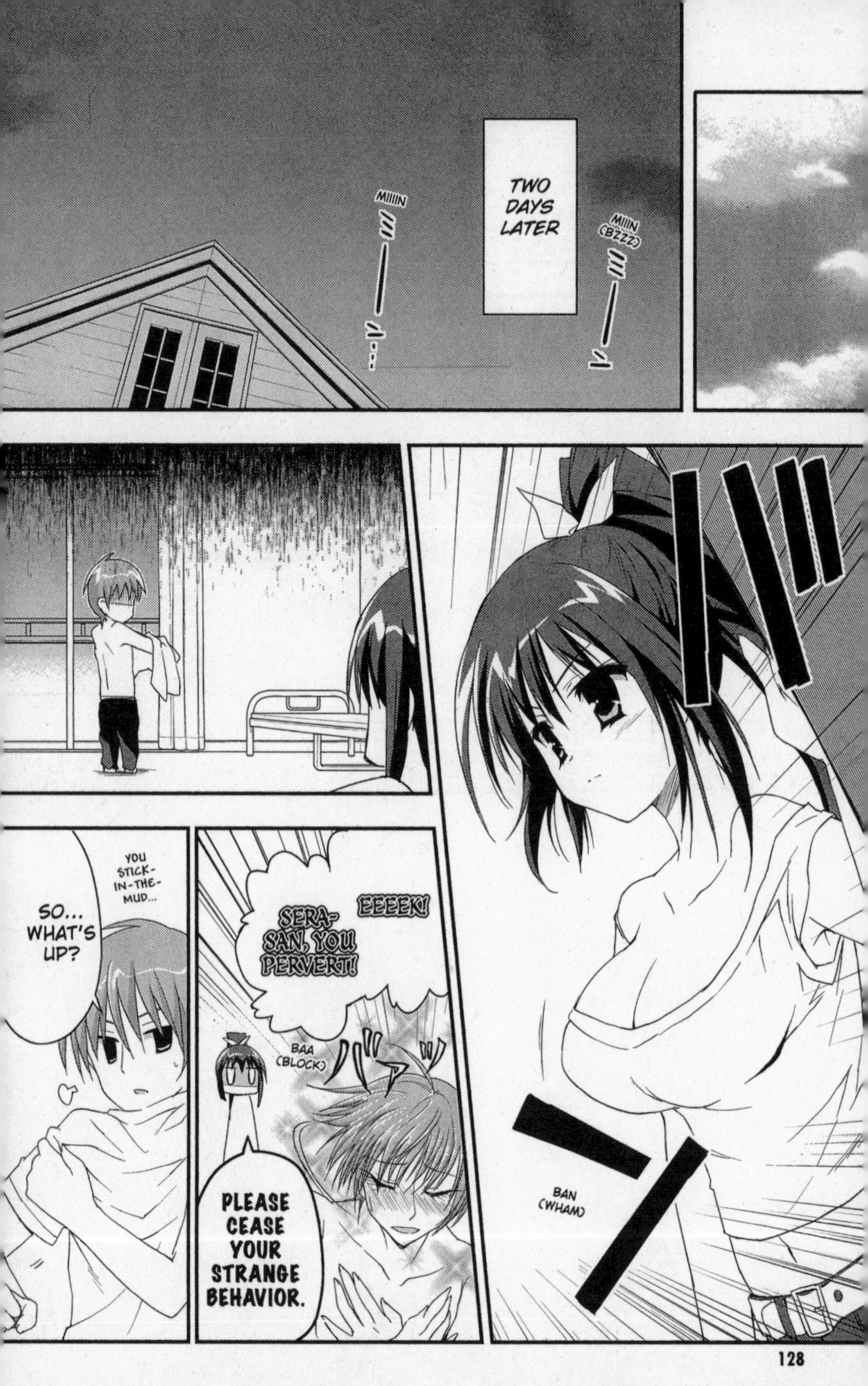
TWO DAYS LATER
MIIN (BZZZ)
MIIIN
BAN (WHAM)
EEEEK!
SERA-SAN, YOU PERVERT!
BAA (BLOCK)
PLEASE CEASE YOUR STRANGE BEHAVIOR.
YOU STICK-IN-THE-MUD...
SO... WHAT'S UP?

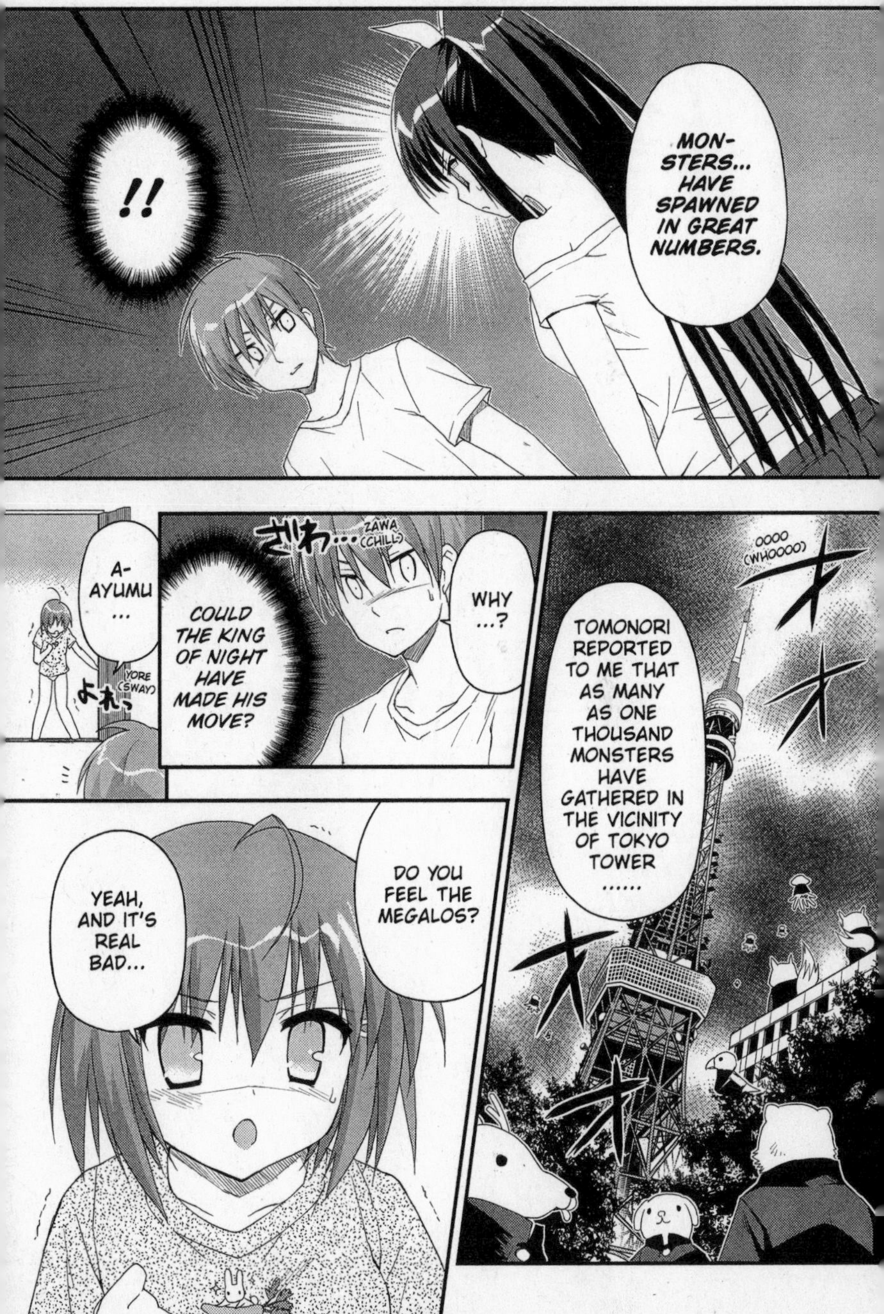

MON-STERS... HAVE SPAWNED IN GREAT NUMBERS.
!!
OOOO (WHOOOO)
TOMONORI REPORTED TO ME THAT AS MANY AS ONE THOUSAND MONSTERS HAVE GATHERED IN THE VICINITY OF TOKYO TOWER ......
ZAWA (CHILL)
WHY ...?
COULD THE KING OF NIGHT HAVE MADE HIS MOVE?
A- AYUMU ...
YORE (SWAY)
DO YOU FEEL THE MEGALOS?
YEAH, AND IT'S REAL BAD...

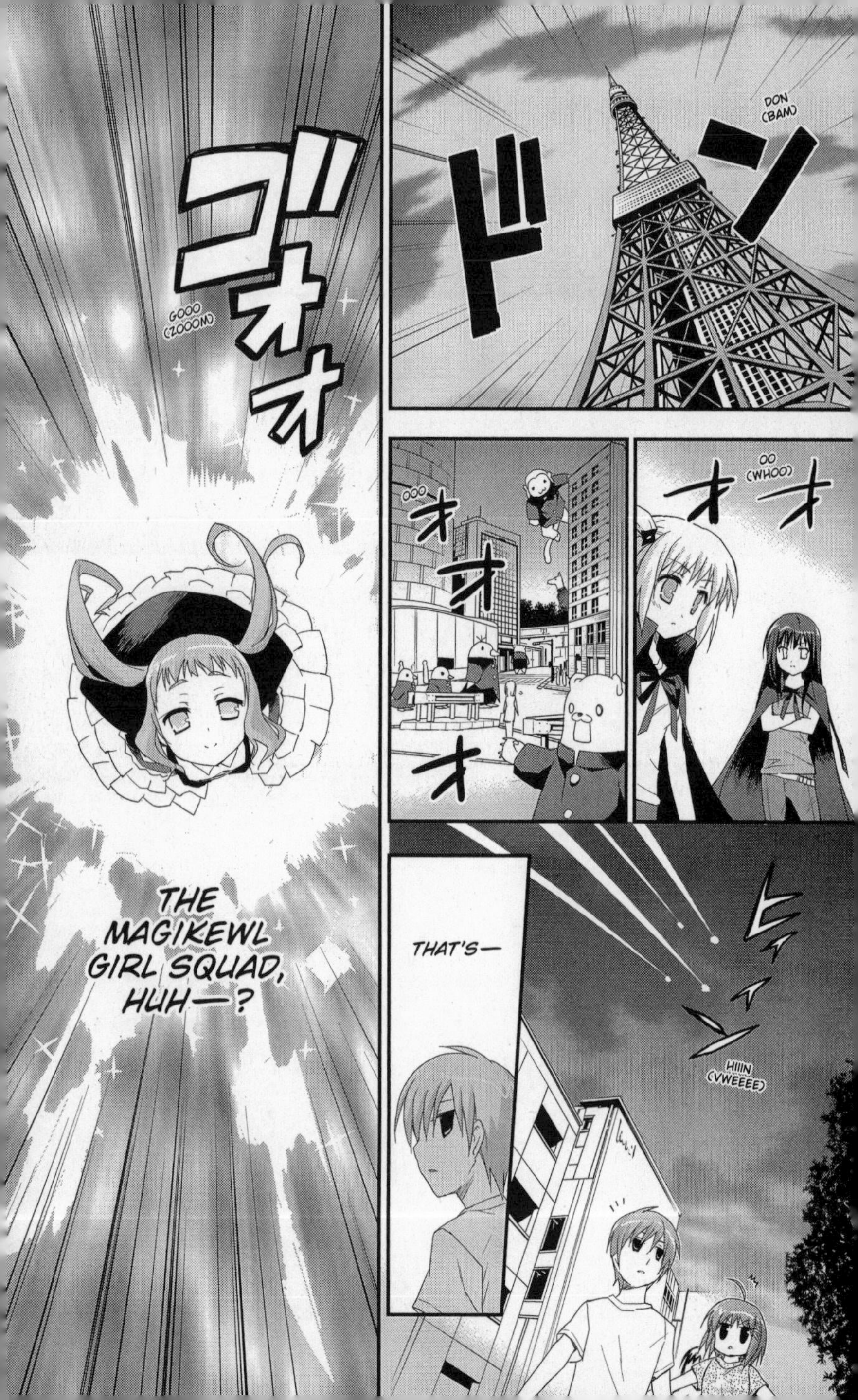
DON (BAM)
OO (WHOO)
OOO
HIIIN (VWEEEE)
THAT'S—
GOOO (ZOOOM)
THE MAGIKEWL GIRL SQUAD, HUH—?

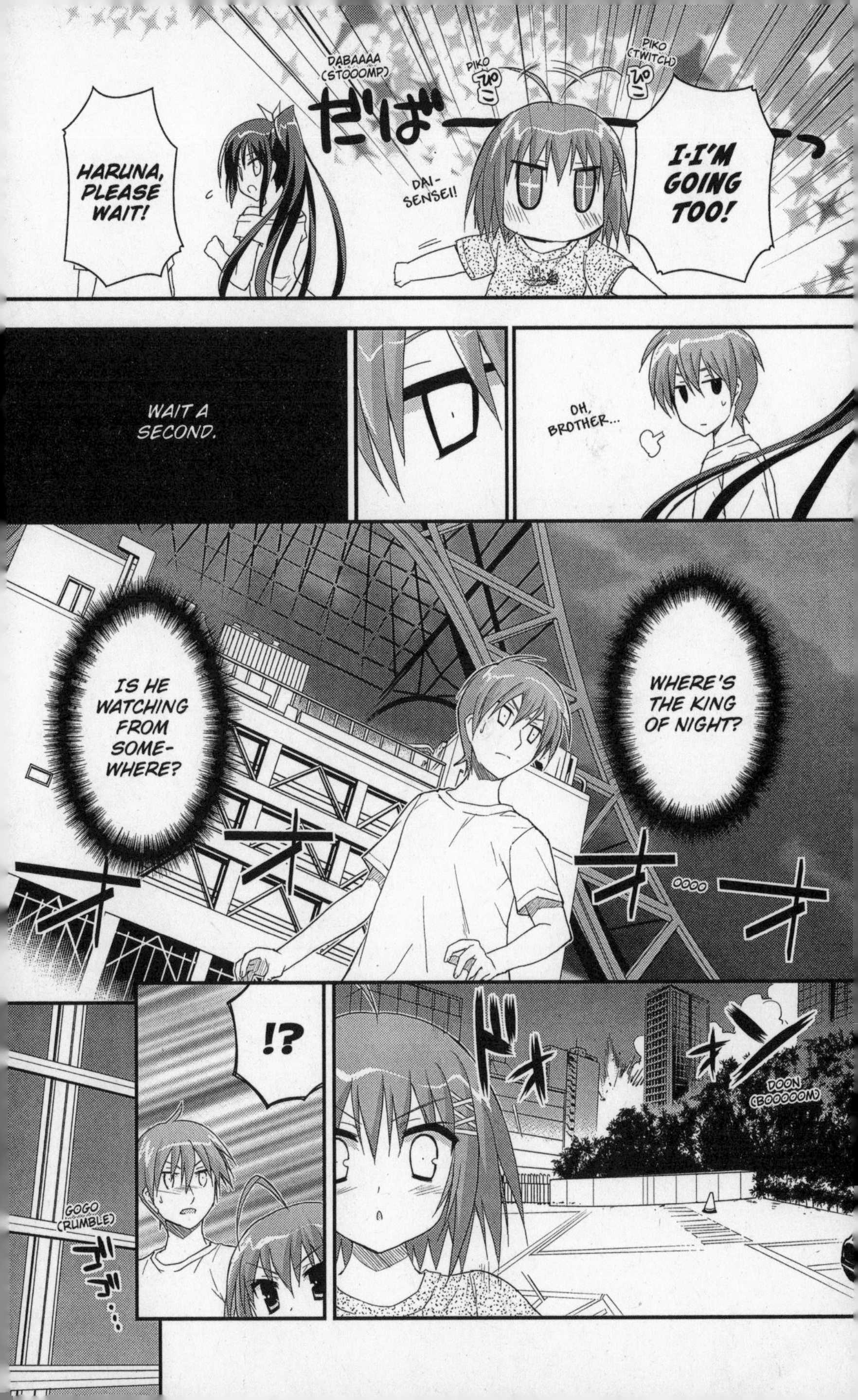
I-I'M GOING TOO!
PIKO (TWITCH)
ぴこ
PIKO
ぴこ
DAI-SENSEI!
DABAAAA (STOOOMP)
だばーーーっ
HARUNA, PLEASE WAIT!
OH, BROTHER...
WAIT A SECOND.
WHERE'S THE KING OF NIGHT?
IS HE WATCHING FROM SOME-WHERE?
OOOO
DOON (BOOOOOM)
!?
GOGO (RUMBLE)

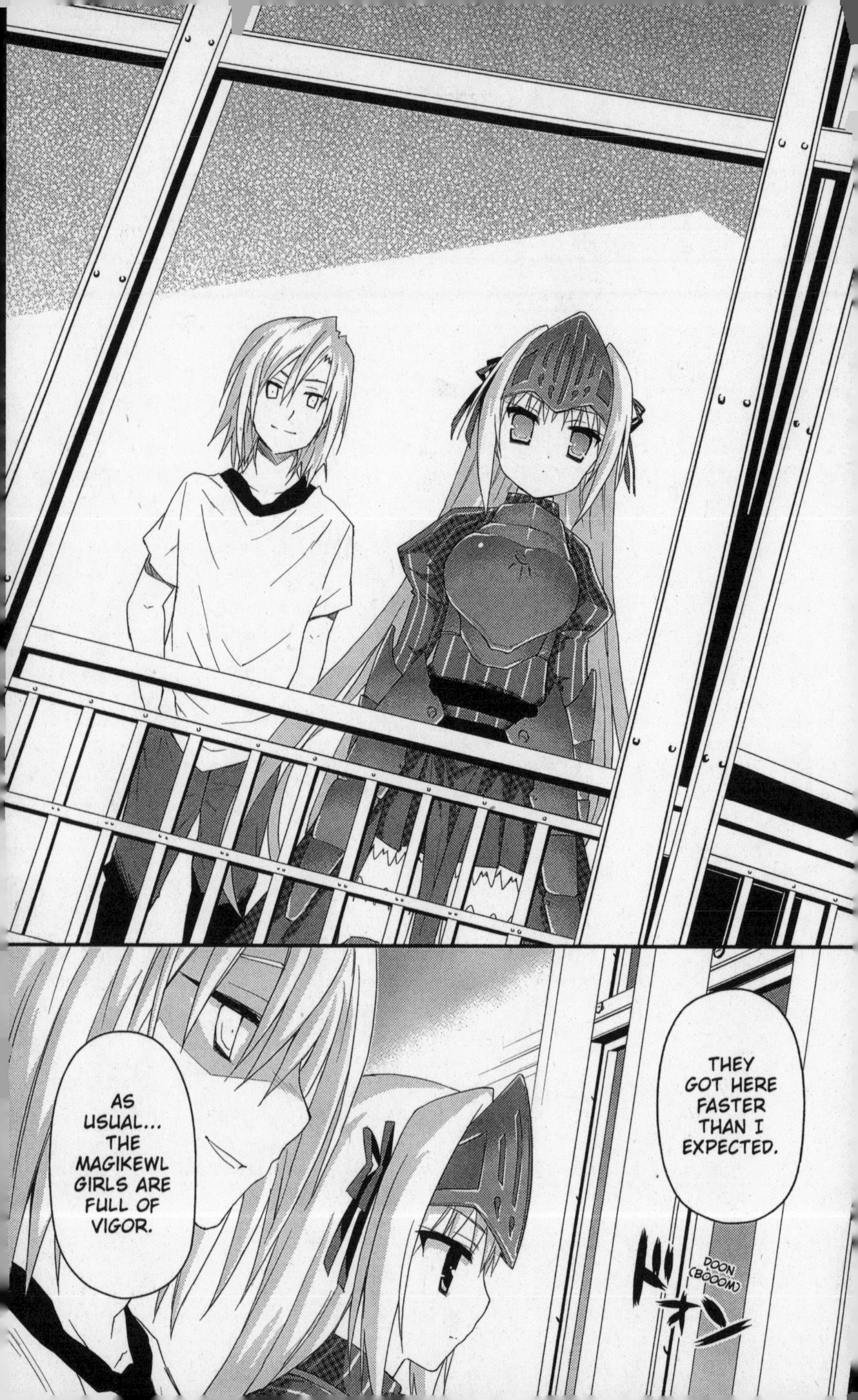
THEY GOT HERE FASTER THAN I EXPECTED.
DOON (BOOOM)
AS USUAL... THE MAGIKEWL GIRLS ARE FULL OF VIGOR.

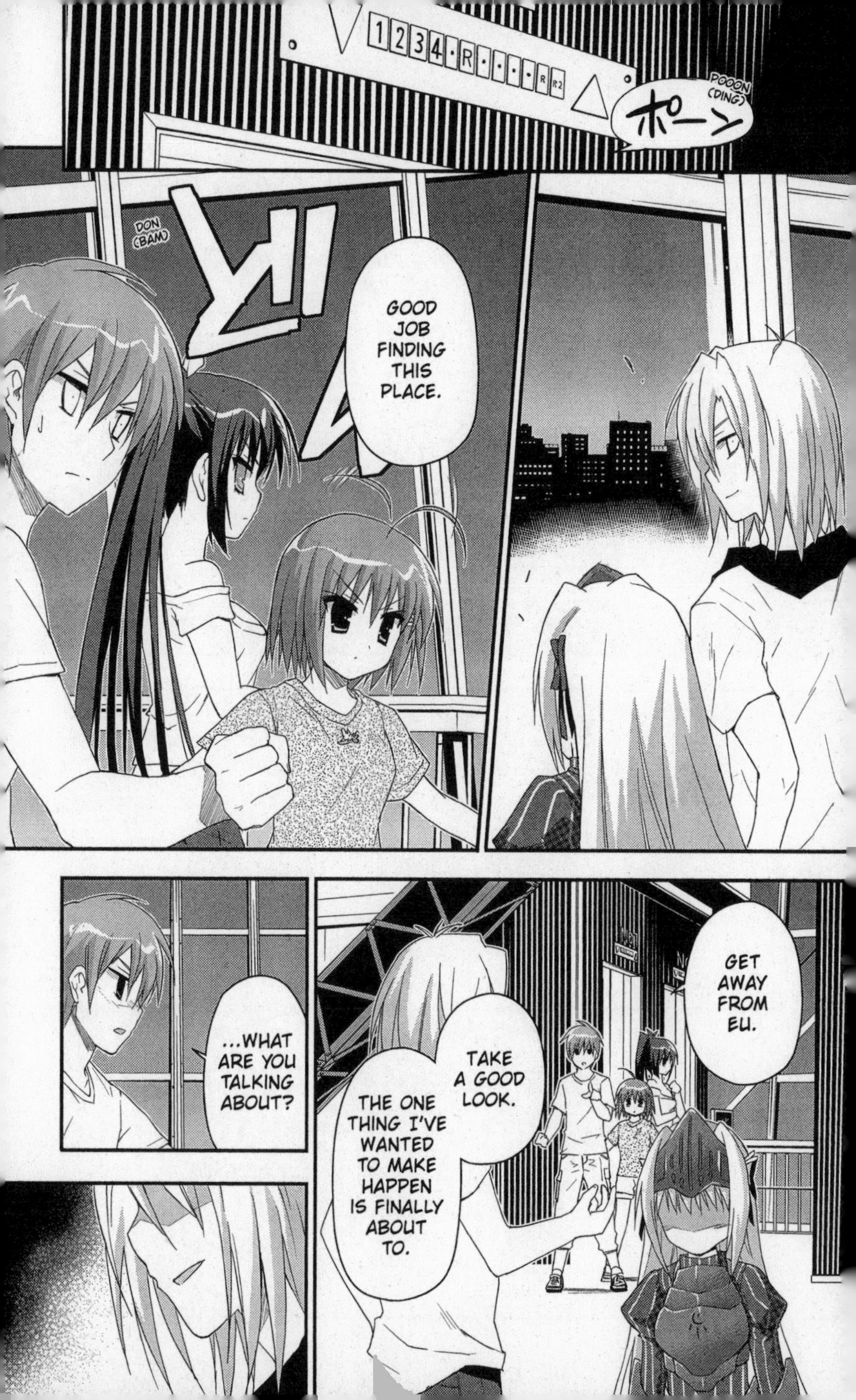

1 2 3 4 R R R2
ポーン
POOON (DING)
DON (BAM)
GOOD JOB FINDING THIS PLACE.
GET AWAY FROM EU.
TAKE A GOOD LOOK.
THE ONE THING I'VE WANTED TO MAKE HAPPEN IS FINALLY ABOUT TO.
...WHAT ARE YOU TALKING ABOUT?

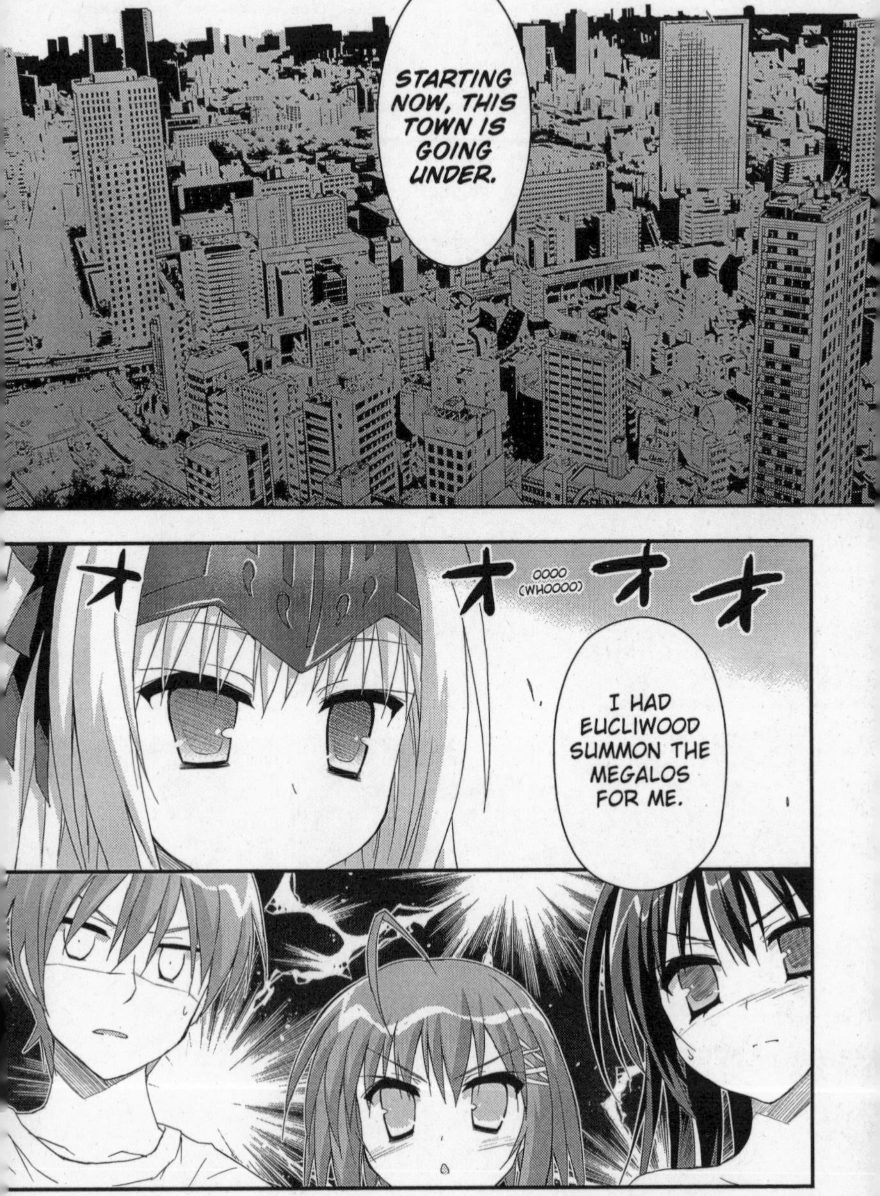
STARTING NOW, THIS TOWN IS GOING UNDER.
オ オ オ オ
OOOO (WHOOOO)
I HAD EUCLIWOOD SUMMON THE MEGALOS FOR ME.

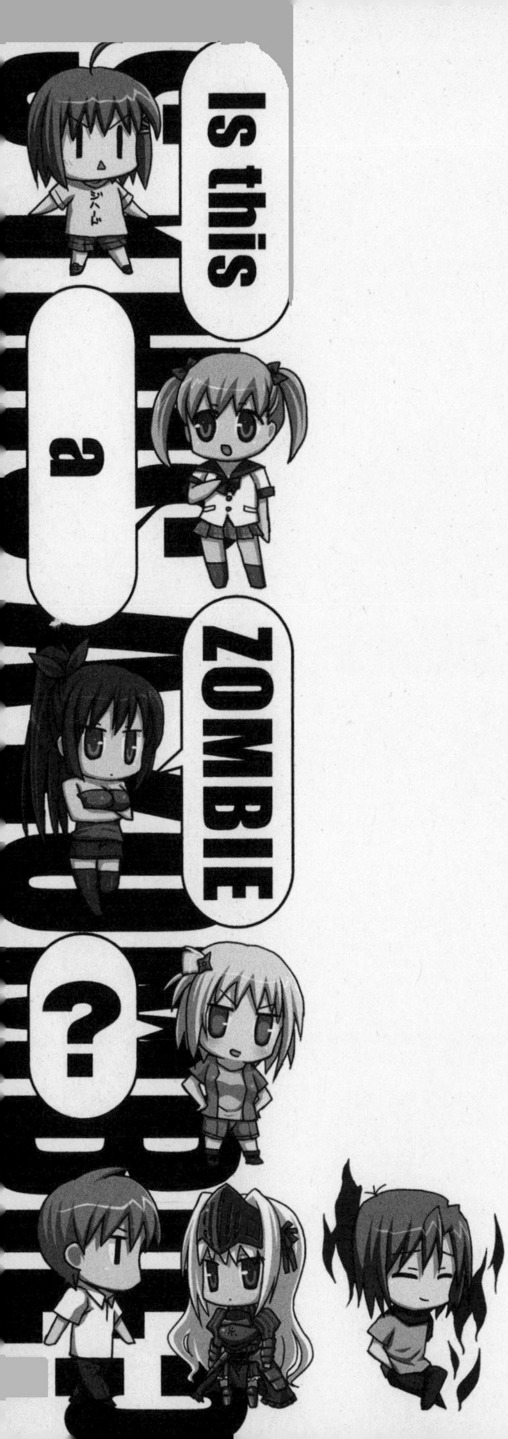
Is this
a
ZOMBIE
?
ジハード

SFX: DOFUU (SMASH)

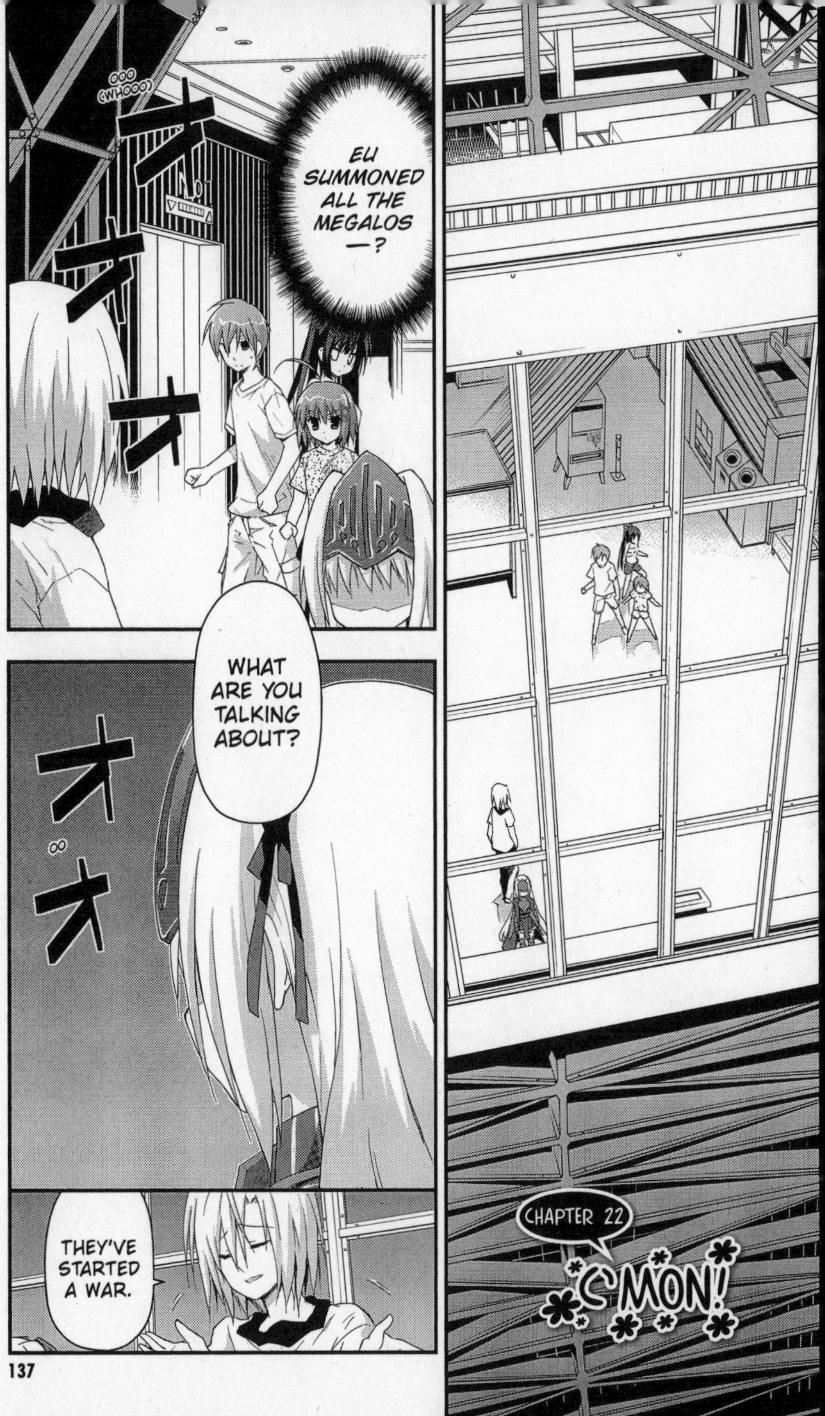
CHAPTER 22
C'MON!
OOO (WHOOO)
EU SUMMONED ALL THE MEGALOS—?
WHAT ARE YOU TALKING ABOUT?
THEY'VE STARTED A WAR.

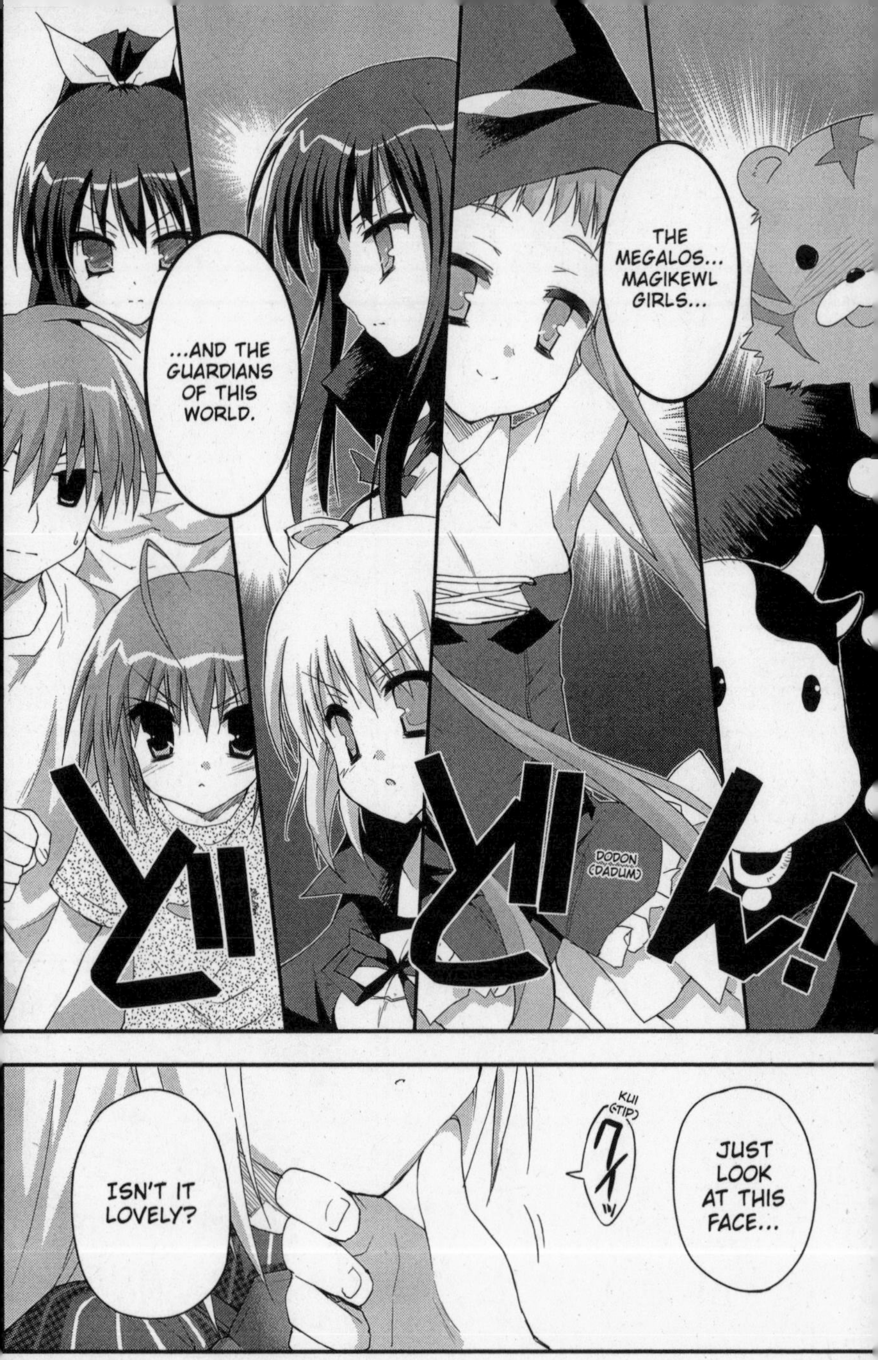
THE MEGALOS... MAGIKEWL GIRLS...
...AND THE GUARDIANS OF THIS WORLD.
DODON (DADUM)
JUST LOOK AT THIS FACE...
KUI (TIP)
ISN'T IT LOVELY?

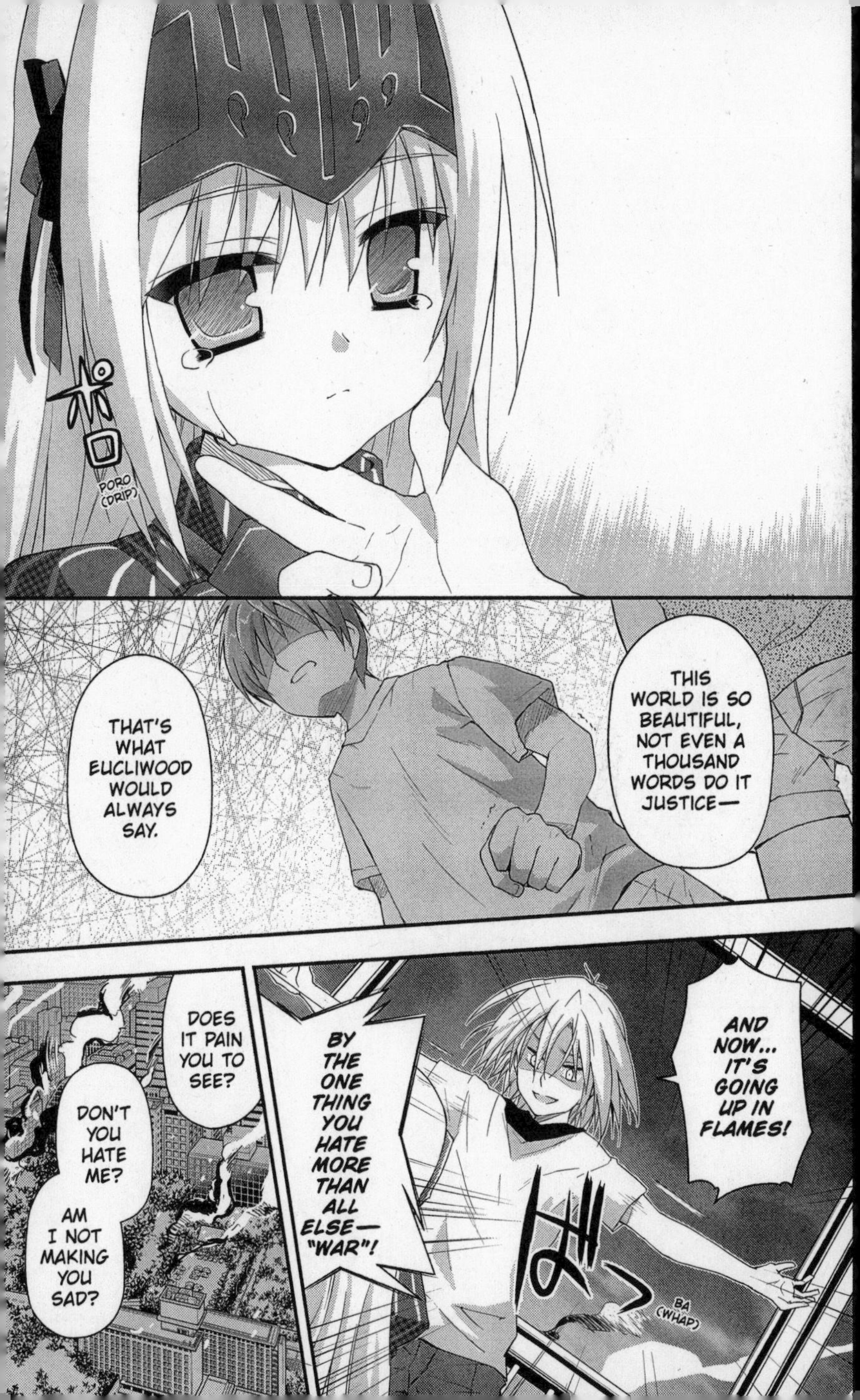
PORO (DRIP)
THIS WORLD IS SO BEAUTIFUL, NOT EVEN A THOUSAND WORDS DO IT JUSTICE—
THAT'S WHAT EUCLIWOOD WOULD ALWAYS SAY.
AND NOW... IT'S GOING UP IN FLAMES!
BY THE ONE THING YOU HATE MORE THAN ALL ELSE— "WAR"!
BA (WHAP)
DOES IT PAIN YOU TO SEE?
DON'T YOU HATE ME?
AM I NOT MAKING YOU SAD?

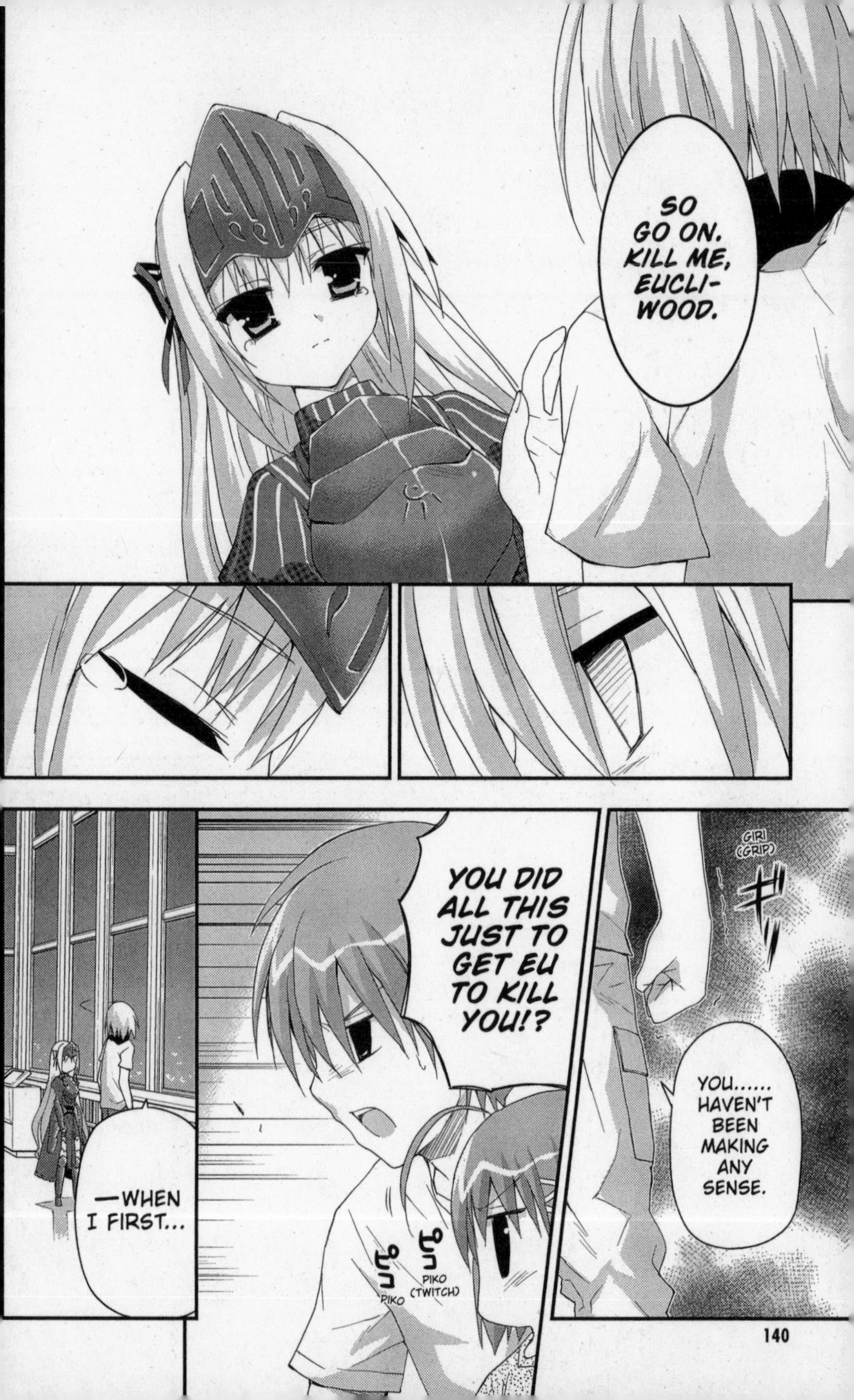
SO GO ON. KILL ME, EUCLI-WOOD.
GIRI (GRIP)
YOU...... HAVEN'T BEEN MAKING ANY SENSE.
YOU DID ALL THIS JUST TO GET EU TO KILL YOU!?
PIKO (TWITCH)
PIKO
—WHEN I FIRST...

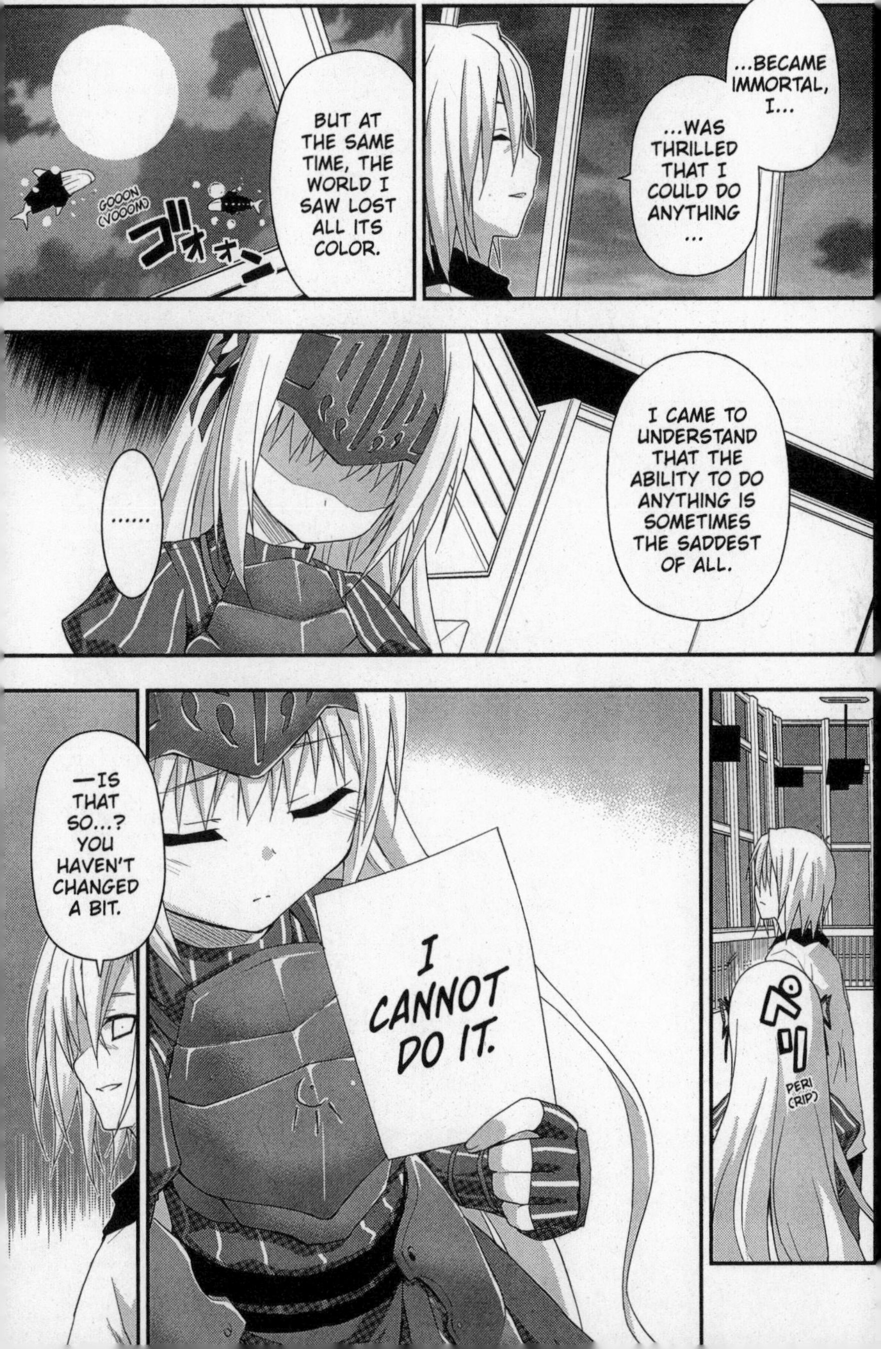

...BECAME IMMORTAL, I...
...WAS THRILLED THAT I COULD DO ANYTHING ...
BUT AT THE SAME TIME, THE WORLD I SAW LOST ALL ITS COLOR.
GOOON (VOOOM)
I CAME TO UNDERSTAND THAT THE ABILITY TO DO ANYTHING IS SOMETIMES THE SADDEST OF ALL.
......
PERI (RIP)
I CANNOT DO IT.
—IS THAT SO...? YOU HAVEN'T CHANGED A BIT.

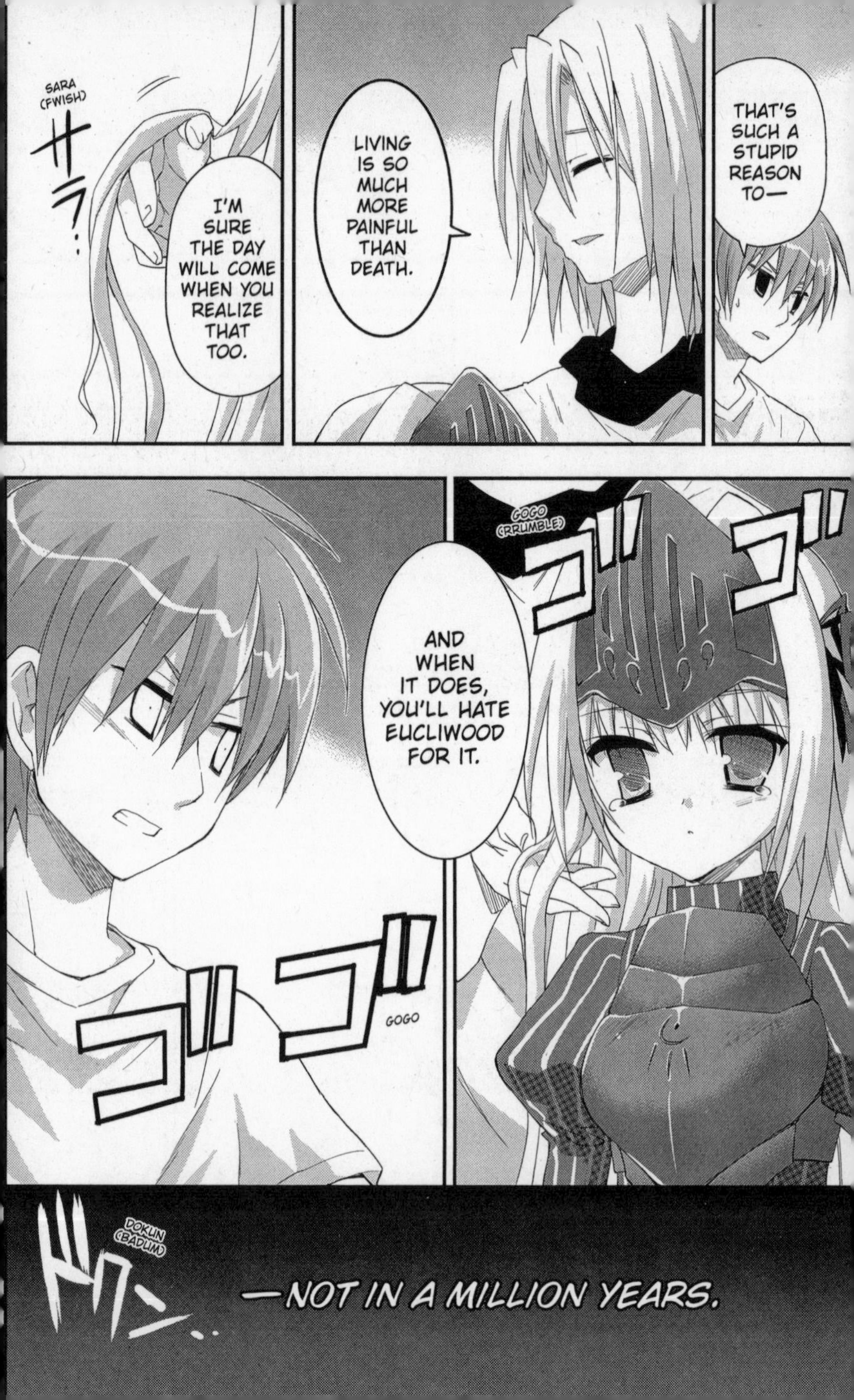
THAT'S SUCH A STUPID REASON TO—
LIVING IS SO MUCH MORE PAINFUL THAN DEATH.
サラ
SARA (FWISH)
I'M SURE THE DAY WILL COME WHEN YOU REALIZE THAT TOO.
ゴゴ
GOGO (RRUMBLE)
AND WHEN IT DOES, YOU'LL HATE EUCLIWOOD FOR IT.
ゴゴ
GOGO
ドクン
DOKUN (BADUM)
—NOT IN A MILLION YEARS.

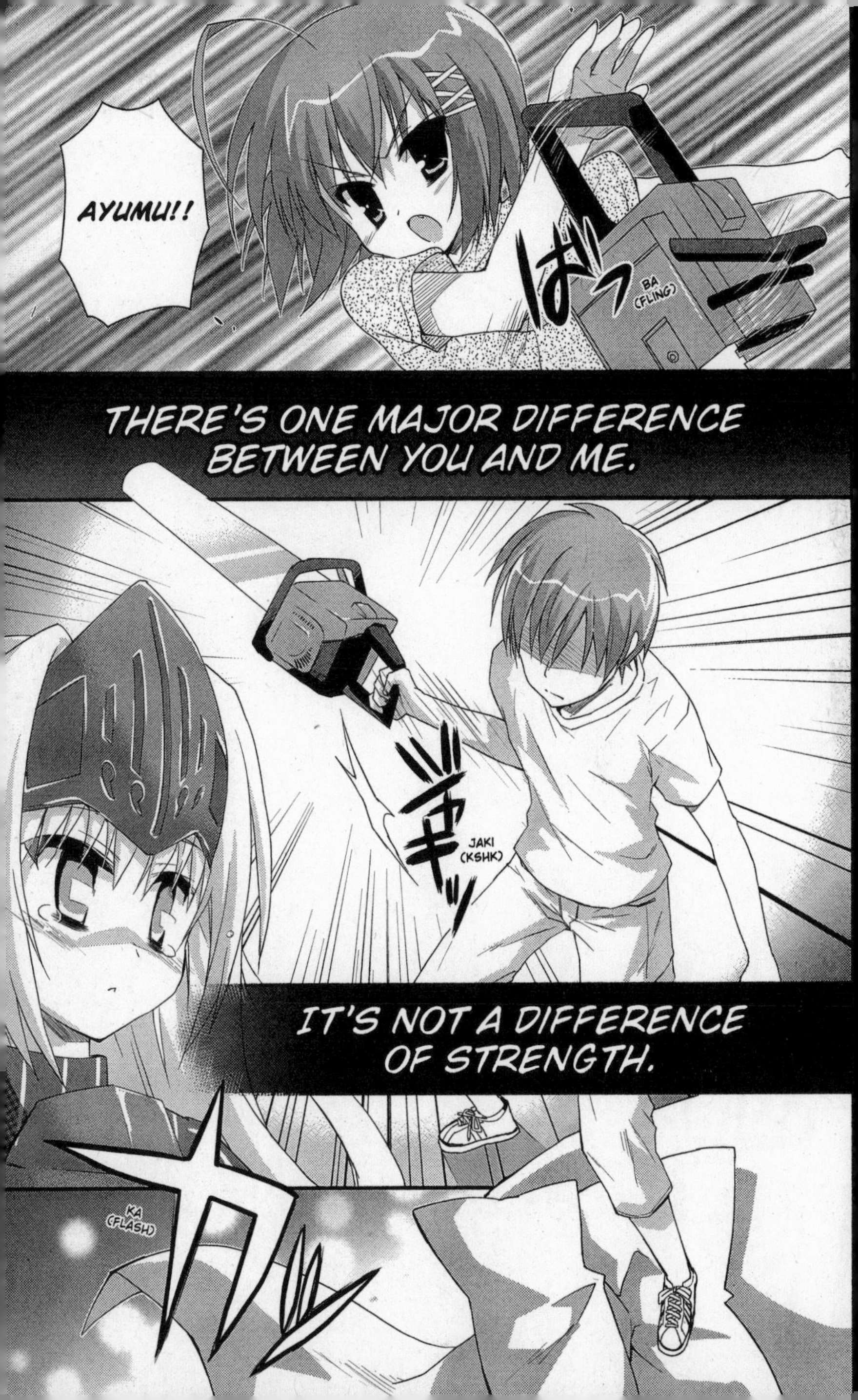
AYUMU!!
ばっ
BA (FLING)
THERE'S ONE MAJOR DIFFERENCE BETWEEN YOU AND ME.
ジャキッ
JAKI (KSHK)
IT'S NOT A DIFFERENCE OF STRENGTH.
カッ
KA (FLASH)

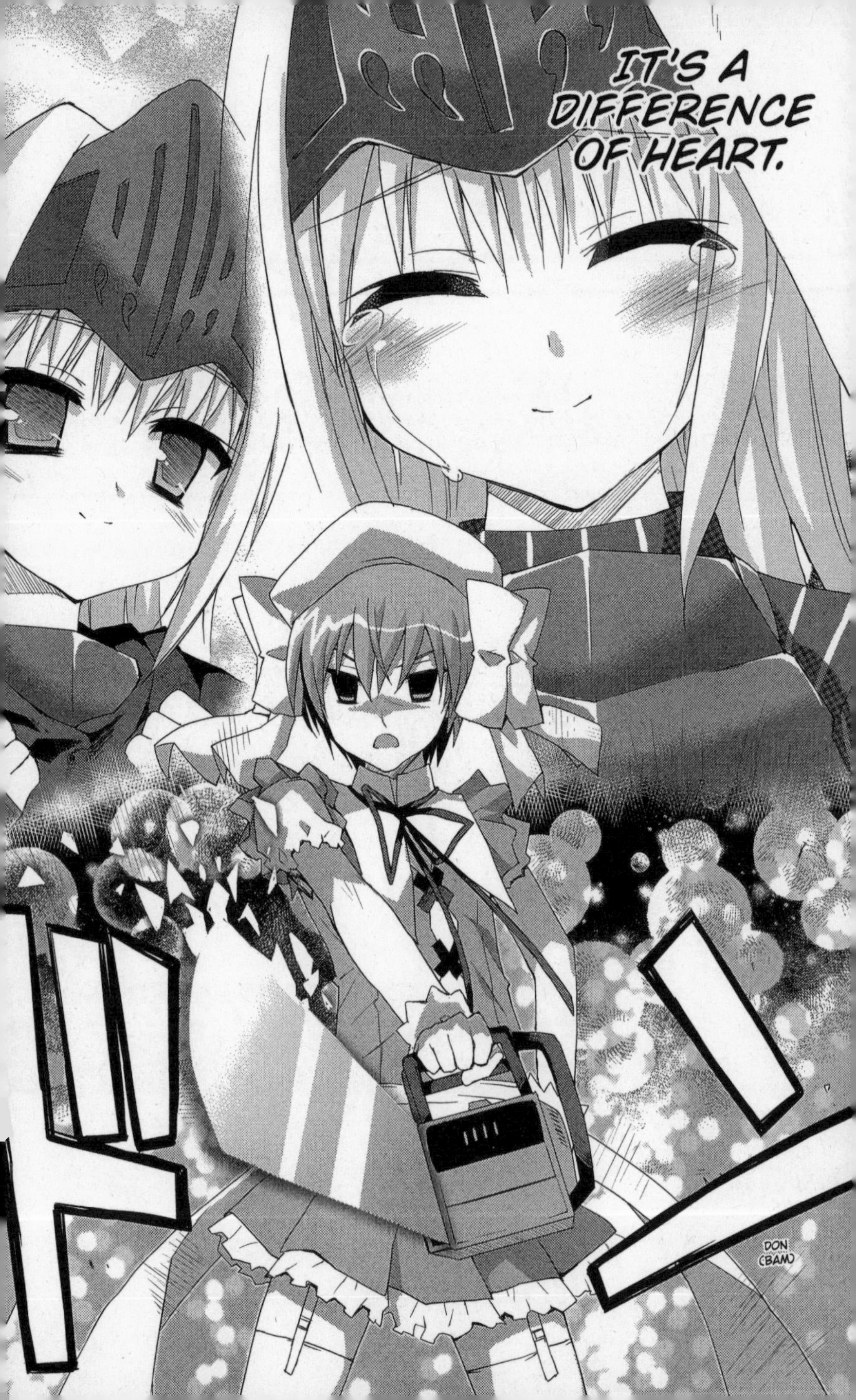
IT'S A DIFFERENCE OF HEART.
DON (BAM)

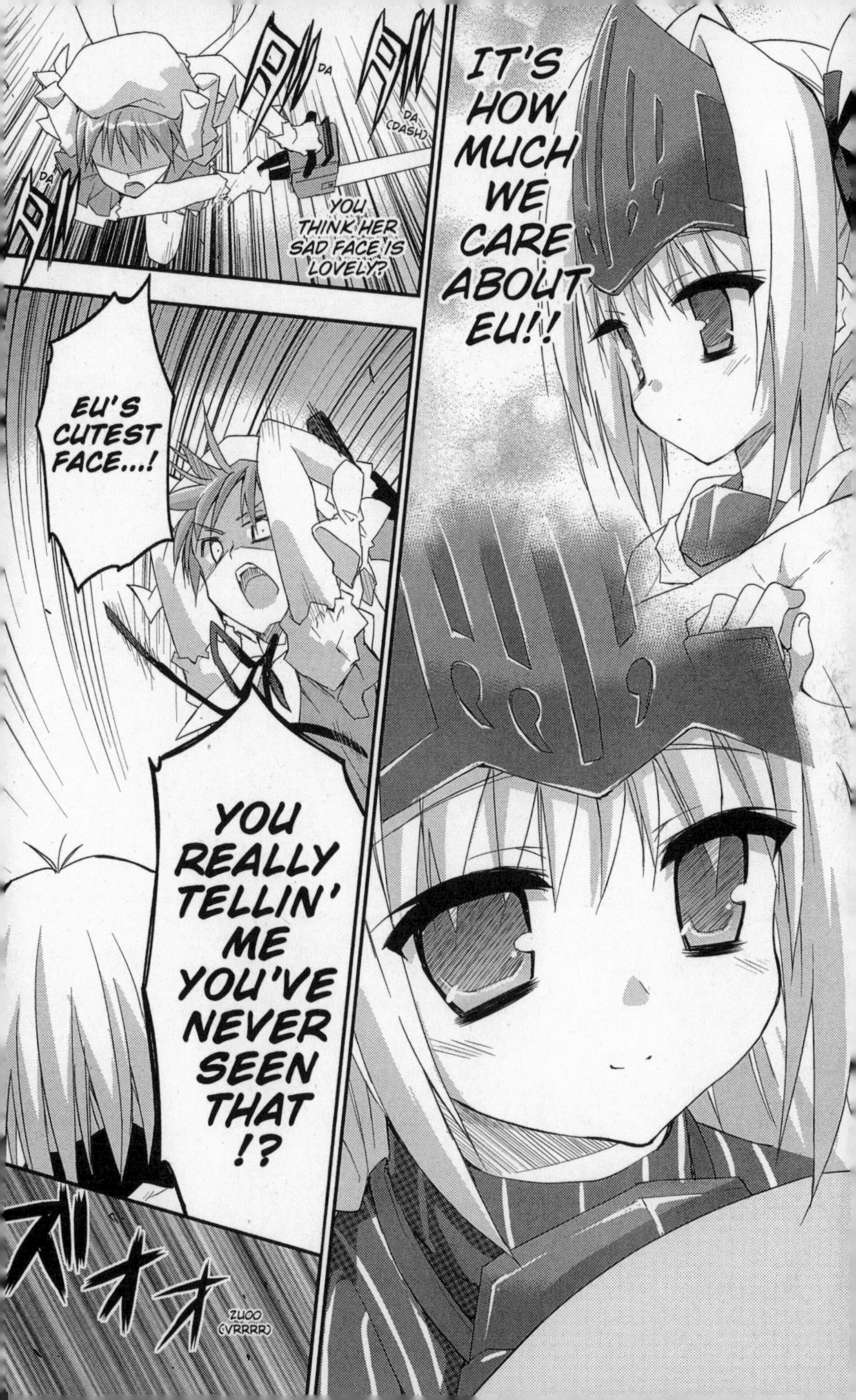
DA
DA (DASH)
DA
YOU THINK HER SAD FACE IS LOVELY?
EU'S CUTEST FACE...!
YOU REALLY TELLIN' ME YOU'VE NEVER SEEN THAT!?
IT'S HOW MUCH WE CARE ABOUT EU!!
ZUOO (VRRRR)

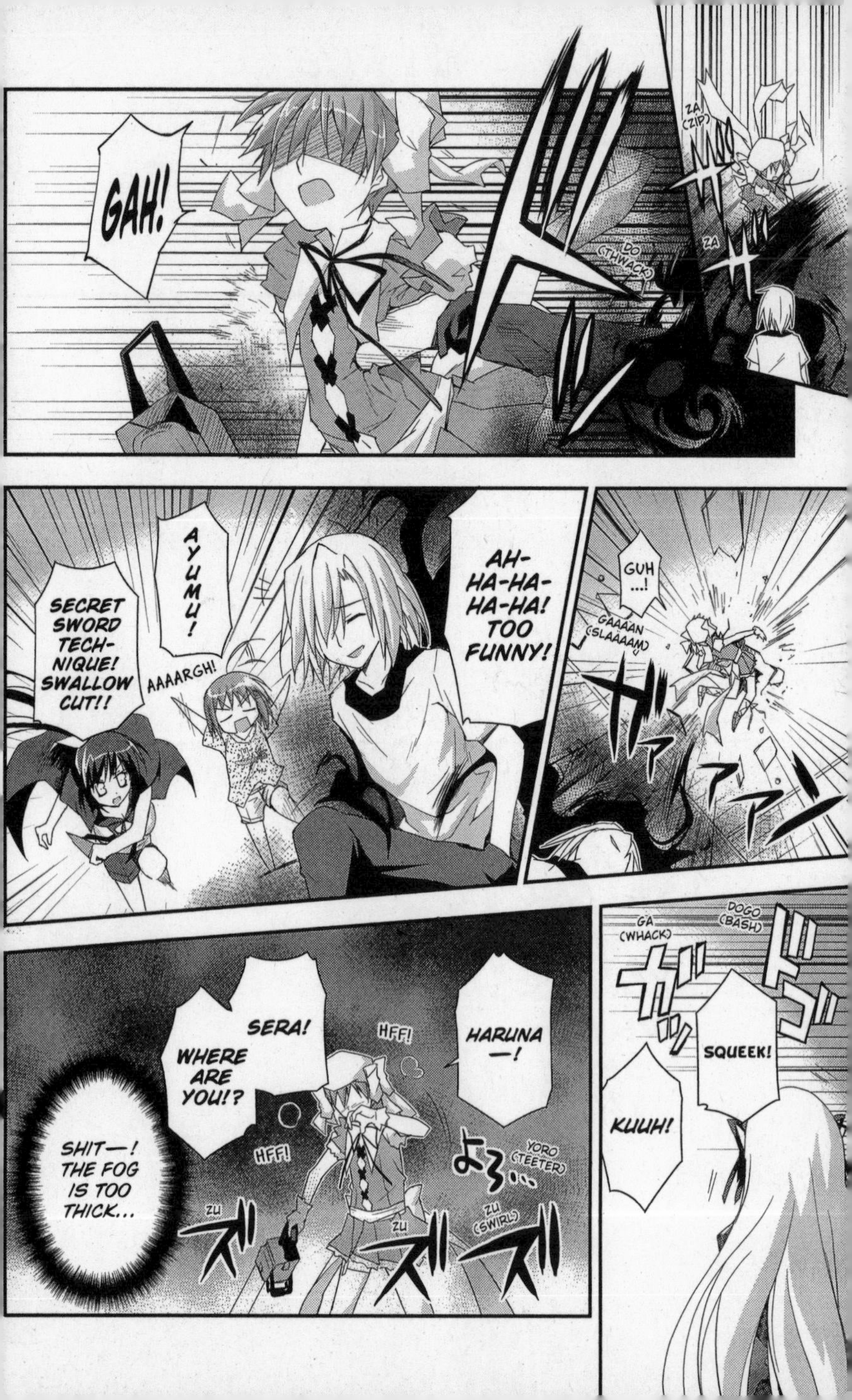
ZA (ZIP)
ZA
DO (THWACK)
GAH!
GUH ...!
GAAAAN (SLAAAAM)
AH-HA-HA-HA-HA! TOO FUNNY!
AYUMU!
AAAARGH!
SECRET SWORD TECHNIQUE! SWALLOW CUT!!
DOGO (BASH)
GA (WHACK)
SQUEEK!
KUUH!
HARUNA—!
HFF!
SERA! WHERE ARE YOU!?
HFF!
YORO (TEETER)
ZU (SWIRL)
ZU
ZU
SHIT—! THE FOG IS TOO THICK...

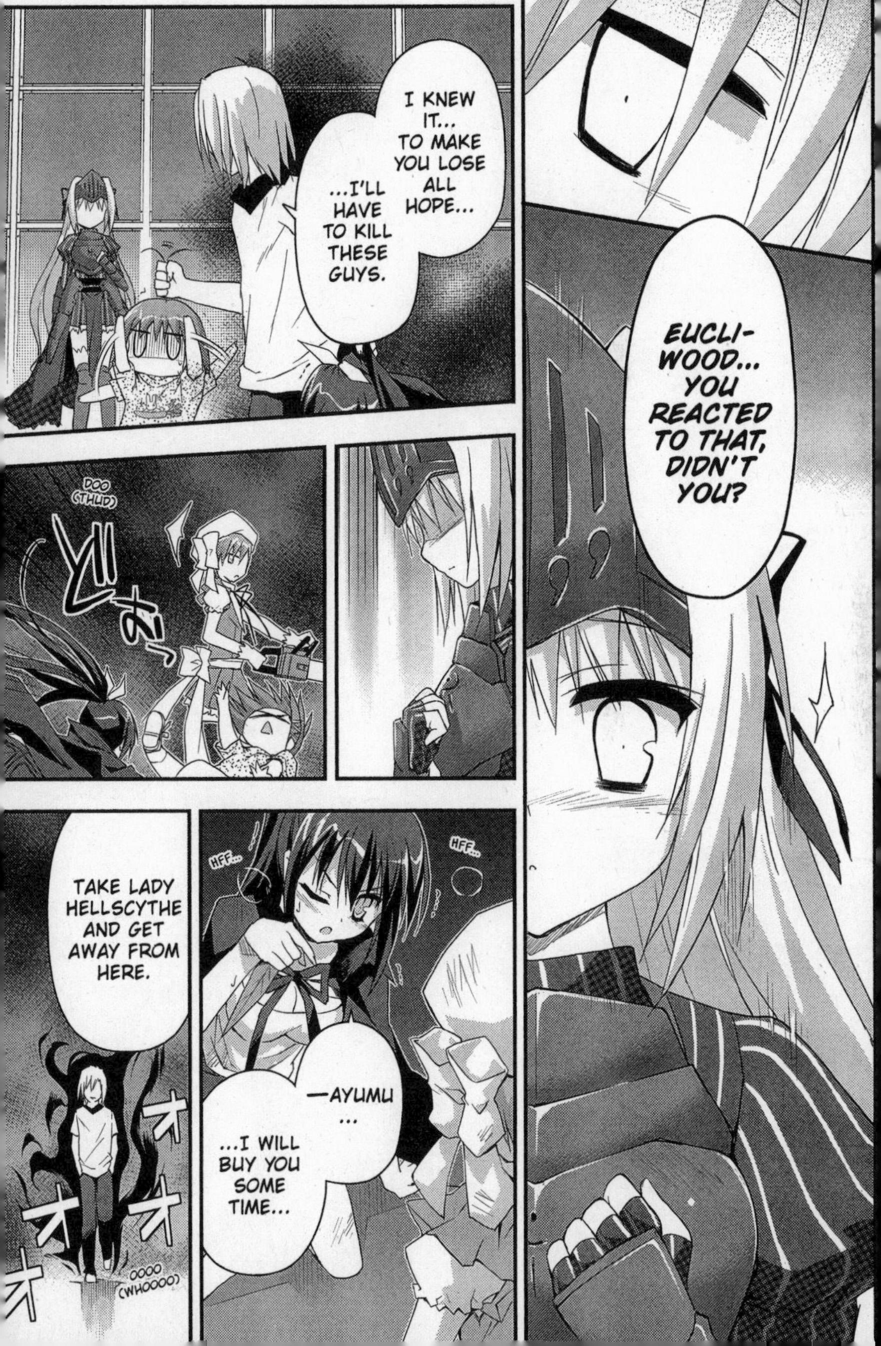
I KNEW IT... TO MAKE YOU LOSE ALL HOPE...
...I'LL HAVE TO KILL THESE GUYS.
EUCLI-WOOD... YOU REACTED TO THAT, DIDN'T YOU?
DOO (THUD)
HFF...
HFF...
—AYUMU ...
...I WILL BUY YOU SOME TIME...
TAKE LADY HELLSCYTHE AND GET AWAY FROM HERE.
OOOO (WHOOOO)

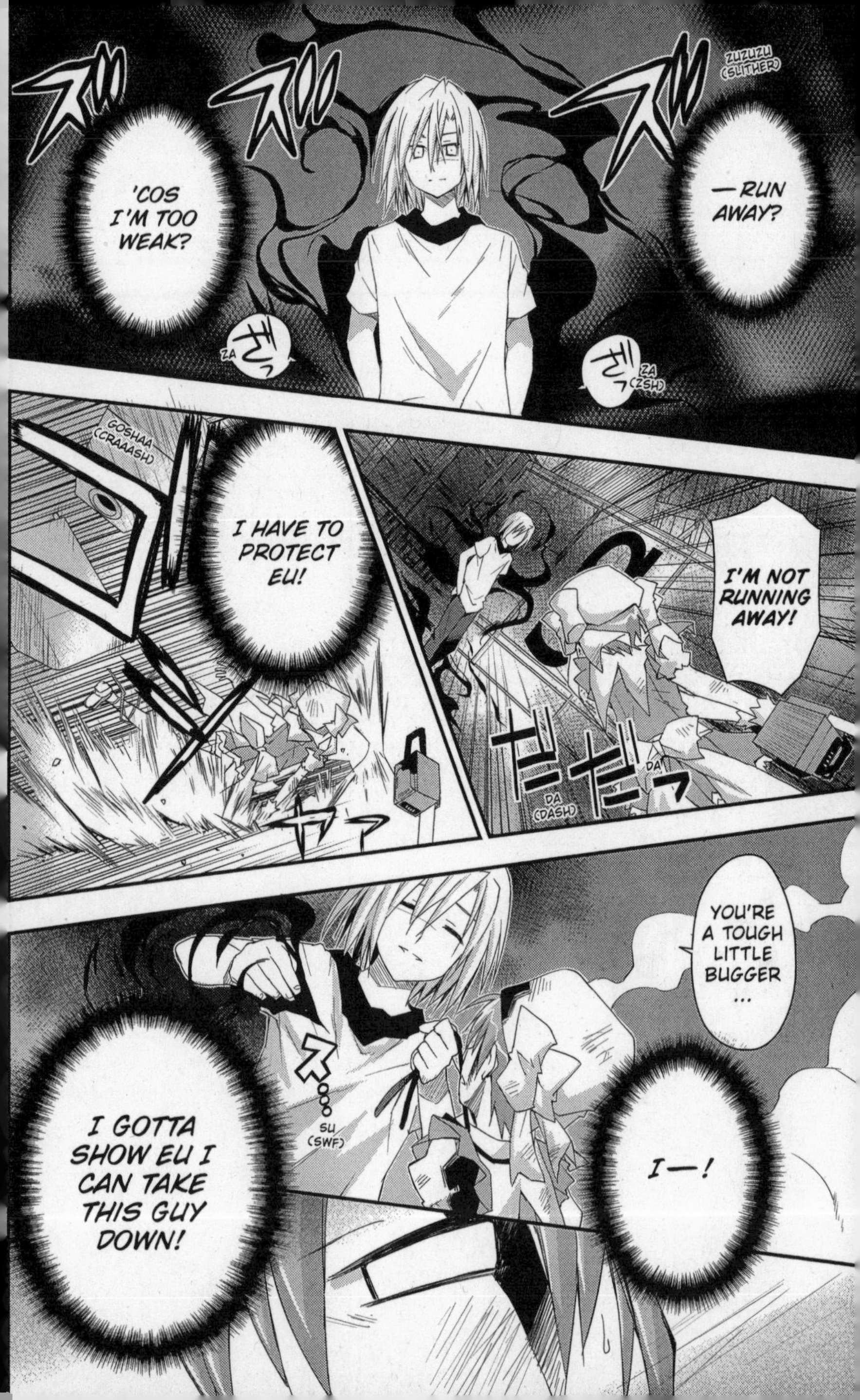
ZUZUZU (SLITHER)
—RUN AWAY?
'COS I'M TOO WEAK?
ZA (ZSH)
ZA
I'M NOT RUNNING AWAY!
DA
DA (DASH)
GOSHAA (CRAAASH)
I HAVE TO PROTECT EU!
YOU'RE A TOUGH LITTLE BUGGER ...
I—!
SU (SWF)
I GOTTA SHOW EU I CAN TAKE THIS GUY DOWN!

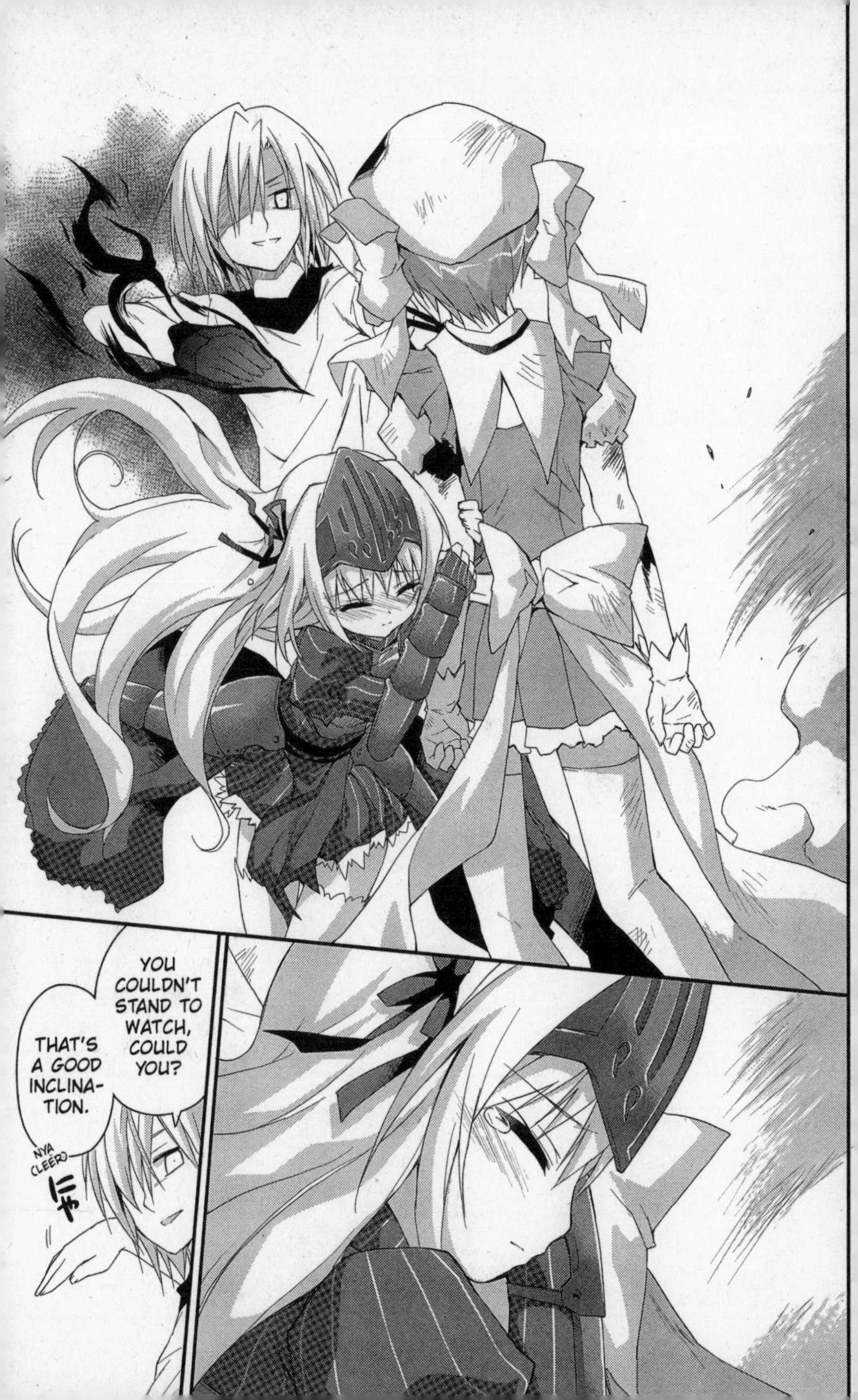
YOU COULDN'T STAND TO WATCH, COULD YOU?
THAT'S A GOOD INCLINATION.
NYA (LEER)
にゃ

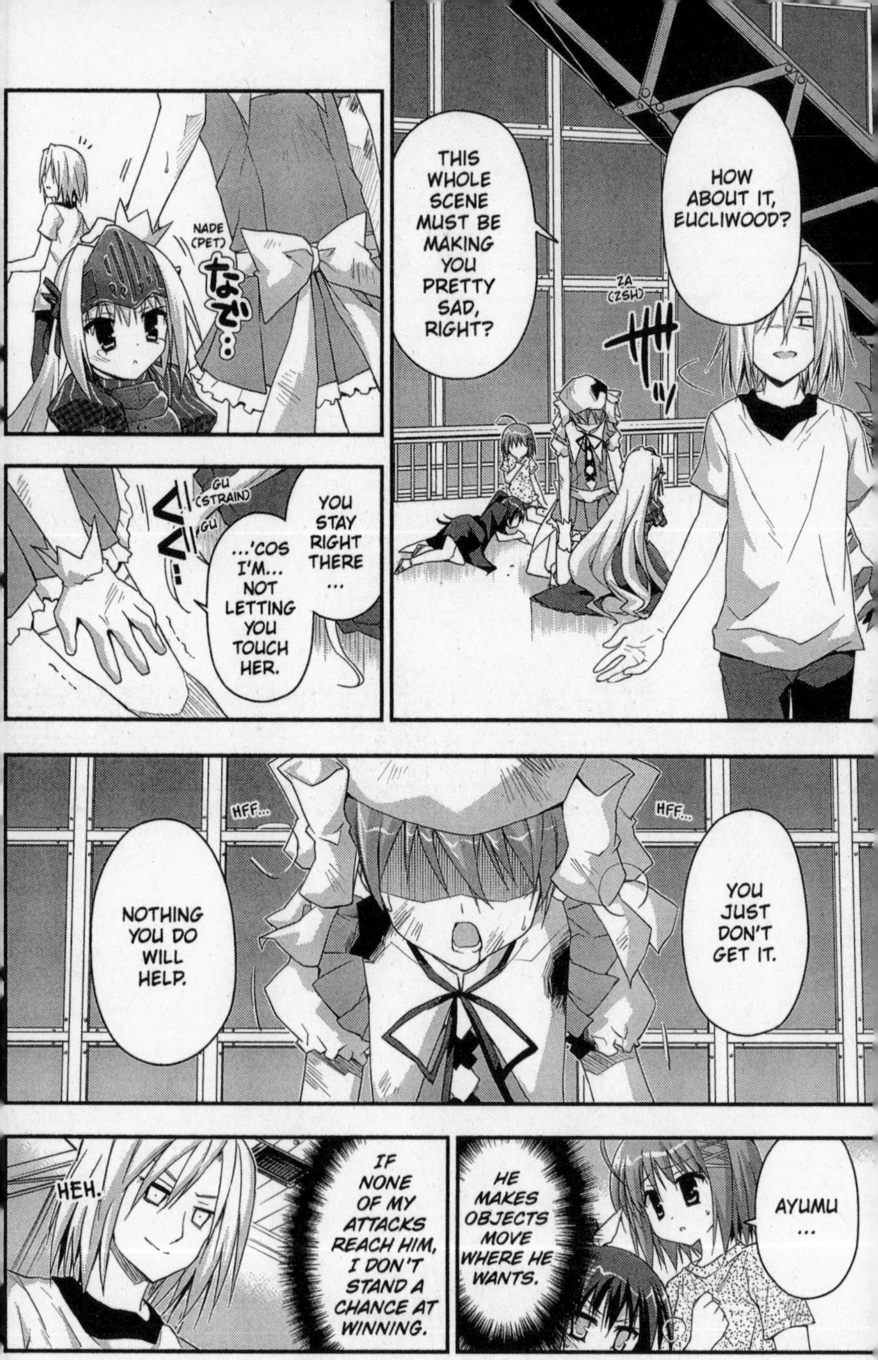
HOW ABOUT IT, EUCLIWOOD?
ZA (ZSH)
THIS WHOLE SCENE MUST BE MAKING YOU PRETTY SAD, RIGHT?
NADE (PET)
なで…
YOU STAY RIGHT THERE ...
GU (STRAIN) GU
...'COS I'M... NOT LETTING YOU TOUCH HER.
HFF...
YOU JUST DON'T GET IT.
HFF...
NOTHING YOU DO WILL HELP.
AYUMU ...
HE MAKES OBJECTS MOVE WHERE HE WANTS.
IF NONE OF MY ATTACKS REACH HIM, I DON'T STAND A CHANCE AT WINNING.
HEH.

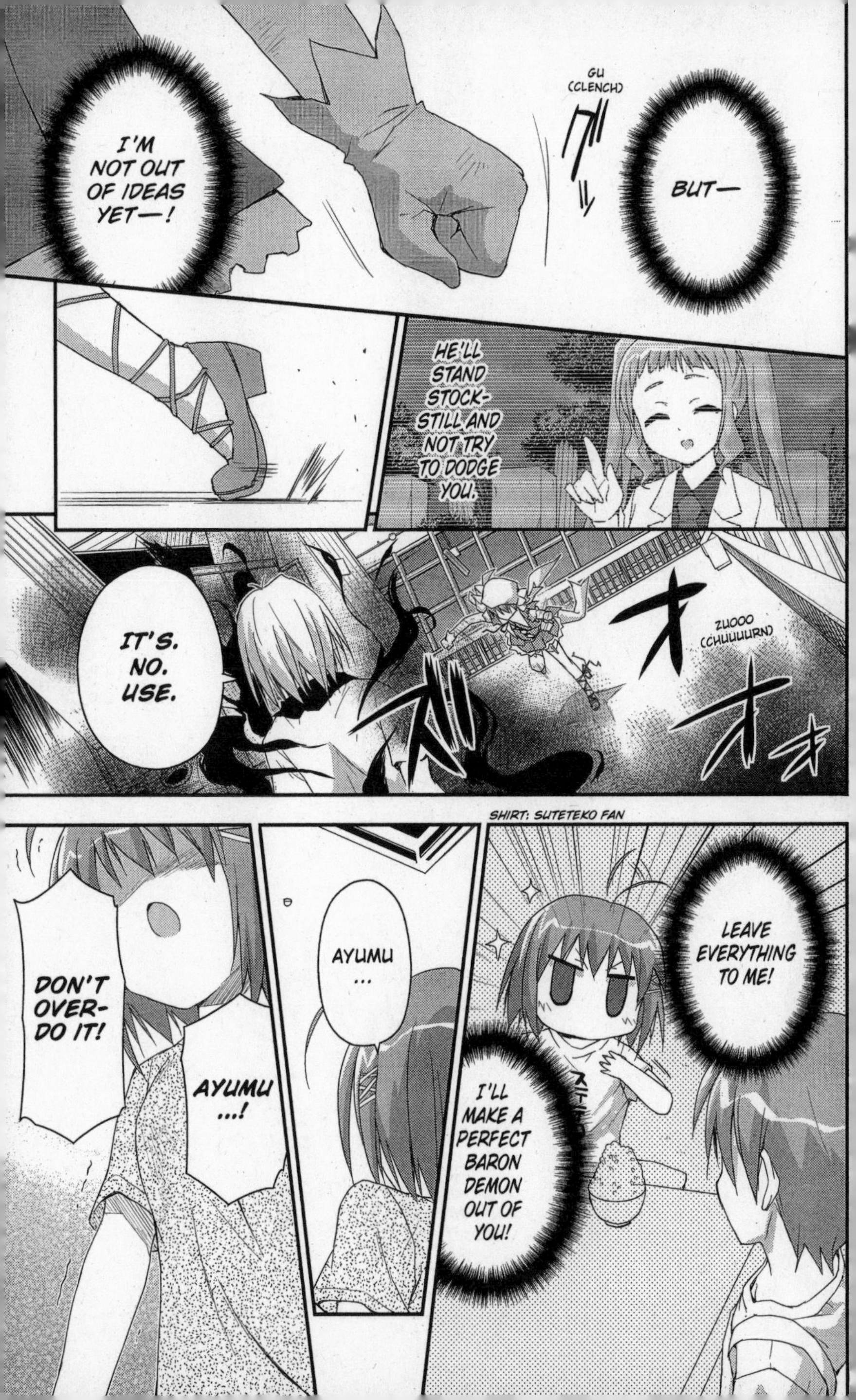

GU (CLENCH)
BUT—
I'M NOT OUT OF IDEAS YET—!
HE'LL STAND STOCK-STILL AND NOT TRY TO DODGE YOU.
ZUOOO (CHUUUURN)
IT'S. NO. USE.
SHIRT: SUTETEKO FAN
LEAVE EVERYTHING TO ME!
I'LL MAKE A PERFECT BARON DEMON OUT OF YOU!
AYUMU ...
AYUMU ...!
DON'T OVER-DO IT!

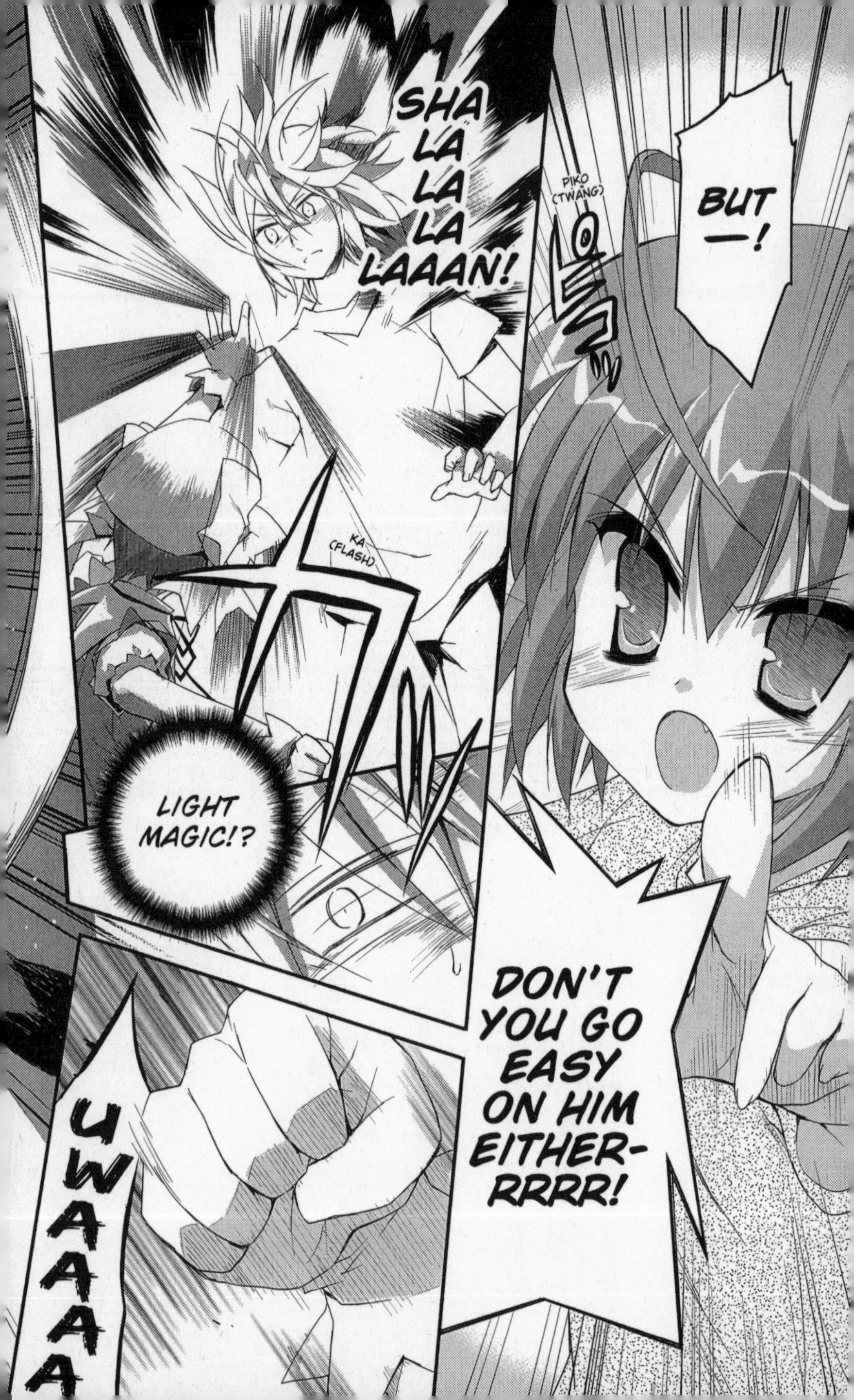
BUT—!
PIKO (TWANG)
SHA LA LA LA LAAAN!
KA (FLASH)
LIGHT MAGIC!?
DON'T YOU GO EASY ON HIM EITHER-RRRR!
UWAAAAA

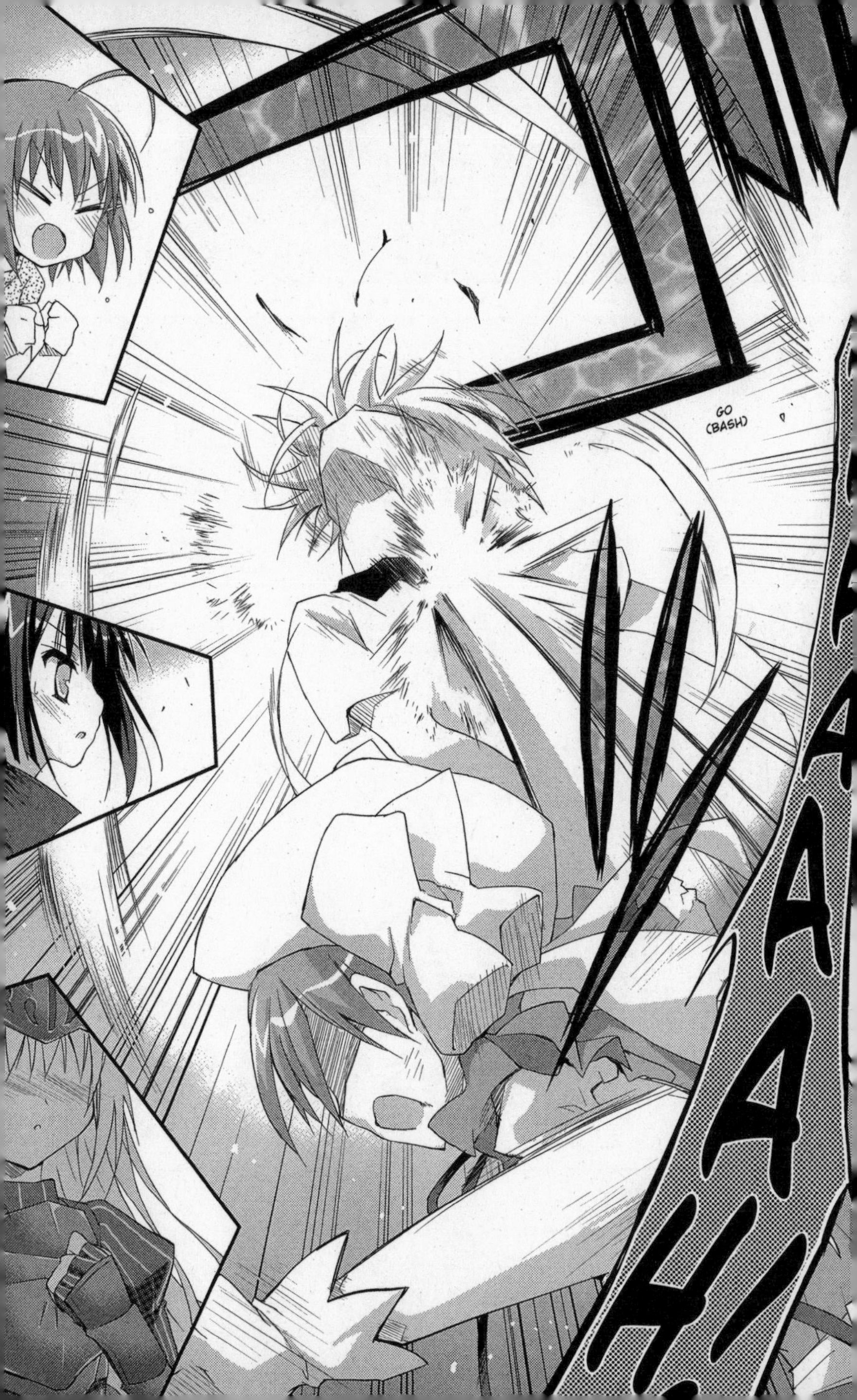
GO (BASH)
AAAAAH!

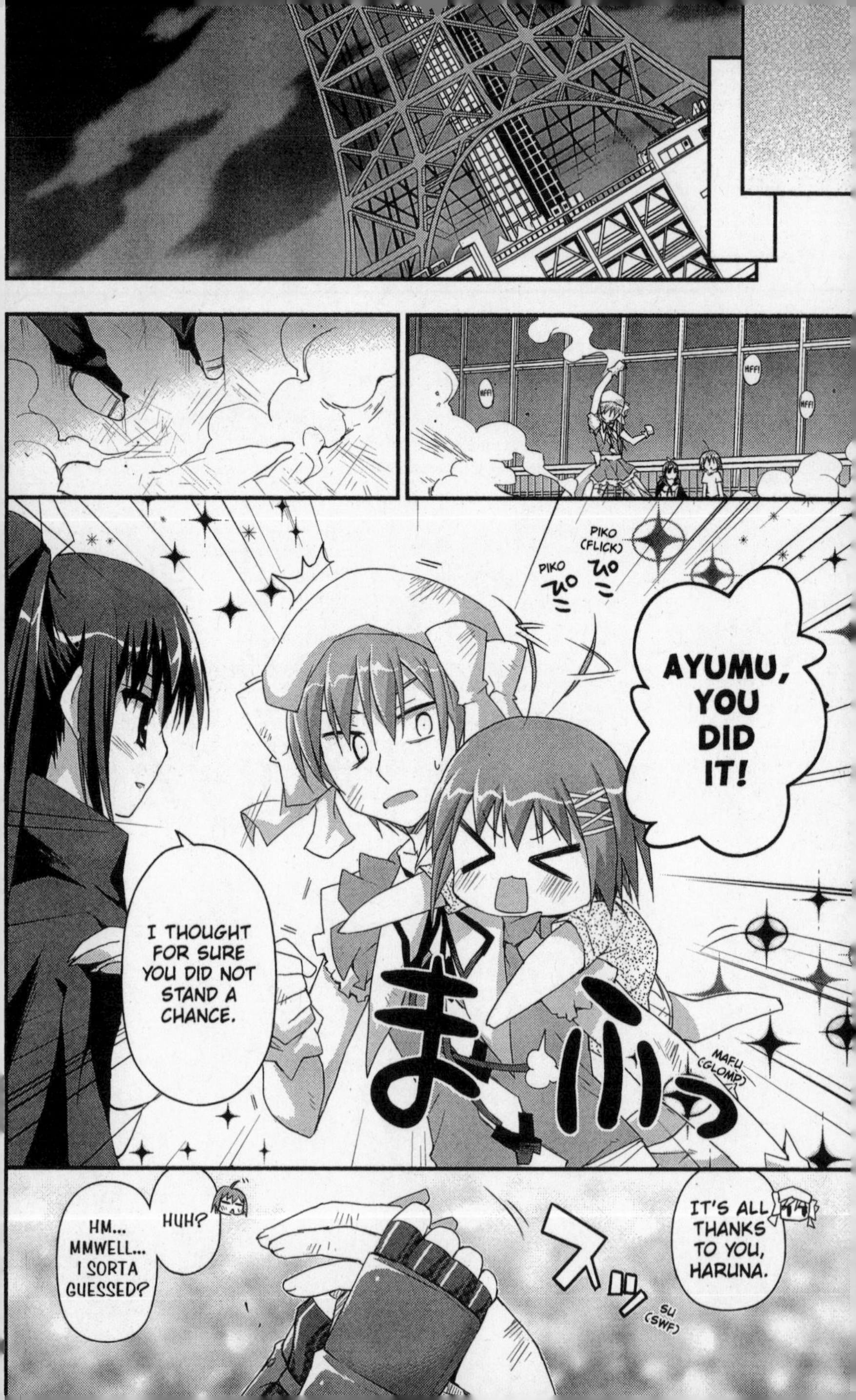
HFF!
HFF!
HFF!
AYUMU, YOU DID IT!
PIKO (FLICK)
ぴこ
PIKO
ぴこ
I THOUGHT FOR SURE YOU DID NOT STAND A CHANCE.
まふっ
MAFU (GLOMP)
IT'S ALL THANKS TO YOU, HARUNA.
スッ
SU (SWF)
HUH?
HM... MMWELL... I SORTA GUESSED?

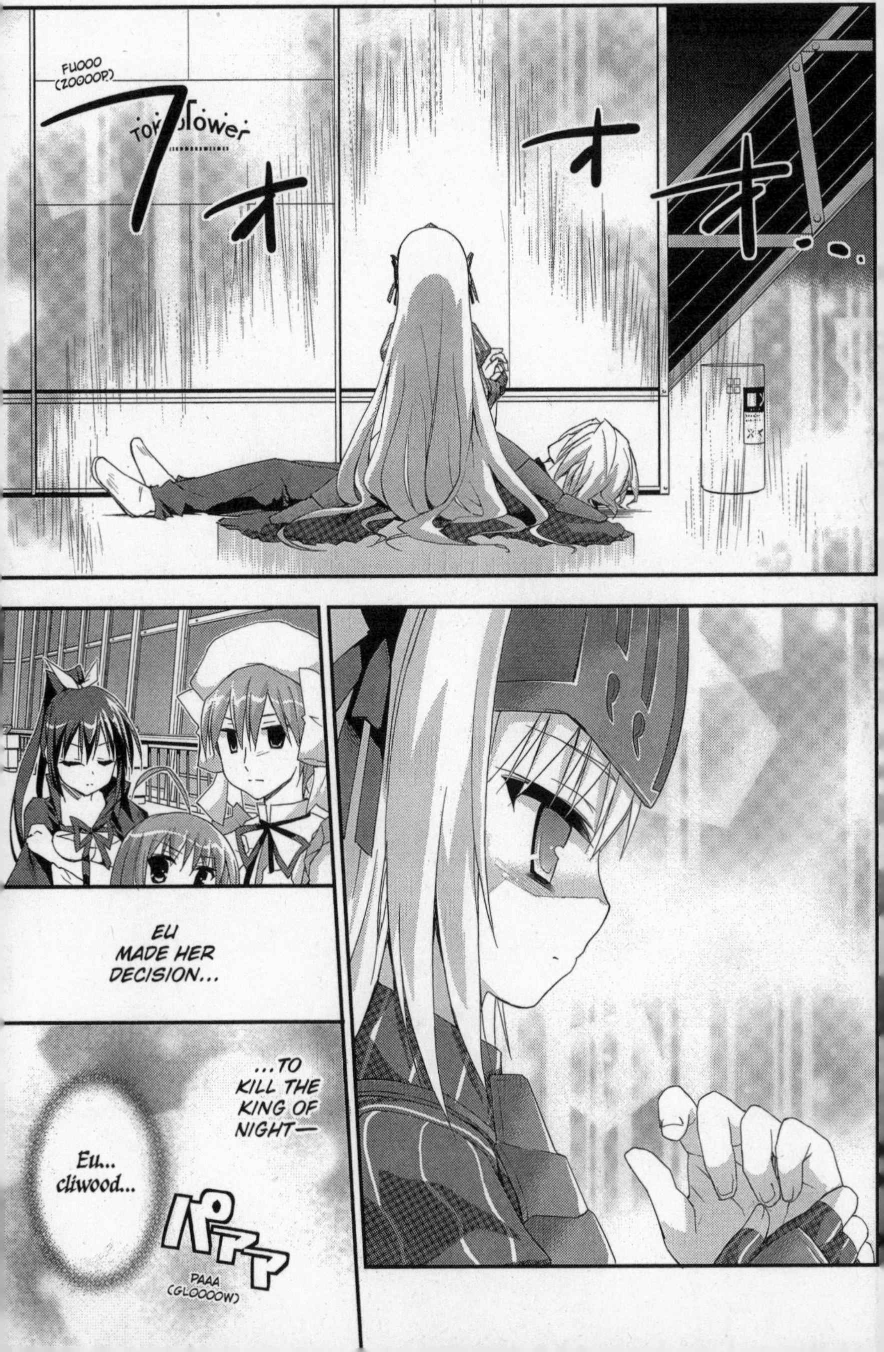

フォオオ…
FUOOO (ZOOOOP)
EU MADE HER DECISION...
...TO KILL THE KING OF NIGHT—
Eu... cliwood...
パアア
PAAA (GLOOOOW)

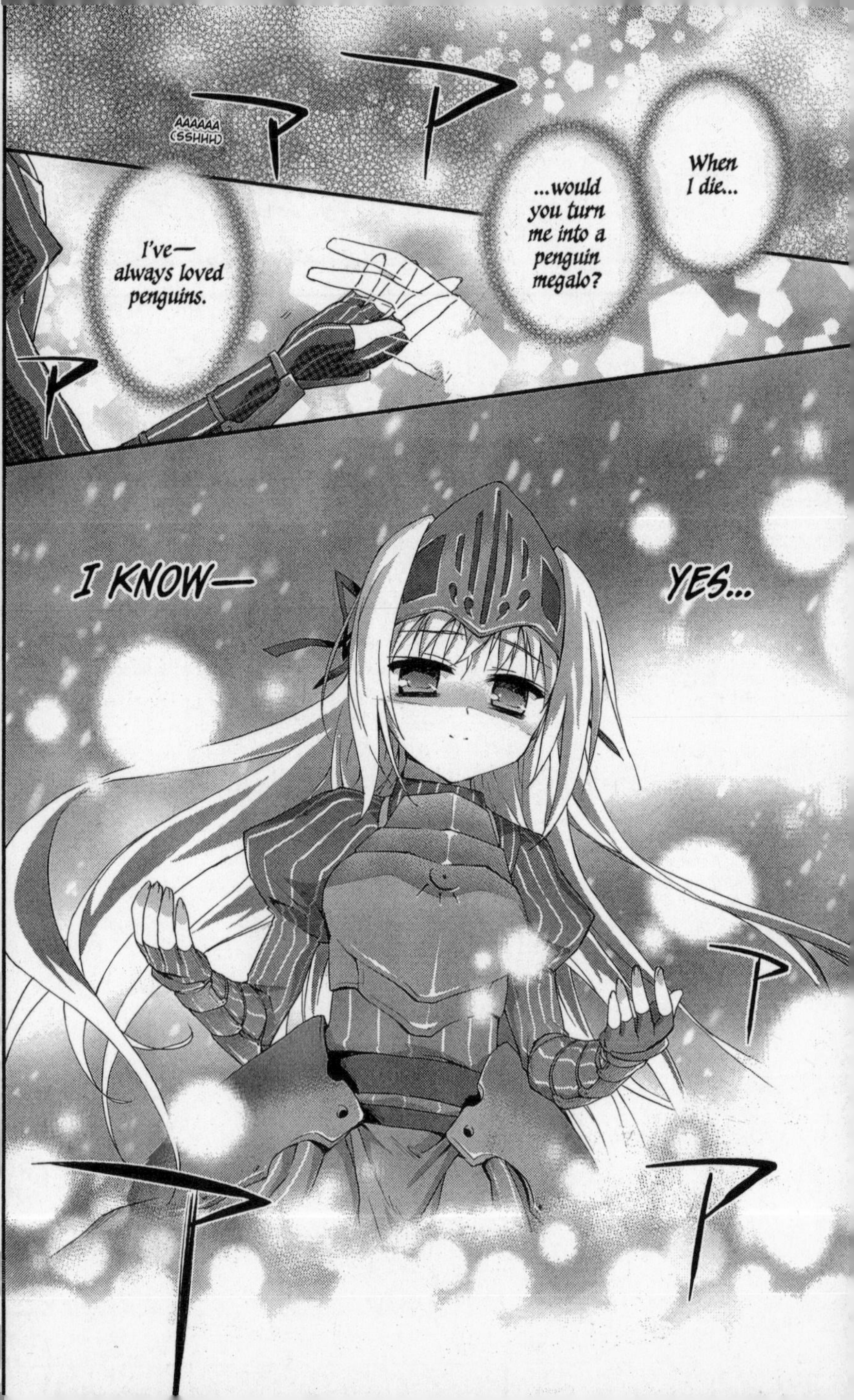
When I die...
...would you turn me into a penguin megalo?
AAAAAA (SSHHH)
I've— always loved penguins.
YES...
I KNOW—

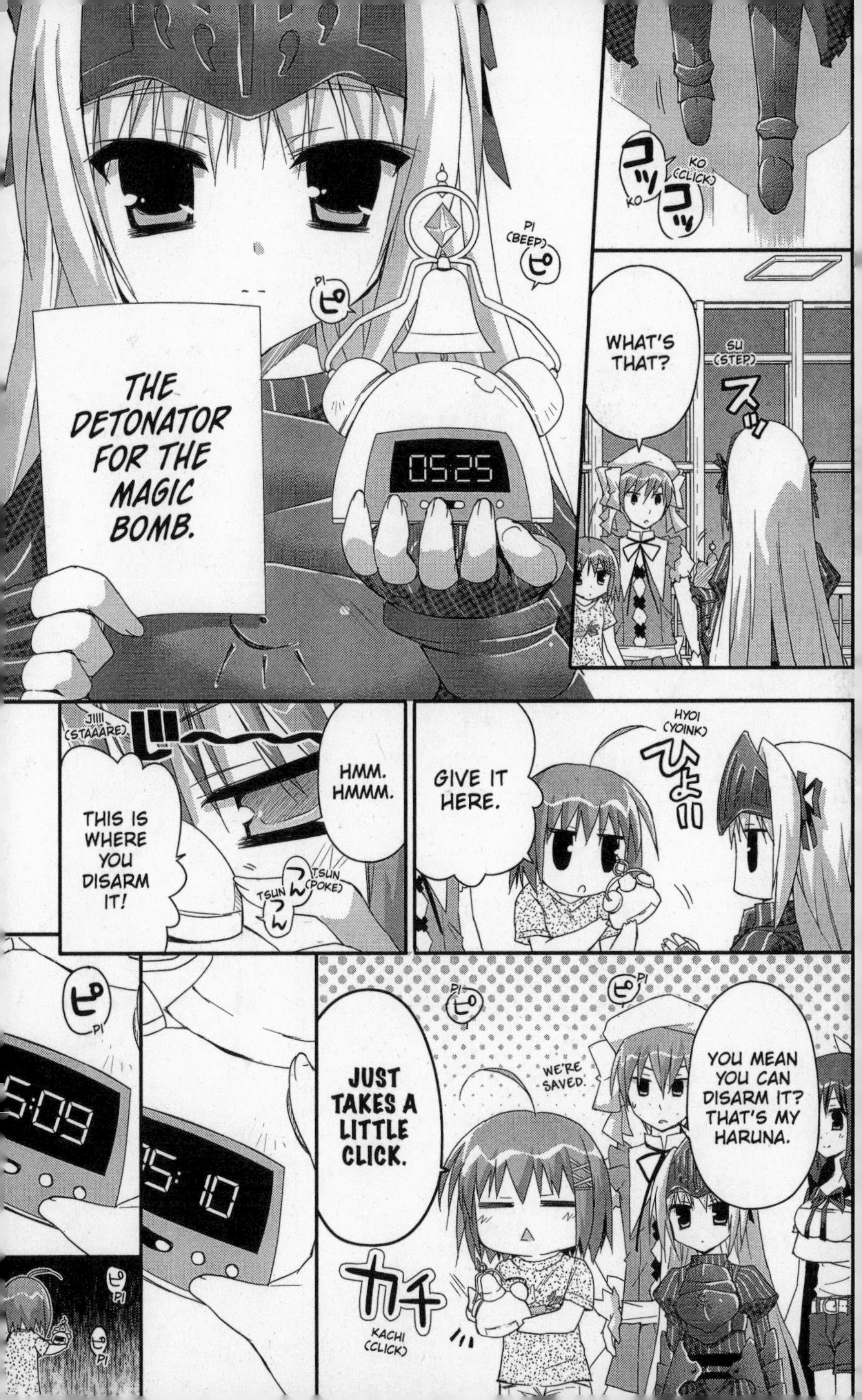

コッ
コッ
KO
KO (CLICK)
WHAT'S THAT?
ス
SU (STEP)
THE DETONATOR FOR THE MAGIC BOMB.
ピ
PI (BEEP)
ピ
PI
05:25
ひょい
HYOI (YOINK)
GIVE IT HERE.
HMM. HMMM.
じーー
JIIII (STAAARE)
THIS IS WHERE YOU DISARM IT!
つん
TSUN (POKE)
つん
TSUN
YOU MEAN YOU CAN DISARM IT? THAT'S MY HARUNA.
WE'RE SAVED.
ピ
PI
ピ
PI
JUST TAKES A LITTLE CLICK.
カチ
KACHI (CLICK)
ピ
PI
5:09
05:10
ピ
PI
ピ
PI

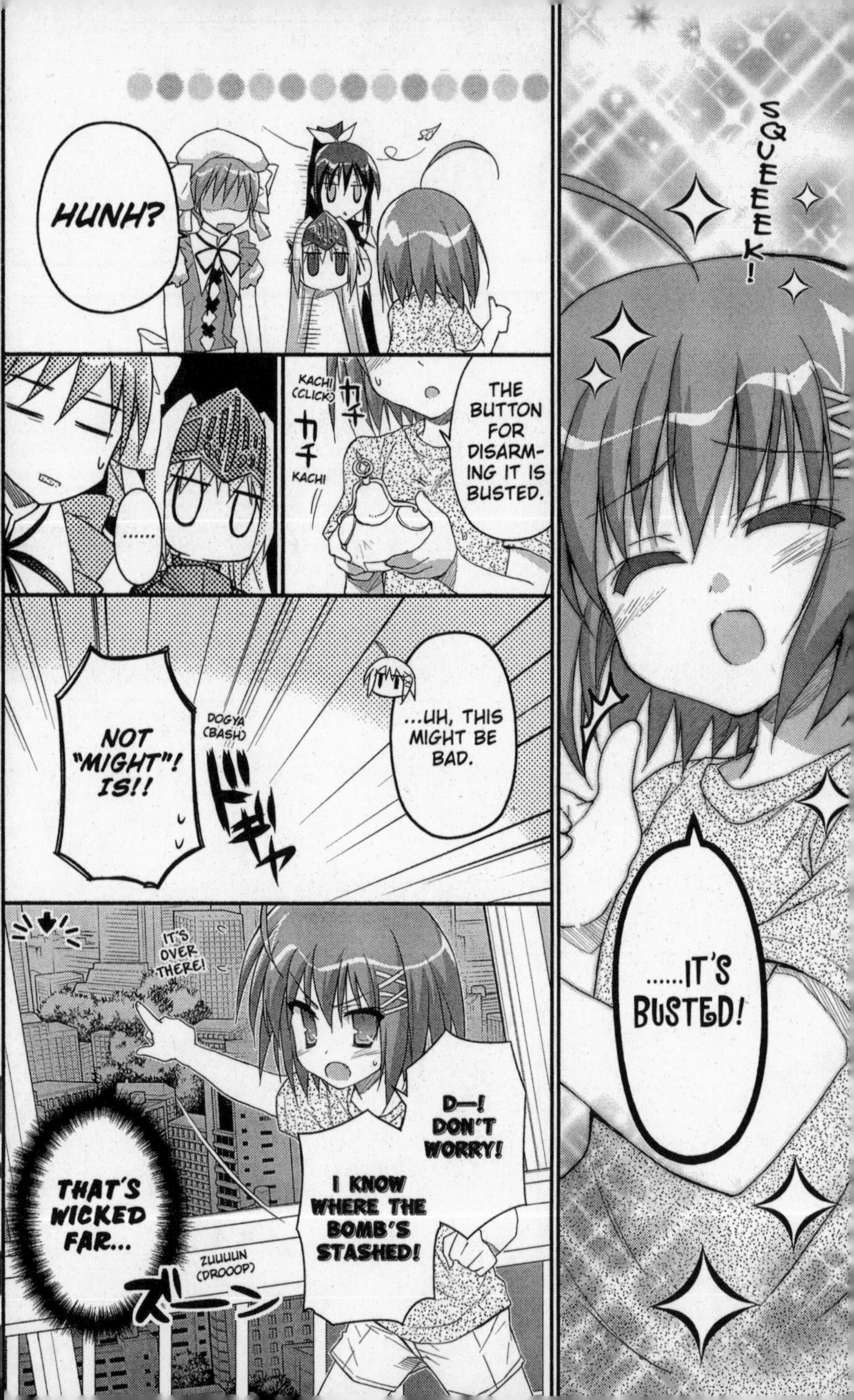
SQUEEEK!
......IT'S BUSTED!
HUNH?
THE BUTTON FOR DISARMING IT IS BUSTED.
KACHI (CLICK) カチ
カチ KACHI
......
...UH, THIS MIGHT BE BAD.
DOGYA (BASH) ドギャ
NOT "MIGHT"! IS!!
IT'S OVER THERE!
D—! DON'T WORRY!
I KNOW WHERE THE BOMB'S STASHED!
ZUUUUN (DROOOP) ズーン
THAT'S WICKED FAR...

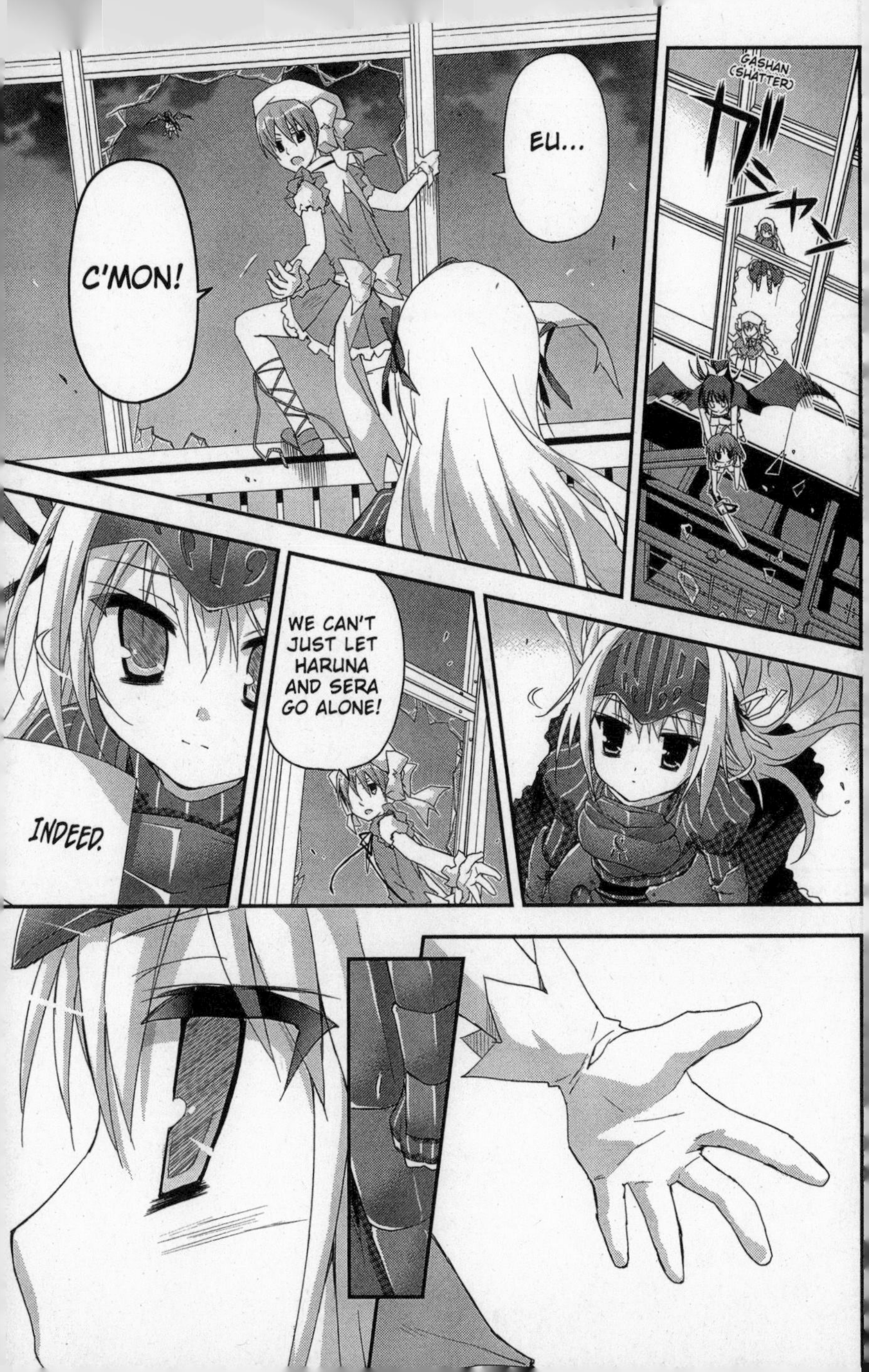
GASHAN (SHATTER)
EU...
C'MON!
WE CAN'T JUST LET HARUNA AND SERA GO ALONE!
INDEED.

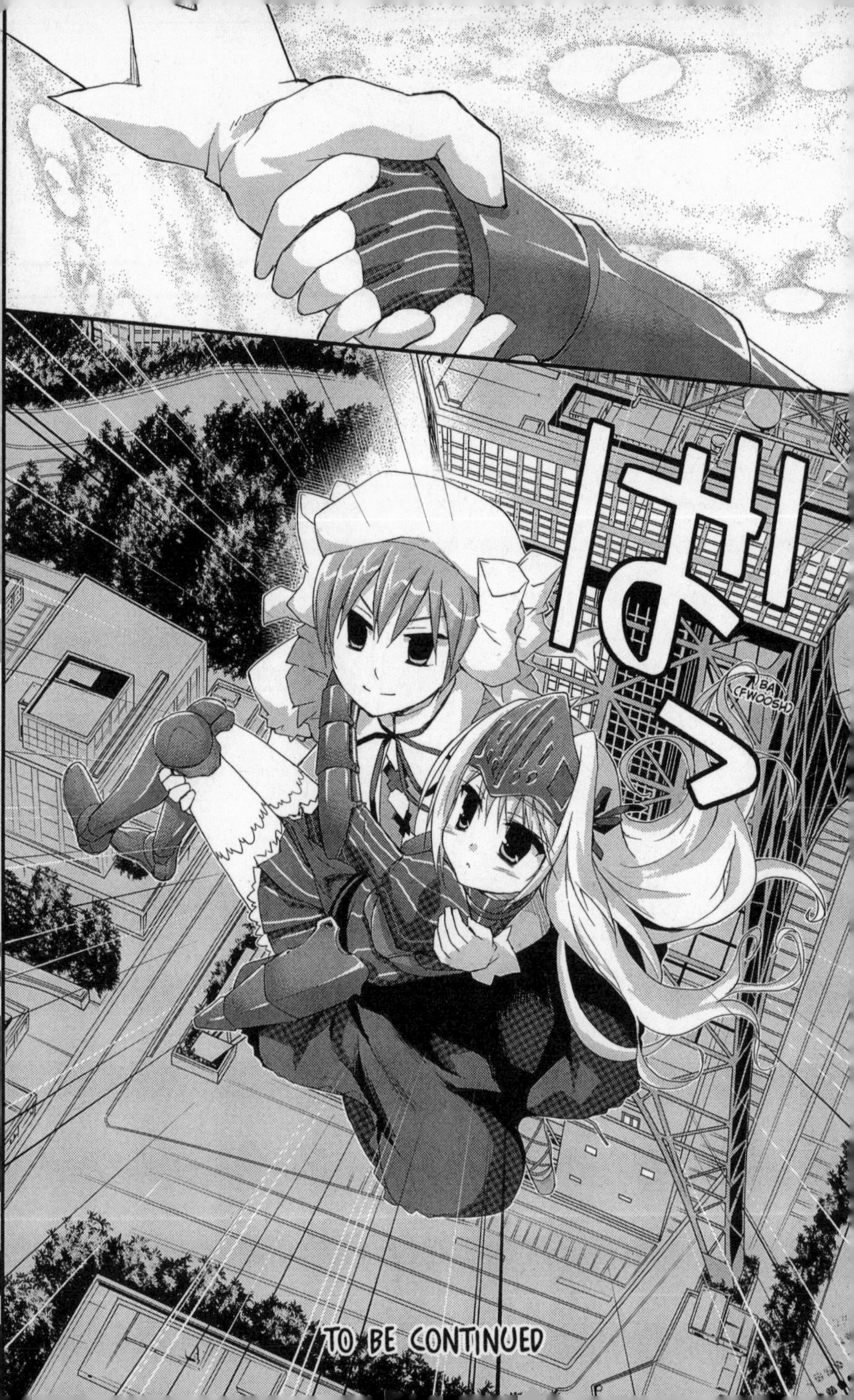
ばっ
BA (FWOOSH)
TO BE CONTINUED

KYOUKO'S JIGGLE LEVEL CHECKLIST

HEE-HEE! ♥

- [ ] To test the myth that "a sixty kilometer wind gives the feeling of boobs," you've stuck your body outside the car window.
- [ ] You think your mom was right all those times she said, "Bigger is better!"
- [ ] You've pondered the many different sounds things make when they tremble.
- [ ] When you talk to your dad, boobs are the first topic you cover.
- [ ] Small boobs are not even up for discussion.
- [ ] You seriously don't wear underwear beneath your yukata!?
- [ ] When you hear the words *greater* and *less than* in regards to numerals, you naturally think about cup sizes.
- [ ] The broader the degree of sway, the better.
- [ ] You've thought countless times about how you can make fake boobs.
- [ ] You can nail someone's cup size based on copping a feel alone! The only problem is there's a conspiracy out there making sure you never get the chance to show your skills.
- [ ] Just hearing the word *Arabia* makes you think of bikinis and gets you horny.
- [ ] Your favorite phrase is "bundles of boobies."

Score	Results
12	Kyouko: "Poor Haruna doesn't even enter the equation. ♥"
6~11	Sera: "Just looking at you fills me with the most severe sensation of chills and queasiness."
1~5	Eu: "A B cup is good enough."
0	Haruna: "You actually get it! I'm appointing you to General of the Tiny Titties!"

IS THIS AN AFTER-WORD?

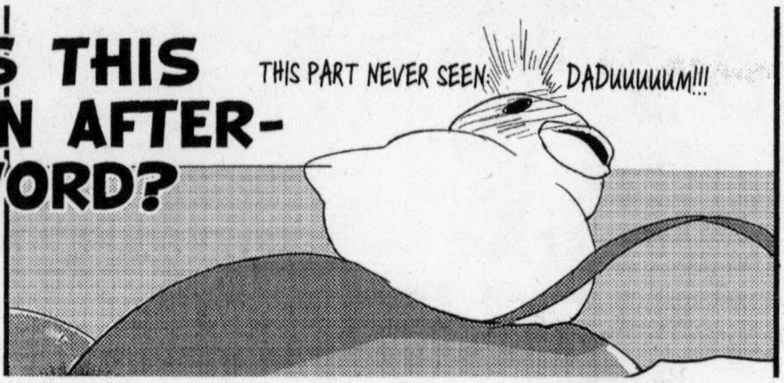
THIS PART NEVER SEEN
DADUUUUUM!!!

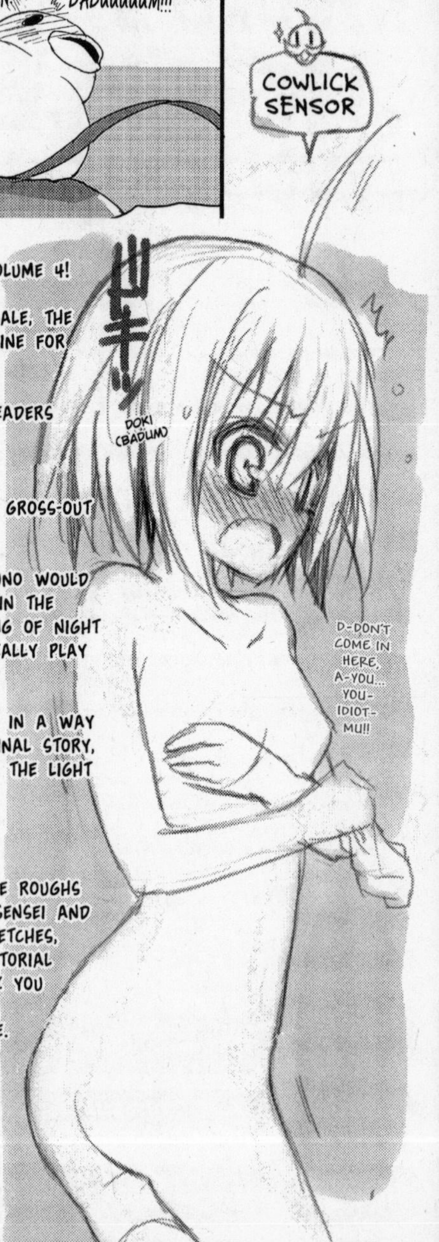
COWLICK SENSOR
DOKI (BADUM)
D-DON'T COME IN HERE, A-YOU... YOU-IDIOT-MU!!

THANK YOU VERY MUCH FOR PURCHASING VOLUME 4!

AROUND THE TIME THIS VOLUME WENT ON SALE, THE STORY HAD BEEN SERIALIZED IN THE MAGAZINE FOR TWO FULL YEARS. HOW TIME FLIES!

THIS IS, OF COURSE, ALL THANKS TO THE READERS OUT THERE WHO SUPPORT THE STORY.
THANK YOU SO, SO MUCH.

I GOTTA SAY, AYUMU REALLY DOES HAVE A GROSS-OUT FACTOR ABOUT HIM.

I'M SURE THE LATE FILM CRITIC HARUO MIZUNO WOULD HAVE SOMETHING TO SAY ABOUT THIS, BUT IN THE NEXT VOLUME, THE PLAN IS TO GET THE KING OF NIGHT AND KYOUKO ARC ALL WRAPPED UP AND REALLY PLAY UP THE ROMANTIC COMEDY ANGLE!

I STILL PLAN ON DOING THE COMIC VERSION IN A WAY THAT DOES JUSTICE TO THE FANTASTIC ORIGINAL STORY, SO IT'D THRILL ME IF YOU KEPT SUPPORTING THE LIGHT NOVELS AND ANIME TOGETHER.

SACCHI

TO KIMURA-SENSEI, WHO ALWAYS CHECKS THE ROUGHS NO MATTER HOW BUSY HE IS, TO KOBUICHI-SENSEI AND MURIRIN-SENSEI FOR THEIR PRETTY GUEST SKETCHES, TO THE EDITORS, AND EVERYONE IN THE EDITORIAL DEPARTMENT, AND TO STUDIO HIBARI—THANK YOU SO MUCH FOR ALL YOU DO FOR ME.
AND THANK YOU FOR GIVING ME THIS SPACE.

★ SPECIAL THANKS TO ★
MIMIZU-SAN, TOMITA-SAN, EKAKIBITO-SAN

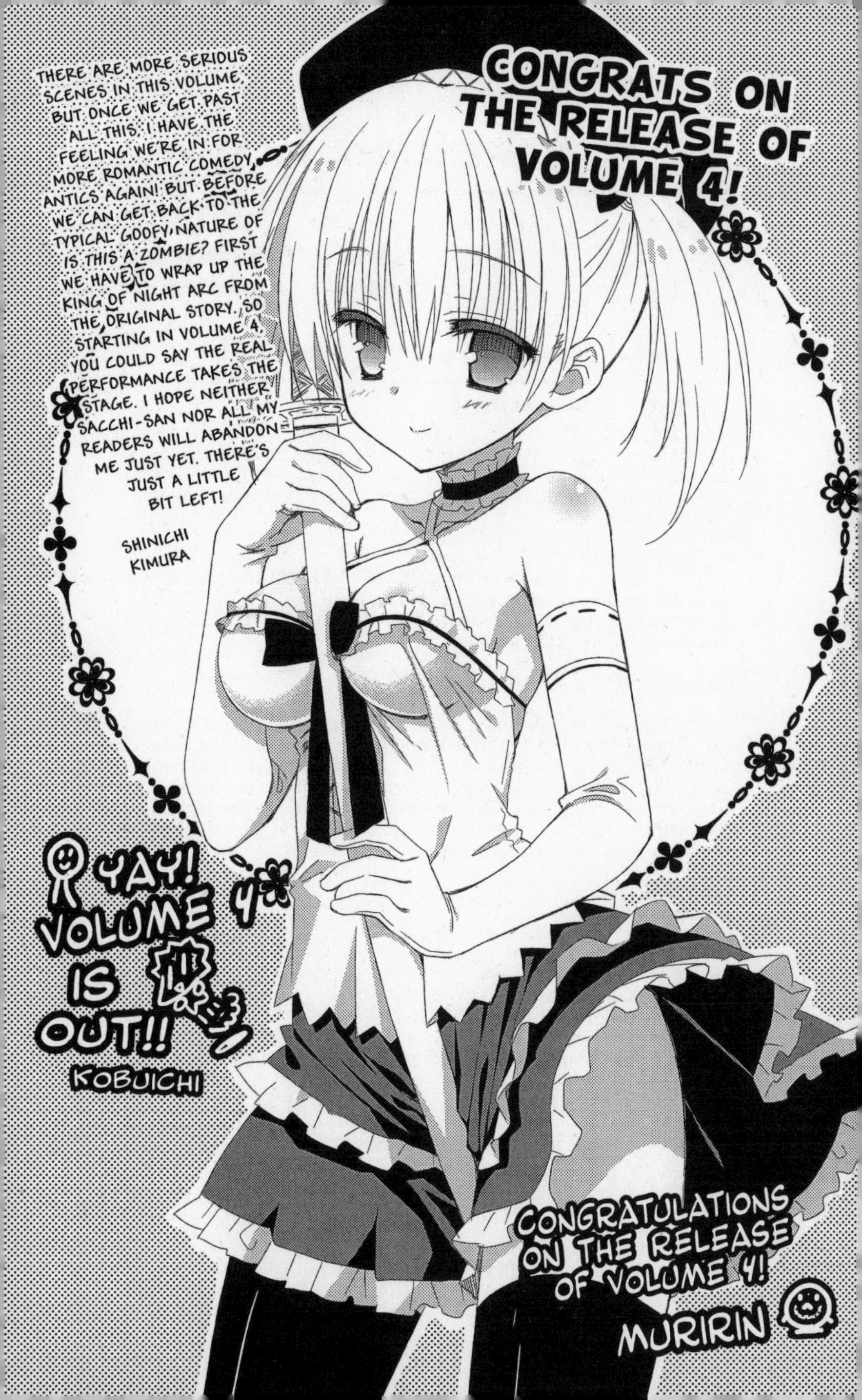
CONGRATS ON THE RELEASE OF VOLUME 4!
THERE ARE MORE SERIOUS SCENES IN THIS VOLUME BUT ONCE WE GET PAST ALL THIS, I HAVE THE FEELING WE'RE IN FOR MORE ROMANTIC COMEDY ANTICS AGAIN! BUT BEFORE WE CAN GET BACK TO THE TYPICAL GOOFY NATURE OF IS THIS A ZOMBIE? FIRST WE HAVE TO WRAP UP THE KING OF NIGHT ARC FROM THE ORIGINAL STORY. SO STARTING IN VOLUME 4, YOU COULD SAY THE REAL PERFORMANCE TAKES THE STAGE. I HOPE NEITHER SACCHI-SAN NOR ALL MY READERS WILL ABANDON ME JUST YET. THERE'S JUST A LITTLE BIT LEFT!
SHINICHI KIMURA
YAY! VOLUME 4 IS OUT!!
KOBUICHI
CONGRATULATIONS ON THE RELEASE OF VOLUME 4!
MURIRIN

IS THIS A ZOMBIE? 4 *

SACCHI
SHINICHI KIMURA
KOBUICHI • MURIRIN

Translation: Christine Dashiell

Lettering: AndWorld Design

KOREHA ZOMBIE DESUKA? Volume 4
© 2011 SACCHI © 2011 SHINICHI KIMURA • KOBUICHI • MURIRIN.
First published in Japan in 2011 by FUJIMISHOBO CO., LTD., Tokyo.
English translation rights arranged with KADOKAWA SHOTEN Co., Ltd., Tokyo through TUTTLE-MORI AGENCY, INC., Tokyo.

Translation © 2013 Hachette Book Group, Inc.

Yen Press
Hachette Book Group
237 Park Avenue, New York, NY 10017

www.HachetteBookGroup.com
www.YenPress.com

Yen Press is an imprint of Hachette Book Group, Inc. The Yen Press name and logo are trademarks of Hachette Book Group, Inc.

First Yen Press Edition: April 2013

ISBN: 978-0-316-24533-3

10 9 8 7 6 5 4 3 2 1

BVG

Printed in the United States of America